Interrogating Development

Interrogating Development

Discourses on Development in India Today

Edited by

Biswajit Ghosh

RAWAT PUBLICATIONS

Jaipur • New Delhi • Bangalore • Hyderabad • Guwahati

ISBN 978-81-316-0476-2

Published by
Prem Rawat for **Rawat Publications**
Satyam Apts, Sector 3, Jawahar Nagar, Jaipur 302 004 (India)
Phone: 0141 265 1748/7006 Fax: 0141 265 1748
E-mail: info@rawatbooks.com
Website: www.rawatbooks.com

New Delhi Office
4858/24, Ansari Road, Daryaganj, New Delhi 110 002
Phone: 011 2326 3290

Also at *Bangalore, Hyderabad* and *Guwahati*

Typeset by Rawat Computers, Jaipur
Printed at Chaman Enterprises, New Delhi

In honour of

Professor M.N. Panini

my Esteemed Supervisor and a Pathfinder in
Sociology of Development in India

Contents

Section III
Gender and Development

Section IV
Science, Environment and Development

Section V
Society, Community and Development

Preface

Nothing seems to be more debated as heatedly as 'development' in our times. This is because all the known canons of development today stand challenged, the radical discourses 'mainstreamed' and the mainstreamed 'radicalised'. Development is no longer a 'word' now but an 'ism' and as with all 'isms' there are well-established 'positions' that has led to an entire body of literature that cautions us of perils and provides hopes of 'alternatives'. Perhaps this untidiness in development is welcome as reflective of a democracy that we witness and most often fail to celebrate. Similarly, one may argue that such messiness is undesirable for the simple reason that we are talking about issues that touch the lives of many. As a corollary, we need to avoid the luxury of a continual flux and thereby decide about appropriate path, model and agencies of development.

The discourse on development is however not new in sociology. The founding fathers of the discipline had broadly talked about development and change of human society, institutions and values. But it is equally true that this discourse has gained prominence in the academic agenda in the last 20 years or so with a new significance and twist. Problems with a given model of development in a local setting and the emerging constraints as well as contradictions have prompted us to rethink about paradigms and agencies of development. These processes of 'learning and experiencing development' in real life with diverse sections and classes of population appear to be an important dimension of the development discourse today. In India too, we are intensely involved in debating and often protesting against development 'pathologies' like disparity, distress, discrimination and displacement.

It is in this context that the present volume seeks to sharpen our understanding about the process and challenges of contemporary development and interrogate its possibilities as well as consequences from multiple, contextual and synoptic points of view. The volume contains sixteen essays and is divided into five sections. After the introduction, the first section begins with a theoretical exploration of the dynamics of development. It also takes stock of Indian alternatives to the Western notion of development. The remaining sections deal with substantive issues of development from the Indian point of view. The second section thus attempts a critical reappraisal of the role and functions of state, market and civil society in contemporary India. In the third section, the issues of gender equality and gender justice are picked up for intense scrutiny and debate. The fourth section on science, environment and development examines our current concern for an eco-friendly and sustainable environment in the path of development. Finally, in the fifth section, the social and cultural issues of development are scrutinised to delineate the linkages between society, community and development in the Indian context. Viewed in totality, our interrogation of the major discourses on development is expected to inform the readers about many vital issues of our life in India today and fill in the gap in knowledge.

Academically, the effort to understand and explore the intricacies of 'sociology development' for me in Burdwan began as early as in 2000 when a course on 'Sociology of Development and Environment' was designed and offered by me for our PG students. But, the idea of bringing out a volume on this emergent and vital issue of contemporary relevance became bright when I along with my colleagues in the department organised a national seminar on *Discourses on Development* during 13–14 March 2010 as a part of the golden jubilee celebrations of our university. In this seminar, we invited noted experts and researchers in the field from all over the country so as to share information and analysis, and thereby delve deep into different aspects of the process of development in the contemporary society.

But the journey to convert the seminar papers into a volume appeared to be very tricky and challenging one. First of all, some noted experts could not make it to the seminar, yet I wanted their contributions to be added in the volume. Secondly, publication is a serious task and I could neither afford to compromise with quality nor postpone my time frame for publishing the volume. However, due to persistent efforts, the volume became a brilliant collection of essays by noted Indian experts some of whom also attended the seminar. But, the articles have been extensively revised and re-written following certain interrogations. I do agree that there may still be certain grey areas that this volume has not addressed. But, in the same spirit, one would agree that it is neither possible nor desirable to include all aspects of development discourse in a single volume. Yet, I have attempted to do justice to my credibility by incorporating as many aspects as desirable and possible in the current context. I hope this will be very useful reading for all those interested in understanding the current discourses on development, particularly in the Indian context.

I acknowledge with gratitude the permission granted by two publishers to reprint the following articles including my own that I revised substantially for this volume:

(i) Oommen, T.K. 2004. 'Development Theory: Rhetoric and Reality', in T.K. Oommen, *Development Discourse: Issues and Concerns* (1–26). New Delhi: Regency.

(ii) Ghosh, Biswajit. 2009. 'NGOs, Civil Society and Social Reconstruction in Contemporary India', *Journal of Developing Societies*, 25 (2): 229–252.

In the course of publishing this volume, I was supported by many people and organisations. At the outset, I must express my gratitude to Indian Council of Social Science Research (ICSSR), University Grants Commission (UGC) and The University of Burdwan for providing financial assistance in organising the seminar. My colleagues in the department, namely Prof. Anirban Banerjee, Mr. Bibhas Bagchi, Dr Ananda Mohan Kar, Dr Sourav Madhur Dey and Mr. Anantya Kumar Biswas immensely cooperated to hold the seminar. The seminar would not have become successful without the cooperation of our MA students and PhD scholars. I also acknowledge the contributions of the chairmen and panelists of different sessions, including the participants, to the seminar. I am especially thankful to Prof. Anand Kumar, Prof. Abhijit Mitra, Prof. Arup Chattopadhyay, Dr Surajit C. Mukhopadhyay, Prof. Satyabrata Chakraborty, Prof. Kalyan Sankar Mondal, Prof. Pradip Bhowmick, Prof. Samita Manna, Dr. Manjula Rathaur, Prof. Amit Hazra, Sri Bipattaran Ghosh, Dr Manish Kumar Thakur, Dr. Roddur Dey, Dr G.C. Rath and Prof. Amritava Banerjee.

This volume would not have seen the light of day without the hard work and patience of our contributors. I am also grateful to Mr Pranit Rawat of Rawat Publications for bringing out this volume in the shortest possible time. I am delighted to find professional acumen and dedication of the editorial team of Rawat Publications in bringing out the volume. My final thanks are reserved for everyone in my family, particularly my wife Tanima and daughter Banhishikha, for their constant moral support and coöperation at every stage of this endeavour.

Contributors

Anup Dash is Professor of Sociology at Utkal University, Bhubaneswar.

Apurba Kumar Mukhopadhyay is Professor of Political Science & Political Studies, Netaji Institute for Asian Studies, Kolkata.

Biswajit Ghosh is Professor of Sociology at The University of Burdwan, Burdwan, West Bengal.

Debal K. SinghaRoy is Professor of Sociology, School of Social Sciences, IGNOU, New Delhi.

Krityapriya Ghosh was formerly Professor of Political Science, Presidency University, Kolkata. He was also Visiting Professor of Sociology at The University of Burdwan, Burdwan.

Maitrayee Chaudhuri is Professor of Sociology, CSSS, SSS, Jawaharlal Nehru University, New Delhi.

Manish K. Verma is Associate Professor of Sociology at School for Ambedkar Studies, Babasaheb Bhimrao Ambedkar University, Lucknow.

Sekh Rahim Mondal is Professor of Sociology and Anthropology, Centre for Himalayan Studies, University of North Bengal, Darjeeling, West Bengal.

Rajkishor Meher is faculty of Sociology at Nabakrishna Choudhury Centre for Development Studies, Bhubaneswar.

Sanjay K. Roy is Professor of Sociology at the University of North Bengal, Darjeeling, West Bengal.

Souvagya Laxmi Saran is Reader in Sociology at Rajdhani College, Bhubaneswar.

Shoma Choudhury Lahiri is Lecturer in Sociology at St. Xavier's College, Kolkata.

Subhasis Bandyopadhyay is Assistant Professor in the Department of Humanities and Social Sciences at Bengal Engineering and Science University, Shibpur, West Bengal.

Swapan Kumar Pramanick has recently retired as the Vice Chancellor of Vidyasagar University, Medinipur. He was earlier Professor of Sociology at Calcutta University, West Bengal.

T.K. Oommen is Emeritus Professor, CSSS, SSS, Jawaharlal Nehru University, New Delhi.

Virginius Xaxa is Professor of Sociology at Delhi School of Economics, Delhi.

Introduction

Biswajit Ghosh

The idea of 'development' has been associated with systematic growth, evolution, advancement and progress. It is presented as opposite of decay, stagnation, retardation and underdevelopment. Therefore, it has been accepted as a positive idea in all contemporary societies, particularly the industrial and post-colonial societies. But, the experience of varied dimensions of 'development' during the last three centuries has given rise to contentions and debate about the possibility of 'development for all'. If any particular model of development has certain avowed advantages, the notion of 'advantage' becomes a suspect in terms of "advantage for whom" and "who determines what 'advantage' means"? In other words, 'development' may appear to be a social construction having a discursive or cultural history. There has been a growing divide among the social scientists about the dynamics of development in spite of faith in the temporal linearity and systemic universality. The sociologists have become alert about the challenges of re-conceptualising the socio-political and economic processes and institutions which have been put together in the last few centuries in Europe and America and in the last several decades in India and the other post-colonial societies. It has been observed that there is clear disconnect between the promises and performance in all the discourses of development. Gender-oriented, eco-centric and culture-focused approaches in social analysis have provided significant support for it. Problems with a given model of development in a local setting and the emerging constraints as well as contradictions have prompted us to rethink about paradigms and agencies of development. These processes of 'learning and experiencing development' in real life with diverse sections and classes of population appear to be an important dimension of the development discourse today.

A reading of the essays in this volume would make one understand that 'development' has no definite boundary, no specific pathways and no universal approach and strategy. Any universal definition of the concept of development is neither possible nor desirable because 'development' is often viewed as an 'ideology' to propagate class rule or hegemony. 'Development' can therefore be viewed as a 'discourse' – a way or framework of thinking and action about things having consequences for power. The term 'discourse' here is used partly following Michel Foucault. As a framework of ideas, behaviour and practice, the discourse on development produces and employs 'knowledge' to make distinctions between perceived and proposed conditions of living in both abstract and concrete sense. It may further be argued that such efforts also attempt to systematically construct the subjects and the worlds of which they speak and thereby act as a medium through which power relations are constructed. It should however be kept in mind that the term 'discourse' here is applied as a methodological device and not as an ideology. 'Developmentalism' itself is argued to be a discourse by the post-developmentalists. In this limited sense, 'discourse' becomes a totality capable of reconciling all tendencies in theorising development and hence to be abandoned. But, as Foucault argued, it is possible to "reconstruct and rediscover the forgotten". For such reconstruction, we need to undo the 'tyranny' of globalising discourses and stress on local knowledge and people's knowledge.

Our treatment of development as a discourse is also helpful to locate changes in the meaning of development over time and space. It has been shown in numerous studies that the meaning, strategy and dimensions of development do change and are changing with the changing passage of time. Even in a given context, 'development' means several things to different stakeholders. In other words, there are several discourses on development and the 'success' of a particular model/strategy should have to be judged keeping in view questions like development 'by whom', 'for whom' and 'at what costs'. Existence of multi-plurality of discourses on development may lead one to refrain from considering any particular mode of thinking, mechanism or paradigm as final or acceptable universally.

In India too, we are today intensely involved in debating and often protesting against development 'pathologies' like disparity, distress, discrimination and displacement. In recent past, we have witnessed the rise of civil society activism and protest movements for different types of rights as well as against corruption, black money, state oppression, market failure or displacement. All these signify a new beginning in the history of development in India. It is now being acknowledged that despite tremendous 'development' since independence, we are still struggling to tackle poverty, unemployment, marginalisation, displacement, gender inequality and violence, rising disparities across caste, community and region. Hence, we need to sharpen our understanding about the process and challenges of contemporary development and analyse its possibilities as well as consequences. Only through such a comprehensive analysis, we would be able to suggest and develop alternative paradigm(s) that are humane in nature, timely in dimension and hold good for a large part of our socially and economically backward/deprived sections of population. It is in this context that the present volume seeks to sharpen our understanding about the process and challenges of contemporary development and interrogate its possibilities as well as consequences from multiple, contextual and synoptic points of view. The volume contains sixteen essays which are divided into five sections: (i) Interrogating Development Discourse, (ii) State, Market and Civil Society, (iii) Gender and Development, (iv) Science, Environment and Development, and (v) Society, Community and Development.

The first section begins with a theoretical exploration of the dynamics and approaches to development. As the concept of development has undergone numerous twists and turns, T.K. Oommen examines the fissure between rhetoric and reality of three major perspectives in the trajectory of development. These are: (a) mainstream perspective on development (MPD), (b) alternative perspective on development (APD), and (c) post-development perspective (PDP). He has argued that the development discourse is very rich in rhetoric but rather poor in coping with reality. Part of the reason for this is that positions and counter-positions in development studies often operate on the basis of simplistic dichotomies – modernity versus tradition, western science versus indigenous knowledge, the global versus the local, the state versus the market, and the like. For development thinking to avoid sterility, Oommen suggests five precautionary measures which include the acceptance of local conditions, reflexivity, equipoise between the concepts of state, market and civil society, holistic approach and multiple models of modernity.

The task of analysing the existing dynamics of development, particularly in the Indian context, is carried further in my own article. I have noticed that 'development' is a qualitative concept involving a qualitative improvement in the general standard of living in any space. The fact that development is complex, contradictory and often contentious does not however nullify the very concept because in spite of much criticism and opposition we are not being able to construct any real 'alternative to development'. One way to solve the perplexity is to combine different angles and approaches to development into 'critical holism'. This means understanding the totality from a critical point of view and thereby using reflexivity to reconstruct 'development'. Another way to reconstruct 'development' is to consider the constructive suggestions of Indian philosophers like Buddha, Vivekananda, Tagore, Gandhi, Aurobindo and Ambedkar. It appears that the best way, in the present context, to materialise 'holistic development' is in terms of the expansion of the real freedoms that the citizens enjoy to pursue the objectives they have reason to value. Hopefully, the discourses of development today are coming to some kind of converging points all over the world. And, this convergence takes place around certain central dreams of humanity, happiness, freedom and participation. Beyond the market-machine as well as state/bureaucracy/political elite guided paradigms, we today require the 'nature-need and people-centric paradigm' to guide us to integrated, balanced and inclusive development. And, such a broad framework has relevance for people across borders and economic frontiers.

Krityapriya Ghosh's essay delves deep into the alternative vision of development by analysing the thoughts of Tagore and Gandhi particularly. Ghosh argues that Tagore was highly critical of the western projection of modernity as 'development'. For him, real development may happen only when the conflict between the individual and the state, labour and capital, the man and the woman, greed of material gain and the spiritual life of man, the organised selfishness of nations and the higher ideals of humanity and all the ugly complexities inseparable from giant organisations of commerce and state and the natural instincts of man crying for simplicity and beauty and fullness of leisure has to be brought to a harmony in a manner not yet dreamt of. Tagore is quite insistent that the object of modernisation is not to gain the material wealth or to furnish the outer grandeur of the social fabric, but to grow one's own treasure from the reserve of his/her own tradition. Here, there is the inevitable and necessary relation between tradition and modernity. Similarly, Ghosh's analysis shows that Gandhi rejected all aspects of the western civilisation based on modern science and technology though he endorsed many key concepts of modernity. Gandhi actually stood for an alternative modernity. And, the principal base or motive of that alternative modernity is ethics and morality. Most of the keen disciples of Gandhi also tried to project that essentially there was no difference of outlook between the two towering personalities; the differences are occasional, sometimes a case of misunderstanding. Although they shared many ideas, they too had some essential differences of attitude towards life and society. The notable area of differences lies on the question of the use of science and technology as well as solutions to the problems of development in India. Yet, Tagore and Gandhi, in their respective ways, stimulate us to think and look for that alternative.

After the initial theoretical discussion about the nature and quality of development discourses, we moved on to discuss substantive issues of development from the Indian point of view. The second section begins the task by attempting a critical reappraisal of the role and functions of state, market and civil society in contemporary India. Apurba Kumar Mukhopadhyay argues that the search for civil society as congeries of de-classed and de-politicised organisations and movements of people as watchdog of India's democracy in a volatile political milieu is theoretically untenable and empirically unsupportable. The author takes a down-to-earth approach to empirical realities about social life and political recognition in India of her teeming millions. As the term 'civil society' is a contested one, he prefers to talk in terms of civil societies, rather than civil society, particularly in the Indian context. The author confronts two distinct civil societal ambiences in the context of Bengal. What is theoretically significant is to note that certain core human values are honoured in one space and grossly violated in another with impunity with or without the intervention of the state. Out of uniform, the state as provider of that sacred and hoary space called civil society by both its adulators and detractors seems no better. By virtue of being democratic, it has been soft to too many institutions and practices, which are uncivil. The 'civil' therefore incorporates the 'uncivil'. The terms of discourse, therefore, argues Mukhopadhyay, may be reset as one of negotiation not between the state and civil society, but between a state that promotes and protects uncivilised ways of life and a state that should not.

Sanjay K. Roy's article deals with the interface between state, market and civil society particularly with reference to ethnic minority groups in the tea gardens of Bengal. Roy's analysis reveals that being a part of the neo-liberal market, the tribal workers of tea gardens in Bengal, with minimal control over material and human resources and cultural capital, are engaged in fierce survival battle. Sandwiched in the power struggle between the Nepalese of Darjeeling striving for a separate state of Gorkhaland and the mainstream political forces which are out to integrate the 'marginalised' into the 'order' and oppose any division of the state, nearly one million *adivasis* in the Dooars and Terai of Jalpaiguri and Darjeeling districts are now engaged in a tribal solidarity movement under the banner of Akhil Bharatiya Adivasi Vikash Parishad (ABAVP) with the objective of finding their own identity and political right over a territory. The shared perception of losing their land and a common experience of marginalisation in the economic, social and political spheres together have prepared the ground for the formation of the tribal ethnic movement. The movement promises the formation of a civil society of the otherwise voiceless *adivasis* of the region on ethnic line although maintaining the solidarity and achieving its political goal prove to be very difficult in the midst of the integrationist efforts and strategies of the systemic forces. This paper therefore not only argues about the negative role of integrationist forces for the rise of ethnicity among members of a class, it also explains ethnicity from a positive point of view. Like many civil society organisations, ABAVP today argues for expansion of democratic rights including right to life and self-determination of the people of Dooars and Terai region and is ready to utilise its ethnic identity and strength for secular gains. In this sense, ethnicity becomes a means to the end of what is commonly termed as 'development'. It appears that in the heterogeneous and hierarchical societies such as India, organised groups and communities should also be recognised as legitimate inhabitants of civil society.

The discussion on the role of civil society will remain incomplete if a critical evaluation of the NGO movement in contemporary India is not carried out. My another article fills this gap. If strong, vibrant and lively civil society is the foundation of modern open democratic polity, NGOs are the very live-force for the civil society. My discussion, however, shows that there are serious inherent flaws in the NGO model of development as they can hardly represent an alternative to the state and the public sector. Like the state, NGOs, barring a few exceptions, have failed at making a substantial impact upon the perceived beneficiaries they were expected to benefit. More importantly, NGOs are the creation of funding agencies and hence their entire existence, not merely dependency, is on donor money, almost always from above. The patron–client relationship emerging out of such a model of development raises numerous questions about their accountability and legitimacy. Charges like corruption, lack of transparency and idiosyncratic, paternalistic and authoritarian organisational structure have made many of them unreliable and unsustainable. So, the hype about NGOs is exaggerated and they are certainly not the panacea for all ills even though we are stuck with them. It should be remembered here that the scope of NGO activism to provide support and relief to the millions of poor, subaltern and weaker sections of people in the world is limited. NGO-isation could hardly prevent growing disparities in income and opportunities of a vast section of masses in post-globalised India. In spite of the relevance of this sector, therefore, we need to look for other viable alternatives. Mere voluntary action arising from the erosion of the modern state and its institutions poses serious threat to the credibility of this so-called 'third sector'.

In the third section, on gender and development, Maitrayee Chaudhuri seeks to focus on the shift in the Indian state's developmental paradigm since the early 1990s. This shift is a deeply gendered process, which she examines at two levels: one, at the specific level of actual policies on gender and development; and two, at the broader level of public discourse. According to Chaudhuri, the broad ideological shift in public discourse is closely linked to the actual policy shifts, and has reconfigured both class and gender in the national imaginary and therefore necessarily in the developmental priority. The paper is premised on the belief that the women's movement has succeeded in making gender a major issue in the public sphere. Yet, with the growing achievements, there has often been not just a de-link with visions of justice articulated by women's movement but often significant reconfigurations of the very ideas of freedom, justice, equity, autonomy, choice, activism, empowerment that it raised. Discernible in the dominant ideological paradigm in India is that an earlier relative privileging of workers is replaced with a rhetoric governed almost entirely by capitalists or 'captains of industry' as nation builders.

In the next article, Swapan Kumar Pramanick sparks off a lively debate on the issue of empowerment of women in India in general and their political empowerment in particular. Admitting that women's position in panchayats has significant outcome, Pramanick doubts that it would be a sufficient weapon to fight against social injustice or gender discrimination. This is because the overall socio-economic milieu in our society still continues to be discriminatory. Women also have to encounter class and caste identities, not just their gender identity. Despite changes in the role of women in the public sphere, their role in the private sphere has not changed. Hence, the current model of 'political empowerment' of women has serious limitations in initiating fundamental changes in either social structure or even in gender relations. But that does not minimise the importance of women's representation in elected bodies at all levels. Given our overall failure to protect the rights of women in every sphere of social life in contemporary India, encompassing political empowerment has the potential to initiate certain positive beginning.

Anup Dash and Souvagya Laxmi Saran argue that micro-finance holds enormous possibilities as a better policy alternative to rebuild damaged lives of poor women and their families in liberalised India. But, there is a lot of wrong in the current landscape of the global micro-finance industry. Given the influence of the hegemonic neo-liberal ideology, the micro-finance industry is behaving more and more like the commercial finance. There is a mission drift of the micro-finance industry. The authors further say that with its distinctive bi-dimensional focus – the economic and the social – the success of micro-finance programmes depends critically on blending values. Micro-credit only moves money to get quick superficial results on the ground, but with little long-term developmental impact. Micro-finance institutions focus only on the single bottom line (of profit), and are more interested in their own sustainability than scaling up their social impact. Such rent-seeking micro-finance institutions, with their minimalist credit programmes, pursuing the agenda of their own institutional well-being, naturally turn blind to the well-being of their poor women clients. The authors therefore are of the view that micro-finance programmes need to be looked into afresh to achieve their social goals of poverty reduction and women's empowerment.

The fourth section reflects our concern for an eco-friendly and sustainable environment. The deleterious effects of 'development' on our environment so far have shaken the faith of modern man. Subhasis Bandyopadhyay, in the light of this gloomy picture, tries to show that be it the issue of environment or development, a political-economic system of capital grossly distorts its code of inception to continue its tattered and cannibalistic existence amidst heaps of self-created ruins. Referring to certain inevitable mark of erosion in the corporate industrial hegemony across the world, the paper locates the smouldering issues of environment and development as watersheds in the 'structural crisis of capital'. Bandyopadhyay also takes a closer look at the neo-liberal attempt to utilise knowledgeable techniques to suit its survival needs at the huge cost of both environment and development. He notes that in the year 2010 three important realities have surfaced in the understanding of the global humanity almost as a postscript to the great economic crisis of 2007–08. These are: (a) the increasing stagnation in the domain of scientific knowledge; (b) the perilous situation of environment across the globe; and (c) the failure of mainstream development programme to reach the target population.

In the next article, Rajkishor Meher makes a critical analysis of the mega-projects taken up in post-independent India in the name of development. He examines the social and ecological impacts generated by them on displaced people and their hinterland economy and society by using case study method, and by making critical review of secondary data. He argues that such a development model initiated in the mineral-rich backward tribal regions of Orissa is ruining the agriculture-based living of tribal people. In the name of development more and more agricultural land is put into urban–industrial use, forest is deforested, water is polluted, people are uprooted and the entire ecosystem of tribal regions in the country is ecologically getting ruined with increasing land, water and air pollution. Such efforts of development mainstreaming generate only namesake benefits for a few relatively better off sections of populations. On the other hand, the majority of the poor tribals are becoming the victims of development. Their status from ecosystem people to ecological refugees in the slums of the large urban centres and grafted urban–industrial towns is a clear manifestation of the development pathologies of our time.

Continuing the debate, Manish K. Verma delves deep into the twin vital issues of rehabilitation and resettlement (R&R). The present investigation was initiated with an effort to locate the historical evolution of R&R policies and various other guidelines, concerned with the acquisition of land in India. The paper focuses on the processes and limitations of development-induced displacement with particular reference to the policies of NTPC in Singrauli region, Land Acquisition Act of India and such other agencies. The author suggests that in the absence of watertight policy, planners went for ad hoc and part-time solutions of the problem depending on their own wisdom. As a result, biases and prejudices erupted into the proceedings of rehabilitation. Verma feels that it is time now to learn from our mistakes and get on with serious R&R planning and execution with the involvement of victims as well as social science experts forming part of the administrative machinery.

Shoma Choudhury Lahiri concludes the discussion in this section by narrating the story of the People's Science Movement in Kerala – a state known for its unique experience of development. The People's Science Movement over its nearly 50 years of existence has worked towards 'taking science to the people' and in the course has intervened in the fields of education, environment, health, and more recently in local level planning and democratic decentralisation in the state. In this paper, the author examines the ways in which the movement engages with the Kerala model, and the extent to which it offers an alternative understanding of development through its interventions. Based on field experience, she argues that these 'alternatives' do not question the larger philosophical framework of development; they in fact create space within the existing framework of the techno-scientific development, thus reaffirming the spirit of developmentalism. Hence, despite its critical currency, development as modernity, with all its ambivalences, continues to be imbricated in the everyday lives, choices, strategies adopted by the various constituencies in Kerala.

The fifth and final section deals with social and cultural issues of development. The facts that social development is an inalienable part of economic development, that economic development is relational and not autonomous of social development and that economic development is a means to social and human development have got wide recognition is recent years. Against this backdrop, Debal K. SinghaRoy delineates the linkages between development, deprivations and social movements in the Indian context. He argues that India lives in paradoxical platform. Contemporary social and economic transition has furthered those paradoxes. While with fast economic development it has emerged to be the world hub of trained manpower and prosperity, it has also remained backward with highest burden of poverty, illiteracy and unemployment. The disjunction between economic growth and social development has contributed to emerging social instability and perversion in many areas of social and economic lives. The dismal state of social development, persisting injustice and inequality have widely resulted from the state failure to adhere to the broad guideline of the United Nations, mandates of the constitutions and increasing gap between the policy formulation and implementations of these policies at the grassroots. As a result, the backward areas of the country have emerged to be the hot beds of protests and resistance of diverse varieties. The author therefore finds positive correlation between social underdevelopment, social deprivations and social movements in the contemporary phase of transition of Indian society.

In the next article, Virginius Xaxa picks up the issue of tribal development in India. He examines the state's agenda towards such long cherished goal and finds that development schemes under the tribal sub-plan (TSP) have been at work now for about 35 years. Moreover, a number of commissions, committees, working groups and study teams have also been constituted from time to time to evaluate the condition and development problems of the scheduled tribes. Yet, the results are still very depressing. Often the failures are falsely attributed to factors inherent in the traditional socio-economic structure and cultural system of the people. Xaxa argues that the reasons for the state of affairs in which tribes are situated are not confined to the problems of implementation only. The reasons are structural too. The most important impact of the policy of national development was that it drastically altered the relationship of tribes with the natural environment and the resources lying therein, viz., land, forest, mineral and other resources. The massive displacement of the tribals from their land and territory following such 'development' has adversely affected the cultural heritage and communitarian life of the tribals. Hence, a great deal of indignation has been shown towards such projects. The resistance against such projects has set into motion not only a critique of development but also a justification for people-centric alternative development. Hence, Xaxa asserts that if we expect plans and strategies of tribal development to be more effective, these programmes and schemes should be evolved in consonance with the ecology, social organisation and cultural values of the tribal people.

Finally, Sekh Rahim Mondal looks into the critical issue of nexus between religion, community and development with particularly reference to Muslims in India. He shows that the state of underdevelopment of Muslims of this country has not been altered significantly even after decades of struggle for national development. Different government reports and research findings clearly indicate that there exist tremendous developmental deficits among the Muslims of this country. In view of this, the author examines the socio-economic status of Muslims of India in general and West Bengal in particular and assesses their problems for future direction of development and change. Mondal argues that the failure of the Muslims to transform their society is not only due to their lack of knowledge, modern skills and capabilities in most areas of intellectual endeavour, but also due to lack of opportunities and resources which are supposed to be available to them as free citizens of the country. Their obligation to the Indian state is also being questioned in some cases. For various reasons, Indian Muslims today have become conscious of their identity and existence. But at the same time it is also true that several 'Muslim factors' are creating obstacles towards their social upliftment. He holds that exclusion and alienation of the Muslims is the outcome of complex factors to which the issues of identity, security and inequality are deeply involved. The state and its political machinery on one hand and activities of some political as well as religious elites of the community on the other hand have played a very crucial role in this process. In order to address the issues of inter-group inequality among the Muslims, any inclusive policy should cover the people of all social categories of the Muslim community except the one who may be called 'creamy'. Under such a context, development initiatives should primarily focus on two factors: (a) increasing standard of living of affected people through socio-economic development, and (b) creating conditions conducive to the growth of people's self-esteem. For a comprehensive and qualitative development of the Muslim community the author puts forward the 'AMP model' (Awareness, Motivation and Participation). He also argues that these issues must be recognised as the problems of the whole nation and not of Muslims alone.

All the essays included in this volume thus present a multidimensional view of the discourses on development particularly in the Indian context. The discussion not only raises certain critical issues related to the major areas of debate on development today, it also suggests certain viable alternatives to resolve the impasse. This is however not to deny that there are many other issues of development confronting the activists and victims. But, one can make use of the wisdom inherent in the core of our discussion about development discourses to analyse a particular problem. Since 'development' is a big challenge for social scientists, administrators, activists and people concerned, there is every need to reconstruct our understanding about the process constantly and through critical evaluation of field experiences and 'local knowledge'. The task is tough, though not impossible.

Section I

Interrogating Development Discourse

1

Development Theory

Rhetoric and Reality*

T.K. Oommen

The career of the concept of development has undergone numerous twists and turns. Its nature and attributes lie in the mind of the analyst, ideologue or reformer. And yet, one can identify three major perspectives in the trajectory development. I shall designate them as mainstream perspective on development (MPD), alternative perspective on development (APD) and post-development perspective (PDP). Admittedly, MPD emerged first and has a long career. In the beginning, the term 'development' was not even invoked.

I

The earliest avatar of MPD could be traced to colonialism and its civilising mission. The colonies of Asia, Africa and the Americas had to be managed and 'developed' by the colonisers for the benefit of the colonised. The export of raw materials from the colonies and their manufacture in West European countries accelerated the latter's industrialisation. This brought about a developmental gap within Europe – the industrialised West Europe on the one hand and the late entrants to industrialisation of Central and East Europe on the other. Establishing primacy of industry over agriculture was the second phase in MPD. Industrialise or perish was the refrain those days.

---

* To compose this lecture I have drawn liberally from Jan Nederveen Pieterse. 2001. *Development Theory: Deconstruction/Reconstruction*. New Delhi: Vistaar Publications.

However, political changes in the colonies and the less industrialised Central and East European countries provided a new twist to the career of development. Development in the colonies was introduced from outside; it was an utterly exogenous project, modelled after the values of the West. Anti-colonial movements rejected the agency of colonial West for development but accepted its goal, namely, modernisation. Modernisation has now become the endogenous project of development to be executed by the 'national' elite. Colonialism was replaced with the modernisation, which in effect was westernisation.

In the case of Central and East European countries the arrival of socialism gave birth to a new model of development. While both capitalism and socialism invoked industrialisation as the primary tool of development, the former combined it with political democracy and the latter with one-party democracy. This gave rise to two competing models of modernisation. The 'natural' modernity of the capitalist democracies initiated the process of economic growth along with equality of opportunity through its welfare states giving birth to the First World. The state was central but adequate space was conceded to market and civil society under this regime. In contrast, the 'enlightened' modernity of socialist stages rolled up the state, civil society and market into one entity and pursued economic growth along with distributive justice. The Second World was created in this process.

The idea of stages of growth crystallised during the Cold War period. However, there were two versions of it – the Right and the Left. Both endorsed industrial urbanisation and modernisation as their goals and advocated that the backward economies should follow the same trajectory. The difference was in the prescription for the backwards, how to acquire capital and technology. The Right advocated an open economy to maximise the technological capacity of the backward economies. The argument was that this will gradually lead to the reduction and final displacement of the traditional sector by the modern sector.

The Left view was that development has to be achieved through endogenous efforts, primarily through the efforts of the state sector through the development of the public sector. That is, the two approaches differed not on the basis of the kind of technology, techniques of production or division of labour, but in the role of state and market. If capitalists gave primacy to the market, the socialists accorded the state with the commanding position.

The Third World countries, largely but not entirely ex-colonial and agrarian, had thus two models of modernisation to opt for. For all practical purposes the Cold War was a project to annex the Third World countries to one of these modernities. Most of the Third World countries opted for one of these but some like India tried to combine multi-party democracy of the First World and planned economic development of the Second World, creating a new model of development, christened as the Third Way.

However, all the three worlds had industrialisation as their aim. But the devastation wrought by industrialisation on environment gave birth to a new trend in development thinking. Development produced the 'risk society' as the whole world is exposed to ecological devastations. Globalisation of risk through global ecological hazards, export of polluting industries and waste materials, the risks of biogenetic engineering, etc., are fast spreading. Understandably, sustainable development became the new refrain.

In the meantime multi-party democracy gained near-universal legitimacy and the Second World got dismantled. The disappearance of the Second World led to the conceptualisation of One World, the global society, as if the Third World did not matter. The bi-polar world gave birth to a uni-polar world and the Cold War disappeared. The new instrument of development is the Structural Adjustment Programme (SAP); modernisation is replaced by globalisation. The two current offsprings of MPD are neo-liberalism and human development.

The high ideological point of neo-liberalism is articulated through the Washington Consensus which maintains that economic growth is best pursued through open trade, export-led growth, greater deregulation and more liberalised financial markets. This market-centred neo-classical approach represents Anglo-American capitalism. And, what is the end product of this process of development? The example of the United States of America, the arch typical neo-liberal economy, is telling. The travails of 'Other America', constituted largely by the Black underclass, are widely reported. The income disparity between the richest and the poorest in the 1980s, in the US, was 350 times. Yet, the US, is invariably designated as the most 'successful' democracy in the world. The assumption that free market and authentic democracy go together is patently wrong. We need to de-couple them. Ensuring political citizenship rights does not ensure basic economic, social and cultural needs.

The other strand of thinking is MPD has come to be designated as human development, which refers to a set of normative orientation – equity, sustainability, productivity and empowerment. That is, mainstream development is no more defined merely in terms of growth and measured by means of per capita income or GNP. Recognising basic needs, distributive justice and growth with equity, it is defined as enlargement of people's choice and human capacitation. Human development claims to put people first catering to their basic needs – nutrition, health, literacy, education and housing. The Human Development Index (HDI) has become the new measure of the people-centred development. It also goes beyond citizenship rights and encapsulates human rights. The newly industrialised countries (NICs) of Asia, particularly Asian Tigers, are taken as the empirical base for conceptualisation.

Both neo-liberalism and human development focus on the individual as the unit of development and neglect social engineering based on groups and communities. It is claimed that in East Asia equity and growth have gone hand in hand. But, the fact is that in these countries pre-growth income inequality was low. This facilitated the achievement of equity in the process of growth. However, ignoring inter-group inequality has had disastrous consequences.

For example, in Malaysia, from 1970s onwards an inter-ethnic trade off is in existence. Citizenship rights for economically prosperous Chinese and economic gains for the politically entrenched *Bhumiputras* were assured by the state. But the state neglected the interests of Malaysians of Indian origin leading to their alienation and large-scale entry into the criminal world. In Indonesia, the Chinese business community was fostered as a trading minority while only limited political rights were conceded to them. The economic prosperity of the Chinese without political empowerment rendered them easy targets of attacks by the 'sons of the soil' in inter-ethnic conflicts, which took a heavy toll of the process of development. The NICs, which are high achievers on the HDI, are weak democracies. Although they have adjusted to the current market-oriented development process, they also play an important role in development. This suggests that global markets and state intervention can co-exist.

The human development perspective (HDP) sometimes becomes a cross-breed between MPD and the alternative perspective on development. Rejecting growth and pursuing development with equity is HDP's refrain. An oft-quoted example is the "Kerala model", which emphasises equity, participation and sustainability. It is true that Kerala has achieved high literacy, better health status and considerable empowerment of women. But there is high unemployment and suicide and crime rates are highest in Kerala among Indian states. And, 30 per cent of population of Kerala remains below the poverty line even today. At any rate, the Kerala model, which focuses on equity without growth, can be only maintained in certain pockets because Kerala's economy is sustained through the flow of funds from regions experiencing rapid growth. For distributive justice to be effected somebody, somewhere, should produce the goods to be distributed. This is to say productivity can be ignored only at the peril of development.

MPD often conceptualises development as a single homogeneous process towards modernisation underestimating the potentials for diversity, complexity and adaptability. In fact, most studies in this tradition undertaken through sophisticated quantitative analyses conclude that growth is positively related to equality. Many of these studies also conclude that inequality is harmful to growth. On the other hand, dependency theory raised the issue of global inequality. But, the fact is that inequality has been increasing even as rapid growth is taking place. The ratio between the incomes of the richest and the poorest country was about 3 to 1 in 1820, 35 to 1 in 1950 and 72 to 1 in 1992. In 1996, 800 million people went to bed hungry every day. How can one explain the gap between the theoretical claim of MPD and the empirical reality?

The narrow economic framework employed by the neo-liberal model is consistent only when it leaves out social, cultural, political psychological and environmental variables. In fact, development was initially understood as economic development. Sociology and Social Anthropology entered the arena of development studies to explain the factors which facilitated or hindered development and launched the notion of social development. Psychology provided insights about the factors which motivated or discouraged development. The concern of Political Science was to provide information regarding political factors influencing development. Finally, environmental concern linked economic development and ecological destruction. It is this moving away of development studies from economics, which heralded the beginning of the alternative perspective on development (APD). APD takes many banners – participatory, appropriate, people-centred, autonomous, holistic, ethno – which erodes its coherence.

II

APD is a critique of mainstream perspective on development. There are two strands of this. First, an alternative approach to development. That is, apparently the goal is the same as that of MPD but the means differ – it is participatory and people-oriented. Here, the agency of development becomes crucial – a shift from state and/or market to civil society is emphasised. A visible manifestation of this shift of emphasis in the agency of development is found in the fact that in the past two decades more funds are channelled through NGOs than through governments by IMF and World Bank. This also hints at the peaceful co-existence of the two perspectives – mainstream and alternative.

Secondly, an alternative goal of development is visualised through APD – people-centred development, geared to satisfaction of needs, which is endogenous, self-reliant and in harmony with the environment. In this rendition, APD incarnates as anti-capitalism, green thinking, feminism, eco-feminism, new social movements, Buddhist economics and post-structuralist analysis of development discourse. Alternative development then is development from below, that is, community-centred and NGO-initiated. APD generally refers to three spheres – agents (NGOs), methodology (participatory, self-reliant, endogenous) and objectives (geared to basic needs).

The hallmark of alternative development methodology is participation, the epistemological root of alternative development is local knowledge, and its implementation strategy is decentralisation of economy and polity. But all these elements are increasingly incorporated by MPD. The society-centred participatory development is now being co-opted by modernists and neo-liberals. What is labelled as indigenous is not always local but that which is locally accepted. Many of the indigenous items have been alien once. Thus, it is the process indigenisation rather than nativity that matters. At any rate indigenous knowledge is often insufficient, inadequate and even inappropriate. Therefore, we need to mutate the indigenous and the alien. It is the process of hybridisation, which renders the alien acceptable. Finally, decentralisation is now widely endorsed by MPD. Even the World Bank advocates putting the people first!

The point I am making is that APD has been increasingly incorporated into MPD. Yesterday's alternatives are today's mainstream. Alternatives then only mean the latest. Institutionalisation of dissent is a perennial possibility. New movements become old, and in turn solidify as institutions. Alternatives interrogate the maladies of mainstream; they do not always provide an alternative goal. Both the mainstream and alternative perspectives pursue development, the quality of which is continuously bettered.

However, APD assumed great importance as manifested in the following trends: First, the importance of environmental concerns and sustainability of development has weakened MPD and gave a boost to ecological economics. Secondly, the failure of several development decades to achieve their goals unsettled MPD. Thirdly, the growing challenges to Bretton Woods institutions led to the question whether these criticisms are merely procedural and institutional (for more participation and democratisation) or they involve fundamentally different principles. Finally, and most importantly, the enormous growth of NGOs in numbers and influence christened APD as a rival to MPD.

What I am suggesting is that there is a dialectical relationship between MPD and APD; they shape and influence reciprocally, giving birth to mutations such as human development perspective (HDP). But the argument often takes the form of a simple binary opposition between the two. In order to emphasise the opposition between MPD and APD, the appeal of the mainstream perspective to various constituencies is underestimated. The fact is APD has been co-opted by MPD, which can be seen either as its castration or celebration depending upon one's perspective.

III

While both MPD and APD pursue development, even if of varying quality, the post-development perspective (PDP) rejects development as conceptualised by MPD and APD. APD advocates the death of development; it is beyond development. Indeed, it is anti-development. PDP emerged with a western critique of modernity and techno-scientific progress such as critical theory, post-structuralism and green movements. An important distinction between APD and PDP is that APD rejects the idea of development equals modernisation equals westernisation, which is often the refrain of MPD. APD refuses to be a mere endorser of the western model of development; it rejects the notion of singular modernity. But it does not reject the notion of modernity as such, it pleads for multiple modernity, the non-west being creators of their versions of alternative modernity. But PDP rejects the very idea of modernity and hence development. Why?

According to PDP, development is not required because poverty is not to be taken for granted, it is a culturally and historically variable notion. Subsistence economies which serve basic needs are not peopled by deprived people. They are defined as poor and deprived by western theorists because they do not participate in the market economy. These people are first labelled as poor by western theorists and then advised to develop. Development is not their felt-need, their natural aspiration. In the rendition of PDP, poverty is first *invented* and development is then prescribed to eradicate poverty.

Colonialism ended and development (modernisation) took over and Coca-colonisation, McDonaldisation and Disneyfication came in. The dream of development is over. What is required is not more development, but a different regime of truth and perception.

The main target of attack by PDP is western science, particularly Newtonian Physics, positivism, Cartesianism and Enlightenment thinking. But it forgets the fact that science has been continuously renewing itself through quantum physics, chaos theory and methodological anarchism. PDP ignores this new science. At any rate, in social science, which deals with the development discourse, positivism is no more the favoured paradigm. A development economist sensitive to the complex social reality cannot afford to ignore politics, society, culture, gender and ecology. Most concepts in currency in development studies – human development, institutional development, good governance, and accountability – are interdisciplinary.

The main limitation of PDP is that it puts a moratorium on human creativity; it ignores the capacity of MPD to adapt. It even denies the agency of South; the importance of dependency theory, the relevance of alternative development, the sensibility of human development. It is trapped by epistemological dualism, the very God that failed, according to its evaluation. It is not true that westernisation displaces everything through development. Indeed, PDP cannot account for Easternisation, Japanisation or a South Asian model of development. Polycentrism is denied, Euro-centrism is upheld, albeit unwittingly. It throws away the baby with the bathwater.

IV

I have identified three major perspectives on development – mainstream, alternative and post – and referred to their numerous incarnations.

Admittedly, there is a substantial volume of studies of differing qualities produced by them. And yet, there are a number of absences or cognitive blackouts, if you prefer. I shall identify four of them, the four Ds, to illustrate the inadequacy of the development discourse. The four Ds are: Displacement, Disparity, Distress and Discrimination.

There seems to be an unquestioned acceptance of the unidirectionality implied in the process of development that hardly draws anyone's attention. Thus, the rural is to be displaced by the urban; low, simple or traditional technology by high, complex or modern technology; the state by the market or the state and market by the civil society in the context of development. This is one of the serious deficits in development thinking. Because displacement is no road to development, often quite the contrary. Consider the following chilling facts. Eighty per cent of couples in Mumbai, the financial capital of India, live in one room, usually with parents and siblings. Most of them manage their lovemaking on the terrace, in guest houses and hotels or in parked vehicles. It is estimated that half of Mumbai was conceived in parked cars owned or hired. Is this hardship experienced by the people of urban Mumbai an indicator of development? If no, is it not atrocious to invoke urbanisation as an indicator of the ongoing process of development?

The state should be displaced by the market under the neo-liberal regime of development; the market should be displaced by the state promoting development under the socialist model. Alternative development wants that both state and market should be displaced by civil society, which should be the prime mover of development. But none of these proposals can work. What is called for is the cooperation between state, market and civil society to bring about balanced development. Similarly, the central tendency in development thinking is to advocate the displacement of traditional technology. Even the advocates of appropriate technology want to displace simple and traditional technology. But what we need is co-existence of all these technologies, that is, technological pluralism.

The second inadequately addressed issue in development studies is disparity. While dependency theory highlighted increasing global disparity, it did not address the issue of disparity within nations. According to neo-liberals, the notion of meritocracy and its motivating engine, namely, 'incentives' legitimises wide disparity between individuals. Both neo-liberals and advocates of HDP take the individual as the unit of development and hence ignores inter-group disparity. Even the APD does not adequately address rural–urban disparity or disparity between cultural communities – religious, linguistic and regional. Only gender disparity attracted some attention in development discourse.

Socialism as such provides no guarantee for reduction of disparities. In Soviet Union, the disparity in wages between the highest and the lowest paid was 33 times in the 1960s. In contrast, in capitalist Scandinavian countries, the wage disparity between the richest and the poorest in the 1970s was only seven times. While a society from which disparity disappears completely is a utopian dream, a society which limits the range of disparity, is in the realm of possibility. While development analysts do discuss the issues of equality and equity, the focus is on equality of opportunities, on providing a level playing ground so that inequality among individuals and between communities can be legitimised.

I need to digress a bit at this juncture to inform you that equality of opportunity cannot be translated into practice except in a very limited sense in so far as deep inequalities on the basis of gender, class, caste and race exist. To cope with the situation we need to create equality of condition for the disadvantaged so that they can successfully compete with the privileged. That is why policies such as affirmative action, protective discrimination and nationality policy are required. But, the vested interest forces from traditionally privileged categories as well as a section of the neo-elite emanating from the traditionally underprivileged categories will oppose the proper functioning of the policies. And yet, the policy should be implemented and society should achieve equality of outcome. The real deficit in development discussions is the silence about equality of outcome leading to the widening of disparity.

The third cognitive blackout in development discourse is distress. Some of the development toppers, which are certified to have good governance (as well as labelled as successful democracies) have an unacceptably high level of human distress. For example, Sweden is among the highest four countries in the rate of murders and rapes and is also among the highest seven countries for suicide, according to Human Development Report of 1991. The United States of America had the highest rate of murders, rapes and prisoners in the same year. Generally, a developed country is believed to have a high quality of life. Can a country where rapes, murders, suicides etc., are rampant have a high quality of life? It seems that we need to re-cast our conceptualisation of 'development' taking into account the distress, which prevails in a society. But development theorists rarely undertake this exercise.

Finally, the issue of discrimination is rarely discussed in devel opment studies. Development necessitates movement of population across rural–urban spaces and cultural regions within countries as well as between countries. The tendency on the part of the 'sons of the soil' to look upon the migrants into their area as cultural strangers and usurpers of their economic opportunities is antithetical to the very ethos of development. Racism, religious persecution, caste discrimination and ethnification are all associated with movement of population in the context of development. And yet, development experts rarely discuss these socio-cultural discriminations. They seem to be impervious to what happens to human beings even as they are propagating the idea of human development and putting people first!

V

I have suggested that the development discourse is very rich in rhetoric but rather poor in coping with reality. Part of the reason for this is that positions and counter-positions in development studies often operate on the basis of simplistic dichotomies – modernity versus tradition, western science versus indigenous knowledge, the global versus the local, the state versus the market. This is a sterile exercise and polemics at its worst. What is the way out of this impasse? I have no illusion to carve out the right path where an army of researchers failed in spite of decades of hard work. However, let me list five precautionary measures so that development thinking need not persist with its current sterility.

First, much of the development thinking is linear. A plausible option is the application of chaos theory to development. Chaos does not mean randomness or the absence of order. It refers to unpredictability of the outcome because of small differences in initial conditions. The small differences in local conditions, across regions, cultures and polities, do determine the final outcome of development.

Secondly, along with the importance of characteristics of the situation referred to above, we must be aware of the role of reflexivity in the context of development. In so far as the development process invites reactions and responses of the people for whom it is meant, their reflexivity should be built into the development enterprises – development plans, projects and outcomes.

Thirdly, the keynote of neo-liberalism is state failure. The complaint of alternative development is the rapacity of the market.

Post-development is suspicious of all, even the civil society. Development, however, should be viewed as a conjoint project of state, market and civil society; it calls for equipoise between all the three.

Fourthly, development is a multi-layered project; it cannot be differentiated into macro, meso and micro projects. The pre-requisite of authentic development is privileging of the different dimensions in their respective spheres. To put it differently, the different layers and dimensions involved in development should be fused into a totality. For this, a holistic approach is required; we need a Tao of development.

Fifthly, if the difference in initial conditions does influence the final outcome, if human reflexivity is to be respected, if the equipoise between the state, market and civil society is to be conceded, if decentring is a necessary developmental strategy, we must expect multiple models of modernity to emerge and developmental pluralism to flourish.

To endorse these proposals is to unthink, not simply re-think, the current development discourse.

2

Understanding Development

Theory and Practice

Biswajit Ghosh

The term 'development' is normally understood to be a process for changing economic and social capacities, priorities and choices. In common parlance, it means well-being and better life for people at large. For many of us, 'development' is also a desire for fulfilment of basic needs both for our sustenance (food, cloth, house, employment, health, education, safety, security etc.) as well as for our comfort (better services, communication, freedom, openness, mobility, dignity, etc.). But, there is little uniformity amongst most of us about what constitute the basic and immediate needs! Measuring development is a thorny endeavour even though we are able to use improvised techniques like Human Development Index (HDI) or Gender Development Index (GDI) today for any comparative and critical estimate. Barriers like class, community, caste, gender, region or country prevent us to arrive at any common minimum understanding. Initially, however, the idea of development was associated with systematic growth, evolution, advancement and progress. Here again, social scientists differed widely about the nature, agency and route to progress. In fact, the 19th century sociologists like Comte, Marx, Spencer, Durkheim, Simmel or Weber offered contrasting solutions to the problems of mankind. Not only this, progress made in a particular period of human history was later turned out to be disaster for all of us. The notion of 'development' has therefore gradually turned out to be a very complex and contentious one, although it is conceived as an optimistic concept in all contemporary societies, particularly in the industrial and post-colonial societies.

In the 19th century, catching up with the advanced industrialised societies was the cherished goal for many developing societies. But, with changing passage of time, the supremacy of the economic model of development is seriously challenged. It is now being realised that even matter like poverty can be and should be measured qualitatively as any simple statistical figure (also GDP/GNP estimates) often leads to suppression and misrepresentation of facts. Not only this, in the name of development, a vast majority of people in different parts of the world witnessed marginalisation, decay, stagnation, retardation, underdevelopment, inequality or violence. In other words, the promise of sustained progress and our journey to a new paradise appear to be more and more remote even after several decades of 'development' sponsored by nation-state and supported by accredited world organisations. The western experience of development since 17th century has been full of disillusionment. Nonetheless, we were very smart enough to shift the agenda of development from industrialisation to structural adjustment and now to Millennium Development Goals (MDGs). Subtle change in the agenda of development however signifies little change in the quality of life and environment worldwide. Surprisingly, neither the capitalist, nor the socialist models of development, could provide any sustainable solutions to the problems of mankind, though there have been some success here and there. Hence, despite import or often imposition of certain models of development from outside, different societies of the world of late have realised the need to develop differently keeping in view their own specific conditions and challenges. During the last 150 years or so, therefore, we have witnessed the rise of different meanings and goals of development over time and space.

Considering the fact that there are many dimensions and approaches to development, a particular model of development is often imposed from above without concerns for its suitability and feasibility in a given context. Hence, development is often viewed as an ideology as well as its propaganda. As a corollary, it is not only difficult to define development, the concept itself has become an issue of considerable debate; a contentious question subjected to variety of interpretations and expectations. J.N. Pieterse has attempted to define development as "the organised intervention in collective affairs according to a standard of improvement". But, that did not prevent him from recognising that "what constitutes improvement and what is appropriate intervention vary according to class, culture, historical context and relations of power"

(Pieterse 2001: 3). Quite obviously, questions like 'development by whom', 'for whom' and 'at what costs' are frequently being raised by even those who talk about development. Any shortcut answers to these queries are neither possible, nor justifiable, given varied and often contradictory experiences of development so far.

In the Indian context, for instance, 'modern' problems like poverty, inequality, unemployment, price rise, illiteracy, displacement or pollution are yet rampant. But, quite contrarily, 'traditional' issues related to caste, community, ethnicity, region, religion and gender, which should have been obliterated with the spread of modern values and institutions, are becoming more sharp and delicate with growing maturity and indexes of socio-economic development. As a corollary, all of our planners, administrators and political leaders have a long list of things to be done because the list of things not done or could not be done so far is also far too long. And this is true for every state, from Bihar to Kerala. How would one explain the development of a society that has retained its tradition in spite of the advent of modernity? Why is child sex ratio declining in those states of India that have witnessed prosperity? Why did social achievements of Kerala fail to prevent its economic slowdown? All these and many more questions open up the Pandora's box for critical evaluation today. This paper attempts to review theoretically the dynamics of development and examine the experience of development particularly from the Indian point of view so as to offer any possible solution to the impasse.

Plethora of Approaches to Development

It is interesting to note at the outset that the term 'development' had originally gained popularity since Second World War. Development was then a western alternative to communism for the decolonising countries of the South. In 1949, the then US President Harry Truman set the frame for *development assistance* (for the underdeveloped countries) from North to South. On the whole, development practice became an instrument to organise post-colonial, backward societies. During this time, development was restrictively defined in terms of economic growth. Cowen and Shenton (1996) however argue that there was yet another meaning of development in 19th century England and that referred to remedies for the shortcoming and maladies of progress. Even before that one can trace the earliest avatar of development to colonialism and its civilising mission. But, with the emergence of independent nation-states and broadening of the meaning of development from economic growth to modernisation, development debate took a new turn. It was then argued that economic growth is dependent on political reform and social engineering from above. Initially, however, modernisation meant the rejection of tradition for the South and adoption of western and more specifically American institutions and culture. But gradually this model of modernisation began competing with the communist model of development proposed by Moscow.

Both the models of development however stressed on industrial urbanisation and modernisation as well as the role of state as the executive agency of development policy even though they prescribed some contrasting path and outcome. But the myth of modernisation gradually lost its appeal in the face of mounting criticism that it has led to accumulation of resources in the North. The idea of the state as the prime mover of development also turned into scepticism following the failures of Third World states in particular. Dependency theorists criticised development thinking for being ahistorical and denying the role of imperialist exploitation in European modernisation. Even in the West, the possibility of social engineering through state action is felt with distrust. Increasingly, the state is looked upon with suspicion if not contempt. Furthermore, the failure of the European socialist states to protect human rights and promote sustained growth became a rallying point. In the Third World, the state is found to be corrupt, oppressive and often anti-poor. Least governance is therefore today seen as the sign of good governance. Due to declining legitimacy of the state and enormous flaws in the functioning of its machinery (red-tapism, apathy, collusion with vested interest, deliberate delay in decision-making or its implementation, etc.) many activists now see certain inherent value in voluntary movements. The entry of non-state associations and voluntary mobilisations including new forms of social movements are to be analysed in this context.

While the undeveloped societies of the East and West have failed to develop or modernise following the footsteps of advanced industrialised countries of Europe, 'development of underdevelopment' became a reality in many parts of the world. The cost of development for the societies of the Third World has been huge as these peripheral societies became dependent on the centre for their sustenance. Even though the debate about the nature of relation and characterisation of 'centre' and 'periphery' in a global society could not be solved, the United Nations Development Programme (UNDP) has acknowledged that the gap between rich and poor countries has actually widened and that the average household in Africa now consumes 20 per cent less than it did about a quarter century ago (UNDP 2001). On the contrary, 200 million of the richest people living in the rich countries (3% of world population) get 40 per cent of total global income (World Bank 2004). In case of South Asia, import of development models from outside is equally seen as inimical to the rich and versatile cultural heritage of these societies. In other words, going beyond the narrow economistic model of development, culture or social structure then gained prominence as an instrument of development. Any effort to development must therefore take into account the cultural distinctiveness of a community or society.

In the West, however, the crisis of developmentalism and an understanding of the 'limits of growth' in a risk society have contributed to the rise of discourses on both 'alternative to development' and 'alternative of development'. Interestingly, the protagonists of mainstream development have advanced many of these alternatives. For instance, the World Bank argued for the non-governmental organisations (NGOs) as the third sector; UNDP talked about Human Development Index (HDI) and Gender Development Index (GDI); World Bank and United Nations popularised the concept of sustainable development (Brundtland Commission); and the goal of women's empowerment was first listed by the UN at Nairobi Conference (1985). The effort to minimise any opposition to the mainstream developmental thinking has also led to the emergence of neo-liberal prescription of development through global market in a post-industrial, post-modern network society. And, the new policy agenda of civil society building and 'NGO-isation' also matches the neo-liberal agenda of government roll back and decentralisation. Civil society is considered to be a space for the enforcement and enhancement of social, economic and political justice. It is a healthy and necessary compliment to democracy. There are however critical questions regarding the possibility of any civil society within the parameters of western bourgeois democracy and class rule. Scholars have also expressed doubts about the possibility of emergence of 'civility' or existence of real democratic CSOs in a society marked by caste, religion or kinship (Mahajan 1999; Béteille 2000; Kaviraj 2001; Ghosh 2009a).

It is true that globalisation, as a distinct phase in capitalist development, has changed the standard units of development, namely, the nation and society, today. The conventional agent of development, the state and its machinery, is being overtaken by the role of international institutions and market forces (Pieterse 2001). To many critics, globalisation is only a new logic of western economic, technological and cultural domination and the process is nothing but a trendy word for advanced capitalism, which faces the crises of accumulation and stagnation. It however took little time for us to understand that irrespective of the irreversibility of technological globalisation, market is not and cannot be the only alternative to state action or civil society activism. It may be noted here that while globalisation has opened up opportunities of several types for even people of developing countries, including the poor, one can also witness a sharp rise in income inequalities in cities and towns. In case of Third World societies, increasing development has rather led to disparities between the rich and the poor, elite and non-elite, between users and non-users of technology, men and women, and rural and urban population. It should be kept in mind that the process of informalisation and casualisation of our economy has serious implications for the cherished goals of social security, quality of life and employment. It is worth noting here that market reform in India since 1991 has led to the growth of a large 'class of losers' along with a small 'class of winners' (Ghosh 2010). Casual and informal sector jobs are hardly rewarding and secured. As such, 'jobless growth' during the post-reform period in India and 'job-lost growth' during the current period of market recession could not mitigate the problems of unemployment and poverty. There is therefore every reason to believe that economic reforms have widened disparity and distress among people. Stagnant agriculture, higher inflation, market recession, increase in the number of casual, marginal and agricultural workers, and higher rates of malnutrition among children – all refer to increasing stress and exclusion in the life of common man. In this context, NCRB (2009) data reveal that more than 17,000 farmers committed suicide in the country in 2009 alone due to economic hardship. Globalisation is therefore argued to be a failed project. Today, even the strong protagonists of market liberalism seek state protection. Instead of our concern for good and transparent governance, the state is required to carry out large-scale welfare activities, particularly in countries like India.

It should however be noted here that globalisation is not a unidirectional one. It is much broader, complex, transformative and multifaceted process. As a corollary, globalisation has increased our 'social reflexivity' (Giddens 2006: 123). Television, newspaper and computer network have given people greater access to information and allowed them to see an extensive variety of forms of life than previously possible. As a dynamic and open process, it has also helped us to organise protest movements globally. Moreover, global environmental crises embrace all of us irrespective of class, region and other socio-cultural differences and hence 'development' requires new agency and institutions globally. There are, however, sharp differences of opinion among activists, scholars and professionals about the nature and role of alternatives offered to cure social and economic evils. This is in spite of the fact that we are convinced about developmental goals like social development, human development, freedom, capacity development, inclusive growth, gender development, empowerment, sustainable development, self-development, participatory development, green ecology etc.

As compared to such optimism, post-development, which is a radical reaction to the dilemmas of development, rejects the optimism that attaining even a middle class lifestyle for the majority of the population worldwide is possible. This school argues that development leads to homogenisation, environmental destruction, exhaustion of natural resources, marginalisation, increasing disparities and displacement. Hence, "it is not the failure of development as such, which has to be feared, but its success" (Sachs 1992: 3). Though their positions are not always consistent, such thinking has led some scholars to reject 'development' totally. For instance, Escobar (1992) and Esteva (1992) hold that development is a 'Frankenstein-type dream', an alien model of exploitation and reflects urban bias. While this discourse analysis has strengthened our reflexivity about development, the question is whether total rejection of development is tenable or possible. On the whole, the development discourse has made us aware about certain critical issues of development across special and socio-cultural boundaries. Let me now discuss a few of them in some detail.

Gender and Development

One major goal of any development agenda is to attain gender equality and gender justice. These issues are today matters of intense scrutiny and debate all over the world. Feminist critique of patriarchy, social structure, culture and values led to the alternative and often revolutionary sensitivity about gender relations and continuation of such socially constructed identities in modern times. The age-old argument of Natural Complementary Theory that masculine and feminine behaviours are biologically determined has lost its appeal. Intellectual discourse on gender inequality during early 1970s had paved the way for the rise of women's development strategy in several parts of the world. The seminal empirical work of liberal feminist Esther Boserup (1970) had helped to produce a distinctive feminist version of the mainstream development process. She showed that the benefits of development do not automatically trickle down to the poor and marginalised women and as a corollary women's status is declining with rising prosperity. The promise that modernisation would deliver greater benefits to women than men, permitting freedom from household drudgery and seclusion in the household, was hardly realised, particularly in the Third World. The upsurge against male domination and oppression during 1970s and early 1980s, therefore, was accompanied by theorising on patriarchy by a host of feminists known as liberal, radical, French, Anglo-American, existentialist, psychoanalytic, Marxist/socialist, post-colonial, post-modern, eco-feminism (Saunders 2004: 2; Harish and Harishankar 2008: xi). The rise of Women in Development (WID) approach in this context has stressed on the productive role of 'invisible' women. From a liberal, modernising perspective, WID advocated legal rights and government policy to prevent gender discrimination and supported the logic for integration of women into development through access to training and employment. Many of national and international development agencies have provided legitimacy to this approach and during the last four decades official UN conferences have played a critical role in mobilising women globally.

In spite of an emerging concern for women's development, the women's point of view is however not singular but heterogeneous. For instance, the Marxist/socialist approach of Women and Development (WAD) has stressed on the overarching influence of structural factors in a class divided society that lead to the subjugation of women. Although, it cannot be denied that sex segregation and women's economic marginalisation are also a reflection of the overall societal economic inequality, there are reasons to believe that gender inequality is not always a reflection of economic inequality alone. Had it been the case, such disparities would have disappeared in the socialist states and there would have been a uniform pattern of gender discrimination in the rest of the world. There are also evidences to suggest that in developing countries economic modernisation and the introduction of electronic technology have rather displaced women from their traditional productive functions.

It is in such a context that the notion of Gender and Development (GAD) proposed by the radical feminists gives due attention to fundamental structures of inequity between men and women. GAD is concerned to unearth gender as an ideological construct in its culturally varied expression. A close scrutiny of social relations between sexes would prove that gender ideology pervades all aspects of life including work, distribution of wealth, income and other resources, decision-making, power sharing, prestige, rights and privileges. The social invisibility of women contributes to the limited perception of their role even as members of elected bodies. As a result, women's contribution to the household or outside work is readily set aside and urbanisation does not seem to be a panacea for solving the gender issues (Ghosh 2001; Ghosh and Choudhuri 2011). There is therefore pressing need for estimating the impact of gender ideology on the construction and reconstruction of institutional practices, gender inequality and subjugation. Consequently, the decade of 1990s had witnessed the rise of women's empowerment perspective so as to argue for an improved social, economic and political space for women. Empowerment is conceived here as "the harnessed, self-generating power of women to act in their own interest" (Saunders 2004: 11).

It appears that a monolithic viewpoint on the issue is not possible; yet recognition of heterogeneity did not prevent feminists cutting across boundaries to recognise the commonality of opposition to gender oppression. This is because, along with problems of nationality, class and race, women more often than not face violence as 'woman'. In other words, both commonality and differences explain women's position in the world today. Similarly, the struggle against gender subordination does not rule out the possibility of struggle against other forms of oppression (Sen and Grown 1987).

In the Indian context, issues of women's development are found to be governed by ideological and gender considerations. The Indian state has however attempted to bring about desirable changes in the status of women and check gender violence through legal reforms. It has been argued that the framers of Indian Constitution have shared a high degree of gender sensitivity at a time when the issue of gender equality was hardly an agenda of socio-cultural reform (Sarkar 2005: 103). They, therefore, affirmed that there would not only be 'justice – social, economic and political' for all citizens, but there would be equality of status and opportunity. Equality before law is a fundamental right and discrimination on the ground of sex is legally prohibited in India. However, the goal of equal pay for equal work for men and women could not be realised and it remained a Directive

Principle of the State Policy to be implemented at a future date. Again, the long cherished goal of a Uniform Civil Code to secularise and homogenise family laws stated under Article 44 of the Constitution is yet a directive principle. The lawmakers have however taken up the Hindu law for making uniformities among the Hindus. They have also reserved 33 per cent of seats for women in local bodies and the effort to ensure such reservation at the highest level of electoral bodies is going on.

Yet, on the whole, the Indian state has maintained contradictory and perplexed positions to ensure or even to maintain gender justice. An analysis of the state response to gender inequality in India has led Sarkar (2005: 111) to conclude that "the state has tended to take a step forward and two steps backwards in its support of legal provisions that favour women". It has also been argued that Indian law has subordinated women in complex and subtle form by reinforcing deeply gendered assumptions, relations and roles (Kapur 2005: 153). The law plays a role in legitimating unequal power relations in society through its recognition of familial ideology, the public/private distinction and the sexual division of labour.

Surprisingly, increasing instances of different types of violence against women in India clearly point to the fact that women of this country, which has the tradition of worshipping goddesses symbolising *shakti* (power), regularly experience humiliation, insult, sexual abuse, molestation, rape, physical torture, and even death in the hands of even 'close relatives' (Ghosh 2007). And, the prevailing ideologies of 'power' provide sustenance to such practices through the transmission of a culture of servility, docility and status quo so that women fall in line with the dominant traditions of the community. The report on 'The Missing Millions' becomes agonising in this context. We all know that the safest place of anybody is the womb of the mother; yet, the girl children are being murdered and this is also pointed out by the Census of 2011. It appears that the strengthening of male-biased norms and values across all castes and classes in India has occurred along with increasing economic development. It is therefore not surprising that child sex ratio (CSR) in India plunges to lowest (914) in 2011 since independence. Similarly, in the economic front, women are over represented in the informal sectors with poor pay, low status, routine and hazardous jobs, temporary, seasonal or casual nature of work (Ghosh 2001). The issue of empowerment of women has been found to be extremely complex and too naïve to be explained in any reductionist way. Obviously, access to panchayat or to credit did not automatically translate into a positive impact.

Concern for Environmental Issues

Along with gender justice, concern for an eco-friendly and sustainable environment has become a major agenda of contemporary life. The deleterious effects of development on our environment so far have shaken the faith of modern man. In the name of progress, we have followed a model of development that has brought the humankind almost to the brink of destruction. Unprecedented advances in science and technology have made man overconfident. Developmentalism, as 'culture', has led to spread of commercial values and conspicuous consumption based on western lifestyle and in particular hegemony of the market (Kothari 1990: 214). The Global Warming Report or the so-called Copenhagen Consensus says that even without any war or mistake, the world is about to end in next few hundred years if not earlier. And, it is not a consequence of any conspiracy; it is rather a result of well-planned development by the top policy makers with total legitimate control. So, the question is where we went wrong. Look at Japan today! Japan's 'success' to industrialise using nuclear energy has led to severe devastations now. It only proves that unlimited economic growth and technology-based model of development cannot always be eco-friendly. There are limits to what we can expect science and technology to do and the Club of Rome had long back voiced this warning to us.

In case of India the planning process since independence has laid emphasis on grounding and building of many mega development projects such as big dams, large industries, large irrigation projects, thermal power plants, large townships, etc. In this process we have done massive exploitation of natural resources such as land, water, forest and mineral resources. This development model undoubtedly helped the country to emerge as one of the influential economic and political powers among the world of nations with a large army of technically skilled manpower. However, as it is now observed, the very process of 'development' in this vast populous country is generating wider socio-economic inequalities across space and people. This model of development has directly been responsible for massive displacement of human populations and decimations of the sustainable subsistence of the ecosystem people in many parts of the country. It is found that in large mining projects tribals lose their land not only to the project authorities, but even to non-tribal outsiders who converge into those areas and corner both land and the new economic opportunities in commerce and petty industry. According to the latest estimate, the total number of people displaced in India during the last 60 years has reached almost 60 million. In recent years this displacement has become more intensified due to the conditions created by globalisation and economic liberalisation. This problem has nowadays taken the shape of a conflict between the ecosystem people and the omnivores, the former fighting to ensure their traditional sustainable form of subsistence and the latter intruding into the territory of the ecosystem people to satisfy their insatiable greed and unmet materialistic needs by exploiting the natural resources like land, forest and minerals.

If our environment has been a victim of industrial capitalism, the socialist or even post-capitalist/post-modern conditions do not differ strikingly in exploiting nature. This is not to deny that in recent times we are frequently introduced to new ideas like sustainable development, sustainable livelihood, eco-friendly technology, eco-forestry, alternative technology, scientific conservation and the like to tackle the crisis. Environmental movements since 1970s have been successful at least to draw our attention to the causes of ecological destruction and possible alternatives to such a catastrophe. Yet, due to misleading diagnosis, our concern for environment has more or less remained restricted to certain efficient methods of resource extraction/use and there is really no move to restrict consumption and market forces particularly in the developed North. Hence, despite a broad consensus among mainstream political and development institutions on the need for sustainable development, the understanding of what it means, in theory as well as in practice, differs. The Brundtland Report has been much criticised on the grounds that continued economic growth is irreconcilable with sustainable development; growth for environmental recovery itself leads to further environmental degradation (Braidotti et al. 1994: 133). The Gandhian prescription of controlled consumption and restricted lifestyle has very few takers in the West.

It would be interesting, in this context, to review the vicious circle of poverty, population and pollution in the developing South. The escalating problem of population explosion in India and the deleterious consequences of such growth on the quality of our life have now been widely recognised. Although human resource is considered very significant in the contemporary world, any sustainable society also requires an optimum population to realise the goals of equity and efficiency. Population is a pre-requisite to development only to the extent that a society requires more manpower to carry out its developmental activities. A huge population can be a blessing only if it can be made productive, literate and healthy. But where this is not the case, as in India, excess manpower is a liability to development (Ghosh 2011). Considering India's achievements and failures during the last six decades, it may fairly be argued that we cannot have both 'population explosion' and 'sustainable society' at the same time. Some optimistic assertions about population growth world wide did not prevent Amartya Sen to recognise that "reducing fertility is important not only because of its consequences for economic prosperity, but also because of the impact of high fertility in diminishing the *freedom of people*" (2000: 226, emphasis mine). While population control alone would not suffice for realising the goal of a sustainable and environment-friendly society, such step should be considered as the most urgent and necessary one at the present moment. However, while analysing the poverty–pollution interface in the South, we must not forget that affluence and consumption have affected our environment even more perniciously (Ghosh 2005).

The foregoing analysis would make one clear that despite tremendous advancement in the application of science and technology in the 20th century, developed and developing countries face contrary realities so far as the problems of 'development' are concerned. The existence of huge backlogs of deprivations, disparities and inequality among countries and regions poses problems for any uniform model of environmental activism in the world today. It is unfortunate that when a concerted and united attack on environmental degradation was urgently needed, politics has crept in this sphere and the world is virtually divided into North and South blocks, the viewpoints of which are quite conflicting. Quite obviously, there is little progress to protect our environment. The recent occurrences of natural devastations (cyclone, earthquake, Tsunami etc.) in many developed countries of the world including Japan and Russia as well as rising incidences of war, violence and terrorism all over the world prove the limits of science and technology to work for the larger benefits of mankind and society at large.

Social and Cultural Issues of Development

The social and cultural issues of development have become very vital today particularly for the developing countries like India. For centuries, development has been equated with economic growth. This growth perspective has been widely nurtured as panacea to all social ills, and accordingly it got a place of paramount significance within the developmental discourses of capitalism, economic modernisation and globalisation. However, with the increasing disjunction between economic growth and social development (that envisages ensuring livelihood security, employment, education, health, clothing, shelter and basic civil rights of all sections of the population), collective endeavour to redefine the course of development has emerged to be a reality.

This is because there is an environment for dissatisfaction with the idea of economic development, argues Anand Kumar (2010). One reason for this is the acknowledgement of the fact that even after so much of proclaimed development, every day out of 6.5 billion people on this earth, at least 2 billion people go hungry and they are mostly concentrated in the southern part of the world, right from South Asia to South Africa to South America. Similarly, the Arjun Sengupta report (submitted in August 2007) says that 77 per cent of people of India are not able to earn or at least spend more than 20 rupees per day. That is their consumption power and there are eight hundred forty millions of such people. Yet, today India has a large number of very rich people. The Justice Rajendra Sachar Committee report (submitted in November 2006) further says that in the last sixty years most Muslims had suffered collective downward mobility and this is in spite of the existence of by and large secular governments in the country. Similarly, it has been observed that tribals in India are victims and refugees of development and their conditions in post-independent India has, in many ways, worsened particularly due to implementation of development projects like dams, factories and mines. The taste of democracy is in the happiness of minorities and backward classes. And, if these groups have been continuously suffering downward mobility, then there must be something wrong in the model of development we have taken. Interestingly, the Bandhopadhyay Committee report (submitted in April 2008) speaks about the pathology of development in this country. This report is about increasing extremism in the hinterland of Indian cities, the so-called Naxalism. The report says that because of the failing government and failing development, at least 400 police stations are beyond the control of our own constitutional mechanisms. More than 125 districts are now under the control of 'extremist' forces.

All these official reports make one thing clear: we are utterly confused today about the direction that development in India has taken since independence. There are therefore valid reasons for disenchantment with modernity and development. Modernisation has not only led to the creation of classes and barriers amongst us, it has also made us loose the community contacts – the resources of tradition. The so-called developed urban space has therefore become a depository of tensions, conflicts, violence, pollution, alienation, selfishness and what not. In other words, development does not necessarily enhance mental, moral and collective happiness. Somebody blames it on capitalism, somebody blames it on consumerism and somebody blames it totally on modernism. But, there is an environment of disenchantment with modernity. Hence, there is a rise in protest movement against the project of 'development' in rural India right from Singur in West Bengal to Kalahandi in Orissa. Surprisingly, one of the abiding tasks before the Government of India since independence was integrated development of rural areas. Hence, a number of initiatives have been taken since then for providing employment, reducing poverty, creation of social and economic infrastructure in rural areas as well as to provide food security and fulfil other basic needs of the rural populace. Yet, people are not convinced about development and it appears that they have lost trust on the idea. They think it is a sweet coated word, a sweet poison. There are many official reports which are staring in the faces of scholars and politicians alike and the people are asking including Queen of England, "where did you go wrong?"

It is in this context that ideas like human development, social development and holistic development have liberated social sciences and humanity from impersonal categories like GDP and GNP. This has also made the process of development interesting once again. The facts that social development is an inalienable part of economic development, that economic development is relational and not autonomous of social development and that economic development is a means to social and human development have got wide recognition is recent years. Given the failures of several economic models of development, social scientists today are showing preference for this 'humane' vision of development that would result in enhancement of the quality of life for all irrespective of sex, colour or creed, meet the basic need of common people, empower them to take active part in the process of development and protect the environment from any further catastrophe.

There is however a debate about the capacity of 'tradition' to promote change. It was earlier proclaimed by the theorists of modernisation school that there are social and cultural obstacles to development. But, at the same time, sociologists have proved that these factors may also promote development. This is in spite of the fact that several aspects of our tradition have been found to impinge on human freedom and capacity development. Max Weber has shown long back how a religious ethic is used to legitimise new patterns of economic behaviour. There has also been research on the role of religion and culture in Japanese modernisation in particular. Many Indian sociologists also rejected the western pessimism about Indian social and cultural institutions. For instance, S.C. Dube (1994) has argued that everything in our tradition is not 'evil' and hence there should be no unnecessary haste to emphasise gross materialism at the cost of social justice. For him, culture cannot be dispensed with to promote growth because it plays a critical role in human life and development does not always offer adequate replacement for it. Similarly, noted Indian sociologists and social anthropologists like Benoy Kumar Sarkar, Radha Kamal Mukerjee, D.P. Mukerji, Nirmal Kumar Bose, Surajit Sinha or Ram Krishna Mukherjee have echoed their thought on certain aspects of our tradition, values and culture that emphasise pluralism and diversity, tolerance and responsibility, non-violence, solidarity, equity and social justice.

Interestingly, the success of orthodox business communities like Marawaris, Jains or Parsis has been a matter of intense introspection by Indian sociologists. Similarly, traditional social institutions like caste, kinship and joint family have been found to be instrumental in influencing trade, business and agriculture. The intricate relationship between tradition and modernity in the Indian context highlights the resilience of Indian culture even after the onslaught of globalisation. Hence, as I have argued elsewhere, cultural globalisation does not mean the possibility of a single global culture; it rather signifies the spread of plural cultural elements across the globe. Such reciprocity also illuminates the strength of social capital approach to understand development. One should not therefore undermine the importance of structural factors like values, customs, traditions, relations and networks for inducing changes in the social fabric particularly in the Indian context. Cultural changes appear to be normal, suitable and positive when they enjoy the support of tradition (Ghosh 2009b). However, cultural determinism is as problematic as ignorance of culture. As Amartya Sen (2004) argued, culture must be understood as one important constituent element of substantive freedoms; at the same time culture can produce exclusionary practices. This calls for the intervention of human agency to eradicate a social evil. In the context of preventing child marriage, I have noticed that it is easy to evolve a top-down strategy of socio-cultural change, but very difficult to implement it unless the people perceive the problem as their own (Ghosh 2009b). In other words, institution building through popular participation – participation of the poor and the marginalised – should become a major focus of any social reform or intervention strategy. The creation of an enabling social environment to resist the prevailing social forces is a challenging task.

Is There any Real Alternative?

There is no doubt about the fact that the meaning, strategy and dimensions of development have changed with the passage of time. Even in a given context, development means several things to different stakeholders. For instance, Abhijit Mitra (2010) argues that development stands for 'a way of life' and there is choice in this way of life, which the middle-class people cherish and enjoy. In this sense, middle class does have a vested interest in development including the academia. But this middle class also suffers because of development. There are emotional costs, social costs and relational costs. As the middle class develops and starts enjoying better part of it, they put themselves into enclaves. In this sense, the principle of social exclusion is not simply a phenomenon of the marginalised. There is a continuous process of marginalisation and exclusion for others, and for the middle class, this is self-made exclusion.

The evident lack of unanimity on universalistic or particularistic development strategies constitutes the core of development debate (Srivastava 1998: 19). Existence of multi-plurality of discourses on development has led us to refrain from considering any particular mode of thinking, mechanism or paradigm as final or acceptable universally. It may be argued that development has no definite boundary, no specific pathways and no universal approach and strategy. It is a qualitative concept involving a qualitative improvement in the general standard of living in any space. As Da Costa (2010: 22) argues, development is "a historical, complex, varied, and uneven experience". The fact that development is complex, contradictory and often contentious does not however nullify the very concept because in spite of much criticism and opposition we have not been able to construct any real 'alternative of development'. As Peet and Hartwick (2010: 3) argue, "when something is heavily criticized yet persists, it probably has real content. Could it be that development is both the best and worst of human projects – best in terms of potential and worst in terms of its sorry contemporary practice?" One way to solve the perplexity is to combine different angles and approaches to development into 'critical holism' (Pieterse 2001: 131). This means understand the totality from a critical point of view and thereby use reflexivity to reconstruct development.

Another way to reconstruct development is to consider the constructive suggestions of Indian philosophers like Buddha, Vivekananda, Tagore, Gandhi, Aurobindo, Ambedkar and the like. Interestingly, the realisation of the limits of the western model of development, particularly for the Third World, and the search for Indian alternatives had long past. Since the time of Gautam Buddha to the 20th century, India has had a succession of persons whose inspiration for their humanitarian activity, social reform and alternative ideals lay the foundation of Indian version of development. Even though the Christian missionaries had stressed the need for modern education and welfare for the Indians in the 19th century, the effort was basically governed by religious pursuits and spirits. The waves of socio-religious movements during the British rule in India however attempted to arrive at a synthesis of the various currents and cross-currents playing upon Indian society under the leadership of social reformers like Raja Rammohan Roy (1772–1833). He was the first to go back to the purity of the Vedic and Upanishadic thought in an effort to defend Hinduism against the criticism of Christian missionaries from outside and the dangers of its being debased by superstitions and ritualistic practices from within. In the 20th century, the Indian response to the western model of modernity in general and development in particular is typically revealed in the thinking of great Indian thinkers like Rabindranath Tagore (1861–1941), Swami Vivekananda (1863–1902) and Mahatma Gandhi (1869–1948). It is worth noting here that Vivekananda's vision of modern India and particularly his notions of work, service, love, harmony, brotherhood and concern for the poor, dalit and women had greatly influenced the thinking of many of his contemporaries including Ambedkar. Swamiji felt that the two fundamental doctrines of Advaita Vedanta, namely, (a) the divinity of all beings, and (b) the oneness of all existence, if applied to society, can lead to revolutionary changes. He was the first to talk about an 'inclusive society' that would put an end to exclusivism. He also realised that nation-building in India cannot be based on the western model and he is therefore called the 'father of modern Indian nationalism'.

For both Tagore and Gandhi, India is a different civilisation – the civilisation not of towns and cities, but the civilisation of village communities – an agrarian civilisation. Hence, in different ways, both of them had concentrated their attention and energies for rural reconstruction. Both of them perceived that economic progress and advancement in India would depend on the liberation of villages and on the thorough reform and reconstruction of our agricultural system. It must be noted that Gandhi objected to the craze for machinery, not machinery as such. Needless to say, Gandhi opposed large-scale industrialisation not only from a practical economic consideration of giving employment to all the villagers, he had a strong ethical argument also. Gandhi always talked about this ethics and morality without which his economics does not get its strong foundation. His ideas of Ahimsa, Sarvodaya, Swaraj, Swadeshi and Panchayati Raj have therefore helped many in the world today to reconstruct development. For Tagore, the root cause of poverty in India is complexly ramified and it dwells within us. Hence, the poet recommended that the leaders of the nation should analyse the problem more broadly and confront the situation in its totality. While, Tagore never denied the importance of science and technology for the promotion and furtherance of civilisation, he insisted on the idea of *Samavaya* or cooperative and self-development as the possible means of panacea in the Indian context. Tagore and Gandhi, in their respective ways and means, therefore stimulate us to think and look for an alternative to unprecedented evolution in modern technology that has enormously dehumanised our world civilisation.

It appears that the best way, in the present context, to materialise holistic development is in terms of the expansion of the real freedoms that the citizens enjoy to pursue the objectives they have reason to value. In this sense, the expansion of human capability can be, broadly, seen as the central feature of the process of development. In other words, "development requires the removal of major sources of unfreedom: poverty as well as tyranny, poor economic opportunities as well as systematic social deprivation, neglect of public facilities as well as intolerance or overactivity of repressive states" (Sen 2000: 3). We all expect that 'inclusive development' would enlarge people's choices at local level and empower them to participate in the process on their own. In this sense, 'self-development' without the mastery of experts has been found to be very effective in the Indian context. The future of development would be governed by our concern for equity and progress in social, economic, behavioural, environmental and cultural conditions where society/community gradually moves away from its economic, cognitive and socio-cultural backwardness and seeks, both locally and globally, to protect ecology, freedom, human rights, quality of life and socio-cultural diversities.

I aver that the discourses of development today are coming to some kind of converging points all over the world. And, this convergence is around certain central dreams of humanity, happiness, freedom and participation. It appears that quality of life is the first parameter for defining development, what development is and what development is not. The second parameter, of course, is its relation with nature; that is the sustainability question. There is need for certain consensus for limits of consumption as well as use of science and technology even while we argue for retaining cultural diversity and individual freedom. The third parameter is to consider people as the real agency of development. In this respect, issues like rule framing and rule implementing, collective ownership, public control, democratic reasoning, rights and privileges of the common man, and their cultural specificity find prominence. All these parameters also create rooms for social movements often at global scale to arouse social consciousness, mobilise opinion and organise opposition. In other words, beyond the market machine as well as state/bureaucracy/political elite/ruling class guided paradigms, we today require the 'nature-need and people-centric paradigm' to guide us to integrated, balanced and inclusive development. This broad framework also has relevance for people across borders and economic frontiers. Such optimism may appear to be idealistic to many in the present context, but let's begin with this new idealism to reformulate our goals and reason for a better future.

References

Béteille, Andre. 2000. *Antinomies of Society: Essays on Ideologies and Institutions*. New Delhi: Oxford University Press.

Boserup, Esther. 1970. *Women's Role in Economic Development*. New York: St. Martin Press.

Braidotti, R., E. Charkiewicz, S. Hausler and S. Wieringa. 1994. *Women, the Environment and Sustainable Development*. London: Zed Books.

Cowen, M.P. and R.W. Shenton. 1996. *Doctrines of Development*. London: Routledge.

Da Costa, Dia. 2010. *Development Dramas: Reimagining Rural Political Actions in Eastern India*. New Delhi: Routledge.

Dube, S.C. 1994. *Tradition and Development*. New Delhi: Vikas Publishing House.

Escobar, A. 1992. 'Reflections on Development: Grassroots Approaches and Alternative Politics in the Third World', *Futures*, June: 411–36.

Esteva, G. 1992. 'Development', in W. Sachs (ed.), *The Development Dictionary: A Guide to Knowledge as Power* (6–25). London: Zed Books.

Gore, M.S. 1965. *Social Work and Social Work Education*. Bombay: Asia Publishing House.

Ghosh, Biswajit. 2001. 'Women's Work and Informal Sectors: Two Case Studies in Burdwan, West Bengal', *Socialist Perspective*, 29 (1 & 2): 1–23.

——. 2004. 'Impact of Market Globalism: Indian Experience', *Bharat Vidya*, Vol. 3: 73–83.

——. 2005. 'Population and Pollution: Concern for a Sustainable Society in India', in A. Das (ed.), *Environment-Science and Thoughts* (167–80). Vol. I, Kolkata: ACB Publication.

——. (ed.). 2007. *Trafficking in Women and Children, Child Marriage and Dowry: A Study for Action Plan in West Bengal*. Kolkata: UNICEF and Govt. of West Bengal.

——. 2009a. 'NGOs, Civil Society and Social Reconstruction in Contemporary India', *Journal of Developing Societies*, 25 (2): 229–52.

——. 2009b. *Delaying the Age of Marriage in Malda*. Kolkata: UNICEF.

——. 2010. 'Cultural Globalisation in Contemporary India: From Homogeneity to Plurality', *Socialist Perspective*, 38 (1 & 2): 1–20.

——. 2011. 'Population Change and Its Consequences: India's Concern in 21st Century', *Man and Development*, 33 (1): 1–18.

Ghosh, Biswajit and Tanima Choudhuri. 2011. 'Gender, Space and Development: Changing Conditions of Tribal Women in Tripura', *Economic and Political Weekly*, 46 (16): 74–78.

Giddens, Anthony. 2006. *Sociology* (Fifth Edition). Cambridge: Polity Press.

Harish, Ranjana and V.B. Harishankar. 2008. *Re-defining Feminism*. Jaipur: Rawat Publications.

Kaviraj, Sudipta. 2001. 'In Search of Civil Society', in S. Kaviraj and S. Khilnani (eds.), *Civil Society: History and Possibilities* (287–323). New Delhi: Cambridge University Press.

Kapur, Ratna. 2005. 'Subversive Sites: Feminist Engagement with Law in India', in Mala Khullar (ed.), *Writing the Women's Movement: A Reader* (153–74). New Delhi: Zubaan.

Kothari, R. 1990. *Rethinking Development: In Search of Humane Alternative*. New Delhi: Ajanta Publication.

Kumar, Anand. 2010. 'Discourses on Development: Some Sociological Aspects', Key Note Address in a National Seminar on Discourses on Development organised by the University of Burdwan, March 13–14.

Mahajan, G. 1999. 'Civil Society, State and Democracy', *Economic and Political Weekly*, 34 (49): 3471–72.

Mitra, Abhijit. 2010. 'Notion of Development and the Academia', Chairman's Address in a National Seminar on Discourses on Development organised by the University of Burdwan, March 13–14.

Nayar, P.K.B. 2008. 'Social Justice in a Globalised World: Encounters with State and Civil Society', *Sociological Bulletin*, 57 (1): 3–29.

National Crime Record Bureau. 2009. *Crime in India 2009*. New Delhi: Government of India.

Oommen, T.K. 2004. *Nation, Civil Society and Social Movements: Essays in Political Sociology*. New Delhi: Sage Publications.

Peet, Richard and Elaine Hartwick. 2010. *Theorising Development* (2nd Edition). Jaipur: Rawat Publications.

Pieterse, J.N. 2001. *Development Theory*. New Delhi: Vistaar Publications.

Sachs, W. (ed.). 1992. 'Introduction', *The Development Dictionary: A Guide to Knowledge as Power* (1–5). London: Zed Books.

Sarkar, Lotika. 2005. 'Constitutional Guarantees', in Mala Khullar (ed.), op. cit. (102–12).

Saunders, Kriemild (ed.). 2004. *Feminist Post-Development Thought: Thinking Modernity, Post-Colonialism and Representation*. London: Zed Books.

Sen, Amartya. 2000. *Development as Freedom*. New Delhi: Oxford University Press.

——. 2004. 'How does Culture Matter?', in Vijayendra Rao and Michael Walton (eds.), *Culture and Public Action* (37–58). Delhi: Permanent Black.

Sen, G. and C. Grown. 1987. *Development, Crisis and Alternative Visions: Third World Women's Perspectives*. New York: Monthly Review Press.

Srivastava, S.P. (ed.). 1998. *The Development Debate*. Jaipur: Rawat Publications.

United Nations Development Programme (UNDP). 2001. *Human Development Report*. New York: UNDP.

World Bank. 2004. *World Development Report*. New York: Oxford University Press.

3

An Alternative Modernity

The Vision of Tagore and Gandhi

Krityapriya Ghosh

The sociologists in the academic circle define modern society as differentiated, pluralistic, broadly participatory and democratic. The criteria as laid down in this explanation of modernity are typical of the western developed society. And, there is no denying the fact that the tradition-bound nations of the Third World accepted this western model unhesitatingly as the universal model. Science and technology, industrialisation and urbanisation, democracy and bureaucracy have become the principal instruments of such modernisation. The broad trends indicative of modernity can possibly be spelt out in this way: First, there is a constant change in the people's commitments and associations from local to universal. The urban populations of the modern society constantly leave aside their parochial local culture and establish close link with the growing global views and ideas. Secondly, the individual as a unit of society has began to play a more important role as against the group or community. Sociologically, this is of profound significance because this bourgeois notion of individuality has torn most of the community links in the relations of the people of the earlier traditional society. This is possibly the most cruel blow to the age-old patterns of the traditional oriental civilisation. Thirdly, as a consequence of the emergence of this new individuality, an individual's work or occupation is less influenced by his/her family, residence or community. All his/her associations depending upon accident of birth is replaced by association of choice. Rational and scientific attitudes of people replace emotions and non-rational approaches. And last, but not least, among other trends of modernity is that in place of fatalistic beliefs, there comes a sense of mastery over nature and other environmental forces.

It is a common knowledge today that the developing societies of the Third World have accepted, by and large, this western notion of modernity not always by choice but by compulsions in many cases. As a matter of fact, in most of the cases, modernity is the offshoot of the colonial domination. The giant exploiting nations of Europe never allowed their colonial people to develop their own culture in their own way. The Enlightenment tradition of the West had a large influence over the making of their nation in many ways. It was out and out, to use Partha Chatterjee's (1986) famous phrase, a 'derivative discourse'. Modernity, in such cases, was composed from outside, it did not evolve spontaneously and freely. One important social scientist of our days S.N. Eisenstadt in his famous book *Modernisation: Protest and Change* wrote:

> Historically, modernisation is the process of change towards those type of social, economic and political systems that have developed in Western Europe and North America from the seventeenth century to the nineteenth and have them spread to other European countries and in the nineteenth and twentieth centuries to the South American, Asian and African countries. (1969: 1)

The spread of modernity in Asia, Africa or Latin America was done extensively by the colonial regimes; it is a historically proven phenomenon now. The only exception was the rise of modern Japan after the Meiji restoration. Since the last decade of the 19th century, Japan, adopting western technology and science, modernised itself at a rapid pace. This is virtually an exceptional lone case in the Asian continent where a particular nation upgraded itself to a tremendous height not by compulsion but by choice. In 1902, the all-mighty Britain had been bound to recognise Japan as a major force in Asian politics and that had been substantiated by the Anglo-Japanese military pact against the possible onslaught of Russian imperialism over the Indian subcontinent. In the post-Second World War history of Asia, Japan is comparable to any prosperous western nation. With its phenomenal rate of growth and consumption, Japan has taken its place among the most developed nations of the world.

The rise of Japan with all its modernity astonished the Asian people with profound awe and admiration. Japan became the matinee idol of the subdued Asian nations. Particularly in India, Japan had been seen as a perfect role model; the national leaders were enthused to establish kin relations with this ever-growing powerful nation. We are to remember here that Okakura's political as well as cultural slogan that "Asia is one" stimulated Vivekananda and Nibedita and many other notable nationalist leaders of that period. The Indian response to the western model of 'modernity' in general and 'development' in particular is typically revealed in the thinking of two great Indian thinkers, namely, Rabindranath Tagore and Mahatma Gandhi. This essay tries to delve deep into their alternative vision of development.

II

The Tagore family of Jorasanko had also become the closest friend of the notable artistic personality of Okakura and through him the painters like Gaganendra or Abanindranath became acquainted with the modern Japanese artistes and the rich heritage of Japanese culture. The Indian art had opened up a new vista since then. Rabindranath too had very intimate relation with him and the other Japanese distinguished scholars, and celebrities came to Santiniketan and stayed there in different capacities in different times. Tagore welcomed Japan as a modern rising star.

But, in spite of this acceptance, Tagore did not appreciate the process of modernisation of Japan. In 1916, during his extensive tour in Japan and the United States, the poet expressed such dislikes. In his famous lecture, 'The Spirit of Japan', Tagore unequivocally expressed his disappointment saying, "I for myself, cannot believe that Japan has become what she is by imitating the West. We cannot imitate life, we cannot stimulate strength for long, nay, what is more, a mere imitation is a source of weakness. For it hampers our true nature, it is always in our way. It is like dressing our skeleton with another man's skin, giving rise to eternal feuds between the skin and the bones at every movement" (quoted in Biswas 1996). Tagore also said that the whole world wants to see what this great Japan is going to do with its immense resources and wealth. The poet does not want to believe that Japan is mere the reproduction of the West, if that be the case then Japan will invariably fail to achieve its missions.

> For there are grave questions that the western civilisation has presented before the world but not completely answered. The conflict between the individual and the state, labour and capital, the man and the woman; the conflict between greed of material gain and the spiritual life of man, the organised selfishness of nations and the higher ideals of humanity; the conflict between all the ugly complexities inseparable from giant

organisations of commerce and state and the natural instincts of man crying for simplicity and beauty and fullness of leisure – all these have to be brought to a harmony in a manner not yet dreamt of.

We need to remember here that this is not a critique of modern Japan only; this is the critique of the concept of modernity itself which the highly developed civilisation of the West tried to project. Tagore saw in it the concept of power – the power of organisation which has made itself manifest in politics and commerce and in coordinating scientific knowledge. If this power of organisation loses the touch of life and the rhythm of beauty and love, then it turns into colossal anti-human power capable of destroying the normal faculties of human life.

Tagore is quite insistent that the object of modernisation is not to gain the material wealth or to furnish the outer grandeur of the social fabric, but to grow one's own treasure from the reserve of his/her own tradition. Here, there is the inevitable and necessary relation between tradition and modernity. Modernity is the continuum of tradition necessarily. The poet also warned that modernising is not affectation of modernism, just as affectation of poesy is not poetising:

> It is nothing but mimicry – only affectation is louder than the original, and it is too literal. One must bear in mind that those who have the true modern spirit need not modernise, just as those who are truly brave are not braggarts. ... True modernism is freedom of mind, not slavery of taste. It is independence of thought and action, not tutelage under European school masters. It is science, but not its wrong application in life – a mere imitation of our science teachers who reduce it into a superstition absurdly invoking its aid for all impossible purposes. (quoted in Biswas 1996: 368)

In this historic address in Japan, Tagore also warned that,

> What is still more dangerous for Japan is not this imitation of the outer features of the West, but the acceptance of the motive force of the western civilisation as her own. Her social ideals are already showing signs of defeat at the hands of politics, and her modern tendency seems to incline towards political gambling in which the players stake their souls to win their game. (quoted in Biswas 1996: 369)

Tagore thus overtly pointed out that the aggressive nationalism of the West – whose other name is organisation of politics and commerce – is all powerful at the cost of the harmony of higher social life. And, this nationalism had engulfed Japan contrary to its legacy of the ancient culture from the East – the culture that has given us the vision of the infinite in all finite things.

Tagore had refused all along to remain stagnant and to be encaged within the walls of old beliefs and habits; he always moved on and on and his voyage had never come to an end. The spirit of modernity was thus embedded in his soul and person and that had been reflected in one of his songs of *Gitanjali*:

> I find they will know no end in me. And where old words die out on the tongue, new melodies break forth from the heart; and where the old tracks are lost, new country is revealed with its wonders. (quoted in Sen 1947: 138)

In 1933 Tagore wrote in Visva Bharati News:

> I believe that the social unrest prevalent today all over the world is owing to the anarchy of spirit in the modern civilisation. What is called progress is the progress in the mechanical contrivances; it is in fact an indefinite extension of our physical limbs and organs which, owing to the enormous material advantage that it brings to us has tempted the modern man away from his inner realm of spiritual value and thus the balance is lost ... today our homes have dissolved into hotels, community life is stifled in the dense and dusty atmosphere of the office, man and woman are afraid of love, people clamour for their rights and forget their obligations and they value comfort more than happiness and spirit of display more than that of beauty. (quoted in Biswas 1996: 665)

If such is the menace of modern civilisation or modernity, what should be the remedial measures? Tagore answered this in myriad ways. The avoidance of organisation of power – manifested in the cult of nationalism – is one such remedy. And that had been emphatically expressed in his lectures on 'Nationalism'. The spirit of the people seeks harmony and order, it wants to revive the best traits of personality, but the methods of the nation are not conducive to the higher ideals of humanity. They improve national efficiency at the cost of human personality. Thus, Tagore described the spirit of national selfishness as 'the brain disease of a people' and according to the poet, it is "the power of self-sacrifice, the moral faculty of sympathy and cooperation which is the guiding spirit of social vitality" (quoted in Sen 1947: 313). The poet suggests that men must forget their idolatry of baser passions and the higher era of civilisation should take its root in our moral ideals – the ideals of beauty, goodness and truth. Tagore called it 'the world of personality'. The foundation of this world of personality is love, because "the most intense consciousness of our own personality comes to us through love, through a realisation of unity with others, which illumines our hearts with a radiance of joy" (ibid.: 317).

The other remedy, we find, in the poet's concept of 'cooperative principle'. The organisation of power is also manifest in the concentration of capital and wealth. This concentration is possible because of unrestrained human greed, motive for profit exploiting other's labour and utter selfishness. Tagore said that this organisation of power should be adequately replaced with an alternative instrument. This instrument believes that out of greed comes sin and sin leads to destruction. Tagore thus argued that greed is an anti-social impulse and it disrupts the social existence of man. In order to restore this social existence, Tagore was in favour of introducing the concept of cooperative principle both in production system as well as in consumption behaviour of human beings. And, Tagore was cautious to point out that delimitation of greed did not suggest stagnation of life or dismissal of novel demands in our daily living process.

On 9 February 1929 Tagore gave an address to the Burdwan Division Cooperative Conference, held at Sriniketan, which was published as a pamphlet under the title 'Samavayniti'. In this lecture Tagore was of the view that the cooperative principle is progressing in the European continent and they have an advantage over the Indians. They have more experience and sense of combination. But, the Indians are backward in this respect. It is argued that the poverty can be rooted out if our living is reduced to bare necessities. Tagore commented that this is hardly any solution because it simply means that one who is lying right at the bottom cannot fall further down.

Tagore said,

> The history of man does not indicate that he will ever retrace his footsteps. His intelligence has to express itself in newer creations through the ages. New times make new demands. Those who cannot meet the demands get dismissed. By his inventive power man goes on creating new opportunities for himself, and his needs multiply. … History tells us of some races who, instead of advancing on the path of newer creations, remained stationary, their faces turned to what ancient possessions they had. They were worse than the dead, because they were dead-alive. (Visva Bharati 1963: 38–39)

Tagore then asked: what is luxury? It is no luxury today to use electric light instead of kerosene lantern. When the bullock cart was first introduced, it was definitely an expression of wealth and the concept of motor car was very much hidden in it. Only the feeble-mind will suggest that poverty may be conquered if one reverts to it. Stagnation is no solution. Regarding this solution Tagore said,

> The remedy lies not in restricting wealth or taking forcible possession of it or giving it away. The remedy is in stimulating in all people the capacity for creating new wealth; in other words, it is in expounding to the people the principles of co-operation. (ibid.: 40)

Tagore did not conceive cooperative movement only by doling out money at a low rate of interest to the needy cultivators; he wanted a full-grown cooperative collective farming by modern tools and implements. He wanted to revive the traditional cottage industries with a new vigour and shape, and in building up the modern industrial production centres on the basis of cooperative creed and instincts. This is also to be borne in mind that Tagore himself had experimented all this since 1890s in his own zamindari estates as well as in his Sriniketan project in later life. The returns he received are in no way insignificant. The post-independence Community Development Programme of Nehru's government was very much indebted to this Tagorean reconstruction programmes and ideas.

Tagore stood for village reconstruction throughout his life and he believed that the village is the life force of Indian civilisation. The poet repeatedly made us understand that the real struggle of independence was not political liberation; the principal task was to liberate the villages from poverty, superstition, malnutrition and lack of education. For this Tagore raised the slogan for building up the *Swadeshi Samaj* on the basis of self-reliance of the people. This self-reliance or the gospel of *atmasakti* became a new form of struggle during the anti-partition movement in 1905. It was popularly known as the constructive *swadeshi*.

It will not be out of context to ask whether Tagore was for industrialisation for the rapid modernisation of his motherland. There is a misconception that Tagore stood against machines and opposed machine-based civilisation. Actually, Tagore opposed soulless industrialisation. His two important dramas *Rakta Karabi* (Red Oleanders) and *Mukta Dhara* (Free Stream) would substantiate his position. Tagore admitted that science has opened up the store-house of power, and technological innovations are always necessary for the advancement of civilisation. But, the development of inner life is also necessary. There must be a process of reconciliation of the material and spiritual life. The West has used science and technology to an enormous extent but the spiritual aspect has been put more and more in the shade. There is a dearth of harmony and balance. Owing to this imbalance, nature also faces a grave crisis. Thus, we can say, in brief, that Tagore not only pleaded for moral basis in material prosperity with the help of science and technology, but he was also keen on accepting the thesis that "moral civilisation cannot be good and final in itself, it can only be healthy when it makes it possible for material civilisation to attain its highest purpose" (cited in Sen 1947: 143).

III

David Hardiman in his book *Gandhi in His Time and Ours* aptly remarked: "Gandhi is often seen as taking an extreme – even eccentric – stance in regard to what is defined as modernity" (Hardiman 2005: 66). Actually, in *Hind Swaraj*, published in 1909, Gandhi rejected all aspects of the western civilisation based on modern science and technology. He characterised the machine-based civilisation as the 'satanic civilisation'. Apparently, this may lead us to say that Gandhi's rejection of modernism would place him in the category of old revivalist thinker. But there are some real difficulties for drawing such conclusion. Because despite his strong reactions against modern technology and science, Gandhi endorsed many key concepts of modernity such as the doctrine of human rights, belief in parliamentary and participatory democracy, fundamental equality of human beings, the principles of governance through persuasion and discussion avoiding all possible means of coercion etc.

Hardiman quite rightly remarked in this context:

> In these respects, he can hardly be said to have been antagonistic to modernity. Rather, he took the position that in these respects westerners frequently did not practise what they preached. The liberal regimes of the West were, for example, far less democratic than they claimed, and extremely undemocratic in a colonial context. When we open up the issue more carefully, we can see that Gandhi was taking up a strategic position within the decades of his day. His relationship to modernity was a dialogic rather than antagonistic one. (ibid.: 66–67)

This characterisation of Hardiman about Gandhi's critique of modernity seems to be quite logical when we find that in 1920s Gandhi accepted the machines for production if they could remove poverty and unemployment in India. Gandhi also endorsed the use of technological implements for the benefits of mass production. In 1940s Gandhi even talked about nationalisation of some heavy industries for the sake of balanced growth of national economy in India. Thus, Gandhi's robust opposition against all sorts of industrialism is not the whole truth; his later compromising attitudes should be taken into counts. These compromises made him realist as against his earlier idealist stance.

But even then Gandhi's concept of modernity does not conform to the typical western idea of modernism. Gandhi actually stood for an alternative modernity. And, the principal base or motive of that alternative modernity is ethics and morality. On one occasion, Gandhi said, "I must confess that I do not draw a sharp or any distinction between economics and ethics. ... Economics that hurt the moral well-being of an individual or a nation are immoral and, therefore, sinful" (quoted in Bhattacharya 1968: 184). In *Young India*, of December 26, 1924, Gandhi declared that the economics which disregards moral and sentimental considerations will ultimately break down. For "that economics is untrue which ignores or disgraces moral values" (ibid.: 184).

According to Gandhi, the material advancement of any nation cannot be undermined and the adequate measures should be taken as and when needed. But this economic advancement cannot be delinked from ethical progress. On another occasion, he thus said:

> By economic progress, I take it we mean material advancement without limit, and by real progress we mean moral progress which again is the same thing as the progress of the permanent element in us. The subject may therefore be stated thus: Does not moral progress increase in the same proportion as material progress? I know that this is a wider proposition than the one before us. But I venture to think that we always mean the large one even when we lay down the smaller. (ibid.: 184–85)

Thus, there is an overdose of ethicality or the primacy of morality in the whole of Gandhian thought and all his theories and techniques are to be understood in the framework of spiritual principles.

Gandhi's critique of colonial rule was essentially cultural. According to him, the British being a trading nation came to India in search of markets and they had been able to consolidate their rule by brainwashing their subjects into thinking that their ways of life were inferior to those of their rulers. Thus, the sword alone was unable to hold, it had been supplemented by an ideology. Colonialism thus killed cultural autonomy of India and the integrity of the subject country. Gandhi, therefore, insisted that the liberation struggle of the Indian people should necessarily be the cultural and not exclusively be political. Moreover, Gandhi sought to preserve values cherished by all pre-modern civilisations. These values were to him universal and all-pervasive. By calling European civilisation modern, Gandhi isolated it in time and space and undermined its universalist claims. He reminded modern Europe of its great historical heritage and to alert it to the growing danger of losing it. Gandhi also assured his countrymen that they were fighters not just for themselves but for the entire mankind.

Gandhi considered our civilisation as spiritual and the European materialist. But, according to him, nothing becomes spiritual or materialist by themselves, the quality depends how they are conducted or conceived. Spirituality necessarily requires self-conquest, self-restraint, mastery of the senses and spirituality is somewhat incompatible with the pursuit of bodily pleasures. Hence, in order to be true spiritual, one must practise *Ahimsa* (non-violence), *Aparigraha* (non-possession) and *Satya* (truth). For the integration of spirit and world, Gandhi talked about love and service to the mankind.

From this spiritual standpoint, Gandhi had given his critique of modernity, i.e., against the modern materialist civilisation. He criticised the large-scale industrialisation because it disrupted the normal rhythms of nature or the inherent laws of cosmic harmony. This giant industrial venture dehumanised human labour, prized bodily pleasures and weakened self-discipline. The large-scale industrialisation gave birth to the evils of concentration of capital and exploitation of labour by a few wealthy owners of huge capital. The modern industrialisation also produced large complex cities which destroyed morally self-sustaining local community bonds.

It was the considered opinion of Gandhi that this giant machine-based production system has given birth to the modern centralised state-craft. This state is highly bureaucratic and impersonal. It is a soulless machine which ruled by means of rigid rules and lifeless legal instruments. It discouraged personal initiative and responsibility; it killed naturalism and provoked artificialities. This industrialised capitalistic state machinery is also individualistic in the sense of stressing rights rather than duties and hedonistic self-interest rather than altruism.

Coming over to India, Gandhi opined that this sort of industrialism is absolutely misfit for this country because India is basically an agrarian civilisation. And, the village is the basic to this polity. The village to Gandhi is a manageable small group which constitutes a unit of society. This village has some other important features which are to be specially mentioned. First, Gandhi's village is a self-governing autonomous community. It should be self-sufficient in the sense that the vital necessities of life, like food, clothing, shelter etc., can be obtained within the village without any external dependence. Secondly, as Jayprakash Narayan pointed out in one of his illuminating article on Gandhi that,

> Gandhi's village was not an exclusively agricultural community; there had to be a balance between agriculture and village industries. Had he been alive now, he might have called it an agro-industrial community. In an unrecorded conversation with one of his co-workers (now Governor of Andhra Pradesh), he spoke of 'urbanising' the villages and 'ruralising' the towns and cities'. (Narayan 1970: 233)

Gandhi himself once wrote about the idea of his 'village swaraj' in his *Harijan Patrika* in 1942:

> My idea of village *swaraj* (self-government) is that it is a complete republic, independent of its neighbours for its vital wants, and yet interdependent for many others in which dependence is a necessity. Thus, every village's first concern will be to grow its own food crops and cotton for its cloth. It should have a reserve for its cattle, recreation and playground for adults and children. Then if there is more land available, it will grow useful money crops. ... It will have its own water works ensuring clean water supply. ... As far as possible every activity will be conducted on a cooperative basis. There will be no castes such as we have today with their graded untouchability. Non-violence with its technique of *satyagraha* (non-violent resistance) and non-cooperation will be the sanction of the village community. There will be a compulsory service of village guards, who will be selected by rotation from the register maintained by the village. The government of the village will be conducted by the Panchayat of five persons annually elected by the adult villagers, male and female, possessing minimum prescribed qualifications. These will have all the authority and jurisdiction required. Since there will be no system of punishments in the

> accepted sense, this Panchayat will be the legislature, judiciary and execution combined to operate for its year of office. (ibid.: 234)

This long depiction of the village *swaraj* suggests that how the common masses of the country can be empowered and enlightened to govern themselves. Instead of the modern elite-ruled democracies in the world, Gandhi visioned an alternative democracy. And, a remarkable fact of Indian social history is that during certain periods of our history these self-sufficient village communities were in operation. This condition was drastically devastated and altered by the British rule. Gandhi wanted to revive and revitalise those lost 'republics' in order to achieve real freedom of the country. Gandhi raised the slogan that our principal objective of national struggle is not to capture the villages, but to reconstruct. Gandhi actually looked forward to a kind of state which is absolutely decentralised, communitarian and non-violent. In 1946 he wrote in *Harijan* that,

> the world society of men will be an oceanic circle whose centre will be the individual, always ready to perish for the village, the latter ready to perish for the circle of villages, till at last the whole becomes one life composed of individuals never aggressive in their arrogance, but ever humble, sharing the majesty of the oceanic circle of which they are integral units. (quoted in Narayan 1970: 228)

This communitarian state, where the thousands of villages have become the principal nerve centre and life blood of the nation, is actually the alternative modernity to Gandhi. Hardiman has pointed out that Gandhi had no blind opposition to the modern West, nor to the forces of modern science. What he has opposed tooth and nail was the instrumental rationalism of the enlightenment tradition and forcefully pleaded for his community-oriented civilisation of the East. We may summarise this discussion with the words of Hardiman: "Gandhi's critique of technologism and a materialistic and instrumentalist practice of science can be fitted into the post-Enlightenment thematic of the divide between what Donald Worster has called an imperialistic science and an arcadian sensibility" (Hardiman 2005: 73).

IV

During his last visit to Santiniketan in December 1945, Gandhi said in an interview, "I started with a disposition to detect a conflict between Gurudev and myself, but ended with the glorious discovery that there was none" (quoted in Ray 1970: 107). Most of the keen disciples of Gandhi also tried to project that essentially there was no difference of outlook between the two towering personalities, the differences are occasional, sometimes a case of misunderstanding. The differences are more of difference of emphasis. But this resolution is perhaps not without some prejudice and bias. In the dispassionate estimate one would rather say that both the stalwarts had some essential differences of attitude towards life and society, and they did never conceal them for any mechanical or artificial purpose. Both Tagore and Gandhi were candid enough to speak out themselves even in the face of any stupendous national debacle. But this does not suggest that they had the lack of confidence and respect to each other. Contrarily, throughout their relation, Tagore and Gandhi held each other in high esteem. Gandhi addressed Tagore as Gurudev while Tagore acclaimed his younger contemporary as Mahatma. The disengagement or the difference between the two giant thinkers was actually a difference of two world views. Romain Rolland correctly spelt out this:

> The controversy between Tagore and Gandhi, between two great minds, both moved by mutual admiration and esteem, but as fatally separated in their feeling as a philosopher can be from an apostle, a St. Paul from a Plato, is important. For one side we have the spirit of religious faith and charity seeking to found a new humanity. On the other, we have intelligence, freedom, serene and broad, seeking to unite the aspirations of all humanity in sympathy and understanding'. (quoted in Basu 2009: 24)

The attitudinal differences between these two great souls became manifest in the non-cooperation movement in 1921 and in the cult of *Charkha* (spinning wheel) in 1925. On the issues of artificial devices of birth control and the Wardha scheme of education Tagore could not share the views of Gandhi. There are some other notable issues of differences either social or political in different periods of time. But these are not directly pertinent to our present discussion. On the question of development, both had some notable similarities along with some subtle differences also.

Tagore and Gandhi had their unique position on the issue of development in India – economic or social. They had a distinct philosophy of their own, an altogether different paradigm, so to say. Both of them considered India a different civilisation – the civilisation not of towns and cities, but the civilisation of village communities, an agrarian civilisation. The self-sufficient village community, we have already noticed, was their point of commonality and the centre of attention. In different ways both of them had concentrated their respective attention and energies for rural reconstruction as their prime objective. Both of them perceived that the economic progress and advancement in India would depend on the liberation of villages and on the thorough reform and reconstruction of our agricultural system. In the pre-industrial society, village was the basis and agriculture was the main occupation of the people. But both Tagore and Gandhi conceived that there should be a certain balance between agriculture and household or cottage industry, which is essential for the stability of the villages. During the phase of staunch de-industrialisation of the imperialist ruler, they urgently felt for the revival of traditional artisan industry with a new vigour and innovation. Gandhi's *Khadi* movement and Tagore's Sriniketan project would substantiate this point. But does it, in any way, crop up the question that this fascination for the village industries would hinder the process of industrialisation with the help of modern science and technology? Does it not contradict the process of capitalist accumulation in the industrialised world system in the 20th century? The questions are relevant and need to be answered.

Gandhi in his own way confronted the question saying, "I have no partiality for return to the primitive methods of grinding and husking for the sake of them. I suggest the return, because there is no other way of giving employment to the millions of villagers who are living in idleness" (quoted in Datta 1970: 245). Replying to the question whether he was against all machinery, Gandhi very simplistically said, "What I object to is the craze of machinery, not machinery as such. The craze is for what they call labour-saving machinery. Men go on 'saving labour' till thousands are without work" (ibid.: 245). It is in the same spirit Gandhi argued for the use of *Charkha*. In 1946, he said, "*Khadi* (hand-spun cloth) will cease to have any value in my eyes if it does not usefully employ the millions" (ibid.: 245).

These statements show that Gandhi had his own evaluation on the state of affairs of his time and he tried to confront the situation most pragmatically. Amlan Datta (1970) has documented that in fifty years from 1881 to 1931 a certain amount of industrialisation along modern lines did take place in India. But, the rise of this modern sector also witnessed the decline of traditional sector and in terms of total employment, the net effect of this was not very positive. Hence, the idea that modern technology creates unemployment has become an important component of Gandhian economic thought. Needless to say, Gandhi opposed large-scale industrialisation not only from this practical economic consideration of giving employment to all the villagers, he had a strong ethical argument also. Gandhi always talked about this ethics and morality without which his economics does not get its strong foundation.

Contrarily, Tagore was quite hesitant to accept this ethical foundation. Through some of his writings and lectures, Tagore opposed the economic efficacy of the *Charkha* programme. He said:

> The question of using or refusing cloth of a particular manufacture belongs mainly to economic science. The discussion of the matter by our countrymen should have been in the languages of economics. If the country has really come to such a habit of mind that precise thinking has become impossible for it, then our very first fight should be against such a fatal habit, to the temporary exclusion of all else if need be. Such a habit would clearly be the original sin from which all our ills are flowing. But far from this, we take the course of confirming ourselves in it by relying on the magical formula that foreign cloth is 'impure'. Thus, economics is bundled out and a fictitious moral dictum dragged into its place. (quoted in Biswas 1996: 422)

Commenting on this observation of Tagore, Sabyasachi Bhattacharya (1997: 10) wrote: "The objection here is not to the substantive point about foreign cloth, but to the terms of discourse, the use of moral language in place of the economic. To this, Gandhi's reply was that he had not drawn any distinction between economics and ethics." It is true that Tagore's objection was, what Bhattacharya said, 'on the terms of discourse'; but it is equally true that the poet could not endorse the programme of boycott of Mahatma Gandhi in 1921 and his cult of *Charkha* afterwards.

In his article "The Cult of the *Charkha*", written in 1925, Tagore pursued the question of economic rationality of Gandhi's programme. Tagore wrote: "If today, poverty has come upon our country, we should know that the root cause is complexly ramified and it dwells within ourselves. For the whole country to fall upon one of its external symptoms with the application of one and the same remedy will not serve to fight the demon away" (quoted in Biswas 1996: 540). Tagore argued that the British swept away our wealth across the seas and that did not happen in the preceding Mughal and Pathan regimes. The destruction and ruin of our native handicrafts was only one of the external symptoms of the total process of impoverishment. If we concentrate only on this and ignore all other forces, give undue prominence to it, then that will be somewhat misleading phenomenon. The poet therefore recommended that the leaders of the nation should analyse the problem more broadly and confront the situation in its totality.

While arguing in such a way, Tagore elaborated his idea of *samavaya* or cooperative as the possible means of panacea. Referring to the experiences and wisdom of great Irish poet and thinker, Sir Horace Plunkett, Tagore acclaimed that the success of this cooperative movement was not confined to Ireland alone, it has great possibility of success in India also. Tagore wrote:

> The cooperative principal tells us, in the field of man's livelihood, that only when he arrives at his truth can he get rid of poverty – not by any external means. And, the manhood of man is at length honoured by the enunciation of this principle. Cooperation is an ideal, not a mere system, and therefore it can give rise to innumerable methods of its application. It leads us into no blind alley; for at every step it communes with our spirit. And so, it seemed to me, in its wake would come, not merely food, but the goddess of plenty herself, in whom all kinds of material food are established in an essential moral oneness. (quoted in Biswas 1996: 544–45)

We all know that Tagore never denied the importance of science and technology for the promotion and furtherance of civilisation. In his article on "The Cult of the *Charkha*" also he put his argument from a moral standpoint. He wrote:

> If the cultivation of science by Europe has any moral significance, it is in its rescue of man from outrage by nature, not its use of man as a machine, but its use of the machine to harness the forces of nature in man's service. One thing is certain, that the all-embracing poverty which has overwhelmed our country cannot be removed by working with our hands to the neglect of science. Nothing can be more undignified drudgery than that man's knowing should stop deed and his doing go on for ever. (quoted in Biswas 1996: 541–42)

The controversy between Tagore and Gandhi on the question of development should not be traced as some archival material for our pedantic discourse. The controversy has its importance in establishing the fact that the concept of development and its necessary corollary 'modernity' has had the multi-dimensional aspects which, in our mainstream popular currency of thought, quite often get submerged. The utilitarian principles of development today must consider the moral and ethical dimensions or in Tagore's language – its aesthetic standards – otherwise the problem of sameness, i.e., lack of variety would pervade our essence and existence. And it is also true that the rapid pace of industrialisation and unprecedented revolution in modern technology enormously dehumanise our world civilisation. If we want to get rid of this gigantic process of dehumanisation, we are to look forward to a better and an alternative model of development and modernity. Tagore and Gandhi, in their respective ways and means, stimulate us to think and look for that alternative.

References

Basu, Sibaji Pratim. 2009. *The Poet and the Mahatma: Engagement with Nationalism and Internationalism*. Kolkata: Progressive Publishers.

Bhattacharya, Sabyasachi. 1997. *The Mahatma and the Poet: Lectures and Debates between Gandhi and Tagore, 1915–1941*. Delhi: National Book Trust.

Bhattacharya, Vivek Ranjan. 1968. 'Economic Thoughts of Mahatma Gandhi', in S.C. Biswas (ed.), *Gandhi: Theory and Practice, Social Impact and Contemporary Relevance* (183–87). Simla: Indian Institute of Advanced Study.

Biswas, S.C. 1996. *The English Writings of Rabindranath Tagore*. Vol. 3, Kolkata: Sahitya Academy.

Chatterjee, Partha. 1986. *Nationalist Thought and the Colonial World: A Derivative Discourse*. Delhi: Oxford University Press.

Datta, Amlan. 1970. 'Aspects of Gandhian Economic Thought', in Sibnarayan Ray (ed.), *Gandhi, India and the World* (242–52). Bombay: Nachiketa Publications Limited.

Eisenstadt, S.N. 1969. *Modernisation: Protest and Change*. New Delhi: Prentice Hall of India.

Hardiman, David. 2005. *Gandhi in His Time and Ours*. New Delhi: Permanent Black.

Narayan, Jayprakash. 1970. 'Gandhi and the Politics of Decentralisation', in Sibnarayan Ray (ed.), op. cit. (226–41).

Ray, Sibnarayan. 1970. 'Tagore-Gandhi Controversy', in Sibnarayan Ray (ed.), op. cit., (107–27).

Sen, Sachin. 1947. *The Political Thought of Tagore*. Calcutta: General Printers and Publishers.

Visva Bharati. 1963. *The Cooperative Principal: Rabindranath Tagore*. Santiniketan: Visva Bharati Press.

Section II

State, Market and Civil Society

4

State and Civil Society

Dialogue between the Deaf and the Dumb in India

Apurba Kumar Mukhopadhyay

> The enlightenment, which discovered the liberties, also invented the disciplines.
>
> —Michel Foucault

> Invoked at the same time, as the diagnosis and as the cure for current ills, deployed by conservatives, liberals and radical utopians alike, by oppositional movements and by international aid donors, civil society has become an ideological rendezvous for erstwhile antagonists.
>
> —Sunil Khilnani (2001)

Up to the 1970s, we the students of social science in India meant by civil society the 'western bourgeois democratic state' – nothing more nothing less. It sounded a bit old fashioned but captured the spirit and the nuances of civil society. We looked back to John Locke, the proponent of classical liberalism and the spokesman for natural rights to realise that civil society was to be the necessary space within the bourgeois state to keep the new ruling classes on the alert about protecting the natural rights of its people so as to ensure that the subjects in a feudal state are merrily transformed into modern citizens of the democratic nation-state in the West. According to John Dunn,

> Civil society for Locke is the state liked. What does the state have to be deservedly likable? ... To deserve liking it has to be as effectively purged of the state of nature as it can be. This is never very effectively purged. The fundamental character of politics for Locke, the problem of politics

> as such is the juxtaposition of individual self-righteous and partial judgments about what is to be done. That is the state of nature; and it is still a state in which all men and women, and hence all groups, smaller or larger of men or women, naturally find themselves. Civil society in Locke's usage is the optimal remedy for the state of nature. But it is a necessarily imperfect remedy; one which cannot in principle be made perfect. (Dunn 2001: 57)

Tocqueville further elaborated the notion by incorporating voluntary associations of citizens occupying the space between family and the state within the ambit of civil society. The wider the space and the more it is allowed to function in tandem with and not in opposition to the state, the healthier and robust is democracy. Tocqueville substantiated his views with insights from his study of democracy in America (obviously prior to the civil war in the south) and by comparing and contrasting the same with mid-19th century political experiences in France, submerged still in the pre-capitalist backwater. A contrasting perspective was presented on the nature and essence of the civil society by Hegel followed by Marx albeit with diametrically opposite political implications. Both Hegel and Marx contextualised civil society in the political economy of the state marked by contending social forces showing little signs of resolution of conflicts and disharmony. While Hegel looked upon the state as the ideal social institution transcending the inadequacies and shortcomings of civil society and presenting a higher level of synthesis following his dialectical triad, Marx located the anatomy of the state in civil society and considered the former to be partisan to the ongoing struggles of classes in modern capitalist society. Gareth Steadman Jones draws our attention to the ambiguous appreciation received by Hegel for conceptualising the dialectic between state and civil society. He observes, "by his admirers he was presented as a prophet, an analyst of the contradictions of capitalism, a critic of liberalism, a clear-sighted realist. By his enemies, he was seen as a champion of totalitarianism, a glorifier of an all-powerful bureaucracy, the mouth piece of an authoritarian state, a blithe apologist of history's juggernaut path, no matter how many victims were crushed beneath its wheels" (2001: 105). Jones' view is that distinction between civil society and the state made by Hegel was substantively addressed "to an ethical ideal rather than a sociological reality, that it formed part of his depiction of the *rational* state and this state itself cannot be understood except as the expression of a new stage of religious enlightenment" (ibid.: 106). To

Marx, the remedy lay not in the state transcending civil society but in the more complex and arduous task of transcending the state along with the civil society that had propped up and upheld the state for perpetrating the interest of the dominant class or classes.

Marx, following Hegel, therefore, problematised the concept of civil society rather than defining it away even within the historically specific western bourgeois democratic milieu. As Sudipta Kaviraj (2001: 300–1) aptly points out, "Marx mistrusts the power of the state to correct and balance by its universality the sectional over enthusiasm of civil society's class strife. Marx is convinced that the competitive principles of civil society (now read as bourgeois society without the benign associations of the public sphere) would either openly or secretly overwhelm the universalistic principles of the state, and in fact the class which is dominant in the economic sphere would use the state's machinery in its own interests. Indeed, that domination would be cognitively more difficult to understand and rectify because it would not be immediately apparent due to the universalistic form of legal rules. Thus, in Marx's reading, the distinction of spheres – between the society and the polity – creates a possibility of intellectual confusion or estrangement". The non-western, predominantly colonised world hardly figured in any conceptualisation of civil society up to the first quarter of the 20th century. This despite Marx's occasional references to the alternative trajectories of social formation in Tsarist Russia or colonial India with communal ownership of land and consequent emergence of peasant communities with potentials for both revolution and counter-revolution. It was the civil society's 'other' that found a space in the revolutionary discourse of Marxism following from the writings of old Marx via Lenin and taking a more rigorous theoretical as well as strategic shape in the writings of Mao, particularly in his discourses on new democratic culture in *On New Democracy* published in the 1930s.

Now, while such alternative possibilities of a non-western civil society were being explored within the tradition of orthodox Marxism, interesting insights into the nature and functioning of western civil society had been offered by Gramsci by way of explaining the contrary experiences of success of revolution in Russia, and its abortion in Italy and Germany giving rise to fascist barbarism. His *Revolution Against Das Capital* was a penetrating analysis of the revolutionary strategy of the working class in the West and not a critique of the Russian revolution. In other words, the small write-up published just after the revolution in 1918 was a bold attempt at contextualisation of the historic event while at the same time pointing towards the impossibility of such quick revolutionary 'leap' in the West precisely because of the ideological hold of the dominant class spread across the length and breadth of civil society in the West. An alternative to the crude armed struggle was called for, a theme that Gramsci would elaborate through the concepts of hegemony and the war of position that would be the necessary strategic choice before the working class to build up counter-hegemony.

To orthodox Marxists, propagated and practiced by ideologues in Soviet Russia, any hint at the impossibility of revolution in the West without revision of socialism in practice would sound heretical and hence Gramsci had few takers up to 1956, pending arrival of the campaign for de-Stalinisation with no less fury and venom than what had marked the crusade against so called renegades till then. Ironically, Gramsci's concept of civil society would henceforth be employed as a stick to beat all existing socialist regimes with. The collapse of Soviet socialism together with socialist regimes in Eastern Europe during the 1980s and 1990s opened up a new vista for the cult of civil society specifically aimed at non-western, post-colonial states with a typical Anglo-American bias that democracy in the West is all hunky dory with the unfettered march of civil society like that of Hegel's god upon earth. The only difference is while for Hegel it was the reason of the state, for contemporary civil society baiters, it was the reason of civil society marching like god upon the vanquished demon of the state. What is more intriguing in this whole exercise of state bashing in post-colonial societies is the overt prodding of the managers of the state to the exercise and deliberate squeezing of the sphere of the state's activities leaving larger space for civil society and non-governmental organisations. For post-colonial democracies like India, wedded to the goal of development and people's welfare, civil society is the new mantra to scare away the spectre of Marx or nowadays even of Keynes. To this changing Indian scenario we may now turn.

II

India is indisputably a land of puzzles; a multicultural and multilingual society accommodating no less than 4,635 discrete communities. According to a study made by the Anthropological Survey of India, it presents "a land of minorities and migrants" to quote the late K. Suresh Singh. That such a complex land mass could manage to survive all provocations to fragmentation and disintegration and sustain and uphold a nation-state for more than six decades with some amount of fidelity to democratic institutions and values arguably points towards the presence of a semblance of civil society in India's post-colonial democracy. One may argue about the nomenclature describing this space and the possibility of a divide between civil society of the middle-class urban elite and political society of the disorganised subaltern. Partha Chatterjee is the chief architect and designer of this conceptual divide between the two categories, applying those in the context of post-colonial democracies like India, bypassing the tradition–modernity dichotomy that remained in fashion for western scholarly work on society and politics in post-independence India throughout the period of intense cold war from the 1950s down to the early 1970s. Chatterjee (2001: 172–173) finds it "useful to keep the term 'civil society' for those characteristic institutions of modern associational life originating in western societies which are based on equality, autonomy, freedom of entry and exit, contract, deliberative procedures of decision-making, recognised rights and duties of members and other such principles. ... By political society, I mean a domain of institutions and activities where several mediations are carried out". He pinpoints the distinction in "the practices that activate the forms and methods of mobilisation and participation in political society", which "are not always consistent with the principles of association in civil society" (ibid.: 176). Tagore, the great Indian poet and philosopher, used the more generic term 'Samaj' without taking the trouble to choose between community and civil society as its appropriate English synonym, to define this space during the early 20th century. Neither conceptual jugglery nor anglomania was his forte. How both these symptoms vitiated the colonised mindset has been depicted most poignantly by Tagore in the following words: "From childhood to adolescence and again from adolescence to manhood, we are coolies of the goddess of learning, carrying loads of words on our folded backs. When at last we manage to enter the realm of English ideas, we find that we are not quite at home there. We find that although we can somehow understand those ideas, we cannot absorb them into our deepest nature, that although we can use them in our lectures and writings, we cannot use them in the practical affairs of our lives" (Tagore 1961: 44–45). Samaj for Tagore constituted an autonomous space neither antecedent to nor consequent upon the state. It had its own logic of unfoldment of interpersonal relations involving cooperation and conflict, being apart and being together, unity but not homogenisation. Tagore's idea of Samaj would express his tirade against both the colonial state and the newly emerging civil society of the English educated elites engaging itself in the unsavoury task of negotiation regarding its place in the colonial state machinery. An identical reaction would be expressed by Gandhi in his *Hind Swaraj* published five years after the publication of Tagore's *Swadeshi Samaj*, taking both the moderates and the extremists within the Indian National Congress to task for fighting over their share in the exercise of colonial state power, for "wanting the tiger's nature, but not the tiger" (Sharma and Suhrud 2010).[1]

The post-independence Indian state that finally emerged in 1947 did not oblige either Tagore or Gandhi. Under Nehru's stewardship it shaped up into a poor replica of western democratic state with a developmentalist orientation. As deliverer of all goods to all men (and women), the state assumed an omniscient and omnipresent aura about itself, leaving little space for Tagore's Samaj or the Loackean civil society that should have normally accompanied the democratic state wedded to the Westminister model.[2] The consequence has been the ambiguity witnessed in the long-term behaviour of the state. As one commentator on India's political economy puts it succinctly, "the Indian state can organise elections for an astounding 700 million voters with less controversy than the United States, it can conduct censuses for a billion people reasonably well, it periodically organises a temporary city for millions of people during the Kumbhamela without mishaps, it runs an efficient space programme and has managed to keep one of the world's largest armed forces away from politics. Yet, the same state does an abysmal job of providing decent primary education and health to its citizens, despite intense political competition, low incumbency and strong electoral participation of the very large number of poor and less educated voters. Its record of providing basic social services has been and continues to be weak and in areas like adult literacy, vaccination coverage and malnutrition, India's performance lags behind many poor countries. ..." (Kapur 2010: 443). Such ambiguities have led many to subscribe to the view that experiences of the Indian state suffice to designate it as a 'flailing', if not a 'failing' state. While the state in India's post-colonial democracy is thus flailing, its civil society is stratified by class and middle class activism is exercising a new hegemony over civil society, generating a 'new politics' of neighbourhood associations which tends to exclude the lower classes in the informal sector and so to perpetuate inequality rather than interrogate it (Harriss 2010: 150–51). There is, therefore, little wonder in the fact that retired civil servants, police officers and army personnel are leading and organising civil society movements in various parts of the country with pretensions of being non-political while waiting with all eagerness to jump into the bandwagon of parties having a brighter electoral prospect. Part of the state machinery as long as holding job in public services, becoming part of the civil society on retirement only to rejoin the state in a new avatar – such is the profile of new politics mediated through civil society and non-governmental organisations which had a rich harvest in the post-globalisation era.

The image of this civil society could hardly be found attractive by millions of India's helpless citizens living in hills and forests, in the fringes of mega cities or booming towns and living below poverty line. Their plight is such that "industries displace them, dams drown them and afforestation starves them". The IMF/World Bank dictated programmes and projects of development penetrating the interiors of the nation-state in India, thanks to globalisation, have intensified exploitation of the marginal men and women, creating in them a sense of despondency that is being utilised by various secessionist and disruptive social forces with overt or covert proddings from foreign countries. According to a Home Ministry report, more than 200 of Indian's nearly 600 districts are infested by Maoists putting up a formidable challenge to the state and civil society in India. The malaise has been aggravated by the intensification of the repressive role of the state with its overarching military and paramilitary presence and with the armed forces habit of picking up wrong targets in a fit of absent mindedness or indulging in terroristic excesses, raping and maiming women as in Manipur or killing civilians as in Kashmir. On the economic front, the story is no less gruesome. Per capita annual food intake of India's citizens went down from 180 kg to 157 kg at a time when India boasted of a projected GDP growth rate of 9.2 per cent per annum. More than 350 million Indians live on a daily income of Rs 12 only; of them 200 million live in villages. Uttar Pradesh, Bihar, Orissa, Madhya Pradesh, Jharkhand and Chhattisgarh have rural people with daily income varying between Rs 6 and Rs 9. As per NSSO data published in 2006, Orissa and Chhattisgarh have 55 to 57 per cent of rural people living on Rs 11 to Rs 12 as daily income. In Madhya Pradesh, they number 47 per cent and in Bihar and Jharkhand, they constitute 46 per cent of the total rural population. Inequality of life has sharpened beyond redemption following economic reforms of the 1990s. The state, despite holding on to its fragile democratic make-up, has been showing signs of growing illegitimacy, corruption and criminalisation.

III

In a recent article published in *The Telegraph*, Kolkata, on August 25, 2010, the noted economist Prabhat Patnaik has narrated a real-life story to underscore the complex nature of state–civil society dialogue in a highly inegalitarian country like India. He writes: "The early years of the Left Front Government in West Bengal in the late seventies had been marked by severe power cuts in Calcutta (as it then was) and elsewhere in the state. One evening, as load shedding began, a little urchin in a slum neighbouring a high rise, jumped up and down clapping his hands, shouting, 'Babuder alo gyalo re (The babus' lights have gone)'. The slum to which he belonged was devoid of power supply and hence not affected by the power cut, while the high rise was. In his excitement, that urchin was expressing an important truth: power supply and hence by inference the concept of infrastructure itself, has a class dimension". Without disputing the fact that this slightly overdrawn picture by Patnaik is not a foolproof argument against class neutral benefits of infrastructural investment in all instances, as for instance the little urchin was not supposed to know that investment in electricity was not meant only for supplying light to the babus in the high rise but also to ensure supply of drinking water to the taps run by the municipality and for a variety of other purposes, there is an important point in the story for state–civil society dialogue that concerns us here. Patnaik's observations suggest the possibility of two diametrically opposite reactions from diverse segments of civil society to the performance of delivery mechanism of the developmentalist state in India. What is cause for one's gloom may be cause for the other's jubilation. The polarities cannot be explained solely through invocation of the dichotomy between civil society of the elites and political society of the marginalised. We have no reason to overlook the fact that the two worlds also share spaces for criminal–politician nexus, for instigating terrorist manoeuvres in collusion with global mafia, for a wide array of frauds and scams. It would be fair to look, rather into the pluralities and fragmentations of a class society where both the ruling classes as well as the ruled are so starkly divided unto themselves and also marked by so many interlinkages and networking run at times on a 'hire and fire' basis. The *Samaj* of the traditional *gram sholoana* still obtained in some tribal hamlets in West Bengal, reorganised through the *Gram Samsad*, the newly created institutional mechanism at the village level to ensure participatory rural development presents a communicative space that is markedly different from what one obtains in a suburban railway compartment where commuters carrying the legacy of the colonial babus share a space amongst themselves. Both can be marked off distinctively from air travellers who share another world of meanings and values even when they descend upon remote villages for purposes of developmental tourism undertaken ostensibly for administering schemes and projects funded by the government or at present mostly by global non-governmental organisations. And, how can one overlook the fact that currently, "business delegations travel with the Finance Minister and the PM on international trips frequently', such public camaraderie 'would have been impossible even a decade or two back when Prime Minister refused to address business associations" (Sinha 2010: 459). The clue to the success of India's fragile democracy marked by the contrary pulls of so many societies (civil or uncivil), divided both horizontally and vertically, lies precisely in such heterogeneity of ruling class coalitions and the compulsion of compromises and mutual accommodation. Thus, factors responsible for India's chronic economic stagnation are ironically contributing to political democracy as no single class or group is in a position to dominate Indian politics (Kapur 2010: 445).

IV

The search for civil society as congeries of de-classed and de-politicised organisations and movements of people as watchdog of India's democracy in such a volatile political milieu is, therefore, theoretically untenable and empirically unsupportable. On crucial policy issues like price increase of essential goods and services, withdrawal of subsidies in agrarian sector, privatisation of the banking and insurance sectors, liberalisation of imports at the behest of global capital, civil society spokespersons maintain studied silence, not to speak of mobilising people in any protest movements against the state. They are rather found to be more active in areas where the state is compelled to initiate some developmental measures for the benefit of the poor and the marginalised. In West Bengal, for example, sections of civil society activists cry foul over terrorism of the state against Maoists while blissfully ignoring the Maoists' daily itinerary of murdering hundreds of unarmed poor victims with sophisticated weapons of annihilation and destruction. The activists enjoy political patronage from influential quarters of the state, receive hefty perks for advising the railway ministry and the Kolkata Corporation, address press conferences to garner political support for political parties' favouring them with tax payers' money and despite all such vulgarities claiming a non-political identity for themselves. They truly match the parliamentary democrats more than 300 of whom are *crorepatis* (millionaires), striving hard for still sharper rise in their pay, allowances and other monetary benefits at a time when several lakhs of peasants had committed suicide under pressure of the chronic debt trap engulfing them and many more are in the queue. The Indian state, sucked into the global capitalist grid, finds itself duty bound to carry the agenda of economic reforms still further braving all forms of popular resentment which are diverted and digressed through the skilful mediation of civil society urging and imploring people to love dogs, expand green pastures in the heart of mega cities or protect rapists and murderers from capital punishment which is terribly inhuman! Such innocuous movements are given wide publicity by the global media to keep both the mentors of global capital and their local protégés in good humour. The dialogue between the state and its civil society is rendered putative in such state craft or stage craft if you so please! It also willy-nilly, dispels the myth about a "supposed link between democracy and the capitalist class", as noted by Kaviraj (2010) in a rigorous attempt at theorisation of the idea of civil society in a non-western context. He writes that "in the European context of absolutism and its rivalry with early capitalist mercantile enterprise, capitalist classes followed a broadly consistent anti-absolutist political strategy. This purely local fact is often generalised into a universal theory which asserts a mysterious essentialist tendency in bourgeois classes everywhere to support democratic movements. As a consequence, political analysts have looked at capitalist classes all over the world with an entirely unreasonable eternal hope that they would side with popular forces instead of an oppressive state, and support restrictions on state power rather than cosy backroom arrangements with its possessors. This was a classic example of a significant but contingent occurrence of European history being turned into a metaphysical truth" (ibid.: 297). Our civil society ideologues and practitioners naively subscribe to this 'metaphysical truth' partly to romanticise their not so heroic actions and partly to keep their middle class conscience clear.

Their ever zealous claim to have an autonomous space carved out for themselves *within* the bourgeois democratic state is mistakenly projected as a struggle for the civil society's right *against* the state encompassing all segments of the marginalised social groups, the destitute and the have-nots, the minorities and women. Since all these groups are involved in a variety of social movements, old or new, with diverse and at times conflicting pursuits, the question that they pose inescapably to ideologues of civil society is, can a pluralistic vision of civil society happily embrace movements, aspirations, struggles, desires and oppositions that are openly hostile to liberal values which saw individuals as essentially autonomous entities, secure in their individuality beyond communal ties and referents? (Femia 2003: 145–46). We may conclude with Femia's observation that "in arguing that the modern idea of civil society is intrinsically linked to a specific way of life and a specific way of thinking, Marx perhaps displayed more insight than his recent 'flexible disciples' and not so recent orthodox detractors as well" (ibid.: 146). Going beyond the universe of this universalised, Eurocentric liberal discourse of civil society calls for an intervention that can hardly be restricted to the realm of pure theory bereft of a qualitatively different form of social practice – of activating the dialogue between the state and civil society in a country like India.

Notes

1. Tagore, interestingly, anticipates Gandhi's views as early as 1906 when he writes, "English models usurp the whole field of our vision and obscure the achievements of our own country. Even in our keenest struggles for freedom from British rule we remain fettered to Britain in so far as we seek no political models other than the British". Tagore (1906) in *Towards Universal Man* (1961: 69).
2. See Paul Brass (2006) and Partha Chatterjee (2010). Post-colonial India's overtures to overstatism in total defiance of Gandhi and Tagore have been registered by Kaviraj in the following observation: "Except for a few odd individuals like Gandhi and Tagore, nationalists did not object to the presence of the modern state, only to its being under European control. With Independence, they did not wish, except in a few cases like Gandhi, to 'abolish' the state, but to use it for their own purposes. After two hundred years of colonialism, the European state receded from India, but the idea of the state brought in by colonialism continued its triumphant career" (Kaviraj 2010: 211).

References

Brass, Paul. 2006. 'How American Political Scientists Experienced India's Development State', in L.I. Rudolph and J.K. Jacobsen (eds.), *Experiencing the State* (110–38). New Delhi: Oxford University Press.

Chatterjee, Partha. 2001. 'On Civil and Political Society in Post-Colonial Democracies', in S. Kaviraj and S. Khilnani (eds.), *Civil Society: History and Possibilities* (165–78). New Delhi: Cambridge University Press.

——. 2010. 'The State', in Niraja Gopal Jayal and Pratap Bhanu Mehta (eds.), *Oxford Companion to Politics in India* (3–14). New Delhi: Oxford University Press.

Dunn, John. 2001. 'The Contemporary Political Significance of John Locke's Conception of Civil Society', in S. Kaviraj and S. Khilnani (eds.), op. cit. (39–57).

Femia, Joseph. 2001. 'Civil Society and the Marxist Tradition', in S. Kaviraj and S. Khilnani (eds.), op. cit. (131–46).

Harriss, John. 2010. 'Class and Politics', in Niraja Gopal Jayal and Pratap Bhanu Mehta (eds.), op. cit. (139–53).

Jones, Gareth Steadman. 2001. 'Hegel and the Economics of Civil Society', in S. Kaviraj and S. Khilnani (eds.), op. cit. (105–30).

Kapur, Devesh. 2010. 'The Political Economy of the State', in Niraja Gopal Jayal and Pratap Bhanu Mehta (eds.), op. cit. (443–58).

Khilnani, Sunil. 2001. 'The Development of Civil Society', in S. Kaviraj and S. Khilnani (eds.), op. cit. (287–323).

Kaviraj, Sudipta. 2001. 'In Search of Civil Society', in S. Kaviraj and S. Khilnani (eds.), op. cit. (287–323).

——. 2010. *The Imaginary Institution of India*. Ranikhet: Permanent Black.

Sharma, Suresh and Tridip Suhrud. 2010. *M.K. Gandhi's Hind Swaraj: A Critical Edition*. New Delhi: Orient Black Swan.

Sinha, Aseema. 2010. 'Business and Politics', in Niraja Gopal Jayal and Pratap Bhanu Mehta (eds.), op. cit. (459–76).

Tagore, Rabindranath. 1961. *Towards Universal Man*. New Delhi: Asia Publishing House.

5

The *Adivasis* in a Liberal Democratic Order and Their Struggle for a Self

Sanjay K. Roy

> A democratic republic is the best possible political shell of capitalism, and therefore, once capital has gained possession of this very best shell ... it establishes its power so securely, so firmly, that no change of persons, institutions or parties in the bourgeois-democratic republic can shake it. (Lenin 1977: 271)

The problem of 'integration' or 'disintegration' of the state or nation emerging from the movements of the subordinated classes and communities could be plausible only if analysed in the context of the Indian liberal democratic order. The present paper aims to analyse the ongoing *adivasi* movement, particularly in Jalpaiguri and Darjeeling districts of North Bengal, which is being spearheaded by the Akhil Bharatiya Adivasi Vikash Parishad (ABAVP). In constructing an account of the genealogy and course of the movement, the paper argues that the crisis in the integrationist mechanisms of the politico-economic order prompts the kind of *adivasi* movement that characterises the region.

Sandwiched in the power struggle between the Nepalese of Darjeeling striving for a separate state of Gorkhaland and the mainstream political forces which are out to integrate the marginalised into the 'order' and oppose any division of the state, nearly one million *adivasis* in the Dooars and Terai of Jalpaiguri and Darjeeling districts, who are highly dissatisfied with the treatment received from the liberal democratic order and its organs, are now engaged in a tribal solidarity movement under the banner of the ABAVP with the objective of finding their own identity and political right over a territory following the provisions of the Sixth Schedule of the Indian Constitution. The movement promises formation of a civil society of the otherwise voiceless *adivasis* of the region on ethnic line, which strives to free the community from the control of the organs of the mainstream political parties, although maintaining the solidarity and achieving its political goal might prove to be very difficult in the face of the integrationist efforts and strategies of the systemic forces.

The present paper locates the *adivasis* of North Bengal against the backdrop of their migration history, their struggle for livelihood, their control over resources – material and human, the history of solidarity movement – all in the wider context of the liberal market and the state which work hand in gloves to integrate and subordinate the 'fringe-people' into the order. The paper argues that the organs of 'biopower' (the state and market) work to achieve the integration function for the liberal democratic order but fail to contain the 'subaltern' forces in search of a greater space within the existing politico-economic frame in order to redefine their rights and self.

The Liberal Democratic Order and the Crises of Integration

In *Capital* (Volume I), Marx outlined capitalist mode of production as an order or system that subjugates the masses by evicting them from the means of production (primitive accumulation) and by turning them into workers, the means of generation of surplus value. The democratic arrangements, the legal and administrative arrangements, extension of workers' democratic rights are termed 'ploys' of the capital to subjugate not only the workers but the entire population. In Marxist analysis, the state and market together make all the arrangements for the reproduction of the capitalist order and legitimise them, legally and ideologically. Marx and Engels' critique of the western capitalist order has been widened and concretised by the later Marxists like Lenin, Gramsci, Althusser and Habermas and the post-Marxist Foucault in one way or the other. Their writings demonstrate that the strategies of integration of the masses flow in the political (and ideological), economic and socio-cultural fields. From the Marxist and post-Marxist critiques of the liberal states of the West, we gather some common features, viz., (1) granting of limited democratic and citizenship rights (Lenin), (2) integration of the masses by the use of social, cultural and ideological means (Gramsci), (3) use of state and as an apparatus of ideological integration (Althusser and Poulantzas), (4) integration of the masses by way of economic governance and promotion of active citizenship (Habermas), and (5) integration by combining the strategies of city-citizen game, pastoral power and biopower (Foucault), and so on. Althusser (1971), taking cues from Gramsci, advanced the thesis of 'ideological state apparatus' spelling out how the post-War II capitalist states use the socio-cultural, educational and ideological routes in integrating the 'revolutionary classes' into the order.

The later Marxist critical thinkers have squarely unravelled the integrationist strategies and the art of population management in modern democracies and produced 'texts' on the bourgeois success in thwarting the counter-hegemonic efforts of the oppressed classes. The social theorists have time and again warned us about the demonic character of the integrationist arrangements (e.g., devolution, welfarism, participatory development, popularisation of consumer culture, symbolic cooption to the leadership of the organs of the civil societies) and integrationist politics of the bourgeois liberal order. In the advanced capitalist systems of the West, according to Habermas, the market works on autonomous and anonymous principles, despite planned attempts by the state and the organised bourgeois to control it. What matters the most, however, is the impact of the market and the system on the 'lifeworld'. Market principles may be anonymous, but one can see their link with life. Prices are fixed not only by invisible factors but also by such lifeworld processes as mob psychology, trust, personal competition, and the like. Conceptual link lies in the fact that the members' knowledge of the lifeworld influences their response to the market. In other words, the systems such as economy and political administration are primarily steered by money and power instead of by people. As the complexity of the system increases, its rationality no longer coincides with the rationality of any individual. This is what Habermas means by the uncoupling of the system from the lifeworld (Habermas 1987: 233).

Michel Foucault, in his non-Marxist interpretation of western capitalist order, argues that 'life and living being' are now at the heart of new political battles and new politics. He analysed the introduction of 'life into history' through the development of political economy. The modern-day liberal democracies subsist on 'biopolitics'. Biopolitics, according to Foucault, speaks of government-population-political economy relationship, which refers to a dynamic of forces that establishes a new relationship between ontology and politics (Foucault 1991). Foucault explains the development of biopolitics as the necessity to assure any strategic coordination of forces, rather than as the organisation of a unilateral power relation. He argues that the problem that arises from the relation between politics and economy in capitalism is resolved by techniques and motivations that come from neither. This 'outside other' which Foucault interrogates is named 'the government of men'. Government is a 'human technology' that the modern state has inherited from the Christian pastoral technique. To govern means to ask the question of how to conduct the conduct of others; to act upon subjects who ought to be considered free (Lazzarato 2010: 1). In the liberal state the men are reduced to economic men, guided by interests, at the cost of their political rights. They are now subjected to the control of the order. Enterprises, the market and labour, Foucault argues, are not spontaneous powers, but rather constitute what liberal government must make possible and real. Modern liberalism invents new techniques (of government) which largely operate through civil society, by continuously reproducing the ideologies and elements of culture that would corroborate the capitalist order. Foucault has elaborated this idea of control and discipline by continuously creating the new knowledge forms by the powerful.

A brief journey into the theories of modern state–market nexus in the western capitalist world was necessary to place the state–market relationship in India in perspective. Power or governance in India is fast taking the shape of biopower and the market is reproduced in the social and cultural spheres, as Foucault has argued. In this arrangement the state is turning out to be the facilitator for the advance of the national and global capital. In this task, the state penetrates into the social and cultural spheres and also in the individual and social psyche, appropriates the cultural symbols and creates new symbols. It is, therefore, absolutely essential to understand the changing equation between economy and power or the rules to 'biopower' in order to explore the integrationist mechanisms of the liberal democratic Indian state.

India in post-World War II period pursued welfarism of a kind and at the same time increasingly performed the function of reproduction of the order and the damage-repairing work by periodically coming up with welfare programmes to support the victims of exploitation, and even by coming up with bail-out packages for the 'capital-in-crisis' in the line prescribed by Keynes. In the Nehruvian model of national development, which was also followed by the latter regimes until early eighties, the state, at least theoretically, had a firm control over the market. The Indian state in the pre-globalisation period combined capitalist growth with 'welfare packages' for the vulnerable in order to defer the legitimation crisis.

The liberal democratic order in India has made an elaborate arrangement for the integration of its otherwise 'excluded' and marginalised sections into the order through schemes like democratic decentralisation, land reforms, capacity building programmes, right to education, Forest Rights Act, tribal sub-plan, the policy of protective discrimination, granting of regional autonomy and formation of regional development authority,[1] special welfare programmes for the marginalised and poor people including the SCs and STs and so on. This is clearly in line with the liberal model of development where (a) the state makes arrangements for the protection of the victims of the market forces, (b) reproduces and prepares the labour force for the market, and (c) ensures peace and stability to facilitate smooth sailing of the manufacturing and business activities. In the recent years one can see that the Indian state is adopting a kind of 'rights-based approach' by recognising 'right to employment' enshrined in the Mahatma Gandhi National Rural Employment Guarantee Act (MGNREGA), the right to information enshrined in the RTI Act, being now succeeded by the Right to Education Bill, a Right to Health Bill waiting in the wings and a Right to Food Bill, which is under consideration (see Patnaik 2010: 35). But such rights acts are argued to be merely 'eye wash' and the state does not take any serious measure to make them effective organs of empowerment. As Patnaik argues, '... while the government talks about conferring 'rights', they are not 'rights' in the true sense of the term' (ibid.: 35).

As opposed to this pro-poor, pro-people approach, the Indian state since the 1990s has turned aggressive by withdrawing much of its 'welfare packages' and thereby leaving the victims of capitalist exploitation to the mercy of the national and global capital. During this new phase of 'market globalism', it has been striving for a growth-oriented model of development, which has been termed by Patnaik (2010: 34) as the 'means-based approach' (which runs on the premise that the growth in GDP and taxation of rich will generate resources in the public exchequer which is to be spent on the welfare of the poor and the workers). The equation has turned so much in favour of capital that the state has passed on much of its responsibility to the market. And, the market has grown so autonomous and powerful that it does eat up much of the advantages meant for the masses via the welfare programmes. The growing market leaves a negative impact on the welfare character of the state and its ability to arrest the resulting exclusion and marginalisation, particularly of the vulnerable sections like the *adivasis* who have very little control over material resources and skills. When the market rules reign supreme the *adivasis* who have not experienced much of capacity building stand the risk of further exclusion.

Economic and Demographic Logic of the Movement

The *adivasi* (tribal) population in North Bengal is largely constituted of the migrants from the Chotanagpur region of Central India, who moved out of their original abode in the second half of the 19th century because of exploitation by the *dikus* (aliens), land loss, loss of forest rights, imposition of land rent, and the colonial oppression, particularly in the post-Santhal rebellion period. The expanding tea gardens in the Dooars and Terai region (along with parts of Assam) offered them livelihood although they found themselves in another exploitative and oppressive economic and power arrangement. The expanding *zamindari* estates in the districts of the region, particularly in Malda and Dinajpur districts, in the latter half of the 19th and first half of the 20th century also accommodated these migrants, primarily as tenant-cultivators. The expansion of rail links later also encouraged migration of tribal labour force from Central India. The migration flow stopped by 1940s when the tea gardens stopped expanding and as the land management system underwent major transformation after the abolition of the *zamindari* system in the 1950s. In the Dooars and Terai region the surplus labour force, ejected from the tea gardens, took hold of the fallow land or cleared forest land and took to settled cultivation. Lack of access to material resources or education (and skill) made them depend on agriculture and tea almost exclusively.

Tribal economy, largely defined as subsistence economy, is based on agriculture in four districts of North Bengal, namely, Cooch Behar, North Dinajpur, South Dinajpur and Malda, and on tea in Jalpaiguri and Darjeeling districts. Census data show that over the years the percentage share of cultivators (owning cultivators) has declined sharply in these districts with corresponding rise in the number of agricultural labourers. Reading these two trends together one can discern the massive land alienation the tribal population in the region has experienced. And, this has happened despite the government efforts to protect tribal land and also the much acclaimed redistribution of land among the landless *adivasis*, as a part of land reform programmes (see, Roy 2008: 41–42; Roy 2009).

Another trend in tribal economy has been a decline in significance of household industry over the years. In the districts, the share of the 'main workers' engaged in household industries hover around 0.5 to 1 per cent in 2001 (Roy 2008: 42). The 'other workers' category, which includes jobs in the tea gardens, in the offices or other organised sector, did not grow expectedly. Interestingly, such growth is higher only in Darjeeling and Jalpaiguri districts where the *adivasi* workforce is primarily engaged as tea garden workers; the growth of jobs in other districts has been less than 0.5 per cent per annum. Even in Jalpaiguri district which accommodates most of the tea gardens, the growth of jobs has been only by 16 per cent in four decades.

The slow growth of jobs in 'other workers' category has to be understood in the light of stagnation and the planters' refusal to recruit in the permanent worker category. The strength of permanent workforce in tea gardens has declined in Jalpaiguri and Darjeeling districts although there has been some increase in the number of casual workers. It has been a feature of the tea gardens that the strength of male workers has declined while there has been a marginal increase in the number of female workers, both in the permanent and causal categories – a feature that can be termed as 'feminisation of workforce' (Roy 2008: 46–48). The increase in work participation as 'other workers', although meagre, is the only positive development the *adivasis* of North Bengal have achieved.

Four factors are primarily responsible for the economic plight of the *adivasis* in the region: (a) meagre control over material and human resources, (b) their incapacity to take advantages of the market opportunities, (c) inadequate state support, and (d) exploitative penetration of the market forces and the groups which control them. The increase of control over the material and human resources could have enhanced their 'capacity' to take greater advantage of the market opportunities and to thwart the penetration of the more powerful exploitative forces. But what the state has done so far is to initiate some relief work here and there and some reservation which have failed to enhance the quality of tribal life. The low rate of literacy (while total ST literacy is 43.4 per cent, ST female literacy is only 29.15 per cent in West Bengal in 2001), high rate of dropout at the school level and very little spread of higher and technical education have hampered the process of human resource development over these years (see Roy 2008: 26–27). The penetration of the outsiders into the tribal belt with the spread of communication and market forces has contributed to land alienation and economic marginalisation of the *adivasis*. The artificial crisis created by the tea garden owners including a distinct strategy of casualisation and the threat of closure as a measure to deprive the tea workers and weaken the trade union movement have conversely brought miseries for the *adivasis*.

When the 'protector' state is in a mood to recede and the market on the rampage, it is quite natural that the powerless and voiceless people who live on the margin would find themselves more vulnerable. Being a part of the neo-liberal market, the *adivasis*, with minimal control over material and human resources and cultural capital, are engaged in fierce survival battle as the dominant sections with greater control over resources not only do not give them much economic and socio-political space but often intrude into whatever small space they occupy. With very little effort to human resource development initiative, the *adivasis* cannot reap the benefits of the policy of protective discrimination or the special development initiatives of the state. The corrupt yet inefficient bureaucracy and the panchayat functionaries come in the way to their reaping the benefits of development initiatives. The over-exploitative arrangement in tea gardens and loss of land (because of division of holdings among the heirs and alienation by the manipulative and resourceful neighbours) perpetuate their marginalised existence in the region. The market uncertainty, the penetration of the forces of globalisation and crisis in the tea gardens make them even more vulnerable as a social category.

Being a part of such a depressing reality, the *adivasis* in the region have all reasons to lose confidence in the state and in the conventional organs of the civil society (trade unions and mass organisations) which they had trusted for so long as the protectors of their rights. The in-migration of more resourceful non-*adivasis* (Nepalese, Bengali refugees and Rajbanshis) into 'their territory' has additionally created a sense of insecurity in the collective psyche of the *adivasis* in the form of being reduced to an insignificant minority and insecurity relating to livelihood. Neither the state nor the expanding market has any mechanism to free the *adivasi* psyche of this sense of insecurity. It may be noted in this context that though the *adivasis* constitute a significant part of the population and the electorate in the blocks claimed in the proposed Sixth Schedule, they are not in the majority in any of the blocks. The agricultural land and the business opportunities in the area are controlled almost exclusively by these non-*adivasi* migrants in the area. These migrants, because of their greater control over the resources and business strategies, often establish exploiter-exploited nexus with the *adivasis* who are largely confined to tea gardens and to small plots of cleared land. The demographic and ethnic heterogeneity factors have therefore weakened the demand for Sixth Schedule of the *adivasis*. It is in such a context that *adivasi* movement in Dooars and Terai has gained prominence.

Adivasi Movement in Dooars and Terai

Shaping of the Movement

Mr Kartik Oraon, an engineer by profession, and a Congress MP, founded the Adivasi Bikas Manch in Ranchi in 1966–67 and visited the Tarai and Dooars region of North Bengal to bring all the *adivasis* under the umbrella of the organisation. Although he did not meet with much organisational success, he could spread the message of a need for an *adivasi* identity and unity. The leaders of Jharkhand statehood movement visited the region on occasions to draw support for the movement. In recent past, Sibu Soren of Jharkhand Mukti Morcha visited the area to spread his organisation but without much success. One common feature of these efforts is that they had all originated in Jharkhand and aimed to integrate the *adivasis* of North Bengal into their Jharkhand-based organisations. These efforts failed to cut much ice because the leaders were outsiders to this region and could not strike a common cord with the aspiration of the *adivasis* of the Tarai and Dooars region of Darjeeling and Jalpaiguri districts of North Bengal.

The other important reason which blocked the tribal solidarity movement has been the strong association of the *adivasis* of the region with the locally dominant parties. The trade union wings of the left parties, particularly the Communist Party of India (CPI), the Communist Party of India (Marxist) and the Revolutionary Socialist Party and the Indian National Congress, had spread their organisational network among the *adivasis*. The organised parties also penetrated into the tribal villages which fall outside the tea gardens through their frontal organisations. The early leaders, particularly of the left parties, were strongly committed to the revolutionary ideology and worked for the organisation with missionary zeal. They sacrificed their life working for the organisation and mixed with the *adivasis*. The first generation leaders were uncompromising and committed to the cause of the workers. Their missionary style of operation earned them a respectable place in the hearts of the workers. They could speak the language of the workers and could adjust with their lifestyle at ease.

The *adivasis* in turn extended wholehearted support to the trade unions and the mainstream left political parties. The left parties and their trade union wings retained the unquestionable support of the *adivasis* because of their early initiative and also because the other all-India parties did not give them much challenge. The mainstream political parties made efforts to integrate the *adivasis* into their organisational fold by spreading wings of frontal organisations and by involving them in the democratic processes at the grassroots level. In 1998, tea gardens, which were outside the panchayat system so far, were brought under the three-tier panchayat system. This was another opportunity to incorporate the *adivasis* into the democratic polity and in the organisation of the parties. The *adivasis* participated in the panchayat bodies with great enthusiasm and helped consolidation of the hold of the mainstream political parties over the *adivasis*. Not only most of the panchayat seats but all the Lok Sabha and Vidhan Sabha seats in the tribal dominated regions have been consistently won by the left parties, such as the CPI (M) and the Revolutionary Socialist Party. As a result of these political processes, a section from amongst the *adivasis* emerged as local level leaders; a few of them were MLAs, MPs, and even ministers in the state government. Spread of education and opportunities for organised sector employment helped the emergence of *adivasi* leaders. There were thus some early signs of formation of neo-elite among the *adivasis*.

However, an important slag in the process of class formation was that the average *adivasis* remained supporters and only supporters; they were far from becoming a 'class for itself'. The trade unions of the national political parties had their wings at the garden level and a few *adivasi* men workers were inducted into the leadership who in turn mobilised support for the party and the trade union. The average *adivasi* workers, women workers in particular, had no ideological training. The other important slag was that the *adivasis* carefully and distinctly nursed their tribal and *adivasi* identities, which might have come in the way to class formation. The domination of the non-tribals in the leadership of the trade unions and political parties also prevented an organic integration of the *adivasis* with these organisations. The insurmountable crises in the tea gardens created by the market and the ownership and the repeated failure of the trade unions and political parties to overcome them have resulted into loss of faith in their effectiveness. The trade unions and political parties remained hapless spectators to the deepening livelihood crises and other crises that resulted from the closure and sickness of the tea gardens. Sharp drops in the quality of the present generation leaders and their mode of mixing with the workers also have brought about a gap between the two. The present generation leaders, who are also busy political leaders, now operate with bureaucratic attitude and they no longer live in the workers' quarters; they in fact maintain a distance from the workers. The proximity of the leaders with the owners and their ineffectiveness in realising the demands raised from time to time have also contributed to workers' loss of faith in the leaders. It is in such a context that the leaders of the ABAVP nurse a deep-rooted grudge against the leaders of the established political parties for failing to reciprocate the unqualified support for the *adivasis* in the region. In their assessment, tribals are used as a captive vote bank by the left parties and the Congress. A lack of understanding of this structural strategy of captivation had to a large extent blocked the emergence of an *adivasi* front, a political self of the *adivasis* in the region.

The leaders of the ABAVP have attributed the following factors for the emergence of the movement: (1) the threat of their territory and self being swallowed by the advancing Gorkha Jana Mukti Morcha (GJMM), (2) the fear of losing their hold over the territory to the non-adivasi settlers, (3) the loss of faith in the established political parties and trade unions, (4) the long perpetuating crisis in the tea gardens and their unsettling effect on the life of the *adivasi* tea workers, (5) the plight of *adivasi* workers in the Bodoland area of neighbouring Assam and the continued atrocity against the tribal women there, (6) their long subdued aspiration for a distinct *adivasi* identity, and (7) absence of any perceptible development in the existing framework.

The Organisational Efforts

The leaders of the movement[2] inform that the ABAVP has a four-tier structure with a National Committee, State Committee, Regional Committee and Block Committees. The Terai-Dooars Committee is a regional committee of the ABAVP. Within the regional committee again there are block level and village level committees. The Terai-Dooars Committee is comprised of 31 members with John Barla as the President and Rajesh Lakra as the Secretary of the Committee.

The effort to form ABAVP began in early 2008 when a long march was organised from Sankosh to Naxalbari in which 200 tribal youth took part, and a motor cycle rally was held in the month of April from Ghoshpukur to Sankosh to press the demand for autonomy and to protest the plight of the *adivasis* in the neighbouring state of Assam at the hands of the Bodos and the Assamese. The rally covered the entire length of the area the ABAVP wants under the Sixth Schedule. Agitations followed opposing GJMM rallies in the area, protesting the different acts of atrocity and injustice against the *adivasis* by the police and administration and the members of non-*adivasi* communities.

The Parishad released a map comprising the tribal belts of the Dooars and Terai region demanding Sixth Schedule status, which it believes, would help develop the backward tribal region. The ABAVP leaders submitted a memorandum in support of the Sixth Schedule to the Chief Minister and the Prime Minister on 25 July 2009 and subsequently held several rallies to reiterate its demands including opposing the inclusion of the region in Gorkhaland.

It should be noted in this context that the GJMM's movement for a separate state has threatened to rob the tribal population in the region of their claim over the land and their identity. The Gorkha statehood movement is a strong sub-nationalist movement which is considered to be an imposition from the above over the minor ethnic communities, such as Lepchas and the *adivasis*, who are keen on retaining their ethnic and cultural identities. Apart from being distinct communities, with some sense of sharing similar objective conditions, the emotive bonds and political interests help ethnic community formation in the present case. The major shared objective conditions include similar position in the production relations, their common place of origin, history of migration, position in power relations, religious and traditional belief system and the sense of being *adivasis* including confrontation of the similar constraints of development.

The ABAVP fought the GJMM tooth and nail against the latter's efforts to spread its organisational network in the Dooars and Terai region. The public rallies and agitations organised by the GJMM were physically opposed by the supporters of the ABAVP. The GJMM initially underestimated the strength of the ABAVP and confronted the latter with an attacking posture. But, by the middle of 2010, the GJMM worked out a policy shift to woo the *adivasis*. It started showing some respect to the *adivasi* leaders and recognised the existence and strength of the *adivasi* outfit. The GJMM tried to please the *adivasi* youth by inducting them into the Gorkha Land Police (GLP) and floated a compromise proposal to the ABAVP. The name of the proposed state in Darjeeling Hills was also changed to Gorkha-Adivasi Pradesh in an effort to persuade the *adivasis* opposed to the idea of inclusion of Dooars and Terai in the map of the Gorkha state. The ABAVP leadership however showed no intention of joining the Morcha or expressing solidarity for the so-called demand of Gorkha Adivasi Pradesh. They rather felt that "it is a conspiracy to derail their movement and again create tension in the brew belts as they will not part with any portion of the Terai and the Dooars for the separate state" (*The Telegraph,* 1 June 2010).

Apart from pressing for their right to land, autonomy and identity, the ABAVP has demonstrated its keenness to raise the issues of civil rights as a part of their solidarity movement. They often raise issues like the rights of the tea garden workers, rights to proper education, development of infrastructure, and their entitlements according to various government sponsored development schemes. The issues like non-development of the *adivasis,* closure of tea gardens, starvation, out-migration in search of income, women trafficking and the spread of prostitution often find prominent place in the political and non-governmental organisations that are opposed to the Left Front in the state. In the anti-left media the Left Front government in the state is held solely responsible for the non-development of the *adivasis* both in southern and northern districts. The leaders of the left trade unions are levelled as corrupt, self-seekers and indifferent to the problems of the workers. The ABAVP has taken up some of these issues and raised the ante against the constituents of the Left Front and its trade unions.

Peeved at the silence of the state government on its demand for Sixth Schedule status for Terai and Dooars, the ABAVP decided to take up the demand with the Centre. "Considering the state's apathy to the Parishad demands, it is only autonomy that can save the region from backwardness", Mr Tirkey said (*The Telegraph,* 15 January 2010). The organisation observed one day strike in Dooars on 27 January to protest against the nomenclature of a government-sponsored *adivasi* festival and to press the demand for Sixth Schedule. It was argued that "the fest has turned into a platform of the ruling CPI (M) and does not serve the purpose to portray the ethnic culture of the tribal population residing in this part of the state" (*The Telegraph,* 28 January 2010).

To step up pressure on the administration, the ABAVP prepared for intensification of its agitation. It announced to organise a rally at Malbazar and called for another strike on 29 January. However, after the strike on 27 January the administration cancelled the fest citing security reasons. Following this the outfit suspended its agitation programmes for two days and decided to organise a mega rally at Malbazar on 29 January. The ABAVP also organised a public rally at Banarhat on 9 June 2010 to mark the 110th death anniversary of the tribal icon Birsa Munda. The rally was attended by nearly 30,000 Parishad supporters from the Dooars and Terai region. The movement spearheaded by the ABAVP has not always been peaceful. There have been incidents of conflict between the ABAVP supporters and the supporters of other political organisations including management of tea estates. It is worth noting here that the *adivasis* in Terai and Dooars region are a heterogeneous lot; there are about 30 tribes, each of which is distinct in terms of name, language, social structure and rituals. They nurse a sense of hierarchy and a feeling of difference in terms of religious faith. Yet, a common geographical root, migration history, common socio-economic standing and common sufferings have united the tribals under the term *adivasi*. The leaders of the movement understand the value of *adivasi* unity and they are out to exploit some cultural symbols to this end. In their effort to revive some of their otherwise insignificant festivals they have demanded holiday on the day of Karam festival (on 20 September every year) and Sarhul festival.[3] The leaders are hopeful that their demand will be met by the state government and this will go a long way to consolidate the *adivasi* unity.

Medium of instructions in schools and colleges has been identified as one of the major problems of education of *adivasi* children in the region. Every *adivasi* community has its own dialect and because of this heterogeneity they use *sadri* as their lingua franca. But *sadri* does not have a script, nor is it used as a medium of instructions in schools. The ABAVP therefore has demanded opening of Hindi medium schools and colleges in the region.[4]

Participation in Democratic Process

The organisation contested the by-election to Kalchini State Assembly seat (ST) in 2009 and lost by a slander margin to the GJMM candidate. It polled more than 30,056 votes against 36,091 votes secured by the GJMM candidate. The RSP and Congress candidates have been relegated to third and fourth position respectively. In the 2006 election, the RSP had won the seat securing 52,748 votes defeating the Congress candidate who got 47,759 votes. One can thus notice significant erosion in support base of the mainstream parties. The *adivasi* members in the three-tier panchayat bodies representing the mainstream parties have now switched their allegiance to the ABAVP. The organisation has tested huge success in the election of local bodies as well; its candidates have won a good number of Panchayat Samiti and Gram Panchayat seats at the cost of Congress and CPI (M). It may be noted here that many local-level leaders of the mainstream political parties have joined the ABAVP which helped the latter gain strength. Most of the leaders of the ABAVP had association with the CPI (M) and the RSP.

With the intensification of Gorkhaland agitation and growing strength of ABAVP, the tea workers in Dooars and Terai, who were earlier members of trade union wings of the National Trade Unions like INTUC, CITU and AITUC, have now switched their allegiance to the trade union wings of the GJMM and the ABAVP. While GJMM has strong support base, particularly among the Nepali-speaking workers, the ABAVP has taken control of the *adivasi* workers. The disillusionment of the workers with the national trade unions has prompted this sudden shift of allegiance. ABAVP has been able to form its own trade union wing, namely, Progressive Tea Workers' Union (Terai-Dooars) (PTWU) in all the 200-plus tea gardens in the Dooars and Terai region. It had submitted a membership list claiming recognition of PTWU.

Areas of Success

Even though there are doubts about the prospect of achieving territorial autonomy under the Sixth Schedule by the ABAVP, the movement has so far been able to put enormous pressure on the mainstream political parties, their trade unions and the state to take issues of *adivasi* development far more seriously. A stock-taking of the following success areas of the movement would substantiate this point:

1. It is largely because of the *adivasi* movement that the GJMM is now prepared to restructure its proposed boundary to include only those parts of Dooars and Terai which have Nepali domination; instead of statehood it is now prepared to accept an interim arrangement of autonomy and it no longer demands the inclusion of entire Terai and Dooars region within the map of the proposed interim arrangement.

2. The ABAVP has succeeded in exerting enough pressure on the state and district administration to take their organisation seriously and agree to frequent meetings and dialogues even on the smaller issues raised by the outfit.
3. The fear of *adivasi* consolidation in the region has put the left parties and the Left Front government under pressure. Leaders of these parties and their ministers now stress on proper implementation of development programmes to retain support base among the *adivasis*.
4. The ABAVP's demands for enhancing the daily wage of the workers to Rs 250 has forced the Coordination Committee of the Tea Plantation Workers (which include all the major trade unions) to equally demand an interim hike in wages.
5. The mainstream trade unions have been put on alert by the movement and with growing popularity of the ABAVP among the *adivasi* garden workers. Under pressure the mainstream trade unions have taken initiative to resolve the long pending PF-related problems. About 102 garden owners in Terai and Dooars have been reported defaulter in depositing the owners' share of workers' provident fund to the tune of Rs 7 crores.
6. The movement has given an effective voice to the otherwise voiceless *adivasis*, who are now learning to articulate their demands and rights in an organised manner and more forcefully. The pressure is felt by the established political parties and their workers' wings. The garden authorities and the state administration too feel the pressure to gear up and take the issues raised by the ethnic outfit more seriously. The government now recognises the fact that the development-related issues of the *adivasis* have long been neglected and it has stepped up its developmental initiatives in the areas of *adivasi* concentration. The central government too has come up with a special allocation for speeding up the development works in the tribal dominated remote districts under Maoist influence.

Fissures Within

ABAVP has not been able to wipe out dissent from within. A breakaway faction of the ABAVP, mostly from its Nagrakata unit, formed Progressive Peoples' Party (PPP) on 25 July 2010 under the leadership of Kiran Kalindi. The split took place on the question of support to the GJMM which offered the ABAVP to be a part of the proposed state of

Gorkha-Adivasi Pradesh. The ABAVP leaders complained that its Nagrakata office has been captured by the PPP and following this Rajesh Lakra, the Secretary of the Terai-Dooars Committee resigned from his post. Three more office bearers of the Terai-Dooars Committee followed Lakra. They complained about the undemocratic style of functioning of the unit and alleged that norms of the Parishad were being violated by some leaders heading the outfit.

It appears that ABAVP is yet to form a solid unit organisationally and ideologically. The commitment of the leaders and workers to the altruistic cause is still questionable. Their ideological, moral and economic vulnerability is not difficult to notice. There are developments that suggest that the leaders individually are being lured with lucrative doles to sabotage the organisation and join hands with them. The formation of the PPP is a clear illustration of the point. The breakaway leaders seem to be frustrated not being able to make any headway with their demand for autonomy.

The experience clearly reveals that an ethnic movement may find it very difficult to sustain itself for long, particularly when the state, market and all the integrationist forces are out to derail it. When their demands fail to draw any attention of the state and central governments, the leaders and supporters lose heart and soon depression grips them. They then fall easy prey to the manoeuvring tactics of the organs of the government and the state (e.g., the trade unions, political parties, panchayats and district administration) and often they are lured by the welfare programmes which matter a lot for their survival. In other words, the strategies of 'biopower' work perfectly.

The tribals of the region, being the 'poorest of the poor', are preoccupied with a perpetual struggle to make a living, always hovering around a subsistence economy. They are haunted by the fear of disturbance in this minimalist living by a long-drawn battle with the order. They just want to redefine their rights within the frame of the order and the movement so far does not talk of liberation from it. It will be a big challenge for the tribal leadership to hold the folk together for long as they would be vulnerable to manipulative strategies of the 'agencies or forces of integration'.

Conclusion

The ethnic movement in the Terai and Dooars region of North Bengal spearheaded by the Akhil Bharatiya Adivasi Vikash Parishad (ABAVP) strives to unite a group of culturally distinct tribes highlighting their collective experience of similar systemic exploitation, oppression and exclusion. The prime objective of the movement is to project a united self of the otherwise distinct tribes in the name of their common roots and shared symbols and their claim over a territory they have dominated for nearly one and a half century. Another objective has been to expose the hollowness of the integrationist organs of the liberal state and to counter the forces that are out to threaten their security and claim in the region.

Being a part of the neo-liberal market, the *adivasis* in North Bengal, with minimal control over material and human resources and culture capital, are engaged in a fierce survival battle as the dominant sections with a greater control over resources have left little economic and socio-political space for them to cultivate. The state, armed with its welfare package, does try to do repair works here and there, but ends up extending support to the liberal market. With very little control over human resources the *adivasis* cannot access the benefits of the policy of protective discrimination or the special development initiatives undertaken by the state periodically. The corrupt yet inefficient bureaucracy and the panchayat functionaries come in their way to reaping the benefits of development initiatives. The overexploitative aırangement in tea gardens and loss of land (because of division of holding among the heirs and alienation by the manipulative and resourceful neighbours) perpetuate their marginalised existence in the region. The market uncertainty, the penetration of the forces of globalisation and crisis in the tea gardens make them even more vulnerable as a social category. Being a part of such a depressing reality the *adivasis* in the region are now showing signs of losing confidence in the ability of the state and other systemic organs to protect them.

The economic marginalisation and livelihood threats that face the tribal communities in the region and which are in-built in the liberal democracy prepare the ground for tribal dissent. The inability of the pre-existing civil societies such as trade unions, mass organisations and political parties – the systemic organs of integration – to create enough social and political space also prompts the *adivasis* to form their own civil societies on ethnic line, asserting tribal identity. However, the fundamental question is whether the 'alternative civil societies' put up by the tribes will work as anti-systemic organs or would settle with a greater space in the existing politico-economic frame.

Besides systemic marginalisation, a new threat in the form of the Gorkha Jan Mukti Morcha faces the *adivasis* in Dooars and Terai region.

The expanding influence of the Gorkha statehood movement in Dooars and Terai and the demand of inclusion of these *adivasi*-dominated areas into the proposed Gorkha state pose a serious threat to the tribal attachment and right to their land. The shared perception of losing their land and a common experience of marginalisation in the economic, social and political spheres together have prepared the ground for the formation of the tribal ethnic movement. Consequently, expanding influence of ABAVP among the *adivasis* in the Dooars and Terai region prompts the decline of the influence of welfare state and its ideological apparatuses like the political parties and their trade union wings. The ethnic outfit has also been able to consolidate its political base in the region by unifying the tribals against the 'other' – the GJMM and the integrationist forces of the 'order'.

The present *adivasi* movement, which is barely two-year old, appears well scripted as it (1) takes care in avoiding the violent course, (2) takes the ethnic route to mobilisation, (3) has already formed a strong trade union, (4) resorts to crafty cultivation of a set of factors that contribute to ethnic formation, (5) participates in democratic and electoral processes, (6) seriously pursues the issues of ethnic interest with the state administration, (7) physically resists the attacks by the GJMM and uses its muscle power for strategic counter offensive, and (8) pursues the development issues with the administration. Given its overall adherence to democratic norms and methods the ABAVP movement stands a fair chance of success, although its demand for autonomy under Sixth Schedule seems unrealisable especially on demographic count. The movement has already tasted some success by way of electoral gains and by way of forcing the administration and the state to concede many of its 'development' demands.

The movement may gradually turn out to be an effective civil society movement of the *adivasis* because of its flexibility in framing demands and strategies, because of the consolidation of the ethnic tribal communities by one *adivasi* identity, because of its ability to create pressure on the state and its organs to pursue the development programmes with greater care and seriousness, and because of its ability to put up organisational challenge to the established political parties and trade unions.

The movement hints at the formation of civil societies via ethnic mobilisation by the hitherto voiceless *adivasi* population in North Bengal. Like many civil society organisations, ABAVP today argues for expansion of democratic rights including right to life and self-determination of the people of the Dooars and Terai region and is ready to utilise its ethnic identity and strength for secular gains. In this sense, ethnicity becomes a means to the end of what is commonly termed as 'development'. It appears that in the heterogeneous and hierarchical societies such as India, organised groups and communities should also be recognised as legitimate inhabitants of civil society. Hence, the meaning of civil society has been widely used to delineate upsurge of popular movements against the state (Chandhoke 1995: 28). Although there are varied definitions of the term 'civil society', most writers agree that it has an institutional core constituted of voluntary associations outside the sphere of the state and the economy. Such associations range from, for example, churches, cultural associations, sport clubs and debating societies to independent media, academies, groups of concerned citizens, grassroots initiatives and organisations of gender, race and sexuality, all the way to occupational associations, political parties and labour unions (Habermas 1992: 453).

The fundamental act of citizenship in a pluralist democracy is that of forming associations of this kind. Keane (1988a: 14) ascribes to these associations the task of maintaining and redefining the boundaries between civil society and state through two interdependent and simultaneous processes: the expansion of social equality and liberty, and the restructuring and democratising of state institutions. This explains the importance of civil society to democracy. Keane (1988b: 21) argues that inequality and domination has been built into the concept of 'civil society' right from the beginning. In this sense, groups defining themselves on the basis of sexuality, gender, ethnicity, civil rights and environment constitute the modern-day civil societies. Clearly, if presently we are to build anything – and something as important as democracy – on the concept of civil society, we need to deal with the problems of exclusion, difference, diversity and the politics of identity. In other words, the civil society organs are diverse enough to include the tribal movement in North Bengal, which is aimed at redefining the political self of the excluded within the democratic arrangement. The movement provides a collective critique of the existing integrationist political economic arrangement and strives for a redefinition of the democratic arrangement within the constitutional frame.

Drawing from his African experience Jean-Francois Bayart used the term 'civil society' as "society in its relation with the state ... in so far as it is in confrontation with the state" or the process by which society seeks to 'breach' and counteract the "simultaneous totalisation unleashed by the state" (Bayart 1986: 111–12). There are however moments in history when civil society becomes the collective will of a people – say during a revolutionary moment – when it is meaningful to speak of entire civil society being in opposition to the state. In such a moment, the civil society can effectively bridge what Bayart calls "certain epistemic gulfs across cultural, religious and linguistic rifts" and "to confront the state with appropriate conceptual weapons" (ibid.). It is in the first sense that civil societies work to reform the integrationist democracies, upholding the liberal democratic values, and in the process preserve and expand the civil space for themselves. Civil society in the second sense takes shape in special situations in history and can effect some lasting structural change in the politico-social arrangement. Since what separates social space from civil society in organisational capacity, civil society cannot be an all-or-nothing phenomenon (Barua 1999: 10); civil society formation is a process which exists and operates in diverse scales, with integrationist as well as disintegrationist repercussions for the liberal democracies.

The *adivasi* movement in Terai and Dooars is distinctly in the first phase, where it is in critical engagement with the state and the conventional integrationist civil societies. We will have to wait to see if the present movement takes the second (revolutionary) course in future. Even at this stage the movement has addressed the inter-tribal differences in terms of race, language and region and contributed to the formation of a collective *adivasi* self. The leaders of the movement are strategic enough to effectively use the common cultural symbols and a shared perception of exclusion and marginalisation in shaping and intensifying the movement. Even if the present *adivasi* movement does never reach the 'revolutionary moment', it promises a strong united *adivasi* voice which will redefine their rights and entitlements within the constitutional frame and will keep the internal dialectics between the hegemonic and counter-hegemonic forces alive.

Notes

(*Acknowledgement*: I am extremely thankful to Prof. Biswajit Ghosh, the editor of the present volume, for his valuable comments on the first draft of the paper).

1. The Government of West Bengal has set up the Dooars Development Authority for the development of the *adivasi* dominated areas of Jalpaiguri

district and Paschimanchal Development Authority covering Bankura, Purulia and West Midnapore districts, which have concentration of sizeable *adivasi* population. The central government too has decided to set up a National Tribal Council, headed by the Prime Minister, to monitor implementation of the many policies and schemes for tribals so that they could be freed from the influence of Maoism and brought within the organisational fold of the Indian National Congress.

2. I tried to grasp the course of shaping the movement and have a feel of the *adivasi* mindset that prompted the movement and sustain it by talking to some of the leaders of the movement. I had long discussions with two top leaders of the ABAVP, namely, John Barla and Raju Ekka also spoke to some local leaders of the organisation, namely, Jerom Lakra and Peter Minj of Athalbari – all from the Dooars of Jalpaiguri district.
3. Karam and Sarhul are considered holy trees by the *adivasis* of Chotanagpur; they offer *puja* to these trees in continuation of their tradition of nature worship.
4. In a letter to the Editor, *Ganasakti* (9 February 2010), Parag Mitra regrets that although the Left Front government has secured recognition of Santhali, helped inclusion of the language in the Eighth Schedule of the Constitution and encouraged the introduction of Alchiki in schools, the ABAVP is demanding introduction of Hindi medium schools and colleges and not showing any interest in Santhali or Alchiki. He regrets that when the small languages are losing out with the encroachment of global language (English in particular), there is no effort on the part of the smaller communities to protect their own language and culture. Mitra further opposes the aggressive ethnic mobilisation by the ABAVP also on the ground that the area has a mixed population and the ethnic movement will result in disharmony among the communities and will affect the unity of the poor and middle class inhabitants of the region. Mitra, it seems, has missed the point that the Santhals are an insignificant minority in the Dooars and Terai region and Santhali is not used even as a spoken language by *adivasi* communities in the region.

References

Althusser, L. 1971. 'Ideology and Ideological State Apparatus', in *Lenin and Philosophy and Other Essays*. London: New Left Books.

Barua, Sanjib. 1999. *India against Itself: Assam and Politics of Nationality*. New Delhi: Oxford University Press.

Bayart, Jean-Francois. 1986. 'African Civil Society', in Patrick Chabal (ed.), *Political Domination in Africa: Reflections on the Limits of Power* (111–12). Cambridge: Cambridge University Press.

Chandhoke, Neera. 1995. *State and Civil Society: Explorations in Political Theory*. New Delhi: Sage Publications.

Foucault, Michel. 1991. 'Governmentality', in G. Burchell, C. Gordon and P. Miller (eds.), *The Foucault Effect: Studies in Governmentality* (87–104). London: Harvester Wheatsheaf.

Habermas, Jurgen. 1987. *The Theory of Communicative Action. Vol. 2: Lifeworld and the System: A Critique of Functionalist Reason*. Boston, MA: Beacon Press.

——. 1992. 'Further Reflection on the Public Sphere', in C. Calhoun (ed.), *Habermas and the Public Sphere*. Cambridge, Mass: MIT Press.

Keane, J. 1988a. *Democracy and Civil Society: On the Predicaments of European Socialism, the Prospects for Democracy and the Problem of Controlling Social and Political Power*. London: Verso.

——. 1988b. 'Introduction', in J. Keane (ed.), *Civil Society and the State: New European Perspectives*. London: Verso.

Lazzarato, Maurizio. 2010. 'Biopolitics/Bioeconomics: A Politics of Multiplicity' (translated by Arianna Bove and Erik Empson), *PLI The Warwick Journal of Philosophy*. http://www.generaion-online.org/p/fplazzarato2.htm (Accessed on 9 August 2010).

Lenin, V.I. 1977. 'The State and Revolution', in *Lenin's Selected Works*. Moscow: Progress Publishers.

Patnaik, Prabhat. 2010. 'A Left Approach to Development', *Economic and Political Weekly*, July 24: 33–37.

Roy, Sanjay K. 2008. *Work Participation of Tribal Women and Marginalization: The Case of Tribes in North Bengal*. Kolkata: Levant Books.

——. 2009. 'North Bengal Tribes in Development Perspective', *Journal of Anthropological Society*, 44: 5–27.

6

Development Through Voluntary Actions

The Paradigm of NGO-isation

Biswajit Ghosh

Increasing concerns for social justice, inclusive growth and empowerment of the poor and marginalised, particularly in the wake of 'market globalism' in the world today, have paved the way for spectacular rise of civil society organisations (CSOs). Civil society is considered to be a space for the enforcement and enhancement of social, economic and political justice. It is a healthy and necessary compliment to democracy. The concept of civil society draws heavily on the liberal intellectual tradition to stress on 'civility' as its core. The notion of civility considers "others as fellow citizens of equal dignity in their rights and obligations as members of civil society" (Shils 1991: 12). In more positive terms, the concept of civil society, according to Hall (1998: 33), upholds voluntarism and freedom and offers individuals, irrespective of their creed, colour or culture, an equal chance to create their own selves. For Béteille (2001: 287), the core of civil society consists of the open and secular institutions that mediate between the citizens and the state in modern democratic societies. Arguing from a different angle, Kothari (1988) equates civil society with non-state, non-government organisations. There are also critical questions regarding the possibility of any civil society within the parameters of western bourgeois democracy and class rule. In the orthodox Marxist framework, neither the state is supersession of civil society, nor does it transform civil society into something else. The bourgeois state incorporates civil society (Dhanagare 2001: 169). Gramsci, however, conceded the autonomous space of civil society, which is a (self-)regulated society of the dominant social class and is capable of making its own 'hegemony' universal (Gramsci 1976: 53). It is however argued that "the search for civil society as congeries of de-classed and de-politicised organisations and movements of people as watch dog of India's democracy in a volatile political milieu is theoretically untenable and empirically unsupportable" (see A. Mukhopadhyay in this volume). Scholars have also expressed doubts about the possibility of emergence of 'civility' or existence of real 'democratic' CSOs in a society marked by caste or kinship (Mahajan 1999; Béteille 2000; Kaviraj 2001; Ghosh 2009). However, given the heterogeneous and hierarchical nature of Indian society, organised groups and communities are also recognised as legitimate inhabitants of civil society in addition to individual (Oommen 2004: 128). Consequently, in India, "the meaning if not the terminology of civil society has been widely used to delineate the upsurge of popular movements against the state" (Chandhoke 1995: 28).

Given such differences of opinions, it would be interesting to review the role of CSOs in a society like India. It is worth noting here that cutting across intellectual boundaries, arguments in favour of CSOs are linked to the failure of the modern state to guarantee autonomy of individuals, protection of individual rights, equal citizenship and access to decision-making apparatus and participatory framework. These 'necessary conditions' of civil society promote development of certain kind within both capitalistic and socialistic systems of government (Sen 2000). It is to be kept in mind that the contemporary discourse on civil society has its roots in the political upheavals of new nation-states during the second half of the 20th century. Ruling classes in most post-colonial states found democracy to be too slow to respond to the rising expectations of people. Similarly, under the global regime, not just civility but even civilisational identity faces threat of extinction (Lim 1992). The entry of non-state associations and voluntary mobilisations including new forms of social movements are to be analysed in this context.

The concept of civil society as a space between the family, the market and the state, however, comprises of a plethora of groups of all sorts ranging from charities to advocacy groups. CSOs vary widely in membership and geographical coverage. They espouse all shades of causes and concerns (Nayar 2008: 19). NGOs constitute an important component of civil society as they work in the space of civil society although all CSOs are not NGOs (ibid.: 28). The salience of the NGO sector within civil society is understood from the fact that civil society needs a great variety of associations whose members have to relate to each other open-endedly, without exclusion on grounds of religion, gender, and so forth (Saberwal 2001: 193–4). If strong, vibrant and lively civil society is the foundation of modern open democratic polity, NGOs are the very live-force for the civil society. Civil society and NGOs seem to go together and one cannot exist without the other (Baviskar 2001: 7). NGOs are considered to be a means of strengthening civil society and fostering good governance (Bebbington and Riddell 1995). They are essential for the dissemination of new ideas and concepts with regards to social and economic development and fostering participation and democracy in order to improve civil society.

NGOs have become a part of a new development paradigm or New World Order in the today's world. NGOs and particularly international NGOs (INGOs) are a part of globalisation as enormous amount of development funds are being channelled or rechannelled through them during the past three decades. The new policy agenda of civil society building and 'NGO-isation' also matches the neo-liberal agenda of government roll back and decentralisation. Simultaneously, the emergence of a new paradigm of 'society-led development' (Pieterse 2001: 17) so as to compensate for the failures of state as well as market-led growth has contributed to the great wave of 'NGO-isation' since 1980. As the post-Cold War considerations led to the diminishing importance of development aid for strategic and military importance for the western industrialised countries including the United States, the donor community found it better to channel development aid through NGOs under the New Policy Agenda (Wagona 2002). Thus, between 1970 and 1985, the total development aid distributed by international NGOs have increased ten fold and in 1992 international NGOs channelled over $7.6 billion of aid to developing countries. It is now estimated that over 15 per cent of total overseas development aid is channelled through NGOs (http://library.duke.edu). It is worth mentioning here that since 1990s the World Bank has not only encouraged member-governments to work with NGOs on development projects, but has also increased its direct funding of such projects. As a result, approved World Bank projects in Third World countries involving NGOs in 1997 were found to be 84 per cent in South Asia, 61 per cent in Africa and 60 per cent in Latin America and the Caribbean (World Bank 1997: 49). Several other international agencies including the United States Agency for International Development (USAID) and United Nations Development Programme (UNDP) have increased their flow of fund through NGOs during the period (Wagona 2002).

Simultaneously, with the onset of alternative development thinking, the focus of development has shifted to alternative agenda like human development, community development, sustainable development, capacity building and the like. As NGOs plead for all these, it is quite commonplace to argue for the entry of this 'third sector'[1] for the 'enlargement of people's choices' as well as 'people-friendly' grassroots movement. The new development strategies perceive poor people including women as active agents of their own development and instead of a top-down, hegemonic character of development under both the capitalist and state socialist models, it calls for a bottom-up participatory approach like participatory rural appraisal (PRA) – one where development 'experts' become 'facilitators' working with poor rather than directing them (Chambers 1997). It would be interesting to review whether NGOs in India today really qualify for the distinctions, methods and goals they are supposed to perform or cherish. This paper seeks to critically review the role of NGOs as CSOs in social reconstruction of our life today on the basis of certain real-life experiences from India. The Indian experience can as well be used to understand similar other context in South Asia.

Concept and Nature of NGOs

A non-governmental organisation (NGO) is normally defined as a non-profit, voluntary citizens' group that is organised on a local, national or international level. The World Bank has defined NGOs as "private organisations that pursue activities to relieve suffering, promote the interests of the poor, protect the environment, provide basic social services, or undertake community development". A World Bank key document, *Working With NGOs* (1995), goes on saying that,

> In wider usage, the term NGO can be applied to any non-profit organisation, which is independent from government. NGOs are typically value-based organisations that depend, in whole or in part, on charitable donations and voluntary service. Although the NGO sector has become increasingly professionalised over the last two decades, principles of altruism and voluntarism remain key defining characteristics.

The World Bank has classified NGOs into two major types: operational and advocacy. Operational NGOs are concerned with design and implementation of development-related projects while advocacy NGOs defend or promote a specific cause.

The distinguishing features of NGOs lie in their being autonomous, non-profit, relatively independent and self-propelled organisations. These characteristics differentiate NGOs from both the state and the market, and establish their claim being the 'third sector'. Even though governments fund NGOs partially or completely, they maintain their non-government status by excluding government representatives from their membership. NGOs, however, differ from each other in terms of size, membership, funding, approaches, strategies and outcomes. Hence, a generalised statement about NGOs is difficult and consequently scholars have attempted to classify NGOs differently (Baviskar 2001: 5; Oommen 2004: 15).

One may, however, argue that the ethos of voluntarism is not new in the Indian context. It is rather woven into the very fabric of Indian social structure. According to Kothari (1998: 183), "it is closely tied to the fundamental plural nature of our society". We may trace them back to the efforts and ideologies of Buddha, Vivekananda, Gandhi, Tagore, Phule and Ambedkar. Organisations like Ramakrishna Mission, Bharat Sevashram Sangha, Jesuit Mission, Harijan Sevak Sangh, etc., have carried out relief and welfare activities relentlessly as first generation NGOs.[2] Later on, a renewed interest in decentralised, participatory and local model of development has led to the growth of a sizeable number of NGOs in India like many other parts of the world. Along with international efforts to provide fund for voluntary action[3], the Government of India has equally begun welcoming NGO participation first in the Seventh Five-Year Plan and later more openly in the Eighth Five-Year Plan (1992–1997) and the fund allocated to such development with NGO participation increased incessantly after that.[4] The Council for Advancement of People's Action and Rural Technology (CAPART), the government body to fund grassroots NGOs, has sanctioned about Rs 330 crore to about 7,500 NGOs in the last nine years in addition to grants from other ministries.[5] As a result, the Central Statistical Organisation (CSO) has estimated in 2008 that the number of NGOs in India has increased to 3.3 million and there is one NGO for every 400 Indians (Jerath 2010). Even though the CSO report has acknowledged that many of the NGOs are defunct, this estimate puts India on the top of map of NGO movement in the world and the phenomenal expansion has taken place after economic liberalisation in 1991.

Arguments favouring NGOs

It is not just coincidental that the decline or retreat of the state as well as the triumph of the market is accompanied by increasing attention to CSOs. It is rather based on a new found expectation that NGOs are better placed as compared to the state bureaucracy or private capitalists to provide leadership for social reconstruction of the societies of the developing world particularly. As Baviskar (2001: 7) argues, "the growing prominence of NGOs in the field of development is strongly related to the declining legitimacy of the state. Increasingly, the state is looked upon with suspicion if not contempt. It is considered to be corrupt, oppressive and anti-poor. Least governance is seen as the sign of good governance". Flaws in the functioning of government machinery (red-tapism, apathy, collusion with vested interests, deliberate delay in decision-making or its implementation, etc.) have led many to see certain inherent value in voluntary movements. NGOs are favoured because they are supposed to facilitate 'participatory management', encourage local initiative, maintain link with grassroots, reach the poor effectively, promote popular participation, react to any calamity immediately, remain accountable and cost effective, emphasise sustainability, remain responsive and committed to the cause of people, perform with greater efficiency and dedication and the like. Apart from such advantages of the NGO sector, voluntary actions also help to increase diversity of opportunity in society. By providing variety and autonomy in associational choice, they promote the formation of interest groups that can challenge monopolistic tendencies and the poor performances of state enterprises (Bebbington and Riddell 1995: 56). From such a point of view, NGOs do not just attempt to replace the state; they rather try to democratise and politicise the civil society more than any other institutions. Hence, the key justification for the expansion, growth and importance of NGOs seems to be "their ability to be what the state is not and cannot be" (Zaidi 2004: 191).

The upswing of a 'new form of voluntarism' as a catalyst of human liberation and genuine freedom has led to a redefinition of the concept of politics as 'multidimensional'. It now seeks to go beyond narrow political or economic demands and cover ecological, feminist and cultural aspects, including a sustained attack on any decay or degeneration (Kothari 1998: 188). NGOs have engaged themselves in activities related to poverty eradication, removal of illiteracy, preventing human trafficking, domestic violence or child marriage, income and employment generation, tribal development, rural development and many other issues of social reconstruction in contemporary India. And, it can fairly be argued that there are some brilliant examples of NGOs in India playing the model role in social reconstruction in contemporary India. Let me now discuss, in brief, the success stories of some of the 'harbingers of silent revolution' (Sharma 1992).

Success Stories

Let me begin by discussing the case of Self-Employed Women's Association (SEWA) of Ahmedabad (Bhatt 1998: 146–61). As a women's wing of Textile Labour Association, SEWA had begun it journey as a trade union in 1972, but gradually it has been able to expand its activities and serve as a true representative of self-employed women in the unorganised sector. Today, its membership has crossed 2.2 lakh and it has been able to come close to achieve two of its basic goals of full employment and self-reliance. SEWA now provides diverse opportunities to the families of its members including food security, income security and social security. In the initial years, SEWA attempted to collect loans for its members from nationalised banks, but faced with several difficulties to do so, the organisation under the leadership of Ila Bhatt had formed SEWA Bank in 1973. Ila Bhatt is therefore considered a pioneer of the microfinance movement as the Mohammed Yunus founded Grameen Bank was formed three years later. Interestingly, unlike the Grameen Bank, SEWA has been regulated by the Reserve Bank of India, staying strictly within the law and seeking no special dispensations. After its formation, each of 4,000 SEWA members paid Rs 10 as capital share. Initially, it acted as an intermediary to enable its depositors to secure loan from nationalised banks. But, later on, SEWA Bank has begun advancing loan from its own fund. It has encouraged women to form groups in different localities and work as a team to cultivate the culture of continuous savings for withdrawal of loans for domestic and productive needs. The Bank has charged interests between 12 per cent and 17.5 per cent per annum for loans taken for a maximum period of 36 months. But is has distributed dividends of 9–12 per cent annually each year since its foundation. Simultaneously, it has provided technical assistance to its members for the use of loan money and closely monitored progress. As a result, the Bank has achieved 96 per cent repayment rate leading to improved income, employment and access to social security for its members. In the 2002–03 fiscal year, SEWA had a working capital of nearly Rs 85 crores and its audit classification has been consistently 'A' grade. SEWA has successfully linked microfinance movement with much needed support services like insurance, health care, child care, legal aid, and training to reduce women's vulnerability. Sato (2009) has found that the livelihood approach of SEWA in the slums of Ahmedabad has not only mitigated women's work burden, but also increased the self-worth of women in the slums. Yet, her research and many others (see Dash's article in this volume, for details) prove that microfinance movement has certain limitations in improving the conditions of the marginalised women. The high rate of interest charged by SEWA and similar other celebrated institutions[6] is a source of worry for many of their clients. Moreover, as Oommen (2004: 120) argues, civil society organisations like SEWA are not always and necessarily anti-state; sometimes they are neutral and occasionally they are even pro-state. Therefore, to posit that civil society is necessarily and always anti-state as is widely believed is at variance with facts.

The experience of Swadhyaya, an NGO started by Pandurang Shastri in 1958, depicts yet another success story of a socio-spiritual movement in organising two million poor people and mainly the dalits and fisherman in Gujarat and Maharashtra (Shah et al., 1998: 57–73). It has propagated the concept of 'impersonal wealth' generated through collective efforts. It has organised collective projects such as fishing cooperatives, deepening of wells, collective farms and orchards on which members of neighbouring villages work with a spirit of harmony and brotherhood. Thus, the members of Swadhyaya Parivar could achieve the twin goals of social transformation and community development with one stroke. Swadhyaya primarily works for self-development and its different centres create a climate for such development, civil society and a rich associational life in their respective locales. It has created a new 'relational revolution' and despite some limitations, Swadhyaya continues to inspire many to come together and contribute to social and cultural revolution (Giri 2008). A notable feature of this movement was to uplift the 'transformers', the elites, as well as the 'transformed', the poor and the deprived. The elites as motivators and catalysts had to maintain discipline and spend a part of their wealth, talent and time for rural development. Many Swadhyayis have given up smoking, drinking and other harmful habits. Apart from spiritual activities, the organisation also utilised science and technology for economic and social development of rural people. As a result of improved farming practices, better environment and sustainable resources, the Swadhyaya movement has gained popularity and crossed its geographical limitations by inspiring even people of other countries to initiate similar movements.

The case of Ralegan Siddhi, a tiny drought-prone and liquor affected village of Ahmednagar district of Maharashtra, is another interesting instance of social development through voluntary efforts (Awasthi 1998; Baviskar 2001; Hazare 2003). Anne Hazare, a retired army personnel, was the leader of the movement. His selfless leadership and moral appeal mobilised the 2,000 odd villagers. He formed a *Tarun Mondal Volunteers* to impress upon the villagers to utilise the government grants for rural development with free labour. The important point to be noted here is that people of Ralegan did not receive any external help except the usual government grants to develop them. Hazare used Gandhian tactics to impress upon those who opposed the move. He attempted to unite the villagers morally before undertaking any developmental task. In his own words, "development does not mean just tall, modern buildings. The people themselves have to develop a new attitude" (ibid.: 15). Villagers dig wells, construct check dams, plant trees, build schools, hostels, temples and community halls through voluntary contribution of physical labour. Apart from *shramdaan*, the village contributed Rs 30 for every 100 rupees of government grants. One-fourth of the surplus generated went to a village fund, from which other community schemes were implemented. As the guiding principle of economic development in Ralegan was 'growth with equity', special attention was paid to eradicate social discrimination. Thus, new houses were built for dalits in the centre of the village and they were also given loans and subsidies for sewing machines, irrigation pumps, biogas plant, common toilet, and children were provided with free textbooks, notebooks and uniform. Due to such collective efforts, people of Ralegan gradually experienced increased crop and milk production, poultry farming, development of watershed, availability of safe drinking water, opposition to alcoholism, abolition of dowry, increased status of women, removal of caste divisions and superstitions as well as a sustainable ecology. It was, therefore, declared as a 'model village' by the Government of Maharashtra. Inspired by such outstanding performances, the government also persuaded Hazare to create 300 more 'Ralegan Siddhis' across the state. But, political competition and bureaucratic corruption belied the expectation of Hazare and his experience could not be replicated.

There are plenty of other successful NGOs in the country which have made their presence felt in the society through constructive social work. Thus, the Aga Khan Rural Support Programmes (AKRSP) has achieved notable success in implementing a participatory watershed development project funded by the Government of India in 35 village of Bhavnagar district, Gujarat (Shah and Iyengar 1998: 92–112). The organisation has been able to complete a lift irrigation project and built a percolation tank in a very short time in 1985 with actual cost being less that that estimated by the government. The success of AKRSP has also put pressure on the government agencies to improve work standard when people start comparing the quality of similar works. Again, the National Institute for Rural Integrated Development (NIRID) has persistently worked in the Sahyadri hills of Maharashtra to prevent deforestation and consequent soil erosion and slitting of riverbeds for 20 years (Patel 1998: 113–29). By this, it has not only arrested environmental degradation in the effected area, the tribals could also be motivated to become self-reliant farmers, develop community assets, conserve water, generate income, regenerate natural resources, preserve forests and wildlife and above all become active participants in the process of development. NIRID has even gone beyond its objectives to improve provisions of social services like education, health and family planning. It is unusual for NGOs to adapt to such challenging goals. Similarly, the Sumangali Seva Ashram (SSA) of Bangalore was set up in 1975 to provide shelter to women and children in need (Pulavarti 1998: 130–45). From a modest beginning as a home for the destitute, the SSA has today grown into a district-wide organisation with extended facilities and wider scope of activities for the upliftment and empowerment of urban women and children. Again, the Social Work and Research Centre (SWRC) of Tilonia at Ajmer district in Rajasthan has achieved the rare distinction of going for general scrutiny of its activities and fund through public meetings. Banker Roy of this organisation has also initiated a move to formulate a code of conduct for voluntary organisations (Sethi 1998: 174–75). The experience of Women's Thrift Cooperatives (WTCs) of Hyderabad in raising small and regular contribution from their members with 1 per cent interest per month and distribute loan with 2 per cent interest per month is equally interesting. Like SEWA, it has achieved excellent loan recovery rates due to group discipline since 1990. Nearly 33,000 members of 101 WTCs could collectively generate savings up to Rs 26 million by the end of 1998 (Baviskar 2001: 6–7).

The contributions of many other small and big NGOs in India are conspicuous by their salience. Thus, to name only a few, organisations like Narmada Bachao Andolan, Centre for Science and Environment, Working Women's Forum, Society for the Promotion of Area Resource

Centres, Lawyer's Collective, Kerala Sastra Sahitya Parishad, Bandhua Mukti Morcha, Shakti Vahini, Child In Need Institute, Sanlaap, Durbar Mahila Samanwaya Committee, Bhartiya Patita Udhar Samiti, Prerana Bhoruka Public Welfare Trust, Tagore Society for Rural Development, Sachetna, Paschim Bangla Kheria-Sabar Kalyan Samiti, People's Union for Civil Liberties, Voluntary Action Network India, Society for Participatory Research in Asia etc., have quite successfully intervened in protecting and preserving our environment, enlarging the rights of women and children, preventing the onus of illiteracy, trafficking and dowry and the like. It is worth mentioning here that Mazdoor Kisan Shakti Sanghthan, an NGO in a Rajasthan village, had started the campaign for right to information in 1990 and it is one of the pioneers of RTI movement in India. The success of the Association of Voluntary Agencies for Rural Development – North East in organising the people of Majuli Island in Assam to fight corruption by contractors in anti-erosion work had ironically led to the kidnapping and killing of its secretary Sanjoy Ghosh.

These examples should not, however, lead one to conclude that the NGO sector, as a whole, has no problem. Irrespective of the achievements of some NGOs in India, there are vast areas of darkness, shortcomings and failures. Niumai (2006: 235) has found that two out of five NGOs she studied in Tamenglong district of Manipur were "more accountable to the government and foreign funding agencies than to the local community and beneficiaries". Hence, it is important to evaluate the nature of NGO sector as a whole, rather than look at certain successful or failed NGO projects. Because of heterogeneity and complexity of this sector, we should be careful in making generalisations by looking into some individual cases (Kaimowitz 1993: 1139). But ironically the dominant thrust of the literature on NGO is either to praise or to malign them. Let me now discuss the failures of NGOs in brief to arrive at a balanced conclusion.

Arguments Against NGOs

It is now being widely recognised that the NGO sector has serious limitations in turning into a true alternative of the state or private sector. Logically speaking, NGOs cannot and did not replace state or market in each and every aspect of our living today. Hence, the hype about NGO is exaggerated. Like the state, NGOs, barring a few exceptions, "have failed at making a substantial impact upon the perceived beneficiaries they were expected to benefit" (Zaidi 2004: 191). Even the successful NGOs have their limitations. Moreover, NGO advocacy often fails to grasp the fact that "if every soil is not equally conducive to the growth of open and secular institutions, it is not equally conducive to the growth of civil associations" (Béteille 2001: 299–300). In spite of very high credible achievements of many NGOs in India in the fields of health, education, childcare and so on, "the question of what they contribute to the creation of civil society, and in what way, still remains open" (ibid: 303–04).

The reasons for the failure of a large number of NGOs to come up to the desired level of expectation are numerous. The major argument against many NGOs is that they are the creation of funding agencies and hence "their entire existence, not merely dependency, is on donor money, almost always from above" (ibid.: 192). There are nearly 40,000 international NGOs in the world today and some of them have annual budgets worth billions of dollars. Being a 'favoured child' (Edwards and Hulme 1996: 961) of western donors, they are capable of exerting pressure on national governments with enormous power in terms of money, technology, cyber strength and knowledge. Hence, they are argued to be the "handmaidens of global imperialism" (Karat 1984). A UN sponsored publication has warned about the "potential (of INGOs) to undermine the sovereignty of constitutional democracies" (Bendell 2006: x). The publication has also documented that "in countries newly independent of the Soviet Union, and in Russia, the NGOs are often perceived as covers for organised crimes, in Bangladesh and Pakistan NGOs are sometimes seen as fronts for fundamentalist causes and in Central Asia they can serve as platform for failed politicians" (ibid.: xii).

Use of NGO fund for purposes other than 'development' is often cited as an argument against them. It is worth noting here that recently India's home ministry has blacklisted more than 800 NGOs in the country's north-east for alleged links with separatist groups. Meghalaya, a state of only around 2.5 million people, has more than 8,000 NGOs. They received nearly Rs 1.5 billion from the government in 2008–09 out of the Rs 5 billion pumped into the state by Delhi. More than 300 of the blacklisted NGOs are in Meghalaya (Bhaumik 2010). I have found that tribal insurgents in the north-eastern state of Tripura have utilised foreign donations send to Baptist church for ethnic mobilisation and insurgent activities (Ghosh 2003: 237).

It has recently been estimated that in India this sector raises anywhere between Rs 40,000 and Rs 80,000 crores annually (southasia.oneworld.net/india-more-ngos-than-schools-and-health-centres—2010). Most of this funding comes from the domestic sector, of which the government is the largest donor. There is however little or no effort to map the voluntary sector and there is yet no objective system to monitor their activity or performance. Consequently, the Home Minister of India Mr P. Chidambaram has expressed doubts in the parliament about the total volume of foreign donations received by the NGOs (Jerath 2010). Moreover, the philanthropic funding of NGOs in India from the rich countries of Europe and North America appears to be devoid of the civic virtues of mutuality, rationality and collective interests as "support flows more easily into temples than into universities, libraries or laboratories" (Béteille 2001: 306). It appears from Table 1 that due to the 'spending spree' initiated mostly by foreign donor agencies in liberalised India, thousands of NGOs are just formed within the last one decade or so and the amount of contributions received by them had propelled equally even though there has been some decline in such receipt in 2007–08. Surprisingly, however, the number of apparently transparent associations reporting their accounts to the government is not much and in 2007–08 only 54 per cent of such associations have done so.

Table 1

Trends of Foreign Funding to Indian Voluntary Associations, 1996–2008

Financial Year	*No. of Registered Associations as on 31st March of Year*	*No. of Reporting Associations*	*Amount of Foreign Contribution (Rs/crores)*
1996–97	17,723	12,136	2571.69
1997–98	18,489	12,198	2864.51
1998–99	19,834	13,775	3402.90
1999–00	21,244	13,986	3924.63
2000–01	22,924	14,598	4535.23
2001–02	24,563	15,598	4870.52
2002–03	26,404	16,590	5046.51
2003–04	28,351	17,145	5105.46
2004–05	30,321	18,540	6256.68
2005–06	32,144	18,570	7877.57
2006–07	33,937	18,996	11336.97
2007–08	34,803	18,796	9663.46

Source: FCRA, Annual Report, Ministry of Home Affairs, Government of India, 1996–2008.

Experience proves that several retired government officials, politicians and people with vested interests have formed NGOs or GONGOs (government-operated NGOs). Obviously, this extraordinary mushrooming is linked to "donor's likes" and even to "fudge data to suit the client's needs"; hence such NGO-isation hardly enhances the ideology of civil society activism (Zaidi 2004: 193). For instance, Bill and Melinda Gates Foundation has donated over $9 billion between 1998 and 2007 to a handful of NGOs with a focus on malaria in areas where other diseases cause more human harm, creating perverse incentives for politicians, policy makers and health workers (Jerath 2010). Again, in Tentulikhaanta village under Kalahandi district of Orissa, a crèche, which people sorely needed, had to be closed down for lack of funds. At the same time, a microfinance scheme introduced in the area made the people fall in debt trap (Sengupta 2010). So, an agenda of 'non-priority' for the people may find 'priority' for NGO activism. As a consequence, the presence of nearly 10,000 NGOs in the infamous Kalahandi-Bolangir-Koraput belt of Orissa could not mitigate the problems of malnutrition and malaria (ibid.). It is quite obvious that under compulsion to adjust with the desires of donors, many of the new generation of *Project NGOs* create hypothetical beneficiaries say, AIDS patient, for meeting targets within a stipulated period. A World Bank study has acknowledged that in 57 per cent cases NGOs have worked like 'technical transfer agents' (Bebbington and Farrington 1995). Surprisingly, the governance mechanism of the donor agencies is largely managed through informal system of personal networks and relationships rather than by a more transparent process based on independent and technical peer review. Starting from NGO registration to project proposal writing and finally account verification, NGOs rely on the services of consultants, experts or bureaucrats and a cycle of corruption sustains at every level. Often big NGOs are favoured by donors because of their good connections and 'power' and not on the basis of efficiency and accountability (Jerath 2010). Valid questions are necessarily raised about the capacity of such NGOs to spread either civic virtues of mutuality and self-reliance or to represent the views of vulnerable social groups.

The patron–client relationship emerging out of such a model of development raises numerous questions about the accountability and legitimacy of NGO activity. A 'puppet' NGO, in spite of its best records, is bound to betray the very spirit of civil society activism and replace accountability by accountancy (Edwards and Hulme 1996: 968). This also reduces NGOs to the position of mere 'sub-contractors' who have to rely on external agencies including the government for launching and managing a project and shift from one problem to the next depending on fund availability and donors choice. It has also been argued that donors choose to spend their money in different areas from those in which most NGOs function (Farouk 2002). Table 2 provides a glimpse of the purposes for which foreign fund was made available to Indian NGOs during 2003–04 to 2007–08. It appears that there is lack of consistency in foreign contribution to different purposes. Yet, a large chunk of foreign donations in India went to religious organisations, both Christian and Hindu, even though the identified purposes of such funding appear to be primarily 'secular' in nature. This is because the prominent donors include religious organisations like Gospel For Asia Inc, USA, Fundacion Vicente Ferrer, Spain, Brahmanand Saraswati Trust, Gospel Fellowship Trust, USA, and Christian Aid, UK. Thus, in 2006–07, out of a total of Rs 2,305.69 crore received by top fifteen NGOs in the country, Rs 1,225.90 crore (53.17 %) went to religious organisations. In 2007–08, Rs 531.15 crore or 39 per cent of fund went to such organisations.[7] Moreover, states like Delhi (Rs 1,716.57 crore), Tamil Nadu (Rs 1,670.93 crore), and Andhra Pradesh (Rs 1,167.21 crore) were among the highest recipients of foreign fund during the last three years. One would wonder why such donations are little for NGOs operating in poor states like Bihar or Orissa.

The issue of external funding also gives the state a convenient leverage over NGOs and there are instances of government threatening NGOs for supporting anti-communal campaign during elections (Baviskar 2001: 12). Services of NGOs are also used by business houses to discredit rivals (Datta 2010). This implies that donors, business houses and government policies dictate NGO agenda and even their existence. To what extent then NGOs are autonomous institutions? In other words, the much acclaimed autonomy of NGOs is relative and not absolute. When NGO activism is reduced to only time-bound or project-specific 'development', it only results in mechanistic implementation of any top-down decision on temporary basis. NGOs are expected to fulfil physical and financial targets within stipulated time period. The pressure to reach the magic figures quickly often leads to sacrificing quality of the output. If an NGO or a group of NGOs solicits to continue spreading awareness among the members of a target group say, prostitutes, even after 10 years of campaign on the same issue, doubts about its vitality and earlier achievements are validly raised. Contrarily, the success stories that have been cited earlier typically remind us about the need of people-centric and community-based approach to lay the foundation of any long-term and holistic development. But, the new generation NGOs relying solely on external funding for their existence and expansion are far short of this goal.[8]

Table 2

Receipt of Foreign Contribution by NGOs, 2003–04 to 2007–08

(Rs in crore)

Purpose	*2007–08*	*2006–07*	*2005–06*	*2004–05*	*2003–04*
Establishment expenses	3421.95	3058.48	679.46	948.20	639.31
Rural development	1781.38	1956.63	475.18	582.49	494.64
Relief/rehabilitation of victims of natural calamities	1689.08	2534.23	875.67	655.65	162.66
Welfare of children	1333.40	1184.38	323.62	303.20	221.38
Construction and maintenance of schools/colleges	1206.47	1208.92	183.51	295.94	221.63
Grant of stipend/scholarship/assistance in cash and kind to poor/deserving children	719.02	646.58	59.62	210.13	161.40
Awareness about AIDS/ treatment and rehabilitation of person affected by AIDS	708.41	462.44	101.26	88.42	181.58
Construction/running of hospitals/dispensaries/clinics	655.98	528.42	215.47	182.69	173.58
Construction and running of hostels for poor students	608.03	511.02	85.07	113.36	130.24
Welfare of the orphans	593.31	615.07	187.19	189.37	164.56
Research	555.20	461.50	93.13	116.71	117.17
Construction/repair/maintenance of places of worship	487.45	379.28	70.20	137.20	70.20
Religious schools/education of priests and preachers	427.54	726.58	58.24	121.68	58.24
Maintenance of priests/preachers/other religious functionaries	409.85	390.20	81.18	100.90	80.76
Welfare/empowerment of women	380.32	626.72	82.58	100.38	97.51

Source: FCRA, Annual Report, Ministry of Home Affairs, Government of India, 2003–04 to 2007–08.

It appears that reliability and sustainability of NGO activities, the two distinguishing criteria for their success, have also not fulfilled in many cases. This may also be due to the fact that an NGO totally relies on the quality of leadership provided by its founder member. As a result, NGOs often fail to maintain the zeal after the demise of their charismatic leader. Also, the very specific and local factors that led to the success of NGO activity in any region may not be replicable in a different region due to changes in socio-cultural and political aspects of life. Anne Hazare could not create another Ralegan Siddhi in Maharashtra in spite government support. Similarly, the Amul experience at Anand in Gujarat could not be replicated in any other part of the country even with the help of foreign funding (Baviskar 2001: 9–10).

It has been argued that new generation of NGOs is more concerned with programme implementation than policy and political critique. This may be due to the fact that they now seek 'safe' and non-controversial issues including the delivery of government programmes for their existence. Becoming an extension of the government or donor agencies may lead to dependencies of various types including any forced compromise with ideology. If NGOs merely become an agency for 'non-party political work' for some, it may lead to growth of opportunism and corrupt practices. Even the political party sponsored NGOs today seek to play the 'safe game'. Unlike the NGOs of 1960s and 1970s in many parts of Latin America and the Third World, which vigorously fought for curtailment of civic and political rights, the new *Project NGOs* hardly work to enhance the space for civil society. Moreover, not all people working for NGOs are volunteers. Today, the NGO sector provides enormous employment opportunities to young social scientists and those who merely work as paid employee of an NGO, the 'service' is nothing more than an 'occupation' for a living. The PRIA survey (2002) had revealed that as many as 20 million people are associated with the NGO sector and 15 per cent of them are paid staff. One should not expect these paid employees to be either committed to the goal of social reconstruction, or even to the particular task on which a project is launched. Alternately, however, such 'professionalisation' might serve to reduce the dependency of an NGO on kinship and family connections. It may also result in the better delivery of services. Yet, due to such transformation, the *vocation* of social welfare has now transformed into an *occupation* of routine social work to suit individual interest. Niumai (2006) shows that whenever an NGO tries to expand and focus on the rights of its employees, it faces 'routinisation' and consequent decline of voluntarism. One should, therefore, not compare the policies and perspectives of *Project NGOs* with the idealistic notion of altruistic, value-based, people-centric or non-profit voluntarism. Because, NGOs today are being formed with the singular objective to trap and manage money that is flowing in the names of corporate responsibility, sustainable development, equitable growth or grassroots development.

Corruption in fund management is a major argument against NGOs.[9] Data collected by Council for Advancement of People's Action and Rural Technology (CAPART), an autonomous body functioning under the Rural Development Ministry, reveal that around 2,900 NGOs and voluntary organisations in the country have been put on blacklist or under funding restrictions. These include 900 blacklisted by other government agencies apart from CAPART, 907 defaulters, 281 doubtful cases and 1,314 put under funding restrictions (www.consumercourt.in/product-services/25635-blacklisted-ngo.html 2010). There are obviously questions regarding seriousness of CAPART and the Rural Development Ministry in applying 'checks and balances' on NGO-fund irregularities. Otherwise, many NGOs would not have received financial assistance from CAPART and other sources. It is surprising that in a country like India, known for high level of corruption, many NGOs also become defaulters by not bothering to submit grants utilisation certificates. It may be assumed that they appear again under different names to usurp fund in active collaboration of bureaucrats and politicians.

It is only expected that in the contemporary world, market-driven NGOs would prefer to sacrifice their ideology for prudence. While commenting on the functioning of human rights NGOs, Baxi (2002: 12) has alleged that they cannot always be trusted in promoting human rights, as they have become market-oriented. According to Giri (2006), NGOs are one-man show where the leaders behave like a tyrant. On the whole, NGOs lack transparency, as they are not open to scrutiny by others. The leaders never disclose their balance sheet to the public or even to its employees[10] though they talk about the current and future programmes of the organisation. The need for transparency in dealings, democratic accountability in transactions and sensitivity to the concerns and aspirations of the people they serve has forced some to argue for a code of conduct for NGOs (Baviskar 2001: 11).

It seems that NGOs often indulge in a double standard. Thus, on the one hand, they argue for transparency and democratic participation while criticising the state/bureaucracy for their failure to do so. But, while discharging their duties, they themselves fail to observe such norms. It is worth mentioning here that authority structure of NGOs is highly idiosyncratic, paternalistic and authoritarian in nature, and it is almost difficult, if not impossible, to penetrate into that structure.[11] This is because, as Béteille (2001: 314) argues, NGOs in India are not able to escape the institution of kinship even though they are able to escape the influence of caste. The cosier environment of the NGOs, particularly the smaller ones, makes them more indulgent towards the claims of family and kinship and they find it easy to accommodate the wife, the nephew and the daughter-in-law than the civil society. Hence, research on NGOs often gets reduced to only what is being stated formally by the dictatorial patriarch of the organisation. Additionally, religious or political party affiliation of NGOs may reduce them to limited circle. If NGO activities are influenced by caste, family, kinship, religion or narrow party politicking, it would be doubtful to what extent they may fit into our imagined paradigm of alternative development!

The middle class background as well as lifestyle of many of the NGO personalities has also come under serious attack. It has been argued that these professionals have by now transformed CSOs into media-focused protests or well-published marches. In other words, even the 'politics of symbolism' of the NGO sector is now being surpassed by the 'politics of rituals' (Sethi 1993). The 'east money' syndrome is also argued to have led to the growth of a new category of 'airport NGOs' – those who travel from one part of the world to the other to attend conferences, meetings – in the name of poor and grassroots activism (Chatterjee 2001). In the context of serious questions regarding NGO credibility and accountability, it is more pertinent today to revise our understanding about 'what an NGO stands for', rather than 'what it is not' (non-governmental).

Conclusion

This paper has attempted to identify some of the critical flaws of CSOs and NGOs in particular. It appears that a handful of successful NGOs, whose number by any rational calculation would be only a few hundreds or at best a thousand or two, as against the presence of millions of NGOs in the sphere of civil society in recent times have failed to impress us and meet our expectations. This is mainly because the hype about NGOs is exaggerated and they are certainly not the panacea for all ills even though we are stuck with them. The public image of the NGO sector is not good.

In most cases, NGOs are evaluated by 'experts' appointed by their funders, not their beneficiaries. As a result, evaluations are too centred on logistics and delivery mechanisms, not on the satisfaction of beneficiaries. In the current context, third-party evaluation and monitoring of NGOs would certainly increase their credibility. The National Policy for the Voluntary Sector, framed by the Planning Commission and approved by the government in 2007, should be implemented.

One may, however, argue that there are serious inherent flaws in this model of development as NGOs can hardly represent an alternative to the state and the public sector. Contrary to the argument that state is retreating, it is rather co-opting NGOs to regain supremacy. Even the strong protagonists of market liberalism today seek state protection as global recession has proved that the volatile market is more fatal than state control. NGOs are also not seen as a means to correct market failures. On the contrary, the more an NGO becomes successful in expanding its activities, the more it gets alienated from the people and becomes hierarchical. The 'iron law of oligarchy' therefore applies to big and 'successful' NGOs as well. This means that the success of any NGO should not be measured by looking into its size and scale. Similarly, the effectiveness of an NGO should not be judged on the basis of its 'success' in fetching foreign fund alone. Because NGO's capacity to contribute to the growth of civil society would rather get squeezed by such 'achievements'. There are serious questions regarding the so-called 'success story' of many microfinance programmes to have significant and lasting positive impact on women's lives. It should be remembered here that the scope of NGO activism to provide support and relief to the millions of poor, subaltern and weaker sections of people in the world is limited. Because, NGO-isation could hardly prevent growing disparities in income and opportunities of a vast section of masses in post-globalised India. In spite of the relevance of this sector, therefore, we need to look for other viable alternatives. Mere voluntary action arising from the erosion of the modern state and its institutions poses serious threat to the credibility of the so-called third sector. Although there are many pitfalls of state action or inaction, the alternative is certainly neither just privatisation, nor only NGO-isation. It should be kept in mind that there is neither any short cut nor any singular model of any real development, and any one claiming to do this either fools us or makes a mockery of the whole process of development. It is high time that we become serious about agenda of alternative development and assign due responsibilities to genuine agencies.

Notes

1. Several other terms like independent sector, non-profit organisations, voluntary citizen's group, voluntary development organisations (VDOs), community-based organisations, grassroots organisations etc., are suggested to refer to NGOs.
2. Korten (1990: 115–27) has distinguished NGOs into three generations. Apart from the relief and welfare-based first generation NGOs, the second generation attended to small-scale, local development projects, and the third generation consisted of community organisations interested in building coalitions.
3. The inflow of foreign fund to NGOs has gone up from Rs 1,584 crore in 1992–93 to Rs 4,871.9 crore in 2001–02. Notwithstanding the role of factors like depletion of Indian rupee as against dollar and inflation during the period, the escalating volume of foreign funding is also a testimony to the increased activities of nearly 23,000 registered societies in the country.
4. The Government of India has sanctioned Rs 200 crore in the Seventh Plan and Rs 750 crore in the Eighth Plan for NGO funding. In the Tenth Plan, the government has earmarked a total fund of Rs 18,000 crore for the social sector.
5. For the 2008–09 fiscal year, the CAPART's budget strength is Rs 74 crore for different developmental works.
6. The Grameen Bank of Bangladesh, though internationally acclaimed, has recently been charged with corruption charges. The Bank charges as high as 20 per cent rate of interest for disbursing loans to its poor clients. It has also been argued that Grameen Bank has "landed poor communities in a perpetual debt-trap" (for details see, en.wikipedia.org/wiki/ Grameen_Bank).
7. The highest recipients of foreign fund in 2007–08 were World Vision of India, Tamil Nadu (Rs 211.62 crore), Rural Development Trust, Andhra Pradesh (Rs 124.79 crore), Believers Church India, Kerala (Rs 101.68 crore), Action Aid, Karnataka (Rs 91.95 crore), Caritas India, Delhi (Rs 89.56 crore), Gospel For Asia, Kerala (Rs 86.20 crore), Women Development Trust, Andhra Pradesh (Rs 79.82 crore), Plan International Inc., Delhi (Rs 74.06 crore), Shri Ganjanam Maharaj Sansthan, Maharashtra (Rs 70.31 crore) and Oxfam India Trust, Delhi (Rs 67 crore). The amount of donations, however, varies from year to year depending on donor's choices (see, http://mha.gov.in/fcra/annual/ar2007–08.pdf).
8. The case of high-profile Bangladeshi NGOs failing to stand by the sufferings of flood-affected people may be referred here. More than 2,000 NGOs in Bangladesh received fund worth 211 crore US dollars during the 2000–01 fiscal year. But they were hardly seen in proving relief during the two successive floods that inundated 40 per cent of the country in 2007. See, for details, Rahman (2007).

9. It was revealed through a public interest litigation before the Delhi High Court in 2000 that over 30,000 NGOs did not account for Rs 7,535 crore given to them by the government during the past several years (Baviskar 2001: 13). Also, as per government record, 36,561 associations did not submit their statutory annual returns relating to receipt and utilisation of foreign contributions between 2003 and 2006 (http://mha.nic.in/fore. htm). Anil Singh of Voluntary Action Network India (VANI) has claimed that most of NGO funds do not reach the poor. He even argued that CAPART is corrupt and charges commission in return for sanctioning projects. See for details, Prasannan (1996: 31).
10. The employees often complain that the management cuts a portion of their salary shown in the budget as 'development fund'.
11. One of my ex-students working as the coordinator of an AIDS project had complained to me that she is merely reduced to a puppet by those who appointed her to look into the work.

References

Awasthi, R. 1998. 'Rural Development through People's Mobilization: A Case Study of Ralegan Siddhi', in M.L. Dantwala, H. Sethi and P. Visaria (eds.), *Social Change through Voluntary Actions* (74–91). New Delhi: Sage Publications.

Bebbington, A. and R. Riddell. 1995. 'The Direct Funding of Southern NGOs by Donors: New Agendas and Old Problems', *Journal of International Development*, 7 (6): 879–93.

Bhaumik, Subir. 2010. 'India Blacklists 800 NGOs'. *news.bbc.co.uk/2/hi/south_asia/3001458.stm* (Accessed on 9th December 2010).

Baviskar, B.S. 2001. 'NGOs and Civil Society in India', *Sociological Bulletin*, 50 (1): 3–15.

Baxi, Upendra. 2002. *The Future of Human Rights*. New Delhi: Oxford University Press.

Bendell, Jem. 2006. *Debating NGO Accountability: NGLS Development Dossier*. New York: United Nations.

Béteille, Andre. 2000. *Antinomies of Society: Essays on Ideologies and Institutions*. New Delhi: Oxford University Press.

——. 2001. 'Civil Society and the Good Society', *Sociological Bulletin*, 50 (2): 286–307.

Bhatt, Ela R. 1998. 'Empowering the Poor through Micro-Finance: The SEWA Bank', in M.L. Dantwala, H. Sethi and P. Visaria (eds.), op. cit. (146–61).

Chambers, Robert. 1997. *Whose Reality Counts? Putting the First Last*. London: Intermediate Technology Publications.

Chandhoke, Neera. 1995. *State and Civil Society: Explorations in Political Theory*. New Delhi: Sage Publications.

Chatterjee, Patralekha. 2001. 'Civil Society in India: A Necessary Corrective in a Representative Democracy'. *http://www.inwent.org/E+Z/zeitschr/de601-9.htm.*

Datta, Saikat. 2010. 'Unblanking the Tapes', *Outlook*, December, Cover Story on Radiagate: 24–44.

Dhanagare, D.N. 2001. 'Civil Society, State and Democracy: Contextualising a Discourse', *Sociological Bulletin*, 50 (2): 167–91.

Edwards, M. and D. Hulme. 1996. 'Too Close for Comfort? The Impact of Official Aid on Non-governmental Organisations', *World Development*, 24 (6): 961–73.

Farouk, Fazila. 2002. 'Why Donor Fund Don't Reach NGO Coffers?', Global Policy Forum. *http://www.globalpolicy.org/ngos/fund/2002/0808coffer.htm.*

Ghosh, Biswajit. 2003. 'Ethnicity and Insurgency in Tripura', *Sociological Bulletin*, 52 (2): 221–43.

——. 2009. 'NGOs, Civil Society and Social Reconstruction in Contemporary India', *Journal of Developing Societies*, 25 (2): 229–52.

Government of India. 2006. 'Receipt of Foreign Contributions by Voluntary Associations', *FCRA Annual Report 2005–06*. New Delhi: Ministry of Home Affairs.

Giri, Ananta Kumar. 2006. *Reflections and Mobilizations: Dialogues with Movements and Voluntary Organisations*. New Delhi: Sage Publications.

——. 2008. *Self Development and Social Transformation? The Vision and Practice of the Self-Study Mobilization of Swadhyaya*. Jaipur: Rawat Publications.

Gramsci, A. 1976. *Selections from the Prison Notebooks of Antonio Gramsci* (ed. and tr. by Q. Hoare and G.N. Smith). London: Lawrence and Wishart.

Hall, J.A. 1998. 'The Nature of Civil society', *Society* (May–June): 32–41.

Hazare, Anna. 2003. *My Village – My Sacred Land*. Ahmednagar: Ralegan Siddhi Pariwar Publication.

Jerath, Arati R. 2010. 'Grassroots Gold Mine', *The Times of India*, The Crest Edition, September 20, Kolkata.

Kaviraj, Sudipta. 2001. 'In Search of Civil Society', in S. Kaviraj and S. Khilnani (eds.), *Civil Society: History and Possibilities* (287–323). New Delhi: Cambridge University Press.

Kaimowitz, D. 1993. 'The Role of Non-governmental Organisations in Agricultural Research and Technology Transfer in Latin America', *World Development*, 21 (7): 1139–50.

Karat, Prakash. 1984. 'Action Groups/Voluntary Agencies: A Factor in Imperialist Strategy', *Marxist*, 2 (2): 19–54.

Korten, D.C. 1990. *Getting to the 21st Century: Voluntary Action and Global Agenda*. West Hartford, CT: Kumarian.

Kothari, R. 1988. *The State against Democracy: In Search of Humane Governance*. Delhi: Ajanta Publications.

——. 1998. 'The Future of Voluntarism', in M.L. Dantwala, H. Sethi and P. Visaria (eds.), op. cit. (182–89).

Lim, H. 1992. 'International Economic System: Trends and their Effects on Development Strategy', in T. Iwasaki et al. (eds.), *Development Strategies for the 21st Century* (578–92). Tokyo: Institute of Developing Economies.

Mahajan, G. 1999. 'Civil Society, State and Democracy', *Economic and Political Weekly*, 34 (49): 3471–72.

Nayar, P.K.B. 2008. 'Social Justice in a Globalised World: Encounters with State and Civil Society', *Sociological Bulletin*, 57 (1): 3–29.

NGOs India. 2008. 'Online Database and Resources of Indian NGOs'. *http://www.ngosindia.com.*

Niumai, Ajailiu. 2006. Non-government Organisations in Development: A Sociological Study of Selected NGOs in Manipur, unpublished PhD Thesis, CSSS, Jawaharlal Nehru University, New Delhi.

Oommen, T.K. 2004. *Nation, Civil Society and Social Movements: Essays in Political Sociology*. New Delhi: Sage Publications.

Patel, Pinakin. 1998. 'Participatory Development in Adivasi Villages: Experiences of NIRID, 1979–1997', in M.L. Dantwala, H. Sethi and P. Visaria (eds.), op. cit. (113–29).

Patel, Rohini. 1998. 'Voluntary Organizations in India: Motivations and Roles', in M.L. Dantwala, H. Sethi and P. Visaria (eds.), op. cit. (40–56).

Pieterse, Jan Nederveen. 2001. *Development Theory: Deconstruction/Reconstructions*. New Delhi: Vistaar Publications.

Prasannan, R. 1996. 'Most of the Funds They Get Never Reach the Poor', *The Week*, September 15: 31.

Pulavarti, Lalita. 1998. 'Sumangali Seva Ashram: Contributions of a Local NGO in Urban Bangalore', in M.L. Dantwala, H. Sethi and P. Visaria (eds.), op. cit. (130–45).

Rahman, Sayeed. 2007. 'Truth about Bangladeshi NGOs: Visibly Absent in Relief Operation'. http://groups.google.com/group/banglaict/browse_thread.

Saberwal, S. 2001. 'Democracy and Civil Society in India: Integral or Accidental', *Sociological Bulletin*, 50 (2): 192–205.

Sato, Y. 2009. 'Power in Participatory Development: Gender, NGOs and the Unequal Social Relations in the Slums of Ahmedabad', unpublished paper.

Sen, Amartya. 2000. *Development as Freedom*. New Delhi: Oxford University Press.

Sengupta, Nandini. 2010. 'Nil at Ground Zero', *The Times of India*, The Crest Edition, September 20, Kolkata.

Sethi, Harsh. 1993. 'Some Notes on Micro-Struggles, NGOs and the State', *Asian Exchange Arena Bulletin*, 9 (1 & 2), May.

——. 1998. 'Evolving Accountability of Voluntary Organisations', in M.L. Dantwala, H. Sethi and P. Visaria (eds.), op. cit. (174–81).

Shah, Anil C. and S. Iyengar. 1998. 'The Contribution of NGOs to Development: Some Issues and a Case Study', in M.L. Dantwala, H. Sethi and P. Visaria (eds.), op. cit. (92–112).

Shah, Vimal, P.N.R. Sheth and Pravin Visaria. 1998. 'Swadhyaya: Social Change through Spirituality', in M.L. Dantwala, H. Sethi and P. Visaria (eds.), op. cit. (57–73).

Sharma, S.L. 1992. 'Social Action Groups as Harbingers of Silent Revolution', *Economic and Political Weekly*, 27 (47): 2557–61.

Shils, E. 1991. 'The Virtue of Civil Society', *Government and Opposition*, 26 (1): 11–23.

Society for Participatory Research in Asia (PRIA). 2002. *Invisible, Yet Widespread: The Non-Profit Sector in India*. New Delhi: PRIA.

Voluntary Action Network India (VANI). 2008. 'Facts and Figures on NGOs in India'. *http://www.vaniindia.org/inf_NGOfact.asp*.

Wagona, Mokaba J. 2002. 'Nongovernmental Organizations (NGOs) and Third World Development: An Alternative Approach to Development', *Journal of Third World Studies*, Spring. *http://findarticles.com/p/articles/mi_qa3821/is_200204/ai_n9071891* (Accessed on 16th October 2008).

World Bank. 1995. *Working with NGOs: A Practical Guide to Operational Collaboration between the World Bank and Non-Governmental Organizations*. Operations Policy Department, Washington, DC: The World Bank.

——. 1997. *Progress Report*. Washington, DC: The World Bank.

Zaidi, S. Akbar. 2004. 'NGO Failure and the Need to Bring Back the State', in P.N. Mukherji and C. Sengupta (eds.), *Indigeneity and Universality in Social Sciences: A South Asian Perspective* (187–202). New Delhi: Sage Publications.

Websites

en.wikipedia.org/wiki/Grameen_Bank.

http://library.duke.edu.

southasia.oneworld.net/.../india-more-ngos-than-schools-and-health-centres.

www.consumercourt.in/product-services/25635-blacklisted-ngo.html.

Section III

Gender and Development

7

Gender and Globalisation

Shifts in Developmental Paradigms

Maitrayee Chaudhuri

This paper seeks to focus on the shift in the Indian state's developmental paradigm since the early 1990s. This shift one argues is a deeply gendered process. I attempt to examine this shift at two levels: one, at the specific level of actual policies on gender and development; and two at the broader level of public discourse, made most evident in changes in the media. I argue that the broad ideological shift in public discourse is closely linked to the actual policy shifts. In the early developmental vision such as the first plan document on women in India, one of the 29 sub-committees under the National Plan Committee (NPC) instituted by the Indian National Congress (INC) in 1938 to plan India's development post-independence, labour in general and women workers in particular were privileged in the national imaginary. The document was tellingly titled *Women's Role in a Planned Economy* (WRPE). The state and national capital who worked in close connect to the state were the key agents to propel India's development path (Chaudhuri 1996). The 1990s altered this paradigm. Capital (not necessarily national capital) and market (not the state) acquired ascendancy. This shift in public discourse, I argue, reconfigured both class and gender in the national imaginary and therefore necessarily in the developmental priority. This however was not the only change. The 1990s also saw an increasing visibility of previously marginalised section with their own distinct response to the paradigm shift in developmental visions. For instance, a section within the dalit movement welcomed it while another was critical of it. I shall return to this later.

Understanding the new and changing dynamics of state formation is therefore critical for grasping recent debates on gender and development.

This I attempt to do by foregrounding the close linkages between the increasing vocal international institutions and the state on one hand, and the reciprocal (even if contentious) links between the state and social movements on the other. In some instances one would discern that the two sets of dynamics work in similar directions, in some case they do not. This has to be accounted by the fact that the basic premises upon which social movements rest are themselves at variance. Indeed, women's movements themselves are not homogenous. Not surprisingly, therefore, feminist responses to the 'developments' initiated by globalisation have been varied. This paper seeks to capture the shift in a schematic fashion.

Few processes have had perhaps a more dramatic impact in recent times than globalisation or the neo-liberal model of development. It is perhaps no exaggeration to state that it has in many ways transformed the social, cultural and political landscape of India. Not surprisingly, serious transformations have taken place in women's movements and concomitantly in gender and development scholarship. The paper is premised on the belief that the women's movement has succeeded in making gender a major issue in the public sphere. Major actors such as state, civil society, market, international institutions have had to take cognisance of gender inequality. Yet, with the growing achievements of the women's movement, not least which has been a certain 'mainstreaming' of gender whether in developmental programmes or in the corporate sector or in the media, there has often been not just a de-link with visions of justice articulated by women's movement but often significant reconfigurations of the very ideas of freedom, justice, equity, autonomy, choice, activism, empowerment that women's movements raised. Many of these developments are new. And many have to be understood in conjuncture with the rise of an assertive new middle class. This class itself is not a homogeneous entity with the rise of a very vocal new middle class from castes other than the traditional 'upper caste' middle class.

Some of these developments can be linked directly to the global rise of a neo-liberal vision and India's own tryst with it. But not all trends evident in the growing body of studies broadly on gender and development can be attributed to the rise of neo-liberalism. Many fundamental interrogations of both women's movements and women studies are linked to the challenges thrown up by new movements that have focused on the rights of 'the discriminated and socially excluded'. These interrogations have brought fresh insights to our understanding of central categories such as the nation and caste and therefore also of possible ways of looking at 'globalisation' itself. It is in this context that the first part of the paper revisits histories of the women's question. For the many interrogations of conventional accounts of the history of the women's question have emerged from both women's movements and women studies. This revisit to the now increasingly debatable history of the nation and of gender throws up contentious perspectives on the class/caste character of national development itself.

The structure of the paper is in keeping with the attempt to develop and put across the broad argument articulated above. Part I therefore sets out to do a very quick and essentially schematic history of movements that raised the women's question in India and the corresponding perspectives of women's studies on questions pertaining to development. It is a quick, sweeping account of the major trends from the colonial period into early years of independence to the mid-1970s that witnessed a range of movements including what is often termed as 'the second wave of women's movements'. This broad etching has two purposes. One, it will help us better appreciate the nature and direction of changes in recent years. Two (and this purpose is critical to this paper), it will foreground how new perspectives are emerging from new movements and how they narrate histories of development differently. Part II involves an overt focus on the contemporary period, focusing primarily on the changes that have come with the New Economic Policy of the Indian state since 1991. The effort will not be towards an exhaustive treatment of either studies or movements but will be more in the nature of an illustrative treatment of what one identifies as distinctive features of the current phase of both social movements and studies on gender and development. Significantly here too new narratives emerge with the increasing presence and role of new actors, especially that of international institutions. The beginning of women studies, indeed the women's question itself, is assumed to have begun with the declaration of the International Women's Year and Decade in 1975 by the United Nations. Such narratives focus on how women have emerged as a target group in agency programmes/projects of various UN organisations such as the UNFPA, UNIFEM, UNICEF, and UNDP. This is the dominant storyline of development practitioners. One thus alludes to more recent trends as evident in the new efforts to 'mainstream' and 'gender train' or 'gender sensitise' by a wide set of actors such as the state, NGOs and increasingly by corporations. Much of this is also evident in mainstream media, whose manifold expansion in recent years cannot be overemphasised. My own study of the portrayal of 'feminism' in the media since the 1990s suggests a clear disengagement with earlier notions of women's movements and an affirmation of the individuated, entrepreneurial woman (Chaudhuri 2000). Here I argue that there are two strands at work: one, a backlash and two, illustration of both an aggressive assertion of class, gender and nation (albeit a refurbished one) that is very typical of a globalising corporate India. Ascendancy of the new individuated entrepreneurial middle class women in the public discourse is accompanied by a celebration of the strength and capabilities of the poor woman. The 'empowerment' discourse becomes the dominant developmental language. This period is also marked by the retreat of traditional left-led mass movements of workers and peasants and by the growth of new social movements. Perhaps the most notable of them has been the dalit movement that has raised some of the most challenging questions to women's movements. Not yet so visible in public discourse but likely to become so increasingly is the 'adivasi' or 'indigenous' or 'tribal' movements. Indeed some very interesting debates emerge from the naming process itself (Xaxa 2010; Omvedt 2005). Such interrogation has meant that the plural and diverse nature of women's movements has come to be accepted. Responses to globalisation from women's movements and studies have therefore been very different – a point that I would discuss below. What is curious at this juncture is that we witness a retreat of both class and capital as categories of analysis, particularly in an era of an almost unchallenged pre-eminence of capitalism.

I

Reading Development: Reading Histories of Women's Movements

My effort is limited to garnering what one would think are largely well-established ideas about the way the women's question emerged in modern India and evolved over time. The story has been written and rewritten, each time as responses to challenges of movements and re-conceptualisation (this has been one of the salient contributions of both women's movements and women's studies). It runs roughly like this (and I attempt to build in the mainstream account and the challenges): a mandatory mention of the 19th century social reform movements and the articulation of the women's question; the growth of women's writing and voices in the same period; the emergence of women's groups in the early part of the 20th century; the links between the women's movement, the national movement and the early left movements; the caste and gender question within and outside the national movement that history writing had excluded for long; independence and the state domestication of the women's question; the 'second phase' of the women's movement in the 1970s, its character and its interrogation, and new issues and institutionalisation of women's studies; the new economic policies, the new social movements and the gender question from the 1990 onwards.

India's tryst with modernity has been inextricably linked with India's entry within British colonialism. The two cannot be disengaged much like the manner that the women's question cannot be severed from our complex relationship with colonial development. The complexity is rendered more so not just because of the nature of colonialism but also because of 'our' differential relationship with colonialism. This difference could be on the basis of regions, classes, castes and communities. Not surprisingly, therefore, there has been considerable interrogation from the dalit viewpoint about the nationalist framework as well as about the purported role of colonialism.[1] One finds that similar interrogations are being made about the present role of globalisation.[2] A significant current from the past, not talked about much today, is the left's own mixed and uncertain response to independence from colonialism in 1947 that raised issues of nationalism, capitalism and class. An interesting comparison may be made with some trends within the dalit movement and dalit studies, both to the issue of colonialism and capitalism.

British colonialism entered and spread over much of India at different stages, impacting different regions differently both because of the stage of colonialism as well as the nature of different regions. Thus, there were periods of reluctance to meddle with India's social customs such as those related to women, periods of active involvement to intervene such as abolition of *sati* in 1829 or raising the Age of Consent for Women in 1863 which brought forth a fury of hostile reaction leading again to a phase where the British preferred to rely more on their conservative allies. What one can however infer is that the colonial rule, the humiliation of the subject population, the impact of western education, the role of Christian missionaries, growth of an English knowing Indian middle class all led to an intense and contested debate of the women's question in the public sphere. This debate itself has been scrutinised carefully from different perspectives. We thus have a Lata Mani (1989) questioning whether the debate on *sati* was about women or about reconfiguring tradition and culture; we have as Rege (1998) points out questions on why dalit women's public initiatives and intervention went unwritten about; we have arguments that suggest social reforms were more about efforts to introduce new patriarchies rather than about women's right and gender justice. Much of this questioning is of recent times. And importantly scholars of women studies have been at the forefront of this. I think this needs reiteration to challenge widely held ideas about the ghettoisation of women's studies.

Commenting on the kind of studies done on gender in the pre-independence period, Vina Mazumdar observes:

> The *objective of pre-Independence research* was often to justify social reform or to provide a backbone for India's cultural pride, which had been battered by colonial rule and the onslaught of western culture. *The focus of such research was on the minority of women in the upper classes.* For a variety of reasons such research declined after Independence. (Mazumdar 1994: 42; emphasis mine)

However, one did have other accounts and orientations, even if they were not the dominant strands. What readily comes to one's mind is the WRPE, mentioned earlier, which revealed a curious mix and contestation of the dominant ideas of liberalism, socialism and notions of cultural revivalism within the same text. It contained substantial data on conditions of women workers in the unorganised sector, in agriculture and the public and private issues that they faced (Chaudhuri 1996). It could be argued, however, like Rege does, that even such accounts of labour and other subaltern groups still privileged the role of nationalism.

Early Years of Independence

There is a general sense of dismay that the women's question, so central to colonial India appeared to retreat from public discourse with independence in 1947, which also marked the unprecedented violence of partition. We are aware that the Hindu Code Bill was returned repeatedly, that a committee for abducted women was formed and that feminist scholars have etched out from the tragic narratives how the women's voices were violently brushed aside before the decisions of the state and nation (Butalia 2000; Menon and Bhasin 1998).

The other paradigm that seemed to dominate notions of gender in this period was the 'modernisation'-driven vision that was premised on a simple dichotomy between 'traditional' and 'non-traditional' societies.

Traditional societies were rural, stratified and 'backward', while non-traditional societies were urban, dynamic and progressive. This privileged a certain 'modern' domesticated woman and studies of women largely operating with a role conflict paradigm. The central question of the private–public dichotomy returned to be a naturalised entity as in Talcott Parson's analysis of the family in an industrial society. Indian Sociology from the late 1970s had a body of works inspired by this model (Chaudhuri 1982). The language of the WRPE seemed a distant forgotten legacy. As we know far more conservative programmes of community development came to be implemented in the 1950s and 1960s:

> Instead, the 1950s and 60s saw the re-emergence of 'women' in the community development programmes (financed by the Ford Foundation) whose projects were geared to enable village women to become, in the words of the director of the Women's programme in 1959, 'a good wife, a wise mother, a competent housewife and a responsible member of the village community'. Women's work and labour are not alluded to. (cited in John 1996, note 6)

A question often raised in this context is how did the left-oriented WRPE completely disappear from public discourse on development and gender? Why did transformation of gender relationships disappear when the other aspects pertaining to social equity and state planning, characteristic of WRPE, persist? I offer two sets of explanations. One that is specific to gender. There was a clear retreat from a more radical questionings of sexualities and sexual division of labour of an earlier period to a time when the Hindu Code Bill was being opposed not just by conservatives but by many within the INC. Significantly, one should recall that much of the 19th century middle class social reform were self-consciously seeking to refashion the family in an ideal typical modern, western bourgeois family with a male breadwinner and a domesticated genteel mother and wife (Chaudhuri 1993). Feminist scholars have worked on conduct books that were written at that time. The challenge clearly stemmed from a patriarchal notion of social order, identity and tradition, heightened in the aftermath of unprecedented violence of partition. This period also marked the confrontation of the Nehruvian Congress government and the communists with the Tebhaga and Telengana movement and a little later by the 1962 war with China. Reference to such international developments, I think, is critical for a great deal of manoeuvrings of the state vis-a-vis strategic moves with a global order that had its own strategies,[3] may be in the form of Community Development Programmes in a Cold War era. In the contemporary period I argue that women studies can provide a vantage point to understand these moves of global politics and dominant global frames of development, be it in the rapid growth of micro-credit and self-finance groups or in shifts in higher education policies or in new discourses of choice and autonomy.

Women's Studies in the Post-1975 Context

Vina Mazumdar iterates time and again the embryonic relationship between women's movements and gender studies. She writes:

> The *revival of the women's movement in the late 1970s brought new dynamism and directions to women studies.* Issues of *violence* – domestic and social, sexual exploitation in old and new forms, identification of *complex structures of domination* and their reassertion in new forms in the *ideology of revivalist, fundamentalist, communal and ethnic movements* – are some of the most significant of these new dimensions that the movement has brought into women's studies. Similarly, investigations of *peasant women* in the rural economy and of their undiscovered history have prompted new questions and drawn women's studies closer to issues being also raised by *ecological and environmental* movements. Investigations into *women's marginalization and exploitation in the economy, formal and informal, in the educational process, in communication and media and, also in the political process,* have turned women's studies into one of the *major critics of the pattern of 'development'* and the choice of strategies. (Mazumdar 1994: 44, emphasis mine)

Significantly, this focus on women in the rural economy and in the unorganised sector brought forth new conceptualisation of 'work' as well the meanings of the public and private domain. The report of the Committee on the Status of Women in India *Towards Equality*[4] presented a grim picture of social reality that sharply contrasted with the goals of equality laid down by the Indian Constitution. The result of the report was to define a new agenda for women's studies in the country – an agenda that stressed the dynamism and pluralism of an Indian society in contrast to the often monolithic discourse of the nationalist or development schools. A new programme for Women's Studies, initiated by the Indian Council of Social Science Research (ICSSR), emerged after the report with three distinct objectives: (1) to identify and work for needed policy change; (2) to persuade the social science community to re-examine the methodology, concepts, theories and analytical apparatus of social research, which had successfully excluded women's role, status and situation from the entire arena of social investigations; and (3) to revive the social debate on the women's question which had emerged as a major issue during the freedom struggle but had faded in the post-independence period (Mazumdar 1994: 43). Further, Mazumdar argues that "the extension of the post-1975 research to peasant women and women in the informal sector generated new sources of information for the fast growing women's movement". Ironically, these studies were then used by the developmental agencies and the state in the neo-liberal era to legitimise a form of development that rested on an unregulated informal economy of flexible labour – an argument that I will return to later in this paper.

II

The Paradigm Shift from the 1990s

The 1990s in a fundamental sense brought in changes that can be clearly seen as a break with the earlier periods. A neo-liberal vision[5] emerged to capture governmental imagination and much of public discourse. The role of the media cannot be overemphasised here.

I attempt below to identify few features pertinent to understand changes in women's movements and women's studies during this period. What I attempt to touch upon are: (i) a developmental vision that privileges the role of the informal sector and encourage initiatives such as micro-credit; (ii) new popular discourses in the media about new ideas about class and gender assertions; (iii) corporate visions on gender justice; and (iv) the appropriation of gender concerns by the entertainment industry, which has been sometimes termed as 'infotainment of gender' and interestingly a professionalisation of both 'feminism' and 'activism'. In many ways all these trends flow from the fact that from the early 1990s the Indian state has moved away from a language of growth with equity – standard hallmarks of an earlier Nehruvian period – to a language almost exclusively of growth and growth rate.

In consonance with the neo-liberal paradigm the discourse for alleviating the conditions of the mass of people has shifted from a vision of state support, development and social support to a language of poverty alleviation through micro-credit and self-finance groups. Crucial discursive shifts have thus taken place in the developmental discourse generally and the manner that gender has been reconfigured within the discourse. I first seek to address this before looking at some of the different ways that the women's movements and women's studies have looked these new developmental initiatives.

Development and Gender

One has already referred to the new energy with which the women's question re-emerged with the women's movement in the mid-1970s. New debates and new issues emerged. And, as noted, a concerted attempt was made to build up a body of research on women studies questioning fundamental categories of social science. Categories such as work, family, sexualities were interrogated and with fresh data and new perspectives such as links between gender and caste, the need for women's reservation bill emerged. Violence was a major issue that was raised and significant theorisation took place (Omvedt 1990).

A very remarkable development that emerged in this period was an appropriation of findings of women studies for purposes that went fundamentally against the models of development and notions of social justice that women's movements were premised upon. This happened as Mary John has argued with a body of literature that women's studies produced from the mid-1970s onwards which was used for quite another purpose in the 1990s by developmental agencies and the state. And, as I have argued elsewhere, a similar process happened with ideas of autonomy and freedom raised by the women's movements (Chaudhuri 2000, 2001).

One of the crucial texts to come out of the subsequent decade of the 1980s was the *Shramshakti* report on self-employed women and women in the informal sector that was published in 1988.

> Drawing from a now vastly expanded literature and from extensive field surveys in different parts of the country, the authors produced detailed studies of women in the informal sectors of urban and rural India. The report was intended to show women's extremely vulnerable working conditions across diverse occupations under high levels of discrimination, as well as the range of health hazards women were exposed to on an everyday basis. The recommendations of the report – addressed to various ministries and departments at the central and state levels, but possibly also international agencies – run to almost a hundred pages.

> Their demands included enlarging the definition of work to encompass all women engaged in production and reproduction, recognizing women's position as major rather than supplementary wage earners, and finding strategies to enhance women's control over and ownership of resources. Also important was the demand to extend the rights and benefits for the privileged 10 per cent of the general labour force who make up the formal sector (in the case of the female workforce the corresponding figure is barely 7 per cent) to the rest of the working population. (John 1996: 247)

Mary John takes off at this point to argue that:

> The special focus of this report on the informal sector, it seems to me, can help serve as a bridge for the 1990s. The *World Bank Gender and Poverty Report,* with which I began, followed only a few years later. The World Bank report draws directly from the efforts of the National Commission on Self-Employed Women and Women in the Informal Sector as well as from most of the literature on women and development produced in India and elsewhere over the last decades. In other words, it is not based on case studies of its own. *By drawing upon the past years of research, activism and government action in India however, it is able to perform a remarkable feat; lay claim to an overall consensus on the nature of women in poverty, while in fact coming to often diametrically opposite conclusions from prior feminist concerns.* (John 1996: 247, emphasis mine)

In the neo-liberal framework, the informal sector is at the heart of the market economy and represents its prime model. And, most important of all, since women are seen to predominate in this sector, it is their creativity and potential that needs special attention (see Kalpagam 1994). The World Bank report, drawing upon this kind of understanding, focuses on "the incredible range of tasks poor women perform, their often greater contribution to household income despite lower wage earnings, their ability to make scarce resources stretch further under deteriorating conditions, all of which were documented and debated in the past, are now reworked: through a crucial shift in signification, these findings are no longer arguments about *exploitation* so as much as proofs of *efficiency*" (John 1996).

Not surprisingly, therefore, a great deal of gender development discourse is now exclusively addressed within the micro-credit framework, premised upon the idea that women are efficient managers and can be trusted to repay. A recent work by Deshmukh et al. (2005) is a collection of micro-finance activities and women's empowerment interestingly initiated by UNDP and ICICI Bank. It says:

> Micro-credit as a tool of poverty alleviation and empowerment, particularly of women have gained credence in development dialogue the world over. The provision of micro-credit involves initiatives on the part of the state and non-state organizations in making available very small amounts of credit to poor citizens. There is an acute need among the poor for credit, both for consumption and production, which often forms the deciding line between survival and succumbing to poverty. In other words, credit is sought for basic requirements such as food, as well as for income generation activities. *The rationale of micro-credit is based on the hypothesis that the poor can be relied upon to return on time the money that they borrow. It has been proved that the poor are capable of thrift and savings.* (Deshmukh et al., 2005: 31, emphasis mine)

Other studies have also suggested that it develops banking habits among poor women and leads to increase in deposit accounts (Varman 2005). In the discourse of micro-credit and self-help groups, the categories of class and production relations disappear. The 'poor' and 'poverty' appear to be self-contained entities with no structural connection with production relations.[6] In a great deal of research a few indicators is all that is required to collect data whether it be 'poverty alleviation' or 'empowerment' to assess the impact of any intervention to alleviate 'poverty' or lead to 'empowerment' of women (Krishnaraj 2005). Often deep-seated patriarchal assumptions persist even as new ideas like gender budgeting are included, for example, the idea that anything that has to do with children and contraception is for the exclusive benefit of women (Mishra and Das 2006). Research on development interventions suggests that often the programmes fall short of both progress towards gender equality and broader social equity. Nitya Rao writes:

> While several projects have encouraged women to participate in development and decision-making processes by specifically targeting them, it is now recognized that a more gender-focused approach is necessary ... Women's groups do provide a forum for women to come together, share ideas, exchange information and develop a social network. Yet, strategic shifts in access to resources and benefits (linked as they are to responsibilities for maintaining them) can only emerge if men support a shift, and take on a more equal share of both productive and

> reproductive work. In the context of structural reform, poor men too are facing a crisis in terms of accessing productive assets, markets and income, leading to a crisis of masculinities that is often reflected in growing trends of violence against women. (Rao 2005: 4707)

Naila Kabeer, who has a more careful take on the role of micro-credit, however, does not dispute the point that it is the "imperatives of cost-recovery and financial sustainability which drive the financial systems approach clearly resonate neo-liberal orientation to market principles" and that "it is not surprising therefore that it has come to assume a hegemonic position in international development thinking about micro-finance as a tool for poverty reduction" (Kabeer 2005: 4709).

Contending Takes on Women and Globalisation

Central to the neo-liberal frame is the informal sector as we saw and one needs to foreground the political implications of this. The political implications of making the informal sector where the greater proportion of women workers are the hub of the new economy are as Jan Breman argues:

> ... the informalisation of gainful employment which has become a major trend especially in developing countries in this late phase of capitalism hampers steady increase in the wretchedly low wages and regular employment with casual, spasmodic work arrangements, paid not in time-based wages but on piece rates. *An economic regime of this kind discourages militancy and obstructs the mobilization of the labouring poor into other unions and other representative organizations.* (Breman 2004: 3872, emphasis mine)

Not all within the women's movement have a similar take on a neo-liberal driven globalisation. Gail Omvedt contends that "being anti-globalisation" has become the correct standard of political correctness. She agrees with Rohini Hensman who argued that in a globalised world, labour needs global regulation, and therefore the left should argue for the extension of these and not of withdrawing from the world system (Hensman 2004). But if one looks at what Breman and John are arguing, the very assumptions of the growth of a global labour movement need to be rethought. The debate on outsourcing in the US is illuminating. Indeed, there have been some labour regulations introduced in India not at the insistence of the labour movements but because of pressure generated by the First World consumers.[7]

Positions within the women's movement on the impact of the new developmental paradigm are seriously divided. For instance, Omvedt contends that:

> The only meaningful question is, for a Marxist (or dalit, or feminist) activist, what advances the revolution, that is, the movement towards a non-caste, non-patriarchal, equalitarian and sustainable socialist society? (Omvedt 2005: 4881)

And, according to her, the present model of development does precisely that. On extraction of natural resources and local control by *adivasis*, she argues that:

> ... the increasing extraction of natural resources and their channelling to the world market via multinationals, the state and local power-holders. ... The problem regarding local control (community control) and the extraction of resources is precisely that the two may go together. Anti-globalisation activists often do not see this; but in fact gaining local control will at best mean that resources will be extracted more sustainably, that local people will get a share of the profits and raise their standard of living. It does not mean that they will resist the world market and extraction or listen to the activists when they try to tell them to do so; self-determination after all does mean just that, that they will do what they want. And *this will primarily mean getting a better deal from world capital.* (Omvedt 2005: 4883, emphasis mine)

In arguing for the need to revisit narratives of women's movements, I had emphasised both a dalit take on colonialism, nationalism and now globalisation. What I would like to argue is that in this late stage of capitalism, a class understanding of nationalism has to take note not just of transnational labour as Hensman does but the transformation of an earlier era of national capitalist to a transnational capitalist class as well as the new dynamics of international institutions. Not to mention how globalisation does not lead to an automatic retreat of states but of 'failures' of some states and incredible flexing of powers by other 'states'. Significantly, with major 'global economic meltdown' in 2008 voices began to be raised about the need for state intervention. However, critiques of state initiated developmental model are not confined to either some sections within the dalit movement or to the corporate world. There are, for instance, views from within the women's movement who speak differently. For instance, Shilpa Phadke argues that the market rather than the state is a better as " 'a potential turf for negotiation', for *unlike the state, where the citizen is largely a client, for the market the individual is first and foremost an actor-consumer.* Can the women's movement use the strategies of the market to re-sell itself to a larger audience and reclaim its right to speak on behalf of a larger constituency of women? Can we reclaim the language of choice and restore its radical edge?" (Phadke 2003: 4575, emphasis mine).

Reconfiguring Feminism: New Popular Assertions of Class and Gender in the Media

If in the developmental arena, findings of women studies were turned around for quite another purpose, we find in the media notions of women's feminism being given new meanings. I have argued for long that the media since 1991 has played an incredibly important role in changing the public discourse on development and gender, on the nation and notions of national pride and shame. I use the vantage point of media to foreground how gender has been used in the overall production of a new discourse and developmental model partly because I have worked on it. But more significantly because the media has increasingly occupied an overarching space in public discourse and has a key role in legitimising the new developmental model in the national imaginary. There has been a celebratory mood since the early 1990s of an India at last free from the shackles of a mistaken project of Nehruvian socialism. There is a transformed visibility of the public; new possibilities of the growing middle class and fractions of the lower middle class; new sensibilities and aspirations; new gender identities; and new ideas of leisure, pleasure and consumption. Together they have tangibly worked towards producing new aspirations of success and freedom, a heightened sense of individuated selves so critical for a consumption-driven society. Along with these major recasting of gender and class identities in the media,[8] gender issues resurface also in a new fashion directly in the corporate world which I look at, albeit sketchily, below. I draw from an earlier writing of mine to illustrate this 'reconfigured' idea of 'feminism'. Readers would note that the discussion below rests on the theme *women and work* – key feminist issues from the early days of WRPE (Chaudhuri 1996) and central to women studies since the mid-1970s. The issue here is however starkly different:

> ... A writing on *'women at work'* initiates the discussion by suggesting that 'dressing for work must rank high in the list of life's arduous-but-inescapable chores ... a dilemma' but suggests that better

days are here now for 'Savio Barretto presents workwear that will ease your journey into the boardroom'.

> ... women over the ages have learned to use their ingenuity, creativity, even daring to adapt – centuries ago, a cave woman somewhere would have discovered that soft fluffy rabbit fur, while nice for a stroll through the jungle, was no good near the cooking ire. Quite the same way, one imagines that a woman today would discover, that the sari while a sophisticated ensemble, isn't refined after a train journey, or a drive through hot, grimy city roads. *So, is the Indian woman condemned to a lifetime of endless inevitabilities? Must she quietly resign herself to helplessness when choosing to dress to work?* Not really. Especially not if designer Anita Dongre has her way ... And while what you choose to wear is really a very personal choice ... it's up to us designers to cater to that ... *Today's Indian woman is different from her predecessor. She is more comfortable with herselj and her body. She doesn't find a need to shy away from expressing herself. She is not afraid of trying new things, even what the close-minded call 'western'. And what's more, she is doing it all looking good.* (eLan August September 1999, emphasis mine, cited in Chaudhuri 2000)

The phrase which reiterates that "what you choose to wear is a very personal choice 'but' it's up to us the designers to cater to it" is illustrative of the thesis that the concept of identity is necessarily defined by two opposites – sameness and difference. To be unique is to be the same in two senses – to be identical to others in your class (and different from those in 'other' classes) as well be identical to yourself over time. What for us here is important is to note how the idea of women's work itself shifts away from an earlier centrality accorded to labour of the working class and peasantry. What also shifts is a focus from collectivities to the individual.

The Corporate Vision: Brand India or India Incorporation

Often today the nation itself is referred to as India Incorporation or Brand India and there has been an incredible move towards corporatisation in all spheres including that of the academia and other domains of knowledge production. The corporate language has acquired a legitimacy that has increasingly been difficult to challenge. Not surprisingly, the gender question and feminism itself has also been subject to reconfigurations. Advertisements and sponsorships have played a huge role in redefining dominant public discourse. We have seen above how the very term 'feminism' has undergone a shift that moves it away from a collective emancipatory project to a lifestyle statement of choices.

There are other moves within the corporate sector to implement what they perceive more gender-friendly work space. One would like to describe it as a kind of corporatisation of gender rights. I draw upon just one example from the January 2008 issue of the magazine *India Today Woman* to illustrate this. How does one look at such moves? Mainstreaming? What does this imply for the women's movement? A two full-page advertisement with three shelves of shoes, placed some distance (space) from each other, has a brief write up. The title is 'Match Point'.

> Four companies redefine gender equality and are recognized by the Nasscom INDIA TODAY *Woman* awards for excellence in gender inclusivity as they strive to create work paces for women that enable them to excel.
>
> The IT industry has been busy wooing women. And why not? A Nasscom study predicts that the percentage of women in the IT industry will grow from 30 to 45 per cent by the year 2010. *Gender inclusivity aims at creating work spaces to entice a college graduate, a career woman and a mother.* Recognizing this change, Nasscom and *India Today Woman* announced winners of the corporate awards for *Excellence in Gender Inclusivity*, recognizing companies that have implemented outstanding practices in promoting gender empowerment. The independent team of judges choosing the winning companies was a veritable who's who: N.R. Narayana Murthy, Chairman, Infosys Technologies Ltd; Aroon Purie, Editor-in-chief, India Today Group; Kiran Karnik, President, Nasscom; Vinita Bali, Managing Editor, Britannia Industries Ltd., Hema Ravichander, Strategic HR Advisor and Rekha Jain, Professor, IIM, Ahmedabad. (emphasis mine)

Quite clearly, 'gender' has been increasingly mainstreamed which was a desired intent of women's movements. What however has happened in the course of things is that the broader vision of a just society and a developmental model that underscored the role of a welfare state (and which was sought to be gendered) itself has been radically redefined. And significantly in a socially transformed Indian society we have had not just expected support for the new model from beneficiaries such as corporations and a section of the middle class. But also from some sections of social movements which saw an increasing integration of India into world capitalism as potentially liberating for marginalised sections.

III

Conclusion

Discernible in the dominant ideological paradigm in India is that an earlier relative privileging of workers as nation builders is replaced by a rhetoric governed almost entirely of capitalists or 'captains of industry' as nation builders. The Finance Minister and Prime Minister of India have been routine participants in award ceremonies to captains of industries in recent years. In one the Finance Minister made an interesting distinction between what he called an earlier era of organic development of capitalism where Indians built industries and the present stage where they should buy off already established industries in major global take over. NDTV broadcasted live its awards for the Indian of the Year 2008, hosted in Taj Mansingh Hotel on 17th January 2008 attended by among others industrialists, politicians, the Prime Minister and Finance Minister. The anchor introduced the event mentioning that "India's best and brightest have come together in the room" and that today it is economics, not politics that drives the world. I think both statements emerge as the apparently unproblematic common sense of the neo-liberal era. Indeed politics is seen as disruptive to development. Not surprisingly, 'women's empowerment' is viewed as constructive, 'women's unionisation and political movements' as obstacles to the furthering of neo-liberal policies, now termed 'reforms'. Yet at this very juncture there are restless claimants to the party. Indeed Indian nationalism is broader than ever before with more sections engaged with it. Yet, at the same time, the language of nationalism has changed both because the nature of capital has changed and the social base of capitalists has changed. The globe is the playing field even as the regions and marginalised groups stake claims. Debates on gender and development clearly reflect this.

Notes

1. Sharmila Rege writes: "History of late colonial India has always prioritised Indian nationalism, such that it came to be assumed that the world of political action and discourse can be comprehended only through the categories of nationalism, imperialism and communalism. The radical historiographies of colonial India, though they emphasized the autonomous role of peasants, labour and other subaltern groups, equated the historiography of colonial India with that of Indian nationalism .... The non-brahmanical

re-constructions of historiography of modern India ... have underlined the histories of anti-hierarchical, pro-democratising collective aspirations of the lower caste masses which are not easily encapsulated within the histories of anti-colonial nationalism. In fact these histories have often faced the penalty of being labelled as collaborative and have therefore being ignored in a historiography which is dominated by narratives of nationalism" (Rege 1998).

2. In other words, there are differences not just about its differential impact on a beneficiary middle class and impoverished masses but of the differential impact on sections such as dalits, tribes, and even fractions of the lower middle class.
3. Interventions in Afghanistan have often sought to be legitimised by all the "good things" that it has brought to Afghan women. The global attention on trafficking of women itself has been debated intensely, with some arguing that strict controls over western borders is an issue that has driven some of the western policy makers to focus on it. Debates on reproductive health have been yet another issue.
4. Mary John writes: "Unbeknownst to its team of authors, this report was meant to be the country study for India at the first International Year for Women in 1975 organised by the UN". See John 2004 (note 12: 131).
5. What defines neo-liberalism? Neo-liberalism is not a unified economic theory or political philosophy – it is a label denoting an apparent shift in social-scientific and political sentiments that manifested themselves in theories and political platforms supporting a reform of largely centralised post-war economic institutions in favour of decentralised ones, seeks to shift control of the economy from the public to the private sector, pushes for free trade, removal of tariff barriers, 'undistorted' market prices, i.e., governments would refrain from policies that would alter prices, export-led development to mention some features.
6. In an interview, Radha Kumar said: "I would say that the women's movement in India has grown so hugely that it is difficult to categorise it as one movement; rather there is a focus on women at different levels by almost every social and economic group. *Perhaps the one defining distinction of the past decade has been a thrust towards encouraging women's self-help and entrepreneurship skills – this is a trend that is reflected in the corporate world, government planning, NGOs and women's groups*" (2008, emphasis mine).
7. See Archana Prasad on Social Compliance Audit in Chaudhuri (2010).
8. See Maitrayee Chaudhuri (1998, 2000, 2001, 2010).

References

Breman, Jan. 2004. 'Return of Social Inequality: A Fashionable Doctrine', *Economic and Political Weekly*, 39 (35): 3869–72.

Butalia, Urvashi. 2000. *The Other Side of Silence: Voices from the Partition of India*. Durham, NC: Duke University Press.

Chaudhuri, Maitrayee. 1982. 'Sociology and Women's Studies', *Social Scientist*, October: 21–29.

——. 1993. *The Indian Women's Movement: Reform and Revival*. Delhi: Radiant.

——. 1996. 'Citizens, Workers and Cultural Emblems: An Analysis of the First Planned Document in India', in Patricia Uberoi (ed.), *State, Social Reform and Sexuality* (211–35), New Delhi: Sage.

——. 1998. 'Advertisements, Print Media and the New Indian Woman', *Social Action*, 48 (3): 239–52.

——. 2000. 'Feminism in Print Media', *Indian Journal of Gender Studies*, 7 (2): 263–88.

——. 2001. 'Gender and Advertisements: The Rhetoric of Globalisation', *Women's Studies International Forum*, 24 (3/4): 373–85.

——. 2010. 'Indian Media and Its Transformed Public', *Contributions to Indian Sociology*, 44 (1 & 2): 57–78.

Deshmukh, Ranadive et al. 2005. *Micro-credit, Poverty and Empowerment: Linking the Triad*. New Delhi: Sage.

Hensman, Rohini. 2004. 'Globalisation, Women and Work: What Are We Talking About?', *Economic and Political Weekly*, 39 (10): 1030–84.

John, Mary E. 1996. 'Gender and Development in India, 1970s–1990s: Some Reflections on the Constitutive Role of Contexts', *Economic and Political Weekly*, 31 (47): 3071–77.

Kabeer, Naila. 2005. 'Is Microfinance a 'Magic Bullet' for Women's Empowerment? Analysis of Findings from South Asia', *Economic and Political Weekly*, 40 (44 & 45): 4709–18.

Kalpagam, U. 1994. *Labour and Gender: Survival in Urban India*. New Delhi: Sage.

Krishnaraj, Maithreyi. 2005. 'Research in Women Studies: A Need for a Critical Appraisal', *Economic and Political Weekly*, 40 (28): 3008–17.

Kumar, Radha. 2008. 'Defining Development'. *infochangeindia.org*. (Accessed on 15th October 2008).

Mani, Lata. 1989. 'Contentious Traditions: The Debate on Sati in Colonial India', in Kumkum Sangari and Sudesh Vaid (eds.), *Recasting Women: Essays in Colonial India* (88–120). New Delhi: Kali for Women.

Mazumdar, Vina. 1994. 'Women's Studies and the Women's Movement in India: An Overview', *Women's Studies Quarterly*, (3 & 4): 42–53.

Menon, Ritu and Kamla Bhasin. 1998. *Borders and Boundaries*. New Jersey: Rutgers University Press.

Mishra, Yamini and Subrat Das. 2006. 'Gender Budgeting Statement: Misleading and Patriarchal Assumptions', *Economic and Political Weekly*, 41 (30): 3285–90.

Omvedt, Gail. 1990. *Violence against Women: New Movements and New Theories in India*. New Delhi: Kali for Women.

——. 2005. 'Capitalism and Globalisation, Dalits and Adivasis', *Economic and Political Weekly*, 40 (47): 4881–84.

Phadke, Shilpa. 2003. 'Thirty Years On: Women's Studies Reflects on the Women's Movement', *Economic and Political Weekly*, 38 (43): 4567–76.

Prasad, Archana. 2010. 'Sociology and the Practice of Social Compliance Auditing', in Maitrayee Chaudhuri (ed.), *Sociology in India: Intellectual and Institutional Practices* (298–319). Jaipur: Rawat Publications.

Rao, Nitya. 2005. 'Women's Rights to Land and Assets: Experience of Mainstreaming Gender in Development Projects', *Economic and Political Weekly*, 40 (44 & 45): 4701–08.

Rege, Sharmila. 1998. 'Dalit Women Talk Differently: A Critique of 'Difference' and Towards a Dalit Feminist Standpoint Position', *Economic and Political Weekly*, 33 (44): WS 39–46.

Varman, Mahendra P. 2005. 'Access, Use and Contribution of Microfinance in India: Findings from a National Study', *Economic and Political Weekly*, 40 (17), April 23rd: 1705–13.

Xaxa, Virginius. 2010. 'Tribes as Indigenous People of India', in Maitrayee Chaudhuri (ed.), op. cit. (340–59).

Websites and Newspapers

www.countercurrents.org September 30, 2004.

www.infochangeindia.org October 15, 2008.

Hindustan Times, February 1, 2005.

8

Political Empowerment of Women in India

Discourse and Reality

Swapan Kumar Pramanick

There is a lively debate and discourse on the issue of empowerment of women in India in general and their political empowerment in particular. On a global scale, from the middle of the 19th century, there was a sustained debate over whether women should have voting rights at all. Even in the established democracies of the West, the hesitation against giving voting rights to women was deep and extensive. In 1867, in Great Britain, when the House of Commons was discussing a bill wherein women were to be given equal voting rights, the motion was defeated by 73 votes to 196. This was even after J.S. Mill, a passionate advocate for equality of women, had argued most effectively to grant voting rights to women. At the beginning of the 20th century, New Zealand was the only country in the world where women had got the right to vote throughout the country (Verma 1997: 39). In Switzerland, men did not grant franchise to their women till 1971.

India was comparatively in a better position, as with the dawn of independence full voting right was granted to women on a par with men. The debate today is not whether women should get voting rights or not. This has been settled globally in their favour. The debate now is what more can be done to increase the representation or visibility of women in public life. As a device of emerging political representation for women, India is debating extensively on a quota system or a reservation system for women in elected bodies. Ever since the Constitution (73rd Amendment) Bill was accepted in 1993, giving one-third representation to women in the Panchayati Raj Institutions (PRIs), the debate has been continuing on whether and how far women are capable of exercising this right, the relation between reservation and empowerment, in what form this right can be extended to assemblies and parliament and whether women's empowerment can really be ensured by this type of device.

In the background of this debate, I intend to analyse the issues related to participation of women in politics in India. The issues involve are: (1) increasing marginalisation and peripherialisation of women in politics, (2) conceptualisation of empowerment, (3) paradoxical attitude of male-dominated politics in India, and (4) the nature and effect of 33 per cent reservation of seats and offices of women in panchayats. Of late, in some states, reservation has been extended up to 50 per cent for women. We need to closely examine these issues from a comparative perspective with empirical evidences.

Let me begin by noting that, unlike in many western countries, right to equal political participation for women including their right to vote was granted to women in India almost automatically with independence. This support for women's rights was the result of a historical legacy where women participated in the political process and fought valiantly along with men against British rule. Gandhi had a big role to play in encouraging women to participate in the freedom movement. To him, the struggle for women's equality was an integral part of the movement of *swaraj*. His method of non-violent *satyagraha* as a form of movement was particularly suitable for women. No wonder, women joined in large numbers in this form of movement as compared to the radical stream of movement sponsored by the extremists. Not only the elitist sections of women, even ordinary women joined in thousands as the forms and messages of movement were nearer to their heart. Nehru (1982: 110) therefore wrote: "Our women came to the forefront and took charge of the struggle. Women had always been there, of course, but now there was an avalanche of them which took not only the British government but their own men-folk by surprise. There were women, women of the upper and middle classes, leaving sheltered lives in their houses, peasant women, working class women, rich women – pouring out in tens of thousands in defiance of government orders and police lathis." As a result of this, mass participation by women characterised freedom movement in the 1930s and 1940s.

From this high position, women's participation in politics began to decline since independence. Even in 1952, when a large number of women freedom fighters were active and in the fray, the Congress party had only 14 women members elected to parliament. They constituted no more than 4.4 per cent of the total members of parliament. In spite of their tremendous contributions to the party, they were marginalised even within the party and had hardly any say in the decision-making process. Here again, perhaps Gandhiji's influence worked as he demanded that women should enter public life in a selfless manner and that they must not hanker after power. As he said in an inimitable style, "And you sisters, what would you do by going to parliament? Do you aspire after collector-ships, commissionerships or even the vice-royalty? I know that you would not care to, for the viceroy has got to order execution and hangings, a thing that you would heartily detest" (cited in Tendulkar 1985: 61). It is because of this patriarchal attitude that women got increasingly alienated and marginalised. Gender discrimination is however a universal phenomenon and women are excluded from positions of power both inside and outside the households. They are denied opportunities to participate in the decision-making process. Even when the decisions are to affect their well-being, they are only passive observers (Jha 2004: 61).

Applied to the political arenas, politics in India got gradually masculinised along with increasing entry of bureaucrats, criminals and corrupt persons. This is despite the fact that due to increase in literacy and spread of consciousness, women have been able to establish themselves in every walk of life. They have become successful lawyers, doctors, architects, bureaucrats, executives, engineers, and the like. Though they are there in lesser number, they have proved their capabilities in these fields beyond doubt. But surprisingly enough, women are yet considered 'untouchables' in electoral politics. If politics means service to the community, then women are certainly interested as they have joined in large number in transformative politics in community-based action programmes and in associating themselves with voluntary organisations. The nature of political process in post-independent India, the adverse attitude of the major political parties and the norms of patriarchy – all have combined to keep women away from politics. As Madhu Kishwar (1996: 2869) has argued, "marginalisation of women (in politics) is integrally related with the marginalisation of all decent people from our party politics". As regards the representation of women in parliament, she says, "Even after all the major political parties had promised 33 per cent reservation for women in legislatures, they all reverted back to tokenism when it actually came to giving party tickets. For the 1996 Lok Sabha election, the Congress (I) fielded only 49 women out of a total of 530 candidates. The BJP gave tickets to 23 women out of a total of 477 candidates. The CPI (M) gave 5 seats to women out of 77 while the CPI fielded four women out of 43 candidates. The Janata Dal fielded 2 women out of 220 candidates" (ibid.: 2867). This has led some to comment that "it was easier to get arrested for supporting democracy (during the freedom struggle) than it is to get elected to the democratic institutions that Indian nationalists were fighting to obtain" (Chowdhury et al., 1997). The dominant norm of patriarchy is also reflected in the functioning of political parties. Besides, women are found to be even more unrepresented in inner party structures, almost invisible in the actual decision-making bodies and rarely influence the more significant party policies. Nor do the political parties focus on women's issues in their agenda or reflect any concern for gender equality in their day-to-day functioning (Biju 2006: 219).

'Politics of Presence' vis-à-vis 'Politics of Idea'

Anne Phillips (1995) has raised the issue of whether women's representation in legislative bodies through quota system would actually be a subversion of democratic ethos. The assumptions behind this position are: (a) women are only entitled to represent and champion women's issues; and (b) this can be done by ensuring political representation of women in the legislative bodies. This contradicts, it is alleged, the fundamental presupposition of democracy because democracy runs on the principle of 'what' the principles or programmes, policies and plans for action on the basis of which political parties get their mandate and which they are expected to implement irrespective of 'who' the legislators are. In this understanding of representation, the personal identification of the representative, e.g., gender, caste or class, are not that important. What matters is how the programmes, on the basis of which a party gets represented, are implemented and it is on this basis that accountability is enforced.

However, this idea of representation and accountability, though valid, is not universally accepted. People, who have been nurtured in different socio-economic settings, may develop their own perspective of looking at the same phenomenon. That is the reason why the class or ethnic or gender background of the representative may be equally important. As Evelin Hust (2004: 25) argues, "Feminists of colour argued that ethnicity is an important factor in identity formation … . Class came back on the agenda as well, especially through feminists with a Marxist point of view". There are many instances when women face onslaughts as women. In some cases, women have collectively been able to stand against oppression but these are only isolated cases. Such experiments are tiny, fragile islands. The ability to survive, sustain this new found consciousness and influence the thinking, values and social institution that encase women's lives depends on such experiments becoming far more widespread (Mazumdar 1987: 13). This can be done through ensuring and guaranteeing political representation to women.

The Empowerment Issue

In the historic Beijing Declaration, it was argued that women empowerment and their full participation on the basis of equality in all spheres of society, including participation in the decision-making process and access to power, are fundamental for the advancement of equality, development and peace. The question is what is meant by empowerment and what are its parameters?

Empowerment means capacity to influence decision or participating in the decision-making process. A comprehensive definition of empowerment by Kumud Sharma (1998: 7) suggests that the term refers to "a range of activities from individual self assertion to collective resistance, protest and mobilisation that challenge basic power relations .... Empowerment, therefore, is a process aimed at changing the nature and direction of systemic forces which marginalise women and other disadvantaged sections in a given context".

It appears that 'empowerment' is a very broad notion. The question is whether membership of PRIs or even of state legislatures or parliament ensures that women are empowered. In a broad sense, unless the structural forces that lead to disempowerment – social, cultural, economic or political – or in other words, the social bases of patriarchy are challenged and changed, real empowerment will not occur. As Nirmala Buch (2010: 13) points out, "The questions continue to be raised if the 73rd Amendment without change in the socio-economic structure can change this rural leadership or its control. The power system has a tendency to incline in favour of the groups who can control the economic expectations of the people of villages. The view of a new model of open democratic participation, without class or gender as qualifiers of political participation, presupposes a modification in the traditionally highly unequal access to economic and social resources".

Empowerment then is a multi-sectoral issue having its ramifications in all areas of society. The ethical component of empowerment is autonomy – both individual and collective, whereby women as individuals can take decisions directing and shaping her own life and at the social level, women as a group are able to participate on an equal footing with men in all spheres of life – economic, social and political (Ranjana 1992: 143).

Homogeneity and Heterogeneity

The discussion on the need to expand political empowerment of women to 'power centres' of Indian polity took a new turn when the issue of representation of marginalised and backward sections of Indian women was highlighted. In the Indian context, representations of Scheduled Castes (SCs) and the Scheduled Tribes (STs) in political bodies were achieved after independence on the ground that representatives of each and every group should ensure the divergent interests of respective groups, if not the common interest of the nation. A further process of differentiation and recognition of new identities – the Other Backward Classes (OBCs) and the Muslims – has taken place later. All these have created overt rationale for sub-quotas. As it stands now, no political party is opposed, *per se*, to the extension of reservation to parliament or state legislatures. The debate now basically is regarding the introduction of sub-quota for different sections within the broader quota of reserved seats for women in these bodies.

No one would deny that there are internal differentiations among women themselves and often their interests vary. There are all categories of women – rural, urban, SCs, STs, OBCs, Muslims, upper class, lower class and the like. Hence, women's identity as a social category, for which reservation of seats in the national parliament and state legislatures in India is being bitterly contested at present, has also to contend with the differences among women based on class/caste/ethnic groups. This is because, any intervention to break the link between social structures of inequality and their political reflection in the presence and participation in the institutions of government has to address not only women's identity but also the plurality of differences (Buch 2010: 15).

Yet, in spite of the internal differences, there are certain issues which affect women as women and here all women have a commonality of interest. And, the fact that women are expected to articulate their own interests does not mean that, as citizens, they can be indifferent to or unaware of the problems of others. The logic of identity politics in a pluralistic society like ours lies in the fact that people belonging to or sharing some common identities act 'severally together'. The advocates for reservation for women only argue that the presence of a 'critical mass' of women representatives in legislative bodies will have a sensitising and facilitative effect and will be instrumental for bringing in gender equality and justice.

It is true that mere enfranchisement in participation in the legislative bodies may not be a panacea for the problems of discrimination faced by women in all spheres of socio-economic activities. Equality with equity continues to be a distant dream for them even in the developed world where high status of women has not brought about total parity in employment opportunities or non-discrimination in wage structures (Verma 1997: XV). So reservation for women has a limited role in the sense that this will bring about a further consolidation and mobilisation of women. This will also lead to identification and resolution of some additional issues which remained invisible in the domain of politics. Dahlerup, who studied the effect of increased presence of women in Nordic politics, mentions that as a result of this, some changes have occurred like the lessening of the stereotyping of women, the creation of new role models of women in public life, a change in some social conventions or the removal of open resistance against women politicians (cited in Hust 2004: 139).

Fighting Against De-politicisation Through Panchayats

In India, the process of de-politicisation of women continues in spite of constitutional provisions stipulating equal rights for women in every sphere of life. Increasing awareness and concern about women's lack of power became a major public issue since the 1970s. In 1977, the Government of India appointed a committee on the status of women in India to undertake a comprehensive examination of all the questions relating to the rights and status of women. The committee noted the failure of the earlier policy to induct women into local government bodies through reservation of a few seats as a form of tokenism and recommended the establishment of statutory rights of women in panchayats at the village level to ensure greater participation on their part. Several other factors like the declaration of International Women's Year in 1975, International Women's Decade 1975–1985, the formulation of a National Perspective Plan for Women (1988) and the establishment of a National

Commission for Women in 1992 along with the demand of the society including women activists to grant more space for women in public life – all contributed to this increased awareness about the political empowerment of women.

The case for women entering in large number in political decision-making bodies would ensure the demands of equity and justice for them. The other effects of women entry according to Medha Nanivadekar (1998: 792) are: "They will change the whole texture of present day politics. They will bring different values, preferences and perspectives into the political arena. Women's issues will find high priority on the agenda of political parties. Women's presence in decision-making positions will lead to the elimination of discrimination against women."

It was a result of all these that the 73rd Constitution Amendment Bill was passed in 1993. But, the development was not sudden as even before that in various commission/committee reports, recommendations were there for granting more space to women. The Balvantrai Mehta Committee (1957) did not give much of attention to the question of women's participation in panchayats. But, the Committee on the Status of Women (1974) favoured the establishment of statutory 'all-women panchayats' at the village level with resources for the management and administration of women and child development programmes. The Ashok Mehta Committee (1978) recommended reservation of two seats for women in panchayats and to co-opt them, if they did not come through elections in order to ensure greater representation of women in the panchayat bodies and participation in the elective process. The National Perspective Plan (1988), on the other hand, has recommended 30 per cent reservation for women in all local self-government agencies and a similar reservation for executive posts in all the three tiers of panchayats.

Many states had also introduced reservation of seats for women through legislative changes before the 73rd Constitution Amendment Act though the percentage varied from 10 as in Madhya Pradesh to 33 as in West Bengal. Kerala, through an Act of 1984, introduced 30 per cent reservation for women in the District Councils. In Orissa, 30 per cent reservation of seats for women in panchayats was introduced in 1990. In West Bengal, through the West Bengal Panchayat (Amendment) Act, 1992, provision was made for compulsory reservation of one-third of the total seats in panchayats for women. This has recently been enhanced to 50 per cent. In Karnataka, through an Act of 1985, 25 per cent of seats had to be reserved for women in the panchayats (Datta et al., 1998: 25).

The 73rd Constitution Amendment Bill provided for one-third reservation of women in the three tiers of panchayats in all the elective seats and offices. It also envisaged a significant structural change in the process of decentralisation of power and development planning at the local level by assigning to panchayat (a) preparation of schemes for economic development and social justice; and (b) implementation of schemes for economic development and social justice in relation to matters listed in the XI Schedule (which includes 29 items).

It is interesting to note that the same parliament which passed this bill has faced political paralysis in so far as the question of extending one-third reservation of seats in parliament and state legislatures is concerned. In spite of providing lip service to the issue, most of the political parties have faced dissensions within their rank and file on this question of power and privileges of a male-dominated parliament. The bill has been shelved for the last eight years. It seems that our law makers have hastily agreed to reform political institutions at grassroots level, but when it comes to sacrificing their own seats, they remain reluctant. This speaks about double standard and ideological biases of our law makers as charity for them does not begin at home.

Debate on Gender Quota as an Instrument of Empowerment

Doubts are often raised about the effectivity of gender quota as an instrument for equity and equality for women. It is argued that an interventionist strategy like enforcing women's reservation may not be helpful for women themselves. What is necessary is to build up a congenial social environment wherein women will feel empowered. Political power will automatically come out of that. Conversely, to try and push reforms without necessary social support "is mere adventurism, mere symbolism ... the damaging impact of ill thought intervention, even if the intention is noble, is no less serious than inaction and paralysis" (Singh 1997: 12). The real issue is to address the underlying causes of women's exclusion rather than enforcing a reservation. Secondly, questions are also raised about the 'representational' character of women. Given their multiple and different locations in the polity, can there be a common status of women as a group? Will it not trap women in their identity as women? And, what will happen about other identities based on class, religion and caste, for example? Thirdly, it is also argued that too much identification with organs of the state smacks of a 'growing statism' wherein a simple equation is drawn between reservations in the parliament and empowerment of women. Empowerment is a multidimensional phenomenon, an insignificant part of which is in the sphere of political empowerment. In fact, it can be argued that if in the social and economic spheres there is dependence, then political empowerment will only result in proxy figures. As Kishwar (1996: 2873) has stated, "The presence of such proxy figures in Parliament ... is actually harmful. Political socialisation of such women legislators, required for being an effective member of state assemblies and parliament, cannot take place smoothly when women members remain filially attached and politically dependent on the male party leaders". Such proxies, instead of improving the position of women, would further undermine it as, basically, the proxies serve the patriarchal interests of the family and as such their participation in politics is itself patriarchal. Furthermore, proxies enter into the political arena for protecting the constituency of their male relatives and are prepared to vacate the same, once de-reserved. Thus, their involvement in politics is not a means of self-actualisation and self-expression (Nanivadekar 1998: 1815–18).

Notwithstanding some logic in these debates, the arguments given in favour of gender quota in the context of the prevailing socio-economic situation in India appear to be far more relevant. In a forceful argument for introducing quota for women, Vina Mazumdar (1997: 14) has stated that institutionalised inequalities require 'institutionalised counter measures' in the form of reservation. She argues that this legislation has brought about 'political dynamism' of women voters. On the issue of identity of women as a group, it is true that women have also identities other than women. But the idea of group representation promotes the interests of smaller or less powerful groups under a system of majority rule. One has also to make a distinction between 'mirror representation' and 'elected representation'. The point is that women representatives will act as 'elected representatives'. The legitimacy of representation guarantees a certain freedom and flexibility on the part of the representatives to represent the heterogeneity of interests and not simply a particular form of identity. Thus, while identifying with women as women in some arenas of public life, working women can still identify with working men in other (overlapping) areas of public life (Dhanda 2000: 2969). Regarding the capacity of women to act independently, one is reminded of the famous statement of J.S. Mill. He argued that a child cannot walk, cannot be an argument of why he must not be allowed to learn to walk.

The experience of elected women representatives shows that in spite of some initial ambivalence, they have excellently adapted themselves to the requirements of the situation. Thus, as Nanivadekar (1998: 1816) argues, "The presence of women benefited by their family connections should be treated as inevitable part of the initial stage of the process of empowerment and should not be used as a tool against the policy of reservation. We find an equally large number of male politicians benefited due to the political connection of their family .... This may be a transient phenomenon that will disappear with growing involvement of a large number of women in politics. Special measures will be necessary to reduce the proxy element in the women relatives of male politicians". As a result of reservation, hundreds of thousands of women have been elected in various responsible posts. There are enough evidences to show that women can stand on their own, demonstrate their political ability, acumen and farsightedness and can take effective leadership position. The failures, if there are any, are not gender-specific.

Debate on Mechanism of Reservation

Even admitting the logic of reservation for women, the issue of mechanism of this institution is equally debatable. The existing mechanism is that these one-third seats and offices will be allocated by rotation to different seats/wards on a random basis. So, every third seat will be rotationally allotted to women at the time of every election. However, there are several arguments why this arrangement militates against the principle of representational politics.

First, there will be a tendency to ghettoise women's politics in that only women will be pitted against women. Women thereby will be confined within a limited world and not allowed to compete with men. As Kishwar (2000: 4152) holds, "Confining women to fight elections only against other women amounts to declaring that women are not competent to face men. Leadership acquired in such a manner will be seen as unnatural, artificial and as having been fostered on the electorate". Second, this will result in a forcible unseating of two-thirds of the incumbents in every general election. This compulsory unseating militates against the very basic principles of democratic representation. Since the legislators do not know whether they can retain their seat next time, accountability to their own electorate will reduce. The process of building up a rapport between the electorate and their representative will be hampered as a result. Hence, this would make the very purpose of women's representation empty and devoid of substance (Singhvi 1997: 25).

The same applies to women representatives also. Nursing their constituencies on a long-term basis will not be fruitful, because after the de-reservation of that constituency following a term, they are not likely to get a ticket for the same seat. This may be a strong disincentive for them. The principle of accountability in the politics will be lost. Men, being unseated at the last moment, may have a tendency to put their relatives as dummies who will retain their seat till the next election when they can reclaim their seat. This has been known as the '*biwi–beti* (wife–daughter) syndrome'. This is neither honourable for women nor helpful for representative democracy.

The alternative which is being suggested is either the introduction of multi-seat or dual member constituencies or the system of voluntary, party-based quotas as it is found in many democracies of Northern Europe and Scandinavia with extremely successful result. In a multi-seat constituency there can be clubbing of three members, one of which has to be a female member, the other two being elected from those male or female, getting highest number of votes. The advantage of this system is that representatives, either male or female, would not be compulsorily delinked from their constituencies and that electoral accountability can be enforced, while ensuring representation for women.

The other alternative is that, instead of identifying any particular constituency as reserved for women, mandatory regulations for political parties may be made so that at least one-third of their nominees must be women candidates, leaving it to them to choose. This would prevent a situation of ghettoisation where women candidates are pitted only against women candidates. The system would result in 'equality of opportunity' through party-based quotas. The example of Norway is suggested, where through the Equal Status Act of 1988, it is required that the contesting parties must field at least 40 per cent candidates of both the sexes on all public boards, councils and committees. Gender quotas have operated at the level of political parties in Germany also. The 'Greens' operate a 50–50 system whereas the Social Democrats in Germany reserve 40 per cent of party posts for women. Similarly, the Labour Party in UK recently 'twinned' constituencies ensuring one female representative in every two for the Scottish parliamentary elections (Dhanda 2000: 2971). This being the experience in many western countries, the argument being made is that this system is better than compulsory selection on a rotation system of one-third of the women representatives as it is followed in India in panchayat elections. It thus appears that the mandatory regulation on political parties is better than mandatory rotational reservation of constituency as it gives greater freedom to the political parties and to the electorate without compromising the necessity of enhanced representation of women.

Reservation: A Political Space

It is against this background that we can now analyse the effects and implications of reservation of seats for women in panchayats. The obvious benefits of this may be summed up as follows:

1. It has created a space for women to operate in the political sphere and has induced hundreds and thousands of them to join in politics which, otherwise, they would not have done. In West Bengal, for example, in the panchayat election of 1998, about 25,000 seats were reserved for women in the three different tiers of panchayats and assuming an average of three women per constituency, the number was a staggering 75,000. That alone justifies reservation, whatever its side effects may be.
2. A large number of women belonging to the underprivileged sections of society have entered the political arena and have been elected to panchayats. The social base of representative democracy has widened as a result of that.
3. It has legitimised and reinforced the role of women in the public sphere, particularly in formal governmental structures. This is likely to change the prevalent notions of power in a hierarchical patriarchal society. The idioms of politics are likely to change as a result of that. Instead of being based on attributes like conflict, violence and aggressiveness, it is likely to give importance to values like love, sharing and caring etc.
4. The process has increased self-esteem, confidence and motivation of women. It has started creating 'cross hierarchies' that have the potential for challenging the hierarchies of patriarchy in the long run (Nanivadekar 1998: 1818).

Allied Issues

But reservation *per se* does not guarantee much substantial things to women unless it is associated with other features. An artificial measure like reservation will ensure only quantitative participation of women. There is no guarantee that these women would behave in a way conducive to the overall empowerment of women (Nanivadekar 1998: 1818). Hence, several other complementary processes need to be initiated in order to make reservation meaningful. In a thought-provoking work, Anne Phillips shows that in the sphere of politics, the question of what is being represented is being overshadowed by who is being represented. "The separation between 'who' and 'what' and the subordination of the first to the second is very much up for question. The 'politics of ideas' is being challenged by an alternative 'politics of presence'" (Phillips 1995: 5). The dominant concern of politics should be sharing of ideas – political beliefs, goals, aspirations and not who the persons are, like Hindu or Muslim or Brahmin or Dalit or man or woman. The argument goes on that the presence of collectivities like women or SCs or STs may be necessary in view of the contextuality of the situation, but these must not overshadow the substantive issues, viz., the goals or ideals which are being pursued.

So, the issue of reservation of seats for women is related with such other important issues like the extent of power and effectiveness of panchayats, the goals which the panchayat is pursuing and the nature of composition of the leadership structure of the panchayat. Only when the issue of reservation is viewed in the perspective of these aspects, we can assess its effect.

The Situation in West Bengal

It is against this backdrop that we can analyse the performance of women panchayat members in different states of India, more particularly in West Bengal. In West Bengal, the most noticeable feature is the massive participation of women in all the panchayat elections. Whereas in pre-1993 panchayats, women's representation was just 2 per cent of the total, in 1993, out of a total 71,120 seats in the three tiers of panchayats, 24,895 seats were reserved for women – a staggering 35 per cent of the total seats. All these seats were filled up through multi-cornered contests. Certainly, this added a new dimension to the political empowerment of women. This is in contrast to Karnataka, for example, where though officially one-third reservation was made for women, many of the seats could not be filled up due to lack of women candidates (Bhargava and Subha 1995: 115). The second important aspect in West Bengal is the nature of the socio-economic background of the women representatives. Almost all the studies made in the field have shown that panchayat representatives including women come mostly from lower socio-economic classes. Prabhat Datta (1998: 52) writes: "There is no notable study as yet on either the social background of women members or on the role played by women in panchayats. But one can say on the basis of social background of all members studied by a number of scholars that most of the women members come from poor families. One micro-study, done by the State Institute of Panchayats, on the educational background of women in one block in the district of Burdwan, shows that a good number of them have either acted as voluntary trainers or as participants in the literary programmes."

Significant increase in the number of women panchayat members have had their impact on the functional aspects of panchayats – in that panchayats are giving more attention than hitherto upon welfare and developmental functions. The focus of the panchayat has now been shifted onto drinking water, school education, health care and dealing with problems relating to sanitation and fuel. They have also begun to address some of the social evils like alcoholism, domestic violence and child marriage. Expectedly, while dealing with these issues, many faced initial hostility not only within the village community, but also within the family. The struggle is not an easy one but the process of empowerment indicates that the struggle has begun (Pillai 2001: 45). It has also been found that the participation (of women) in panchayats has had an impact on their sense of self. The data on their perceptions, recognition, respect, enhanced status, confidence levels, enhanced levels of mobility and exposure, their increased political aspirations and community's perceptions and evaluation of their performance are seen as markers of empowerment process for this long disadvantaged group (Buch 2001; Datta 2001: 30). To illustrate these points, one can cite a few case studies on the West Bengal situation.

G.K. Lieten, in a study of the socio-economic background of the panchayat leaders in one block in Birbhum district in West Bengal, has cited the instance of one Alema Bibi, a secondary school teacher, who was elected to the 1983 panchayat. But after her husband was murdered, she was forced to resign by her father with the argument that Muslim ladies should not take part in public life. Fortunately, she revoked that decision and volunteered to be a candidate for the next election as well. He also gave the example of one Malati Tudu who was a tribal illiterate but became the *upapradhan* (vice-chairman) of a panchayat (Lieten 1988: 2072).

Such instances before 1993 were exceptional but have now become fairly common. In line with women's participation in other states, movements like the *Chipko* in Himachal Pradesh or the *Gangha Madhan* against BALCO in Orissa or the movement against *arak (liquor)* in Andhra Pradesh have emerged. In West Bengal also, in the Kultikuri panchayat, which was an all-women panchayat, women took an active part in organising protests against and in dismantling the liquor dens to stop alcoholism of men, in fighting against superstitions like the practice of witch hunting, in taking up issues like health and hygienic standards and in taking up development projects for women and children like the DWCRA through which women are being helped to start small-scale agro-based industries as a step to encourage self-employment among women.

The study of Chattopadhyay and Duflo (2001), who worked on 65 gram panchayats in the district of Birbhum, West Bengal, compared the types of public goods provided in reserved and unreserved panchayats. They have shown that reservation for women increases female participation and the investment priorities differ. In the reserved panchayats, there are more investments in road construction, recycled fuel equipment and drinking water.

In another survey, it was observed that (a) 87 per cent of the women respondents were the first member of the family to get represented, so the charge of women as substitute members for their males do not hold good; (b) 78 per cent of the respondents stated that people come to them directly for the redressal of their grievances, not through their family or through the party; and (c) the rate of attendance of women members and their participation in the decision-making process was also found to be very high and effective (Datta 1998).

The study made by D.K. Ghosh on the background and performance of women members of panchayat in the district of Birbhum similarly shows that they participate in large number, irrespective of caste, creed or religion. Mostly women of younger age group come to the panchayats. But, the educational statuses of women members are comparatively low vis-à-vis male members. This sometimes creates barriers in effective interaction. Regarding their economic condition, it was found that 44.12 per cent have land holdings up to 2.5 acres. Thus, there was a convergence of lower caste–lower class syndrome in the women members of the panchayat (Ghosh 1997: 291).

Of course, all the studies on the level of participation of women in panchayats in West Bengal do not reflect this optimistic situation. In one such study in the district of South 24 Parganas, it was revealed that, among 92 elected women representatives, less than 25 per cent used to take part in discussions at the panchayat meetings and those who participated seldom used to speak against the elders. The performance of more than 50 per cent of women was not satisfactory. Family pressure, lack of literacy, lack of awareness – all these factors accounted for this situation (Pramanick and Nandi 2000).

Situation in Other States

Such a mixed situation with regard to the women's empowerment in panchayats is found in other states as well. A study of 12 all-women panchayats in Maharashtra showed that though men generally welcomed the entry of women, there were anxieties also about the impact of this role reversal on the part of women (Datta 1998). A study in Haryana has revealed how the male relatives of the women members rise in prominence in the eyes of the government. A report from Orissa shows the positive impact of women's participation on other aspects of their lives (Hust 2004).

Studies from Kerala show how women are fighting against the traditional patriarchal values and are asserting their rights to stay in office. The story of Bhanwari, a woman panchayat member from Bassi block in Jaipur district of Rajasthan, is now fairly well known. She was gangraped for fighting against the evil practice of child marriage and had also to face boycott by Sarpanchas of the panchayats in that area. So, the profiles and experiences of the women panchayat members are varied. Though one does not get a neat and consistent picture, it is clear that the norms and values of a patriarchal society are being challenged by this type of political empowerment.

Conclusion

One has to remember that political empowerment of women is not an end in itself – it is just a means to an end. The overall socio-economic milieu in our society still continues to be discriminatory. Norms of patriarchy are widespread. Poverty and illiteracy are extensive phenomena and women particularly are the victims of that situation. Violence against women is pervasive and escalating. Women also have to encounter class and caste identities, not just their gender identity. Furthermore, women who come in under gender and caste reservations "have come in with their social and economic disadvantages – mostly non-literate, with little productive assets, largely dependent on wage labour and belong to a society that has fixed places for various castes and gender. These cannot be changed by a wave of the constitutional amendment wand" (Vyasulu and Vyasulu 1999: 3684).

Admitting that women's position in panchayats has significant outcome, it would be too much to believe that it would be a sufficient weapon to fight against social injustice or gender discrimination. The Kerala experience has led Isaac and Franke (2000) to argue that 33 per cent reservation is a necessary but not a sufficient condition for women's empowerment. This has to be accompanied by capacity building programme and an enabling environment within the panchayats themselves. An artificial measure like reservation will ensure only quantitative participation of women. What we need now is qualitative participation and capacity building in a conducive social environment. Massive efforts for comprehensive political education and gender sensitisation are necessary. It is true that despite the change in the role of women in the public sphere, their role in the private sphere has not changed. Proposals for training women in panchayat work are met with typical refrain, "who will make *chapattis*?" Even in West Bengal, Lieten found that the unwillingness to alter the division of labour at home and apprehension that the entry of women into the public domain would mean passing on household chores to males (Lieten 1996: 25). These are the hard realities of a patriarchal society and women as well as men have to confront the situation if women's participation has to be made meaningful.

The role of women's own organisations and the role of NGOs may be made very relevant in such an enabling programme. Women, particularly from poorer households, need their own organisations to help them break the barriers of inequality, invisibility and powerlessness and expand the base for their 'participatory development' (like SEWA in Ahmedabad, WWF in Chennai, CWDS or AIWC). These organisations can generate necessary awareness as well as increase the bargaining power of women and can confront/cooperate with other organisations to represent the collective interests of women. The NGOs may also conduct training programmes involving leadership development, capacity building, group dynamics and the like. Some of the NGOs have successfully done so for members of PRIs (e.g., SEARCH and UMA in Karnataka, FRCH in Maharashtra, CINI in West Bengal, YIP in Andhra Pradesh). In West Bengal, the State Institute of Panchayats also organises such training programmes.

To conclude, political empowerment of women has serious limitations in initiating fundamental changes in either social structure or even in gender relations. But that does not minimise the importance of women's representation in elected bodies at all levels. Given our overall failure to protect the rights of women in every sphere of social life in contemporary India, encompassing political empowerment has potential to initiate certain positive beginning. Governance can be made much more meaningful through participatory process and women's participation is a necessary, though not a sufficient condition for ensuring a smooth transformation to a better social order.

References

Bhargava, B.S. and K. Subha. 1995. 'Political Empowerment of Women: The Case of Karnataka's Experience with Panchayati Raj', in S.P. Jain and Thomas W. Hochgesang (eds.), *Emerging Trends in Panchayati Raj in India*. Hyderabad: National Institute of Rural Development.

Biju, M.R. (ed.). 2006. *Women's Empowerment*. New Delhi: Mittal Publications.

Buch, Nirmala. 2010. *From Oppression to Assertion*. New Delhi: Routledge.

Chattopadhyay, Raghabendra and Esther Duflo. 2001. 'Women's Leadership and Policy Decisions: Evidence from a Nationwide Randomized Experiment in India', IED Discussion Paper 114, Boston University, Institute for Economic Development.

Chowdhury, N. and Others. 1997. 'Redefining Politics: Pattern of Women's Political Engagement from a Global Perspective', in Barbara Nelson and Najma Chowdhury (eds.), *Women and Politics Worldwide*. New Delhi: Oxford University Press.

Dhanda, Meena. 2000. 'Representation for Women: Should Feminists Support Quota?', *Economic and Political Weekly*, 25 (33): 2969–76.

Datta, Prabhat. 2001. 'Women in Panchayats', *Kurukshetra*, December: 30–32.

——. 1998. *Major Issues in Development Debate*. New Delhi: Kanishka.

Datta, S., S. Bandyopadhyay and K. Pakrasi. 1998. *Impact of Women's Empowerment: A Pilot Study of West Bengal Panchayats* (unpublished report). Joshi Adhikari Institute of Social Studies, West Bengal.

Ghosh, D.K. 1997. 'Grassroots Women Leaders: Who are they? A Study in a West Bengal District', *Journal of Rural Development*, 16 (2): 290–95.

Ghosh, B.N. 1999. 'Women Leaders in Gram Panchayat: Prospects and Constraints', *Socialist Perspectives*, 27 (1–2): 38–39.

Hust, Evelin. 2004. *Women's Political Representation and Empowerment in India*. New Delhi: Manohar.

Isaac, T.M. Thomas and R.W. Franke. 2000. *Local Democracy and Development: People's Campaign for Decentralised Planning in Kerala*. Delhi: Left Word Books.

Jha, Ashok Kumar. 2004. *Women in Panchayati Raj Institutions*. Lucknow: Anmol Publications.

Kishwar, Madhu. 1996. 'Women and Politics: Beyond Quotas', *Economic and Political Weekly*, 31 (43): 2867–74.

——. 2000. 'Equality of Opportunities Vs Equality of Results', *Economic and Political Weekly*, November 18: 4151–56.

Kumari, Ranjana. 1992. *Women in Decision Making*. New Delhi: Vikas Publishing.

Lieten, G.K. 1996. 'Land Reforms at Centre Stage: The Evidence of West Bengal', *Development and Change*, 27 (1): 111–30.

——. 1988. 'Panchayat Leaders in West Bengal District', *Economic and Political Weekly*, 23 (40): 2069–73.

Mazumdar, Vina. 1997. 'Historical Surroundings', *Seminar*, No. 457: 14–19.

——. 1987. *The First Six Years and Forward*. New Delhi: Centre for Women's Development Studies.

Nanivadekar, Medha. 1998. 'Reservation for Women: Challenge of Tackling Counter Productive Trends', *Economic and Political Weekly*, 33 (28): 1815–19.

Nehru, Jawaharlal. 1982. *The Discovery of India*. New Delhi: Oxford University Press.

Phillips, Anne. 1995. *Politics of Presence*. Oxford: Clarendon Press.

Pillai, Sudha. 2001. 'Can Panchayati Raj Improve the Scene?', *Yojana*, August, 45: 45–47.

Pramanick, S.K. and N.C. Nandi. 2000. 'Empowerment in Panchayati Raj: A Case Study of Mograhat II Development Block', *Socialist Perspective*, 28 (1–2): 29–38.

Sharma, Kumud. 1998. 'Transformative Politics: Dimensions of Women's Participation in Panchayati Raj', *Indian Journal of Gender Studies*, 5 (1): 23–47.

Singh, T. 1997. 'Empowering Women: A Symposium on Political Reservation for Women', *Seminar*, No. 457.

Singhvi, A.M. 1997. 'The Women's Reservation Bill', *Seminar*, No. 457.

Tendulkar, G.D. 1985. *Mahatma*. Vol. III, Government of India: Publications Division.

Verma, Sudhir. 1997. *Women's Struggle for Political Space*. Jaipur: Rawat Publications.

Vyasulu, P. and V. Vyasulu. 1999. 'Women in Panchayati Raj: Grassroots Democracy in Malgudi', *Economic and Political Weekly*, 34 (52): 3677–86.

9

Women, Poverty and Empowerment

Rethinking Microfinance After the Global Crisis

Anup Dash and Souvagya Laxmi Saran

The Global Economic Crisis

The recent financial crisis, which led to the most severe global recession since the Great Depression, continues to be the centre of intense public debate. Economists are still trying to figure out the causes and the magnitude of the crisis, its consequences, and strategies for its prevention in future, as governments try hard to recover from it. The crisis damaged the global economy, brought it under terrible stress with cracks in the system, and turned to the 'Big Government' to bail it out. Once again, the 'Wall Street Model' of the economy has failed. This crisis is more than just the bursting of a speculative bubble, with prices of real estate, stocks and other assets suddenly dropping. The crisis came in two waves – first the banking system collapsed, and this in turn, affected trade and industry. Stage two of the crisis is about the real economy. After these two waves, as some countries begin to recover slowly, the aftershocks of the crisis are resonating through workforces around the world. The process of corporate recovery has been described as 'jobless recovery'. As Khang argues (2009: 26–29), there is now a third wave engulfing the labour market, leaving millions without work and changing the course of their lives. For the vulnerable poor and the innocent victims in the developing world, "the crisis is not behind, but still ahead", says Dominique Strauss-Kahn, the head of the IMF (quoted in Khang, ibid.). Chen and Ravallion (2009) estimate for the World Bank that an extra 50 million people have been pushed into extreme poverty by the end of 2009 as a direct result of the crisis, and this number is expected to rise to 89 million by the end of 2010.

But, as Queen Elizabeth II, during a recent visit to the London School of Economics, very pertinently asked why no economists had forecast the crisis. The crisis has convincingly demonstrated the inadequacy of the economic model itself. A consensus is now emerging that we need to rethink about the economic system itself. Clearly, the crisis has shown the limits of the current regulatory and supervisory frameworks. The challenge is therefore to design new rules and institutions that reduce systemic risks. Corporate gurus emphasise the need for introduction of more stringent regulations, stronger risk management, and better board oversight with a robust consolidated supervision framework as the bottom line for the global corporate governance. While we do not underemphasise the importance of these debates around the question of how to repair the damaged economy, the focus of this paper is to explore ways to repair the damaged lives of the innocent victims. This leads us to focus on the social impact of the crisis and creatively pursue the promising strands of thought.

From a Gender Perspective

While we are yet to comprehend the full range of the impact of this crisis as well as its depth, duration and magnitude, what is already evident is that the most dramatic sign of the recession's severity is the state of the labour market. Although the impact is not uniform across countries, regions, sectors and different classes of people, it is most clearly *gendered*. It is not something unique to the current crisis. It has been commonly observed that during any economic crisis or restructuring, women suffer disproportionately and the extra pressures generated for coping at the household level are always passed on to women. Feminist scholars have claimed that mainstream economic paradigm is *androcentric* (Beneria and Feldman 1992; Best and Humphries 2003). Obviously, therefore, its offshoot, namely, economic policy planning is not gender-neutral, nor are the institutions which implement these plans. This is abundantly reflected in the WID–GAD debate of the 1980s (cf. Moser 1993). The *Gender and Development* (GAD) approach sought to move beyond the earlier *Women in Development* (WID) approach by focusing on the structural issues rather than merely treating women as an 'untapped resource' for the (androcentric) national economy. But this male bias still predominates our thinking, more so, in the context of the present global capitalism, because capitalism is essentially anchored in patriarchy (Vaughan 2007).

While empirical evidences of the impacts of the current crisis are still very patchy, whatever evidences have been gathered do suggest that, like other previous crises, the women and children in the poorest households bear a disproportionate share of the burden created, or added by the crisis (King and Sweetman 2010). The International Labour Organisation (ILO 2009) has observed that in most regions of the world, the economic crisis was expected to have greater impact on female unemployment rates than male. This is because, women are employed in the most precarious job, and they are most vulnerable to being laid off during economic contraction. Basing on a research conducted by the Oxfam, Dame Barbara Stocking, the CEO of the Oxfam/GB, comments: "Our research in several countries has found women to be most at risk of losing their livelihoods, whether they are garment workers in Cambodia or Shea nut collectors in northern Ghana" (2009: 54). It is estimated that up to one-third of workers in garment factories, construction and tourism in Cambodia have lost their jobs since 2008. It is however easier to estimate and quantify the effects of the crisis in the formal sector. But what makes it even more complex is the fact that it is extremely difficult to track the impact of the crisis in the informal and the *reproductive economy* where women are concentrated so heavily. Ruth Pearson (2009) argues that if we are to fully understand the economic crisis from a gender perspective, we need to explore the impact that it has on the reproductive economy, where the impact is most catastrophic.

Given the multiple constraints women suffer due primarily to the structural discrimination, women have no other choice but to work in the informal employment in spite of the inherent vulnerabilities, lower income and lack of social protection. Women's incomes are especially important for the poor households, as it is on this income the household's subsistence and their children's education and health depends. Therefore, they have to accept whatever job where they can bridge their productive and reproductive roles. In times of crisis, the twin pressures of productive and reproductive roles become overwhelming for the poor women. They are forced to work longer hours, often taking up a second or even a third job in the productive economy, while at the same time, their burden in the reproductive economy increases as the public expenditure squeezes in the social sector. They burn the candle on both ends, their tangible and intangible assets are depleted, and their basic needs for food and sleep are foregone. The lives of the vulnerable women have become more vulnerable (Horn 2009; Oxfam 2010).

The Lessons from the New Deal

In the context of the rapidly eroding livelihood base as a consequence of the global crisis, the most pressing challenge is to create employment opportunities for women. During the 1930s, when the US came under the grip of a Great Depression, Keynes famously advocated the role of the government in stabilising the economy through public investment. President Roosevelt's fiscal and job creation programmes, a result of the Keynesian economics, did help end the Great Depression. The Keynesian view of the macro relationships between the market and the government broadly held sway in most western countries until the 1980s when Milton Friedman questioned the efficiency and the ability of the (already failing) governments to deliver public goods, and championed the ideology of 'market fundamentalism'. The recent global crisis has once again brought Keynes back to the centre of public policy. We now realise that some of the basic truths on which market fundamentalists base their arguments are naïve to the point of absurdity. The events leading to the global crisis do confirm that market cannot be left to itself, and we need devices to ensure macroeconomic stability. The economy needs regulation, management and intervention. We are back again to the 'Big Government' policy. The only way to rapid economic recovery seems to be government bail out with stimulus packages and job creation to immediately deal with the problem of unemployment.

It is argued that the 'Big Government' can act as the 'employer of the last resort' in two ways: one by scaling up wage employment programmes, and second, by scaling up self-employment programmes. Wage employment programmes are certainly very important in a situation like this, but here again, as we know, women suffer a lot of discrimination in the labour market, especially as reflected in gender-wage gaps. For example, As Khitarishvili reports about Georgia, on an average, women earn approximately 57 per cent of what men do (2010: 10). Antonopoulos (2008) study shows that unskilled women in South Africa need to work an extra four hours per day, compared to unskilled men, to earn the poverty-line income in addition to an average of over two hours of unpaid work per day in their non-market (reproductive) activities. Further, in many developing countries of the world, there are already major programmes in place for employment generation designed to boost up the economic condition of the poor households, such as the one being implemented since 2005 under the Mahatma Gandhi National Rural Employment Guarantee Act (MGNREGA). This is a very well-designed programme which provides for the enhancement of livelihood security of the poor households in rural areas by providing at least 100 days of guaranteed wage employment in a year to every household whose adult members volunteer to do unskilled manual work. Under the provisions of this programme, if a person, who applies for work, is not given a job within the stipulated period, shall be entitled to an unemployment allowance from the government. But, given the problems of governance failures (such problems as corruption, lack of bureaucratic will, inefficiency, lack of transparency and other bureaupathologies) the implementation of this programme has a very poor record. Apart from the discouraging track record, governments, while designing programmes to promote employment, are often motivated more by political pressure than by efficient outcomes. I would therefore argue that self-employment programmes constitute a serious policy alternative. Further, poor self-employed women can create jobs for others in their small enterprises.

The Power of the 'Small Money' at the Bottom of the Pyramid

The mainstream attention so far has been focused around policy orientations towards the institutions that are too big to fail. We have also seen what happens when 'Big Governments' and 'Big Banks' operate in secret. In our search for solutions to the crisis we should not undermine the power of the 'small money' – microfinance – in dealing with the impacts of the crisis. We need to now turn to this world of the small money at the bottom of the pyramid and harness its potentials in rebuilding damaged lives and livelihoods. Microfinance is a very powerful and women-centric tool for changing lives of the excluded and vulnerable people through poverty alleviation and empowerment (Dash 2005). It holds enormous possibilities in the crisis-hit global economy to create a second chance for the innocent victims to move out of poverty. However, in order for microfinance to be able to make any real impact in the lives of the victims, it has to be very creatively designed as *money with a mission*. It is 'finance against poverty', or *development finance as distinct from commercial finance*. Its social goal (expressed in terms of gender and poverty) lies at its heart and is the source of its transformative power. The success of microfinance critically depends on blending values – economic with social – in embracing the double bottom line. In the context of the current crisis, microfinance can be an excellent example of how economic and social values may be leveraged through women-centred innovative programmes carefully crafted with transformative potentials. In operational terms, microfinance policy focus is bi-focal: *economic* (increasing economic growth; making markets work better for the poor; and helping poor people create their asset base and build better lives) and *empowerment* (increasing women's skills and capacities; enhancing their access to and control over resources; changing gender relations in the household and in the community; building institutions of the poor women; and enhancing their capacities to deal with oppressive power relations and structures of constraint).

But, a quick perusal of the present landscape of the global microfinance industry does lead one to conclude that microfinance is not a 'magic bullet' and that there is quite a bit wrong with microfinance (Dichter and Harper 2007). Instead of copying the initial breakthrough products, and recycling old-fashioned methodologies, we need to better align ourselves with the changing ground realities, and "stimulate a more reflective microfinance in the future than we have witnessed thus far" (ibid.: 6). Instead of hiding behind anecdotes and rhetoric, or being driven by donor hype, we need to take stock, raise questions, and re-examine the assumptions – some of which are fatal (Mahajan 2007: 243). Just as this global crisis calls for a rethinking the current world of commercial finance, we need also to rethink microfinance in order for us to realise its transformative power as a gender-sensitive tool.

Microfinance as the Lifeline for Poor Women

Microfinance over the years has developed into a world-wide industry as a very compelling tool for development. Its goal is to build better lives and create an emancipatory space for those women who are excluded from the broader institutional framework of the economy through providing a whole range of financial (and non-financial) services and products, designed to help them move out of poverty and grow along the pathways of empowerment. The growth of the microfinance movement in recent years has been enormous, as seen from the numbers of clients, the volume of donor funding to this sector, as well as the numbers and ranges of the microfinance institutions (MFIs). Given its potentials, promise and possible social impacts, especially in terms of women's empowerment and poverty eradication, a broad range of actors – state and non-state, formal and informal, corporate and philanthropic, global and local – are increasingly engaged in promoting it as a strategy to realise the Millennium Development Goals (MDGs) (Dash 2003). The Microcredit Summit Campaign was originally launched in 1997 with the goal of reaching 100 million of the world's poorest families, especially the women of those families, with credit for self-employment and other financial and business services by the year 2005. Based on the encouraging experience of its initial target and the increasing importance of the role of microfinance in realising the MDGs, the Campaign was re-launched to 2015 (to match the target year for the MDGs) with two new goals: (a) working to ensure that 175 million of the world's poorest families, especially the women of those families, are receiving credit for self-employment and other financial and business services by the end of 2015, and (b) working to ensure that 100 million families rise above the US$ 1 a day threshold adjusted for purchasing power parity (PPP) between 1990 and 2015. The first of these new goals relates to expanding outreach (building on the original goal of reaching 100 million families), while the second goal is a new addition to the Micro-credit Summit agenda with a focus on impact (to match the MDG focus on impact, e.g., in terms of reducing poverty by half).

Microfinance programmes especially target women (of the poor households), because of the critical need to move out of the complex syndrome of the growing 'feminisation of poverty'. Further, experience shows that women are a good credit risk, and that women invest their income toward the well-being of their families. At the same time, women themselves benefit from the higher social status they achieve within the home when they are able to provide income (Microcredit Summit Campaign). MFIs thus hold a great promise to make 'another world possible' for women. They can make a difference in the lives of poor women by addressing their practical gender needs as well as their strategic gender needs, through enhancing women's access, control, choice and voice in different spheres and at different levels of the society. Only when do they efficiently achieve these impacts on the ground in a convincing and demonstrable way, can they be legitimately regarded as competing players of a 'Smart Economics' (Buvinic and King 2007).

What is Wrong with Microfinance: A Reality Check

However, the celebration of microfinance as a 'magic bullet' among the donors and microfinance communities is based more often on anecdotes and rhetoric. The knowledge about the real social impacts of MFIs is partial and contested, while the assumptions behind microfinance programmes are not always supported by credible results. There have been, of course, some studies which show that microfinance has some positive economic and social impacts (Otero and Rhyne 1994; Khandkar 1998; Holcombe 1995; Hossain 1988). But, in situations of observed impacts, the question of attribution and causality remains a major unresolved issue. On the other hand, there are others that point to rather negative impacts (Montgomery 1996; Rogaly 1996; Adams and von Pischke 1992; Wood and Sharrif 1997). There are still others to show that microfinance has some beneficial impacts, but claim that MFIs do not reach out to the poorest, as is so often claimed (Mosley and Hulme 1998).

While the microfinance institutions are increasingly faced with the difficult challenges of credibly proving the impact of their programmes in the lives and behaviour of the clients, their households as well as the wider communities, there is, at the same time, a growing concern that MFIs are falling short of their hype. A recent assessment and a stocktaking of the field, made by leading experts who are microfinance 'insiders', drawn from around the world, very authoritatively concludes that in spite of its centrality in the donor policy agenda in the mainstream development paradigm, microfinance still remains 'an immature and unproven field' in some important ways, and we do not really know where we stand (Dichter and Harper 2007: 4). The essays presented in this book, representing the rich diversity of experience within microfinance industry in the global landscape, with the breadth of issues covered and the depth of their analysis, do suggest that *too much is claimed for microfinance, and that expectations are grossly exaggerated*, and they all add up to a powerful argument that *there is quite a lot wrong with microfinance* (ibid.: 257; emphasis added). Exaggerated expectations can and does have serious damaging effects on the poor women clients, as 'feminisation of debt' (the other side of 'credit') can destroy a client's self-respect and even her life.

MFIs are seriously constrained by a limited ability to reach the very poor (Sebstad and Cohen 2001). As Mahajan claims, microcredit, in reality, is "barely adequate as an instrument of poverty alleviation" (2007: 249). Rahman concludes his analysis of Bangladesh with the observation that "(t)he poverty fighting power of microfinance is limited" (2007: 202). Frances Sinha's research of Indian SHGs clearly shows that "even after five or seven years, around half of member households are still below the poverty line" (2007: 76). Microcredit only moves money to get quick superficial results on the ground, but with little long-term developmental impact, yet it is defended with development rhetoric. Their products and services are too standardised to go beyond credit which are more useful, appropriate as well as needed by the poor women (such as savings, insurance, remittance etc.), to stimulate the core of sustainable local economic and social development and become more flexible and innovative to creatively interact with the up-end business market and the mainstream economy, to develop successful coping strategies (among the poor women clients) in times of financial crises and emergencies. There is a growing consensus within the microfinance industry that the relationship between microfinance and poverty reduction is not straightforward. Poverty is multidimensional, gendered, and just as the causes are complex so is its solution. The current global crisis makes it evident that the macroeconomic shocks, structural risks and the negative externalities created by the speculative capitalist economy – all interacting with a complex set of institutions at the global level – can all cumulatively make a complex phenomenon even more complex. Therefore, it is extremely important and timely that we make a critical reality check so that we may reorient this world of the small money at the bottom of the pyramid to be able to grow as a compelling and transformative force in the lives of the poor women.

The Left and the Right Wings of Microfinance

Microfinance institutions are diverse – by type, size, context, goal, programmatic emphasis, approach, methodology and lending technology etc. However, most of them share a core mission of poverty reduction. The success of these MFIs therefore lies critically in effectively blending values – economic with social. Balancing these two goals often proves to be extremely difficult and challenging since they appear to be uneasy bed fellows in practice. As a result, the pendulum within most MFIs tilts towards any one of the two as they navigate in this difficult space. With the mix of goals, the question is how to deepen outreach to poorer household and scale-up their gender impact on a sustainable basis. This has aroused an intense and passionate debate among the microfinance providers, promoters and others in the microfinance field, which, in turn, has given rise to two different camps with their respective paradigms, namely, the 'poverty lending paradigm' and the 'financial sustainability paradigm'. The broad differences between these two paradigms are presented in the following table:

	The Left Wing	*The Right Wing*
Paradigm	Poverty lending	Financial sustainability
Objective	Poverty reduction, advance well-being, empower the poor women, address their multiple constraints through provision of multiple services, bottom-up social transformation	Entrepreneurship building, develop sustainable financial institutions (MFIs), design viable financial services and products, profit at the bottom of the pyramid
Outreach	The hard core poor	The entrepreneurial poor, economically active or the, 'deserving' poor
	The depth of outreach	The cost of outreach
Products and Services	A range of products and services complementary to credit, (credit ++), subsidise	Minimalist (credit only) level playing field
Methodology	Loan ceiling, client development and graduation	Full cost recovery, financial discipline, institutional systems for efficiency
Client Orientation	Clients as 'makers and shapers' of their lives, focus on clients, clients need capacity	Clients as 'users and choosers' of services, focus on institutions, clients need capital
Investments Type	Mix of donations, subsidy and market rate capital, social mission with below market rate financial returns, social return on investment	Market rate capital, risk-adjusted market rate financial return, financial return on investment
Bottom Line	Double bottom line (social and economic)	Single bottom line (only financial)

Source: Dash (2009).

The microfinance industry remains a divided house in terms of the institutional value and the resultant approach and method of MFI – one stream pulling it in the direction of a narrow-focused, minimalist credit only approach, while the other moves in the direction of a broad-based microfinance. As a result, a 'clash of methods' (*Methodenstreit*) has been 'a central feature of microfinance' (Von Pischke 2007: 137).

The Industry Tilts towards the Right Wing Paradigm

Microfinance has gone through a transition in operational emphasis in recent years especially under the hegemonic influence of neo-liberalism. This is being promoted since the 1990s by most donor agencies through the 'Microfinance Best Practices' guidelines developed by the USAID,

World Bank and other multi- and bi-lateral donors. The ideological hegemony of neo-liberalism over donor thinking in recent years has resulted more and more in the commercialisation of microfinance, pressing MFIs hard to gravitate towards the financial sustainability paradigm. The main arguments advanced in this direction are that donor money is erratic and unreliable, there is a huge market for microfinance with 500 million people out of financial system, level the playing field (subsidy creates distortions in the market), microfinance is not a magic answer to global poverty, focus on institutional sustainability as 'the bottom line', institutions have to cover their costs in order to be sustainable, poverty targeting with small loans is expensive and reduces sustainability, efficiency of MFI is judged in terms of financial performance, don't go to people who don't have 'active' economic activity. Microfinance is for the 'deserving poor' only, engage the bottom half in growth, give the poor purchasing power, and create profit at the 'bottom of the pyramid'.

Although strong in terms of the social goals, the major problems with the philanthropic capital market (donor and subsidised funding) are that: (a) the funding generated in the philanthropic capital market is highly inadequate for the current needs to meet the, MDGs fight global poverty and create an inclusive society with empowered citizens (especially those on the wrong side of the wealth divide) to claim their rights and entitlements, and (b) it does not recycle the capital to continue its work on a self-sustained basis.

Therefore, the microfinance industry, in order to fulfil the global aspirations (as reflected in the Microcredit Summit Campaign and the MDGs), is in need of leveraging substantial new capital in order to expand its outreach and impact. This new capital will most likely come from the mainstream capital market. Accessing capital from the commercial market poses a challenge for the microfinance institutions to steer clear of the investment spectrum to show efficiency and results based on a single (i.e., the financial) bottomline. The ultimate institutional focus of the MFIs, then, shifts away from the original poverty and empowerment goals to building up large and efficient microfinance programmes so that they are profitable and fully self-supporting and can compete with other private sector banks and are able to raise funds from the international financial markets rather than depending on subsidies and donor funds from development agencies.

Focus on the institutional sustainability of MFIs has meant a shift away from the poverty focus of microfinance intervention because of the rent seeking behaviour of profit minded MFIs. This creates the danger of a 'client drift' and a 'mission drift' of the MFIs as they tend to go in search of greener pastures by rushing up-market. Martin Greeley (2004: 4) describes this mission drift as a shift from 'compassion to capitalism'. There are inherent trade-offs between poverty outreach and sustainability. The empirical truth is that the further down the poverty scale one goes, the less businesslike becomes the micro-enterprises, and the more expensive becomes the delivery of services. Successive loan cycles do not grow as much as the (commercially-oriented) MFIs would want them to. It is important to accept that the real-life world of the poor women does not move as fast as the logic of the economy assumes. Therefore, microfinance capital, in order to be effective and produce the desired impact, should be understood as 'patient capital', designed for investment for long-term social profits rather than short-term market value. But, more and more, as the industry matures, 'efficiency' replaces 'effectiveness' and 'impact' as the management mantra of the MFIs.

The Rating Agencies and their Tools

A consequence of this misplaced emphasis on sustainability over outreach (largely the result of the perceived trade-off between the two) and the focus on 'efficiency' during the last few years has been the attention given to the process of institutional development in terms of building the managerial, technical and systems capacity within the institutions to drive towards sustainability. The pressure to be 'sustainable' required MFIs to measure, monitor and manage their financial performance very carefully (e.g., in terms of portfolio quality, profit and loss, subsidy dependence etc.) and MFIs needed to build up their institutional health through cost control, 'client' responsiveness to be demand-driven, market innovations, and going to scale in a competitive environment. Thus, we have robust and standardised performance standards, sophisticated tools, and measures for the financial performance of the MFIs, while there is a serious lack of standards and tools to measure the social performance of the MFIs and their impact in terms of building better lives for the poor women not only by enhancing their income, but more importantly by enhancing their 'capability space', 'freedom' and 'agency' to deal with the oppressive structures of subordination. Once again, the focus has been on the means (institutions) and not on the end (the poor women).

The 'rating instruments', currently used by the donors to assess the recipient institutions, suffer from some serious weaknesses. Thus, for example, Lowell et al. (2005: 40) in their study point out three major weaknesses of the rating agencies: (a) they rely too heavily on simple analysis of ratios derived from poor-quality financial data, (b) they overemphasise financial efficiency while ignoring the questions of programme effectiveness, and (c) they generally do a poor job of conducting analysis in important qualitative areas. Further, they argue that "donors make important decisions using potentially misleading data and analysis, and *the agencies' potential to do harm may outweigh their ability to inform*" (emphasis added). In most instances, the donor sees only the score but no explanations, and therefore can easily be misled by these oversimplified scores the way the MFIs report their finances. Lowell et al. in their essay quote Bruce Sievers, former executive director of the Walter and Elise Haas Fund, who says: "Sure these rating agencies are serving the donors, but it is irresponsible not to educate donors on the many aspects of effectiveness, beyond the financials, even if you can't measure them all" (ibid.: 43). Therefore, the rating system needs to capture the realities of the MFIs and the distinct nature of their double bottomline portfolio. They should be able to integrate a social rating with their financial rating in their tools, and thus be able to comment on the important intangibles that are so important to the operations of the MFIs. The rating organisations ought to be able to address the questions of social impact.

The field of microfinance is today strong with performance indicators, mostly in the form of ratios, to measure the financial health of the institution (e.g., portfolio quality ratios, efficiency ratios, profitability ratios, etc.) and sophisticated systems of indicators like the CAMEL system (Capital Adequacy, Asset Quality, Management, Earning, Liquidity) and the PEARLS system (Protection, Effective Financial Structure, Asset Quality, Rates of Return and Costs, Liquidity, Signs of Growth) for rating the health of the MFIs. But it remains very weak in terms of the corresponding measures of social performance. Therefore, the recent growth of the global status of microfinance does not mean that it has reached maturity as an industry, nor does it mean that it has a secure future. Financial performance tools tell us about the health of the institutions, but not about the health of their clients. In the absence of these tools, we cannot say whether microfinance initiatives help the poor women to move out of poverty and build along the pathways of empowerment – whether they help households build sustainable livelihoods or lead them to take risks which they regret later, whether they help women strengthen their position and achieve equity and bargaining power within the household and the wider community, or they are subjected to more tensions and violence, whether they empower women or they increase their vulnerability by feminisation of debt. While there have been a number of studies exploring these questions, the answers remain inconclusive.

The New Breed of 'Efficient' MFIs

While the great debates within the industry (e.g., around poverty reach and institutional sustainability, the vexed topic of subsidy etc.) remain unresolved, the pendulum steadily swings more and more in the direction of the *right* (the 'institutional sustainability' paradigm). The 'rush to do good' has practically been translated to a 'rush to grow'. As a result, the microfinance industry has produced "a pandemic of revenue-maximising institutions, many of which have *forgotten* the social mission they may once have had" (Rippey 2007: 113; emphasis added), breeding a race of financial institutions "with no conscience at all" (ibid.: 115). The interests of the poor women borrowers are often in conflict with the interests of the institutions, and when interests diverge, donors have shown more interest in the well-being of the institutions at the cost of the well-being of the poor women borrowers. The rush to grow with pre-packaged and easily installed microfinance programmes, resulting in a reckless and indiscriminate lending with bad products, could have untoward longer-term effects on the supposed beneficiaries, and may even be anti-development by providing 'unhelpful help' (Ellerman 2007: 154).

'Best practices' are evolved and promoted that clearly argue for commercialisation, which, in effect, has meant a 'mission drift' and a 'client drift' for MFIs. In her recent thought-provoking essay, Kim Wilson rightly asks, "Why incorporate pseudo-business practices and call them 'best' in the name of development?" (2007: 103). Subsidy, so much despised in the name of levelling the playing field and one of the most controversial issues in microfinance, is not always a bad thing. But, perversely, "subsidies never travelled to the poor in the form of low interest rates, great service, or social impact' but stays with the MFI, often off its books" (ibid.: 98). Ironically, the reality of subsidy is that those MFIs that criticise it most vocally are the ones that dispense and receive the most subsidies.

The proliferation of more and more MFIs, one would expect, would give rise to a 'healthy' competition. Instead, it degenerates and distorts the microfinance marketplace as these rent-seeking players vie for the same market and the same client base/territory. In their drive to be sustainable, MFIs do struggle to cover costs. The easiest way for that is to charge high interest rates, and MFIs do enjoy a 'quasi-monopoly position' in terms of loan pricing. The rates of returns are often lower in the enterprises supported through micro loans to women than the interest rates, which means that the long-term impact is impoverishment of the client. Kim Wilson (2007) reflects from her CRS experience that through microcredit the poor were poor twice – firstly, from the initial circumstances and secondly, from high interest rates.

Financial sustainability-oriented MFIs, in their efforts to be more and more efficient in managing the single bottom line (financial), design minimalist credit programmes to be cost-efficient and profitable. The core assumptions underlying their programmes are that the poor are budding entrepreneurs, who, with access to formal financial services, would pull themselves out of poverty through business development, asset accumulation and wealth creation. They do target the women for strategic 'efficiency' reasons (rather than any strategic 'impact' focus), because women save and repay better than men. Small income generation activities can be integrated into their culturally patterned gender roles within the household. Further, as the argument goes, women spend their income for household welfare more than men. Thus, any increase in income automatically enhances household welfare and benefits the entire household. Moreover, group-based microfinance programmes target women because women are easier to organise. The Social Capital Theory suggests that women are stronger in bonding, and that group social mechanisms are stronger among women. Groups themselves are promoted by the microfinance institutions for instrumental reasons: the group has a comparative information advantage about members the groups serve as social collateral and are jointly liable; the groups perform key functions for the MFI through peer screening, peer monitoring and peer pressure against default – thus efficiently managing the problems of adverse selection, information asymmetries and loan defaults. This obviously enhances the efficiency of the MFIs in terms of lowering their credit risks, reducing their transaction costs and ensuring high repayment rates.

Yet, the MFIs hardly invest on the groups to build up their capacity as organisations of the poor women. The groups are not even remunerated for providing these services. On the other hand, the interest rates on loans through groups are higher than individual loans. Groups do impose heavy burdens on the members in terms of time, risk and loss of privacy. Further, the myths about the role of social capital and peer lending have obscured the complexity of group dynamics. In the context of Bosnia and Herzegovina, Bateman (2007: 208) argues that the present model of microfinance "very actively destroys social capital". While community development and support activities are recast as commercial and strict cost-recovery operations, there is "a degeneration of local solidarity, interpersonal communication, volunteerism, trust-based interaction and goodwill" (ibid.: 219). In spite of that clients do repay their loans, albeit under duress, thanks to the social mechanism of peer pressure. Instances of threats, seizure of their household articles by SHG members/MFI staff, arrests by the police, physical violence etc. are common to ensure loan repayment. So, not only that the costs of credit are high for the client, but the risks of borrowing are also great.

The Questions of Impact

The heavy winds of neo-liberal ideology blowing over the world of microfinance push MFIs more and more towards commercialisation, and narrow down their focus to the single bottom line of profit, and seriously constrict the definition of 'good practice'. The microfinance field as a whole finds itself burdened by significant misalignments in goals, strategies, priorities, and methodologies as profit assumes primacy over poverty. They, however, do have a gender focus and do target women (albeit, for practical 'efficiency' reasons). The assumption under these programmes is that increasing women's access to microfinance will (automatically) lead to economic empowerment. Further, they advocate their impact on the clients' lives with the argument that if clients pay back their loans on time and come back for repeat loans (of larger amounts) then the programme must be having a positive impact. In this vein, Elisabeth Rhyne argues that institutional sustainability is the best indicator of impact on the poor. Referring to the Bolivian context, she writes: "When I see clients streaming into MFIs (the Market test) and institutions growing and shedding dependence on subsidies (the institutional market test), and a sustainable financial sector serving the poor emerging in a country (collective impact), that's when I know microfinance is worth it" (quoted in Tawney 2004: 3).

The issue of empowerment, as feminist scholars have shown, is extremely complex and too naïve to be explained in a reductionist way as above. Obviously, access (to credit) does not automatically translate into a positive impact. Focusing on 'access' therefore provides only a partial view of the success, because it ignores the structural and cultural barriers women face in transforming access to resources into control over them (Kabeer 1999). MFIs need to shed more light on the extent to which, if at all, access to financial services enables poor women to address their practical gender needs on a daily basis as well as their strategic gender needs. Although, as Molyneux (1985) argues, strategic gender needs go to the very core of the structure of patriarchal power (abolition of unequal control over resources, of coercive gender division of labour, ending sexual exploitation, male violence, and establishing political equality, women's control over their own bodies etc.) and involves transformations at the structural level over a much longer time period, it does not need to be in opposition with the everyday practical needs of women. The process of transformation may begin more modestly with the constraints that prevent women from exercising their individual agency on a practical everyday basis. Kabeer (2005: 4710) rightly says, "(m)eeting the daily practical needs of poor women in ways that transform the conditions in which they exercise their agency can be seen as part of the process by which they are empowered to take on some of the more deeply entrenched aspects of their subordination". Increasing women's access to income is therefore an important aim of microfinance development, but it is not the sole objective (Mayoux 1995), and should not be used as the sole measure of its success.

Building *Bonsai* Enterprises in the Female Space

Feminist economists have argued that capitalism is patriarchal (Vaughan 2007) and the orthodox mainstream economy suffers from an inherent 'androcentric bias' (Best and Humphries 2003). In making a historical analysis of the women's relationship to the world of money making and investment in the 19th century America, Yohn (2006) describes the women entrepreneurs as 'crippled capitalists' in the otherwise 'male preserve' of financial markets, credit systems and capitalist accumulation. They were crippled under the larger ideological climate that shaped popular beliefs about the 'natural (in)capacities' of women. Women lacked, it was believed, the "element of reason and logic found in men", and thus, they were unable to "reason the way that is indispensable to a successful speculator" (ibid.: 89). Thus, women lacked the 'mental power' for the great operations of the 'masculine precinct'. In the gendered world of moneymaking, female 'invasion' of the bastions of male power (ibid.: 86–87) was actively discouraged, and women were expected to turn their energies to the production of social capital and 'social housekeeping'. Those who dared to enter the male world of finance could expect to "have their reputation and morals questioned" (ibid.: 89). Obviously, women's business in this period remained small, under-capitalised, and limited in their reach and profit potential, as women had to carve out an alternate and female space in which business is to be done by highlighting the connections between their entrepreneurial activities and domestic concerns.

What has changed today from the 19th century scenario is that women are today encouraged, promoted and organised to do business and run enterprises as a matter of public policy – more so through microfinance programmes aimed at poor women. But, what women have still not been able to do is to challenge the gendered nature of enterprise development. Even today, as in the 19th century, in spite of all the efforts and investments to promote women entrepreneurs through the microfinance programmes, women enterprises remain small, under-capitalised and limited in their reach and profit potential, as women have to run them within the 'female space' harmonising their productive and reproductive roles – thanks to the microfinance programmes under the hegemonic neo-liberal ideological order and the 'androcentric' capitalist system.

Women's enterprises are under-funded with smaller start-up capital in the first instance compared with men's enterprises, and the range of their business options is severely limited by the need to integrate the productive and reproductive roles, restricting them to only those kinds of business which provide the needed flexibility. Thus, these enterprises are mostly home-based, because of constraints in their mobility. For these same reasons, women were more committed than men to sticking with their business, even if better wage-paying jobs or more profitable opportunities were to appear. Home (or close to home)-based operations mean that interruptions to their work are frequent (arising out of the need to simultaneously attend to their reproductive work) with the resultant loss in the efficient functioning and loss of productivity in the enterprise. Hence, they dedicate less total time to their business than their male counterparts. They reduce the geographical scope of their business activity to cut down travel time. Women hire fewer employees than men for their enterprises, and again they hire mostly same-sex workers from the known social circles because the relationships are easier, at the cost of efficiency. The proportion of money from the profits reinvested for the growth and development of the enterprise is very low in case of women's enterprises (compared with those of the men's) as women need to spend a major part of their income in ensuring the well-being of the family on a daily basis. It is very common, for this reason, to find that women mix up their business and household finance. They give much less time (than their male counterparts) to their business. Given the limited working capital, lack of time and other constraints on their mobility, women entrepreneurs are unable to procure their inputs and supplies in large quantities at competitive prices from distant markets. Women undervalue their own labour and time (a strong patriarchal imprint on the women entrepreneurs) while fixing the price of the goods for sale. Thus, women's investments were relatively small, and their productive processes were simpler than men's, they are made to restrict the scope of their business small, confine it to activities and locations which they can manage in combination with their reproductive role. The barriers to entry into a competitive market are too many for them – all flowing from their subordination in a patriarchal system. Thus, the neo-liberal minimalist microfinance programmes, by not challenging these structural and cultural constraints of women, promote women's enterprises within the accepted 'female space' within the patriarchal hegemony and do not enable them to challenge this space and overcome patriarchy.

Changing the Lens: From Neo-classical to Feminist Economics

A well-functioning and matured self-help group demonstrates that markets and hierarchies are not the only two alternative modes of coordination as advocated by orthodox economists. It also moves beyond the ontological construct of the *homo economicus* – a neo-classical concept rejected by the feminist economists as an atomistic and under-socialised individual, exclusively self-regarding, autonomous and instrumentally rational. The members of the self-help groups resemble more with the contrastive explanation of the 'human agency' offered by the feminist economists – the model of non-deterministic multi-dimensionality and relatedness, in which both material and non-material motivations drive human behaviour. Interdependent and interconnected group actors (and not isolated individuals) are at the centre of economic activities, and heterogeneity of human needs (and not simply economic calculus) defines human well-being. With the very notion of such a 'separative' self, which is 'androcentric' in its very core, understanding collective action is an endless problem in orthodox economics (Best and Humphries 2003).

Feminist economics informs us better in understanding the phenomenon of these self-help groups getting things done. It is difficult to explain these groups in terms of the Rational Choice Theory. Nor is it desirable to strip the groups off their sociological essence. The members' behaviour is determined by multiple logic, they cannot be reduced to an aggregate of atomistic individuals pursuing their own private goods only. The group is a social entity that enables members to develop their capability space in ways that cannot be bought in the market place or through market mechanisms. The emancipatory goals of the microfinance movement ought to be anchored in the shared interests of the poor women and their situated agency.

A. Sen's influential contribution powerfully argues that capability is a better conceptual tool (in contrast to income) to understand well-being. Well-being is defined as the freedom and the ability of people "to lead the kind of lives they value" (Sen 1999: 18). Processes of development and the relations of power within these processes are central to any gender and development programme. Sen emphasises that women's agency – their ability to be active agents of change, to define one's goals and act upon them – is crucial to ensuring their well-being. Women's well-being can be furthered by highlighting agency amid structures of constraint and thereby directing action to everyday practices of subordination and discrimination. Giving women the freedom to exercise their agency should be the goal of development policy, and microfinance institutions should check how much their services realise this goal.

Credit alone does not enable women to challenge patriarchy, and change the complex structures of subordination, inequalities, and discrimination within the household, the market, or the wider society. Conversely, such technically structured microfinance programmes more often get co-opted into the hegemonic patriarchal structures. In the minimalist credit programmes, women frequently exhibit, what Sen (1990) calls, 'adaptive preferences' – preferences that have adjusted to their second-class status.

If microfinance programmes are to have significant and lasting positive impact on women's lives, they must also work to change the power relations that constrain their abilities to control and benefit from improvements in household income (Kantor 2005: 65). Therefore, MFIs ought to work on strategies and models that draw on the concepts and theories of feminist economics. It is both strategic and more immediately necessary that MFIs move beyond viewing women as recipients, responsible payers or a new market. They need to expand their role in supporting investment in social reproduction while also contributing to do this in ways that change gender relations. There is a need to conceive of microfinance more boldly (Matin et al. 2007) and more creatively in terms of its social promise appropriate to the realities of the poor women in order to unleash the true emancipatory and transformative potential of microfinance as a tool for development. Microfinance institutions ought to change the neo-liberal lens if they want to make another world possible for women.

References

Adams, D. and J.D. von Pischke. 1992. 'Microenterprise Credit Programs: Déjà vu', *World Development*, 20: 1463–70.

Antonopoulos, Rania. 2008. 'The Right to a Job, the Right Types of Projects: Employment Guarantee Policies from a Gender Perspective', Working Paper No. 516, NY, Levy Economics Institute of Bard College Report, January. *www.levy.org/pubs/wp_516.pdf.*

Bateman, M. 2007. 'De-industrialization and Social Disintegration in Bosnia', in Thomas Dichter and Malcolm Harper (eds.), *What's Wrong with Microfinance?* (207–23). Warwickshire: ITDG/Practical Action.

Beneria, Lourdes and Shelley Feldman (eds.). 1992. *Unequal Burden: Economic Crisis, Persistent Poverty and Women's Work.* Boulder: Westview Press.

Best, M.H. and Jane Humphries. 2003. 'Edith Penrose: A Feminist Economist?', *Feminist Economics*, 9 (1): 47–73 (March).

Buvinic, Mayra and Elizabeth M. King. 2007. 'Smart Economics', *Finance and Development*, June. *www.imf.org.*

Chen, S. and M. Ravallion. 2009. *The Impact of the Global Financial Crisis on the World's Poorest: June Update.* Washington, DC: The World Bank.

Dash, A. 2003. 'Strategies for Poverty Alleviation in India: CYSD's Holistic Approach to Empowerment through the Self-help Group Model', *IDS Bulletin*, 34 (4): 133–42 (October).

———. 2005. 'Emancipation through Micro Credit', *Appropriate Technology*, 32 (1): 10–14 (March).

——. 2009. 'Microfinance, Poverty and the Social Economy of Empowerment', in Denis Harrison et al. (eds.), *Social Innovation, the Social Economy and World Economic Development* (83–104). Frankfurt am Main: Peter Lang.

Dichter, T. and Malcolm Harper (eds.). 2007. *What's Wrong with Microfinance?* Warwickshire: ITDG/Practical Action.

Ellerman, D. 2007. 'Microfinance: Some Conceptual and Methodological Problems', in Thomas Dichter and Malcolm Harper (eds.), op. cit. (149–61).

Greeley, M. 2004. 'MFIs with a Poverty Mandate should go beyond 'Knowing the Market' to Assessing their Impact on Clients', *Small Enterprise Development*, 15 (3): 4–7.

Holcombe, S. 1995. *Managing to Empower: The Grameen Bank's Experience of Poverty Alleviation*. London: Zed.

Horn, Z.E. 2009. 'No Cushion to Fall Back On: The Global Economic Crisis and Informal Workers', Inclusive Cities Project, Cambridge, MA: Women in Informal Employment: Globalizing and Organizing (WIEGO): 20.

Hossain, M. 1988. *Credit for Alleviation of Rural Poverty: The Grameen Bank in Bangladesh*. Washington, DC: IFFRI.

International Labour Organization. 2009. *Global Employment Trends for Women*. March, Geneva: ILO.

Kabeer, N. 1999. 'Resources, Agency, Achievements: Reflections on the Measurement of Women's Empowerment', *Development and Change*, 30 (3): 435–64.

——. 2005. 'Is Microfinance a 'Magic Bullet' for Women's Empowerment? Analysis of Findings from South Asia', *Economic and Political Weekly*, XL (44 & 45), October 29–November 4: 4709–18.

Kantor, P. 2005. 'Determinants of Women's Microenterprise Success in Ahmedabad, India: Empowerment and Economics', *Feminist Economics*, 11 (3): 63–83.

Khandkar, S. 1998. *Fighting Poverty with Microcredit: Experience in Bangladesh*. New York: Oxford University Press.

Khang, Hyun-Sung. 2009. 'Surviving the Third Wave', *Finance and Development*, December. *www.imf.org*.

Khitarishvili, Tamar. 2010. 'Explaining the Gender Wage Gap in Georgia', Working Paper No. 577, NY, Levy Economics Institute of Bard College Report, January.

King, Richard and Caroline Sweetman. 2010. 'Gender Perspectives on the Global Economic Crisis', Oxfam International Discussion Paper, February. *www.oxfam.org*.

Lowell, Stephanie et al. 2005. 'The Rating Game', *Stanford Social Innovation Review*, Summer: 39–45.

Mahajan, V. 2007. 'From Microcredit to Livelihood Finance', in Thomas Dichter and Malcolm Harper (eds.), op. cit. (241–49).

Matin, I. et al. 2007. 'Imagining Microfinance More Boldly: Unleashing the True Potential of Microfinance', in Thomas Dichter and Malcolm Harper (eds.), op. cit. (23–34).

Mayoux, Linda. 1995. 'From Vicious to Virtuous Circle? Gender and Microenterprise Development'. Occasional Paper 1, 4th World Conference on Women, Geneva: UNRISD.

Molyneux, M. 1985. 'Mobilisation without Emancipation: Women's Interests, State and Revolution', *Feminist Studies*, 11 (2): 227–54.

Montgomery, R. 1996. 'Disciplining or Protecting the Poor?', *Journal of International Development*, 8 (2): 289–305.

Moser, Caroline O.N. 1993. *Gender Planning and Development: Theory, Practice and Training*. London: Routledge.

Mosley, P. and D. Hulme. 1998. 'Microenterprise Finance: Is there a Conflict between Growth and Poverty Alleviation', *World Development*, 26 (5): 783–90.

Otero, M. and E. Rhyne. 1994. *The New World of Microenterprise Finance*. London: IT Publication.

Oxfam. 2010. 'The Global Economic Crisis and Developing Countries: Impact and Response'. Oxford: Oxfam International (Forthcoming).

Pearson, Ruth. 2009. 'Crisis of Reproduction as well as of Production and Finance (The Human Development Approach)', paper presented at the Gender and the Economic Crisis Workshop, Oxford, 15–16 September.

Rahman, S.M. 2007. 'A Practitioner's View of the Challenges Facing NGO-based Microfinance in Bangladesh', in Thomas Dichter and Malcolm Harper (eds.), op. cit. (193–205).

Rippey, P. 2007. 'Princes, Peasants and Pretenders: The Past and Future of African Microfinance', in Thomas Dichter and Malcolm Harper (eds.), op. cit. (109–20).

Rogaly, B. 1996. 'Microfinance Evangelism, Destitute Women and the Hard Selling of a New Anti-Poverty Formula', *Development in Practice*, 6 (2): 100–12.

Sebstad, J. and Monique Cohen. 2001. *Microfinance, Risk Management and Poverty*. Washington, DC: CGAP.

Sen, A. 1990. 'Gender and Cooperative Conflicts', in Irene Tinker (ed.), *Persistent Inequalities* (123–49). New York: Oxford University Press.

——. 1999. *Development as Freedom*. New York: Alfred A. Knopf.

Sinha, F. 2007. 'SHGs in India: Numbers Yes, Poverty Outreach and Empowerment, Partially', in Thomas Dichter and Malcolm Harper (eds.), op. cit. (73–82).

Sinha, F. et al. 2006. *Self-help Groups in India: A Study of the Lights and Shades.* Gurgaon/Hyderabad: EDA Rural Systems-APMAS.

Stocking, Dame Barbara. 2009. 'The Poor Should Not Pay the Price for the Crisis', *Finance and Development*, December. *www.imf.org.*

Tawney, C. 2004. 'From the Editor', *Small Enterprise Development*, 15 (3): 1–2 (September).

Vaughan, G. (ed.). 2007. *Women and the Gift Economy.* Toronto: Inanna.

Von Pischke, J.D. 2007. 'Methodenstreit and Sustainability in Microfinance: Generalizations Describing Institutional Frameworks', in Thomas Dichter and Malcolm Harper (eds.), op. cit. (137–48).

Wilson, K. 2007. 'The Moneylenders Dilemma', in Thomas Dichter and Malcolm Harper (eds.), op. cit. (97–108).

Wood, G. and S. Sharrif. 1997. *Credit Where Credit is Due.* Dhaka/London: UPL and Zed.

Yohn, Susan M. 2006. 'Crippled Capitalists: The Inscription of Economic Dependence and the Challenge of Female Entrepreneurship in Nineteenth-Century America', *Feminist Economics*, 12 (1/2): 85–109 (January/April).

Section IV

Science, Environment and Development

10

10

Science, Environment and Development

Issues in the Structural Crisis of Capital

Subhasis Bandyopadhyay

> Theory is capable of gripping the masses as soon as it demonstrates ad hominem, and it demonstrates ad hominem as soon as it becomes radical.
>
> —Karl Marx, *Introduction, A Contribution to the Critique of Hegel's Philosophy of Right,* 1843.

When three colossal concepts were bundled into one theme – science, environment and development – at least two of which, environment and development, often took centre stage in any social science forum – there must have been some urgency to understand the *triple helix* from a sociological perspective. Of these three, however, I may add that 'science' aka 'scientific' is a most frequently used term either to substantiate or to refute arguments and propositions in environmental or developmental issues in subjective *ipso facto* manner for rendering the original meaning of the term. Two very recent examples of this ilk are: the Copenhagen Summit (COP15) and the *faux passé* of the R.K. Pachauri-led IPCC (Intergovernmental Panel on Climate Change) report on the condition of the glaciers of Himalayas. The point I would like to stress is that concepts as complex as environment and development with profound economic, political, cultural and psychological significance may use science as a means to understand, debate and construct a reasonable model of application. However, there remains a huge possibility that more often than not it is used in a teleological manner to suit the need of the powers that be. This is important, as it is often useful for the interest groups to blur the original issue at stake behind the smoke screen of 'technical' jargons inaccessible to ordinary men and women of letters. There is, of course, another possibility. Technology, a more convenient component than science, as it is generally perceived as application of abstract formulation into machine forms so far as power-manoeuvring is concerned, may be put to use in the name of science. However, it is the latter possibility which is now transformed into a mainstream practice in this age of neo-liberalism.[1]

Let us take a closer look at this neo-liberal attempt to utilise knowledgeable techniques to suit its survival needs at the huge cost of both environment and development. In the October 30 issue of the leading scientific journal *Nature* (2008) physicist Jean-Philippe Bouchaud rhetorically commented that the flagship achievement of economics is only its recurrent inability to avert crisis. This comment applies equally well to mainstream social scientific approaches to the issues of environment and development – where, for example, ancient forest and hill stretches are seen as non-performing assets to be liquidated, and clean air and water are luxury goods for the affluent to purchase at their discretion (York et al. 2009). This is the predominant view where development is perceived as endless growth of GDP (gross domestic product) – a measurement of 'value added', not of human well-being or the intrinsic worth of ecosystems and other species – that has led to more than the basic fact of an inability to perceive the deterioration of the environment and the societal condition across the globe.

The demonstrated failure of social sciences to offer a solution to the fundamental problem of human society has resulted in a *PLAN B* to save the system through the proliferation of technological silver bullets for carrying out a green operation without altering the social and economic relations of the system, like the orthodox economists who assume that the resource problem of today will force up the prices tomorrow and these higher prices will force the creation of a new technology a day after, as panacea (ibid.: 5). Recent spurt in the petro-product price hike both globally and nationally is given a mandatory logical boost in the same line and the issue of innovative non-conventional energy is given a temporary focus only as part of the politically correct corporate social responsibility (CSR) of the state rulers! State and national governments, in the process, don the robe of industrial capital without any compunction. In the case of overshooting climatic disaster, the most ambitious scheme involve massive geo-engineering proposals to combat climate change, usually aimed at enhancing the earth's *ALBEDO* or reflectivity by releasing reflective materials like sulphate aerosols or aluminium oxide into the upper stratosphere to reflect back the rays of the sun or releasing 'designer particles' that are self-levitating to provide sun shades for the polar regions. Such wonderland technology is yet to protect the capital from its perennial crisis.[2]

The objective of this appraisal is moved by this phenomenon of manipulative technique and my endeavour is to show that be it the issue of environment or the one of development a political-economic system grossly distorts its code of inception to continue its tattered and cannibalistic existence amidst heaps of self-created ruins. The anthropological and historical evidences of the spread of capital as the driving force of modernity (as stated unequivocally first by Saint-Simon and later Toynbee) had to discover sooner than expected that the economic power of capital carried a postscript of ideology – capitalism – in the very sense of Weberian 'capitalism' (Weber 2002). The process of innovation in technology of capitalist production relation since its inception required another in-built, almost instinctive, thrust for horizontal spread across the lands and cultures. Along the line of this proliferation everywhere this dynamic system of production continued to extend an inevitable *aka* latent function of contradiction and conflict. Let me elaborate this point very briefly.

Secondary and tertiary levels of production augmented with the help of synthesised energy from steam and electricity helped capitalism to a large extent to displace the land-based feudal mode of production. Upon this matrix, huge edifices like organised labour, urban sprawl, skill and knowledge-based occupation, science and technology as well as notions such as reasons, rights and democracy evolved. Scientific and technological spurs in the 17th century Europe provided for humanity important intellectual tools like innovation, articulation and critique. But these self-interrogating elements of modernity when applied to analyse the trajectory of the very economic system that generated them are, without exception, everywhere throttled, besieged, misrepresented and usurped by the dominant class, viz., the bourgeoisie. Destruction which has spun out of control now characterises the capitalist system on a global scale and imperils all life of this planet and has its dialectical antithesis in the potential for an acceleration of history through the activation of a genuine struggle for substantive equality.[3] The destruction is evidently triggered by the irrevocable overshooting of the environmental and ecological parameters by industrial (and post-industrial) need for optimal profit. In this blind run for maximisation of profit, there are mandatory collateral damages like climatic disasters and 'expendable trivia' like food insecurity and hunger which do not remain benign in the long run and often come back with a vengeance.

Contemporary economists frequently talk about externalities. Externalities are things that do not affect the corporate balance sheet and therefore firms do not worry about. For example, a firm produces iron and steel. It gets paid for these outputs. It also produces smoke, sludge and acidic wastes all of which are nuisances, but the firm is not charged and it does not bother how much smoke it belches out. Who pays? It is the common people who are in and around the factory pay. They pay through eye, lung and chest discomfort and diseases. The government-run primary health centre pays in treating them (notwithstanding the abysmal state of public health care in India). So, we pay twice as the government exchequer that provides the costs of public health is generally filled by the taxes in various forms paid by the public themselves. But, the firm does not pay. Firms minimise costs because that is the best way to make tangible profit. They do not minimise costs that others have to pay – externalities. These are real costs, just like pig iron and coking coal, only to be borne by the rest of us.

One particular aspect that reflects this condition in a most glaring manner within the global political economy is the comprehensive dismantling of the organised productive labour by the gigantic world corporations. This has been accomplished nearly everywhere under the designer rubric 'strategic human resource development'.[4] It is a process that has far reaching economic, environmental and developmental consequences for the entire habitat of this planet (Ghosh 2010). Further, it calls for new regime of trade union movement based on a new set of conceptual tools. For instance, Dunn (2006: 56) points out that trade union should neither believe in neo-liberal assertions that the state has become irrelevant for strategies of resistance, nor should they fall back into a purely nationalist strategy along traditional social-democratic or socialist lines. He develops an understanding of the 'relative autonomy of the state' and the related understanding of the relation between the national and the global through the concepts of combined and uneven development. An attempt of theorisation like this once more points to the inherent fallibility of the structure of capital as represented in the corporatised world order today.

Following is a generalised depiction on the shift that has taken place in the corporate system across the world.

The Case: To begin with, it would be apt to clarify my position vis-à-vis development. I do not belong to that genre of environmentalism that decries industry in any form. Rather, as I see it, the condition of human development is inextricably linked with the upgradation in the means and mode of production in society in a manner suitable to conserve the ambience that is flexible enough to foster the growth of other flora and fauna of our surroundings and preserve the essential ecological balance. Industry provides us with a composite system of labour, technology and art to fulfil the human requirement in the most prolific manner. The doubt about the efficacy of industry, almost singly, is generated by the profiteering motive (extraction of surplus value) of the owner or the consortium of the owners of the industry – the ruling class.

Experiencing the onslaught of capital is an emotional testimony to violation of every kind. For example, take any three major TNCs involved in producing consumer goods, say, Nike, GE Inc. and IBM. These are the corporations known for their specialised production of commodities of three different kinds, viz., sports goods, electrical equipments and computer and office automation systems. Now, the reality is stark. These corporations, in their effort to maintain and maximise profit, have become lean or size zero. They just own their brands and put all their effort only to enhance the brand value. That means they do not produce the product physically any more. In the special economic zones (SEZs) or export processing zones (EPZs) of poor countries, little known or unknown factories in their nondescript surrounding engage streams of workers to produce renowned brands as per the benchmarking procedure brandished by the corporate headquarters. These corporations still flaunt their R&D facilities only to improve the design parameters and to initiate strategies for foreign direct investment (FDI) in overseas portfolios. In the process they get rid of the hassles of the 'dirty' production process and 'labour unrest'. They can now evade taxation on the home front and pay just a pittance to the 'development' seeking states. Their henchmen in those countries who act as 'wholly owned subsidiary' agents bribe the local government agencies for a favourable EIA (environmental impact assessment) report.

The most contemporary Indian instance in this regard is none other than the Bhopal gas tragedy tainted Mahindra-owned Union Carbide India, a wholly owned subsidiary of Dow Chemical Company, USA. The former is still allowed to run its other chemical manufacturing units in India on the basis of such 'negotiable' EIA reports. Subsidiary units like this generally flout the minimum wage ceiling which is already many times less than in the countries of their parent corporations and with laying off of the skilled hands on a regular basis they decrease it further. Workers in those EPZs or SEZs, many of whom are women, have no insurance, health or social protection scheme. Pregnant women are summarily sacked (Klein 2000). Workers there are not allowed to form unions (www.suite101.com 2010). Migrant workers from the distant countryside are forced to live in make-shift thatched hutments resembling a piggery.[5] These are not pictures of distant places. In our vicinity the SEZ at Falta in South 24 Parganas district of West Bengal that carries the dubious distinction of the first EPZ in India, reflects almost an identical scenario (sanhati.com 2009).[6] A closer look at the employment figures provided by the Ministry of Commerce and Industry, Government of India (fsez.nic.in/glance.html 2009) amply demonstrates the gendered pattern of employment and exploitation in such SEZs:

Strength in Falta Special Economic Zone (Till November 2009)

Permanent Male Staff	:	2,284
Permanent Female Staff	:	157
Temporary Male Staff	:	4,261
Temporary Female Staff	:	6,837
Construction Labour	:	1,417

The aforesaid table shows that women are more favoured as temporary workers (as against permanent positions) over their male counterparts for low-pay jobs in the SEZ by their employers. In addition, the same document shows, there are approximately 4,000 contractual workers out of which above 60 per cent is female. This is ostensibly because women are considered as fragile and dispensable part of the working force in the perception of the recruiters and their agents. Moreover, as women are relatively new entrants in the industrial occupation in the region, the nucleus of collective bargaining is comparatively weak among them.

The story has another side. A majority of such corporations have either faced bankruptcy threats or had a frail profit margin in the face of global meltdown or what *Business Week* called a 'financial icé age'. That is of little wonder as a majority of the mammoth transnational corporations, three of which are mentioned here, were and are still engaged in investing in capital ventures to make runaway profit quickly and getting increasingly shy to produce any physical product. The worldwide economic recession now makes these corporations act more aggressively in the direction of farming out to make manufacturing of their brands more anonymous, cheap and distant. To attain these solemn business objectives, what they need are essentially three things: inexpensive labour, freehold over natural resources, and eager governments in poor countries who are ready to grab any offer of pseudo-industrialisation in the name of GDP growth, technology transfer and percolation of development.

The formation of a dope haze around a triangulated nexus of technology, environment and development, I hope, is now clear. This is not only important to understand in the context of the global South, it is equally important to appreciate the toxicity it generates for the working class of the North or the so-called developed countries.[7] Why has this become an imperative in the Indian context? Because in recent decades precious little sociological research has been done in South Asia to understand the societal implication of the hegemony of the monopolistic capital and generally it is accepted that if any industry is making profit, it is, *ipso facto*, a socially necessary industry and it is beyond the purview of socio-economic study to question its legitimacy. Such an approach, at the practical level, reduces the issues pertaining to environment and development from handles to reform to naught, a perspective that helps to hide the structural crisis of capital behind the shadow of a conjectural financial crisis. From hedge fund to toxic debt of sub-prime lending – all such jargons flooding the magazine and newspaper articles are in reality the self-portrayal of financial giants with an objective to convince the state power as if they have already diagnosed the root cause of institutional failures successfully and only waiting for the curative measures to be taken by the governments. Nevertheless, this structural crisis cannot be seen simply as a shallow transient moment in the timeline. Rather it clearly encompasses the global ecological crisis, the problem of development and the manifold social and cultural contradictions emanating from the hierarchical power relation of the prevailing order (Foster 2009). The structural crisis is, indeed, not a resultant effect of the recent global meltdown. In contrast, it started quite in advance in capital's maiden response to the phenomenon of internal fractures including ecological overshooting in the early seventies of the last century. Istvan Meszaros, who, following Marx for the first time located the endemic nature of this inevitable crisis, also looked at it as one cardinal point of capital's many systemic faults, which is hardly amenable to any kind of curative and reform measures from within.[8]

In the third edition of *Marx's Theory of Alienation* (1971) Meszaros first addressed the problematic of the 'global structural crisis of capital' what Daniel Singer would later qualify with words like: What must be abolished is not only classical capitalist society but the reign of capital (Singer 1996). Why was this so? Because, Meszaros felt, the entire reign of capital was approaching its absolute limits as a result of its increasing inability to displace its internal contradictions. The result is maximisation of waste and destruction, marked by the incessant degradation of human labour, a decreasing rate of utilisation, ballooning financial parasitism and accelerating planetary ecological catastrophe (Foster and Clark 2004). In the face of such a composite imbalance, the historical transformation of the productive economy of capital into a finance-centric 'casino economy' only accelerated the pace of all-round disaster. Already, in 1990, James Petras and Christian Davenport had shown using Forbes 400 data that speculator capitalists had become dominant ruling class in the developed world displacing industrial and petro-capitalists (Petras and Davenport 1990). This new FIRE (finance, insurance and real estate) capital that starts dominating the world political economy understands the financialisation as a secular process, arising in response to the stagnation of production and as such an inevitability for whom science, environment and development are conceptual surrealistic murals for exhibition and sale and nothing else. Such a self-justifying vicious circle of wasteful 'progress' toward the irrational conversion of ever greater productive potentiality into destructive reality can go unhindered until a global catastrophe brings it to a halt. At the root of all these destructive manifestations one may find the insurmountable imperatives arising from the established order's self-perpetuating structural hierarchies where consideration of substantive equality – a goal normatively shared by science, environment and development – cannot conceivably enter capital's framework of decision-making. This makes the structural crisis of our system of social metabolism uniquely acute at the present historical juncture (Meszaros 2008: 62).

Designer terms like ICT (information and communication technology)-driven 'knowledge economy' that is often looked upon as a panacea for every possible sort of crisis is miserably inadequate to make any dent in this lumpen venture of capital. This is simply because in such a thesaurus knowledge is the product of knowledge industry where the owner dictates the boundaries of the legitimate, the research agenda, the domain of acceptability, and the criteria for rejection, for example, 'non-mainstream' or 'ideological' (Levins 2010). Science is armed with self-correcting mechanism to rectify errors as it is always vexed with the possibility of flaws. Science understands that all theories are limited and each has a finite life span before being replaced by a better theory. Science is organised as a sceptic and self-correcting system of knowledge – features that are impossible on the part of capital to bear with. That is why, such a mechanism is completely useless against the subjective control exercised over the domain of science by the market forces and representatives of capital in numerous forms. Also, the institutionalised capital has become increasingly obscurantist anti-science, which ranges from creationism and the mystification of mathematical chaos, to post-modern hoax as exposed by Sokal affairs (Lewontin and Levins 2007: 9).

The structural crisis of capital, as explained and illustrated by Meszaros (2009), has its profound reflection in the realms of environment, science and development. This requires further elaboration as the theory covers intrinsic as well as extrinsic complexities and short-comings of the compound dynamics of capital and capitalist formations. Keeping in mind the recent financial crisis and the consequent stagflation experienced by the major economic forces across the world, one may argue that the dynamic of financialisation in relation to a stagnant economy is the enigma of monopoly finance capital. This increasing monopolisation has been specifically evident within the finance sector itself that lays bare the intense conflict between private appropriation and the social or even survival needs of humanity. In her book, *The Shock Doctrine* (2007), Naomi Klein suggested that the consequences of this conflict extends to ever deepening socio-political instability, expanding militarism and war, and seemingly unstoppable planetary environmental destruction resulting in, what she called, 'disaster capitalism'.

The capitalist economic structures in its neo-liberal ventures have had to radically realign themselves to support the ever-growing desire for goods and services. Since the post-war era, capitalist production has been restructured into a post-Fordist globalised system in which more and more products are more efficiently or cheaply made by workers from the global South.[9] More and more of the economy is based on information and information processing, and that too, mostly about the fictitious finance capital. And finally, many of the contemporary technological changes are devoted to the production of a plethora of consumer goods, the universalisation of the mass-mediated products of the culture industry and a variety of consumable experiences only for a handful urban people with substantial surplus in the name of science and development.

Conclusion

In the year 2010 three important realities have surfaced in the understanding of the global humanity almost as a postscript to the Great Economic Crisis of 2007–08: (a) the increasing stagnation in the domain of scientific knowledge; (b) the perilous situation of environment across the globe; and (c) the failure of mainstream development programme to reach the target population. The entire human society is now more than ever deeply bifurcated. The bifurcation is both ontological and epistemic. It is both contradictory and conflicting. In the words of one observer, "the crisis radically undermined the very concept of unilateral and multilateral economic-political hegemony, which compels one to explore new forms of multilateral world governance" (Marazzi 2010). When such institutional forms are still in the womb of future as the world is running out of time very quickly. The conjectured forms of governance aside, however, all hope is not lost. Now, more than ever before, it is important in the contemporary scenario to understand the dialectics of science, environment and development. The present system has failed and we are given with the task to question its legitimacy of continuance. The project is a tough one. But hardly in the history of human civilisation has the majority ever been given an easier choice. The question is precise: are we ready to join Noah's Ark in the journey of survival once again after the Great Flood? The answer is even simpler: otherwise as a species we are bound to face the Armageddon possibly in the form of World War III.

Acknowledgement: The author sincerely thanks Professor Biswajit Ghosh, University of Burdwan, for giving him the opportunity to present a paper with an identical title in the UGC-ICSSR sponsored National Seminar in March 2010 including editorial assistance in writing this paper. Usual disclaimers apply.

Notes

1. David Harvey (2005: 2) defines neo-liberalism as a theory of political economic practices proposing human well-being that can best be advanced by liberating individual entrepreneurial freedoms and skills within an institutional framework characterised by strong private property rights, free markets and free trade. Here, the state has to play the role of an institutional facilitator providing conducive atmosphere for such practices. The state, for example, must set up those military and legal structures and functions needed to secure private property rights and to guarantee, by force if need be, the proper functioning of markets.
2. It is not only the fairy-tale feature of the given technology that is put to criticism but also the idea behind such a project to display an imaginary technology as a weapon to combat the ill-effects of capitalism itself on the environment. It can be termed as a case of *technological overdeterminism*.
3. The idea of substantive equality as opposed to formal equality has its origin in the juridical reforms in North America as well as in the first wave of feminist movement in the 1960s. In the Marxist parlance, however, it means a comprehensive organic egalitarianism so far as the production relations are concerned.
4. In the present era of irregularity and crisis, organised labour is under severe threat. Be it in the form of widespread poverty, rising unemployment and underemployment, decline in wages and living standards across the industrial societies, predatory features has engulfed the contemporary capitalism that has shrugged off its earlier stance of rationality in its effort to annihilate the organised workers (Ghosh 2010: 195).
5. According to the Chinese National Labour Committee Report *China's Youth Meet Microsoft* – April 2010, a typical shift in Guangdon SEZ in southern China hosting TNCs like Microsoft is from 7:45 a.m. to 10:55 p.m. Many of the young workers are "work study students" who usually work at the factory for about three months. Aside from hiring teenagers, KYE, the local subsidiary unit of Microsoft prefers to hire young women between 18 to 25 years old, 'since they are easier to discipline and control'. Read more at Suite 101: 'Working in the SEZ of Southern China's Guangdong Province' (Winnig 2010).
6. Falta SEZ in West Bengal – a fact-finding report (see, Sanhati.com Nov 26, 2009). The report states: What was established by the Government of India as the Falta Export Processing Zone (FEPZ) in 1984, turned into the Falta Free Trade Zone (FFTZ) and finally appeared in its current avatar as a Special Economic Zone (SEZ) under the West Bengal SEZ Act, 2003, the first SEZ Act passed by any state government in India. Therefore, the Falta SEZ earned the dubious distinction of being the first SEZ in India. After the Government of India passed the SEZ Act in 2005, the Falta SEZ came under the purview of this Act, becoming the pioneer of the 500 odd SEZs set up all over India, becoming

the epitome of the neo-liberal capitalist policies of the central and the nominally 'leftist' West Bengal state governments.

7. The political economy of North–South divide in the contemporary world system is an indispensable analytical tool in the general understanding of the structural crises of capital and particularly regarding the current tension about calculating the economic cost-benefit of environmental issues. For example, the hiatus is quite discernable in the context of industrial emission of green house gases and carbon pool trading.
8. Capital in the 20th century was forced to respond unforeseen and extensive crises by accepting 'hybridisation' – in the form of an ever greater intrusion of the state into the socio-economic production at the cost of the viability of the system in the long run. This is a direct outcome of the three-fold internal fracture within the system of capital, viz., production and its control; production and consumption; and production and circulation of products that results into an irremediably 'centrifugal' system in which the conflicting and internally antagonistic parts pull in very different directions (Meszaros 2008: 63–65).
9. Post-Fordism, in the lexicon of industrial sociology, denotes flexible specialisation in the production process, characterised by specialist units of production, decentralised management, versatile technologies and workforces, to satisfy increasingly volatile and uncertain market conditions.

References

Bouchaud, Jean-Philippe. 2008. 'Economics Needs a New Scientific Revolution', *Nature*, 455 (October 30): 1181.

Dunn, Bill. 2006. 'Globalization, Labour and the State', in Craig Phelan (ed.), *The Future of Organized Labour: Global Perspectives* (37–62). Bern: Peter Lang AG.

Falta Special Economic Zone – A GoI Document. 2009. Available at *fsez.nic.in/glance.html.*

Foster, John Bellamy. 2009. 'Foreword to the Structural Crisis of Capital', *Analytical Monthly Review*, 7 (4 & 5): 152.

Foster, John Bellamy and Brett Clark. 2004. 'Empire of Barbarism', *Monthly Review*, 56 (7): 1–15.

Ghosh, Biswajit. 2010. 'How to Govern Corporate Houses?', in S.K. Pramanick and R. Ganguly (eds.), *Globalization in India: New Frontiers and Emerging Challenges* (191–218). New Delhi: PHI.

Harvey, David. 2005. *A Brief History of Neoliberalism*. NY: OUP.

Klein, Naomi. 2000. *No Logo*. Toronto: Knopf.

——. 2007. *The Shock Doctrine: The Rise of Disaster Capitalism.* NY: Henry Holt.

Levins, Richard. 2010. 'Why Programs Fail', *Analytical Monthly Review*, 7 (12): 39–44.

Lewontin, Richard and Richard Levins. 2007. *Biology under the Influence.* NY: Monthly Review Press.

Marazzi, Christian. 2010. *The Violence of Financial Capitalism.* Translated by Kristina Lebedeva. Los Angeles, CA: Semiotext(e).

Meszaros, Istvan. 1971. *Marx's Theory of Alienation.* London: Merlin Press.

——. 2008. *The Challenge and Burden of Historical Time.* NY: Monthly Review Press.

——. 2009. *The Structural Crisis of Capital.* NY: Monthly Review Press.

Petras, James and Christian Davenport. 1990. 'The Changing Wealth of the U.S. Ruling Class', *Monthly Review*, 42 (7): 33–37.

Sanhati.com. 2009. *Falta SEZ in West Bengal – A Fact Finding Report.* November 26.

Singer, Daniel. 1996. 'After Alienation', *The Nation*, June10.

Weber, Max. 2002. *The Protestant Ethic and the Spirit of Capitalism.* Translated by Peter Baehr and Gordon C. Wells. London: Penguin Books.

Winnig, Heike. 2010. 'Working in the SEZ of Southern China's Guandong Province'. *www.suite101.com* (Accessed on August 27, 2010).

York, Richard et al. 2009. 'Capitalism in Wonderland', *Analytical Monthly Review*, 7 (2): 1.

11

Development or Livelihood Insecurity of Ecosystem People?

The Social and Ecological Costs of Modern Development in Contemporary India

Rajkishor Meher

With the introduction of the country's First Five-Year Plan in early 1950s, India treaded the path of modern development by emulating western development model. By combining both capitalist and socialist models of planned development in a mixed economy framework, the planners and policy makers assumed that the best result of development could be ensured to all sections of population with higher living standard and improved quality of life within a very reasonable time period. As expected, the planning laid emphasis on grounding and building of many mega development projects such as big dams, large industries, large irrigation projects, thermal power plants, large townships, better roads and highways, railways, ports, airports and the like by doing massive exploitation of natural resources such as land, water, forest and mineral resources.

This development model undoubtedly helped the country to emerge as one of the influential economic and political powers in the world with a large army of technically skilled manpower. However, as it is now observed, the very process of development in the country is generating wider socio-economic inequalities across space and people. The present development paradigm has not been able to tackle the problem of mass poverty and derisory form of living for a large section of marginalised people. According to latest estimates of poverty by Tendulkar Committee (Government of India 2009: 17) set up by the Planning Commission, 37.2 per cent of the country's population still lives below the poverty line

(41.8% in rural area and 25.7% in urban area) notwithstanding rapid economic growth in national income during the LPG (liberalisation, privatisation and globalisation) era.

The mainstream development model aims at promoting mega development projects in the country to accelerate the process of economic development by increasing economic growth expressed in terms of Gross National Product (GNP). However, this endeavour has directly been responsible for massive displacement of human population and generation of new poverty by decimating sustainable means of subsistence of the 'ecosystem people'[1] in many parts of the country. According to an estimate, during 1951–1990, around 21.3 million persons in India were displaced by the development projects and among them 8.54 million (40%) were tribals or indigenous people and of those only 2.12 million (24.8%) could be resettled (Government of India 2002: 458). Tribals lose their land not only to the project authorities, but even to non-tribal outsiders who converge into project areas and corner both land and the new economic opportunities in commerce and petty industry. According to the latest estimate, the total number of people displaced in India due to setting up of many modern development projects during the last 60 years has reached almost 60 million (Mathur 2008). Of late, it is found that involuntary displacement of ecosystem people is getting more intensified due to the conditions created by globalisation and economic liberalisation. The facilitating role of the state to promote mega mineral-based industries under the auspices of market economy is found to be generating many unintended effects on the living of ecosystem people. The application of 'eminent domain' principle to acquire land for the multinational corporations (MNCs) and large Indian corporate houses (ICHs) in the mineral-rich tribal regions of the country has led to pushing out of ecosystem people from their traditional ecological niche.

This problem has nowadays taken the shape of a conflict between the ecosystem people and the omnivores, the former fighting to ensure their traditional sustainable form of subsistence and the latter intruding into the territory of the ecosystem people to satisfy their insatiable greed and unmet materialistic needs by exploiting the natural resources like land, forest and minerals (Gadgil and Guha 1995). In the name of modern development and to civilise and assimilate the ecosystem people in the development mainstream, the latter are virtually uprooted from their roots and natural resource base providing sustainable means of subsistence. Such efforts of development mainstreaming through mega projects like multipurpose river dams, industries and mining of minerals and metals generate namesake benefits only for a few relatively better off sections of populations. On the other hand, the majority of the ecosystem people are becoming the victims of development. Their status from ecosystem people to ecological refugees in the slums of the large urban centres and grafted urban–industrial towns is a clear manifestation of the development pathologies of our time (Oommen 2006).

In the light of above experience, the present paper makes a critical analysis of the modern mega development projects taken up in post-independent India. It examines the social and ecological impacts of mega projects on direct and indirectly displaced people and their hinterland economy and society in general by using case study method, and by making critical reviews of published literature and secondary data.

The Logic of Mineral-based Industrialisation

Since economic liberalisation, the mineral-rich poor and backward states of India are found to be treading the unsustainable path of 'resource exhausting model of industrialisation' for faster economic growth. These states with substantial proportion of depressed and illiterate population do not have any strong base of human capital. Majority of the people have land-based subsistence of sustainable nature. There is little scope for these agriculture-dependent unskilled people to integrate with the modern technology-oriented development process. However, the state machinery is in hurry to industrialise and globalise without bothering about the social and ecological consequences of such 'development'. Propelled by these factors, the state's plans in India envisage huge investments by large private corporations, especially Multi National Corporations (MNCs) in mining, industrial and infrastructure development projects (Mathur 2008: 12).

The governments of states like Chhattisgarh, Jharkhand and Orissa that form part of the mineral-rich Chhotanagpur plateau region of India are succumbing to the pressure of market economy. In the name of development, they are playing supportive and facilitating role for the MNCs and Indian corporate houses to expand their empire to earn more and more profits. There is a belief that large-scale industrial expansion would help in rapid economic development and poverty reduction through 'trickle down' effects of growth. As a corollary, the problem of human displacement has aggravated in post-reform India, as more and more land is being acquired for industry and mines.

Notwithstanding the reasoning of 'limits of growth' (Meadows et al. 1972) and the wisdom of many ecological and environmental protest movements all over the globe, the materialistic desires of modern and the so-called civilised man could not be restrained (see Blaser et al. 2004; Taylor 1995). The mainstream development model that aims at homogenisation of human civilisations and cultures in fact marginalises and pauperises the indigenous tribals, peasants and other ecosystem people. The model leaves them in semi-limbo condition and ultimately makes them 'ecological refugees' in the slums and squatter localities of the city.

The Insecure Oustees

In many cases the living conditions of people displaced by modern development projects are found to be worse than that in their past. Many suffer from agonies and estrangement of their kith and kin, breakdown of social capital linkages and support to encounter the problem of transient as well as hardcore poverty in their place of resettlement (Areeparampil 1989; Baboo 1992; Mahapatra 1999; Ota 1999; Pandey 1998a and 1998b; Reddy 1992 and 1994; Sahu 2000). Especially, the mining and mineral-based industries in the tribal regions are exposed to great risks and destitution of the tribals and other ecosystem people in the forms of loss of their hearth and home, access to common property resources, forests, land and water, with little hope of sustainable living. They are becoming the victims of impoverishment, homelessness, social disarticulation, loss of sustainable living and unsecured environmental surroundings due to incomplete resettlement and rehabilitation (R&R) measures (see, for details, Blaser et al. 2004; Cernea 2000 and 1996; CSE 1985; Fernandes 1994; Mathur and Marsden 1998; Meher 2001, 2003, 2004 and 2010; Oommen 2004 and 2006; Taylor 1995).

I therefore call this model of development as the 'livelihood insecurity and deprivation of ecosystem peoples'. There have been little sincere efforts to integrate and assimilate the people displaced and impoverished by the development projects. The development planners assume that displacement-related trauma and dislocation from home and traditional family-based occupations are short-term sufferings of the oustees. They argue that cash compensation and project-based jobs coupled with many invisible benefits finally mitigate the problems of oustee population in their new resettlement areas. However, in realty, the piecemeal and ad hoc approach to solve the problem of the development-displaced ecosystem peoples often works as palliatives and in the long run creates livelihood insecurity for them (Meher 2010). This becomes evidently clear from our brief analysis of the state of living of the ecosystem people displaced or affected by such projects in the post-displacement years.

Hirakud Dam

Hirakud is the first major multipurpose river dam project of independent India. The project was conceptualised during the British rule to control floods and recurring natural calamities in the coastal districts of Orissa. Though the foundation stone of the dam was laid down in March 1946, actual work started after independence. Land for the Hirakud reservoir covering an area of 743 sq. km. in the undivided Sambalpur district of Orissa and the Raigarh district of present Chhattisgarh state was acquired under the Land Acquisition Act, 1894. All land coming below RL 632 (reservoir level) feet of the reservoir was acquired covering around 1,67,377 acres of submerged land, out of which 1,15,128 (68.78%) acres was good agricultural land. The reservoir submerged 249 villages of undivided Sambalpur district and 49 villages of Raigarh district. According to government report, a total of 22,144 families with a population of about 101 thousand were affected by the project (quoted in Viegas 1992). However, it is revealed from the findings of later studies that the official record did not reflect the actual number of villages and people affected by the project, most of whom were people from the marginalised Gond tribe (Baboo 1992; Viegas 1992).

It may be mentioned that despite simmering discontent among the oustee families of the dam to leave their hearth and home resided by them and their ancestors for generations, the people probably due to long years of oppressive colonial rule and the dream of a modern India easily succumbed to the land acquisition notice of the government. Many accepted the compensation as per the price fixed by the government for the different categories of agricultural land such as low, medium and high, which were further categorised into many sub-categories. The price thus fixed for different categories of land varied between Rs 50 and Rs 1,000 per acre. However, the price was fixed and the gradation of the land was made in such an arbitrary manner that the compensation received by the oustee families of a village having similar category of land varied widely. Often the compensation was reportedly paid according to the social status and bargaining strength of the oustee family in the village. More so, as many among the tribal families were not having proper land *patta* (record of rights over the land), they were deprived of cash compensation. Neither the illiterate tribals could oppose the move, nor did any civil society organisation or political party come forward to protect the rights of the oustees. The protests and agitations against the dam that took place at the time of construction of the dam and evacuation of the families were mostly erupted at the village level in a very disorganised, sporadic and spontaneous manner. As there was little transportation and communication network, the disgruntled oustee families could not be united to project their demands and grievances before the government. Only some among them could manage to get better compensation package by filing court cases individually. Overall, the agitations and protests raised by the displacees could not be strengthened and they fizzled out in due course of time (Baboo 1992).

My field survey of some of the villages in present Jharsuguda district of Orissa during 2007–08 revealed that after more than fifty years of displacement, the R&R problems of the Hirakud dam oustees have not been solved. Many oustees, resettled in the new sites and colonies developed by the government, continue to live under the quagmire of poverty and miseries. Surprisingly, many of the 'rehabilitated' oustees were later displaced in the wake of opening up of open cast coal mines and industries.

The Pong Dam

The construction of the Pong dam in Himachal Pradesh was commenced in 1961 and was completed by 1974. This dam was planned when Himachal Pradesh was part of the undivided Punjab to distribute the benefits of irrigation and hydroelectricity among Rajasthan, Punjab and Haryana. In the Kangra district of Himachal Pradesh, the dam submerged 71,724 acres of land belonging to 30,000 families with a total population of 1,50,000 spread over 94 villages comprising 316 *tikkas* or revenue estates. Out of the 316 *tikkas*, 124 were fully submerged and the rest 192 were partially affected. However, the actual number of submerged villages and *tikkas* is not clear and their number in the government reports as well as in the media varies from time to time. As per the agreement, the displaced population was to be rehabilitated in the command area of Rajasthan. For the purpose, the central government constituted a committee comprising three Chief Ministers of the concerned states in 1961. After the formation of Himachal Pradesh, its Chief Minister also became a member of the committee. This Resettlement and Rehabilitation of Pong Dam Oustees Committee, after several meetings and discussions, lay down that each landowner oustee, irrespective of the quantum of land submerged, would be entitled to 15.625 acres of land in the Rajasthan command area. In addition, all the oustees were given cash compensation as per the rate fixed by the government for the loss of land according to its gradation, houses and homestead plots, trees and common property resources. The committee also decided that artisans, landless labourers, tenants, etc., would be given house plots within the *abadi* (residential) areas. But the oustees would have to pay for the houses constructed by the state colonisation department, which was expected to provide housing, roads, water supply and other basic amenities and services in the resettlement colonies.

However, as usual, not all the oustees could be resettled in Rajasthan. The cultural, ecological and geographical factors stood as barriers, apart from the political economy factors that operated against the interest of the oustee population vis-à-vis the host population. As a result, even after more than 30 years of displacement, the oustees of the Pong dam could not be fully rehabilitated and allotted land in the promised command area of Rajasthan, nor could they be rehabilitated and resettled in other parts of Himachal Pradesh. Owing to unfavourable geo-physical set-up, climate and hostile behaviour of the host population, some of the oustees resettled in Rajasthan were forced to return to Himachal Pradesh. For long, the protests of the oustees and demand for adequate compensation and rehabilitation packages went on and the problem was left unresolved.

It is pertinent to mention here that although the people of Himachal Pradesh sacrificed land for the project, the newly constituted state formed in the wake of reorganisation of Punjab in 1966 was not allocated any share in the benefits emanating from the Pong dam. Yet, the state had to shoulder the task of rehabilitation of a large number of displaced families and hence, the problem is yet to be resolved. There was no fixed and stipulated time period, by which the displaced families of the Pong dam were to be fully resettled and rehabilitated to overcome their long years of agonies and wandering life (Bhanot and Singh 1992).

The Tehri Dam

The Tehri dam on Bhagirathi river, a main tributary of the Ganges, is one of the world's largest and most controversial hydroelectric projects. The cost of the scheme, originally estimated at Rs 1,950 million, virtually crossed more than Rs 60,000 million at the time of completion. The project got underway in 1978 and was completed in 2002 and its hydroelectric plant became operational in July 2006. Nearly 5,200 hectares of land is lost to the reservoir. Since its inception, the Tehri dam, because of its ecology and geo-physical features, became highly controversial. It was subjected to numerous lawsuits, demonstrations and hunger strikes by the project-affected people as well as the social activists. The government infamously neglected to fulfil the most basic resettlement and rehabilitation requirements. Basic data about the number of people affected by Tehri dam were not collected, affected people were not informed about the resettlement process, and a resettlement plan for nearly 1,00,000 affected people did not exist. According to Sunderlal Bahuguna, a noted environmental activist and a leader of the struggle against Tehri dam, "the dam was built in the tears of the people of project-affected region and in return the oustees got nothing except miseries and sufferings".

Although most of the displaced were given cash compensation and alternative land, the rehabilitation package failed to satisfy everyone. The oustees felt that the alternative sites provided were too far from Tehri. The State Government had provided them land near Pantnagar in Udhamsingh Nagar district of the Terai area. It was difficult for the oustees to settle in the plains, as they were all born and brought up in the hilly terrain. The problem of the oustees in spite of all possible compensation made by the state in terms of both cash and kind continues to exist. The anger of the oustees and social activists manifested at different points of time is pointer to the fact that the undercurrent of dissatisfaction of project-affected persons have not yet been subsided and it may continue among the descendants of the oustee population for years to come (Shukla 2001; Sharma 2009; Meher 2010).

The Sardar Sarovar Project

India's first Prime Minister, Pandit Jawaharlal Nehru, had conceived the Sardar Sarovar Project in the 1940s. However, the project took very long time for grounding and became a reality in 1979. The goal of the project is to create around 3,200 small, medium and large dams along the length of the river, with the Sardar Sarovar Dam being the largest. The espousers of the big dam project argue that the dam will provide hydroelectric power to the entire region, as well as help in irrigating the arid regions of Gujarat, namely, north Gujarat, Saurashtra and Kutch. The combined benefits would reach some 50 million people in the states of Gujarat, Maharashtra and Madhya Pradesh.

However, since its inception the dam on river Narmada has become highly controversial. It has received unique type of resistance and incessant protests not only by the oustees, the majority of whom are tribals, but also by the civil society organisations and eminent social and environmental activists of the country including Baba Amte and Medha Patker. The oustees of the dam feel totally insecure of their displaced life and livelihood and quite apprehensive of the R&R package, as many of them displaced from Madhya Pradesh region have been planned to be resettled and rehabilitated in Gujarat in a very alien environment having wide linguistic and cultural differences between the host and oustee populations. Under the circumstances, the activists of *Narmada Bachao Andolan* (Save the Narmada Movement) argue that the damage caused by the dam will far outweigh any potential benefits. It maintains that besides causing serious damage to the region's natural ecology (a recognised consequence of large-scale dam construction), the dam will cause displacement of millions of poor peasants and tribals, causing not only a loss of livelihood, but also a loss of a historical way of life. In addition, some among the environmental scientists and geologists apprehend that building of the dam will make the region more prone to earthquakes and the benefits estimated to generate by the dam will be much below than the social and environmental costs of displacement and loss of livelihood of millions of people. Furthermore, the river supplies water to residents in Madhya Pradesh, Maharashtra, Chhattisgarh and Rajasthan, and there are fears that the dam will block the flow of water to these regions, causing widespread devastation in some of the most arid parts of India. The NBA leaders further argue that the actual benefits of large dams are much less as compared to their projections. Thus, for instance, the Bargi dam, built 20 years ago, did not deliver adequate irrigation benefits. Similarly, there was no improvement in the electricity situation even though the Indira Sagar dam had been constructed at great speed. The Sardar Sarovar Project will not equally provide water to the millions of thirsty people in Kutch and Saurashtra. It would rather satiate the greed of rich farmers, industrialists and city people, who need more water and electricity for their luxurious living and higher level earning, instead of providing a lifeline to the drought-hit regions of Gujarat.

This clearly reflects the typical iniquitous development model where the richer and affluent sections conspire to usurp the resources of the poor to satiate their unending greed for wealth and comfort, and to achieve that goal, they use the state machinery in the name of development and people's welfare (for more details see, Kothari 2001; Dreze, Samson and Singh 1997; Baviskar 1995; Engineer 1990; Ghosh 1990).

The Rourkela Steel Plant

The location of the present Rourkela Steel Plant (RSP) in the public sector and the concomitant birth of a grafted township in mid-1950s led to the displacement of many tribal families in the Panposh sub-division of Sundargarh district in Orissa. It is found from the latest record available with the Additional District Magistrate, Rourkela that altogether land in 33 villages was acquired for the steel plant and its township in Rourkela. The total land acquired for the purpose was 19,722.69 acres (7,984.89 ha), out of which 14,824.18 acres (75.16%) were private land and the rest 4,898.51 acres were government land. The total number of families displaced by the land acquisition process was 2,901. Out of that, 1,974 (68.05%) were Scheduled Tribes (STs), and 279 (9.62%) were Scheduled Castes (SCs). The rest (22.34%) were general category households, of which the Other Backward Classes (OBCs) formed the majority. Apart from that, the plant was responsible for the acquisition of land in another 31 villages for the construction of a water reservoir at Mandira in river Sankh located at a distance of 30 km from Rourkela. According to the government record, the reservoir submerged 11,964 acres (4,843.72 ha) of land and the number of families displaced due to Mandira dam was 1,193, most of whom were tribals. On the whole, RSP caused direct displacement of 4,094 families and the total livelihood sustaining land lost for the project was 31,687 acres (12,829 ha), or 7.74 acres per displaced family.

The government records further show that the oustees were given only nominal cash compensation for the land and other lost properties, as per the price fixed by the government for different grades of land at that time. The cultivated lands in this part are of four types, viz., Bahal (best quality paddy land), Berna (terraced paddy land), Mal (up paddy land) and Guda (dry land). The price fixed for compensation at that time for different categories of lands per acre was as follows: (i) Bahal – Rs 900, (ii) Berna – Rs 600, (iii) Mal – Rs 400, and (iv) Guda – Rs 200. For homestead land the price was fixed at Rs 227 per acre. It is also revealed from the records that in the 15 reclamation sites, none of the oustee family was compensated for the loss of Guda land and only 684 families were given 3,983.12 acres of agricultural land, which was in fact the wasteland. Added to that, 625 families were given 155.40 acres for homestead land in the reclamation sites at 24.86 decimals of land per family.

Families displaced for the construction of the Mandira dam were rehabilitated in six resettlement colonies. All the 1,193 oustee families received 149.74 acres of homestead land at 12.55 decimals per family. The amount of agricultural land allotted to them in these resettlement areas was 1,833.22 acres at 1.54 acres per family, whereas the average amount of land lost by a displaced family was around 10 acres. It may be noted here that the Mandira dam oustees did not get benefits like housing plot or job extended to the plant oustees. After many protests later, some of the oustees were considered for steel plant jobs and the problem continues till date.

Initially, when the Master Plan for a new industrial township and blueprint of the project was prepared by the then Hindustan Steel Limited, the local people of the region were mostly indifferent about the development project due to their illiteracy and ignorance. However, when the process of acquisition of private land began, the villagers started showing their resentment and discontentment. To pacify the villagers, the Government of Orissa issued a press note taking responsibility for the rehabilitation and resettlement of the displaced people. The company, set up in German collaboration, also took the help of the German Lutheran Church to prevail upon the tribal protesters, as many among them were converted to Christianity. The people were also loyal to the Church for its charitable activities in the region. This to some extent helped in containing the protests of the tribals. In spite of that, the resentment of people kept on simmering against forced involuntary displacement. The *ganjhus* (village head) of several affected villages in a public meeting in 1951 had passed a resolution that they did not want a steel plant in the region by sacrificing their land. By 1953, the locals had formed an association called, Steel Plant Site People's Federation, and made a representation to the District Collector who assured them that their interest in land would be taken up and they would be given preference in employment in the steel plant. The people were ignorant about the effects of the steel plant on their livelihood and hence they adopted an ambivalent attitude towards it. The intervention made by the then Chief Minister of Orissa, Nabakrushna Choudhury and the state government's promise to provide adequate cash/land compensation and livelihood support including one job to each of the displaced families pacified the protesters (Meher 2004: 67–71; Roy Burman 1968).

It is claimed that among the past oustees of development projects in India, the displaced persons of Rourkela were given one of the best R&R

packages. The displaced families were provided with land-based rehabilitation and job-based rehabilitation. It is, however, found that the effort of land-based rehabilitation of the oustees was half-hearted as there was no uniformity in the principle of compensation paid to RSP oustees and Mandira dam oustees. The decision relating to R&R measures was totally ad hoc and arbitrary. On the other hand, many displaced families were not provided any employment in the steel plant for the sacrifice made by their ancestors in the past. According to Ramchandra Sahoo, President of Rourkela Steel Plant Displaced Persons' Association, about 3,500 tribal families and another 500 other caste families among the oustees of the displaced and affected villages of RSP have not been given job by the plant authority. The total number of un-rehabilitated families of RSP at present is 8,006 including Mandira dam oustees. The RSP authority however claims that the total number of families displaced by the RSP was 4,000 and the plant has given jobs to 6,200 displaced persons by the end of 2007. This claim is, however, frequently contested by the original oustees and their descendants. It has been found from my field investigation that many original oustee families and their descendants could not get plant jobs due to lack of minimum education. In some cases, the middlemen collected the 'displacement certificates' from the oustee families so as to help them getting plant jobs. But actually the middlemen in connivance with the RSP officials misused all such certificates and provided jobs to many non-oustees. That apart, it has been found that only one job was provided against a particular holding, whereas there were three/four legal heirs against all such joint holdings of land at that time. This in reality deprived many from the original oustee families to get plant jobs.

It has also been revealed in some of the resettlement colonies of Rourkela oustees that the RSP authority inhumanely evacuated many of the displaced families during rainy season. Even bulldozers were used to demolish the house and no arrangement was made for the food and shelter of the displaced people in the resettlement sites. People were forcibly loaded into trucks like animals and they were dumped in the reclamation camps located far away from Rourkela in Bonei sub-division area of Sundargarh district and in Deogarh sub-division area of undivided Sambalpur district. At that time, the sites chosen for resettlement of the displaced people of RSP were highly inaccessible as they were in the midst of forest. The land was also not suitable for agriculture. Therefore, people virtually starved and many died of epidemic like cholera and diarrhoea due to intake of inedible food and contaminated water. Till date in many resettlement colonies located in forest area, the demarcation of forest and revenue land has not been made properly and this has left an easy option for the authority to evict them again. Unfortunately, such a fear came true for some oustees. Thus, in village Tainsar, about 27 to 44 acres of land belonging to oustee families have been given in recent times to Jay Balaji Jyoti Industry, a sponge iron plant, without the knowledge of the people. Similarly, another sponge iron plant in Kuarmunda has encroached upon the land given to the oustee families (for more details see Meher 2010).

The Bhilai Steel Plant

The Bhilai Steel Plant (BSP) in present Chhattisgarh state was set up during the Second Five-Year Plan period along with Rourkela and Durgapur as central public sector undertakings. In mid-1950s, before the setting up of the steel plant, Bhilai was a small unknown village adjacent to Durg, the district headquarters town in the then Madhya Pradesh. According to Srinivasan (1984), on 1 April 1984, the total land acquisition by BSP in the region including its captive mines was 12,086.6 hectares (29,853.90 acres). Altogether 94 villages and 5,703 families were affected due to land acquisition. Before the setting up of the steel plant, the acquired villages were characterised by subsistence agricultural economy vulnerable to weather God. Life of people in the village was placid and peaceful. There was little contact with the outsiders, except among the kin confined to a limited kinship territory in the region. However, the main village Bhilai boasted of a small railway station on Mumbai–Kolkata railway line passing through it.

Given such a context, people in general welcomed the setting up industry and fostered much hope on it to make the livelihood of their progenies much better in future. There was very little organised resistance against the project by the involuntarily displaced people of the villages. Although there was minor and sporadic protest by the oustees relating particularly to arbitrary fixation of the compensation price by the state, expecting brighter hope for all in future the oustees finally yielded to development euphoria of the time. Even the oustees of the project did not demand 'land for land' settlement package and separate resettlement colonies for all displaced families. The assurance given by the plant to provide industrial job to at least one adult member of every displaced families was a great consolation for all. The oustees settled down on their own nearer to the plant area in the villages according to their own choice and some bought agricultural land in the neighbouring villages by utilising the compensation money. However, as the compensation was far below the prevailing market price of land in the region and since the price for land increased to almost twofold due to setting up of the plant, the oustees could manage to get around one-third of the lost land assets in their new set-up. Many even failed to procure that much assets, as the amount received by the landless and sharecroppers was too low and it was spent mostly in meeting consumption expenditure of the oustee households. Some of the oustee families even spent the compensation money in wasteful consumption, as they were all ignorant about the future. There was nobody to guide them to make right use of the compensation money.

The land in the plant site region of stratum I and II villages that were most affected was of different grades carrying different values per acre according to its agricultural importance. According to the survey conducted by the then state government of Madhya Pradesh, the land was locally classified into ten different types and the prevailing market price of such lands per acre was fixed (Government of Madhya Pradesh 1959 and 1967). The land acquired from the oustees was compensated accordingly. But, as the majority of the oustee families were illiterates, they could not know how their land was graded and how the compensation amount was determined. Nobody questioned the price given by the authority and the oustees were exploited by the petty land revenue officials while fixing and making payment for the compensation value.

It has been found from my recent study that the oustees of BSP suffered equally like the oustee families of RSP. About 56 per cent of the original oustee families are found to be living in poverty. Even those who were employed in the steel plant could do little to improve the socio-economic condition of their progenies. After retirement from the plant service many such families witnessed downward mobility and fell into the vicious circle of poverty as they did not have adequate savings or developed human capital to sustain themselves in the changed urban environment. Owing to lack of quality education, many of the progenies of retired BSP workers now work as contract workers in various work sites of BSP and its township in Bhilai (Meher 2010: 55).

The Mining and Mega Industrial Projects of Post-1990s

In the post-reform years, the mineral-rich backward states such as Orissa, Jharkhand and Chhattisgarh have laid stress on massive exploitation of mineral resources and development of mineral-based heavy industries such as iron and steel, aluminium and super thermal power plants. They have become the development facilitators for the private corporate sector and the MNCs without any concern for long-term environmental and social consequences of such 'development'. In the name of promoting industries to increase the living standard of people in their respective state, the state governments have been competing among themselves to attract foreign direct investments (FDI) and investment by the large Indian private sector companies to facilitate access to their unexplored mineral resources that are found in the areas resided mostly by the tribals.

Orissa, by the end of 2005, had signed Memorandum of Understandings (MoUs) with many MNCs and large Indian corporate houses to facilitate the setting up 43 iron and steel as well as aluminium industries in the state. The MoUs include the giant Posco of South Korea that proposes to establish a 12 million tonnes export-oriented steel plant with its own port near Paradeep with a total investment of Rs 510 billion. Interestingly, if all such units start operating in the state then all the iron ore and bauxite ore of so far proven deposits are likely to be exhausted within next 30 years leaving little for the next generation population. According to the estimates of Orissa Bureau of Mines, the state has total iron ore deposits of 4,177 million tonnes. However, according to information provided by the Minister, Steel and Mines, Government of Orissa, the Orissa Mining Corporation (OMC) has already given on lease to exploit 3,133 million tonnes of iron ore from its various mines to various agencies like SAIL (Steel Authority of India Ltd.), TISCO (Tata Iron and Steel Company), Nilachal Ispat Nigam Ltd., Jindal Steel Company, etc.

Further, according to the MoU signed with the Posco, the state has to supply 1,000 million tonnes of iron ore at a royalty price of Rs 400 per tonne, as against the prevailing international market price of Rs 2,600 per tonne. Again, as per the MoUs signed with another 37 large, medium and small companies, the state has agreed to supply 2,016 million tonnes of iron ore to them. That means the state is already in supply deficit problem, in so far as its promises to the national companies as per the earlier MoUs and existing proven deposit of iron ore in the state are concerned. If the Posco starts operating in spite of its controversial MoU, the situation may worsen further in terms of environmental degradation, displacement and livelihood insecurity of the poor. The area in which the Posco project is proposed to be set up is a highly fertile agricultural zone nearer to the sea coast. It has been reported that more than one lakh people will lose their agro-based sustainable living in case land is acquired for the steel plant. As against that, hardly 5,000 families of the region shall be benefited by the linkage effects generated by the steel plant, as it is planned to go for high-tech driven production employing directly about 12,000 persons to produce 12 million tonnes of steel per annum. In half an acre land of betel vine people manage to earn about Rs 50,000 to Rs 60,000 per annum by selling and exporting betel leafs to far off places. Besides, the area is famous for high yield rate of paddy and marine fish. So to say, this area is an oasis in the poverty-stricken state of Orissa, where everybody subsisting on agro-based living has reasonable level of earning free from the scourge of poverty. It is obvious that the location of a steel plant in such agro-climatic zone will ruin agriculture and pisciculture due to increasing pollution of land, air and water. That apart, the people displaced from their hearth and home shall not be in a position to have non-agriculture based sustainable living for them and for their progenies in the future by working in the steel plant or in the urban informal sector economy (Meher 2006).

Notwithstanding the Posco stalemate and controversy, the state on 21 December 2006 signed another MoU with the ArcelorMittal of the UK (United Kingdom) to set up another 12 million tonnes steel plant in Keonjhar district of Orissa with an investment of Rs 400 billion. According to the MoU, the plan consists of building coke oven, steel making, rolling mills, and a 750 MW captive power plant. Mittal has asked for 8,000 acres of land at the proposed location. The land requirement is almost double the size of the land sought by Posco, as the company has planned for further expansion of the plant capacity in future.

Similarly, it is found that in between 2001 and 2007, the government of Jharkhand has signed 66 MoUs with the MNCs and corporate houses for large-scale investment in mineral-based industries like iron and steel, sponge iron, cement, etc. The list includes big players like ArcelorMittal, Tatas, Birlas, Jindal Steel, Essar, etc. It is found that all such industries will require acquisition of 3,37,798 acres of land and consumption of around 300 million tonnes of iron ore per annum (Ekka 2008: 33–38).

In Chhattisgarh, the number of MoUs signed by the state government for mineral-based industries like iron and steel, sponge iron, aluminium, cement, thermal power plant, etc., between 2001 and 2008 is as high as 73. The proposed investment of all those industries is Rs 908.22

billion. Besides several MNCs and corporate houses signing agreement to set up industries in Chhattisgarh state (Government of Chhattisgarh 2008), many sponge iron, thermal plant and aluminium units have already gone into operation in the state since early 1990s.

In the wake of plan to mine bauxite and to locate aluminium industries by the MNCs, the tranquil tribal belt of the undivided Koraput and Kalahandi districts of KBK[2] region in Orissa has been undergoing the trauma of massive tribal unrest and people's protests since early 1990. The majestic plateaus of the north-west part of the present Rayagada district in Orissa carry almost one-third of the bauxite deposits in India. The misty mountaintops and the plateaus covering Kashipur block of Rayagada district and Thuamul-Rampur block of Kalahandi district have nearly a thousand perennial streams and good tree coverage. But, mining and industrial activities have engendered a unique eco-climate in these two blocks.

Among the MNCs and corporate houses eyeing for the bauxite deposits of the region, UAIL (Utkal Alumina International Limited) Vedanta Alumina Limited and Aditya Aluminium Limited have already made their presence felt in the region. These companies have begun their work notwithstanding several protests and resistances to the involuntary displacement and the inadequate compensation packages including R&R benefits provided to the project-affected people. The Vedanta Alumina Limited, a subsidiary of Sterlite Industries (India) Limited, has also proceeded with its plan to exploit the Niyamgiri bauxite reserve located on top of Niyamgiri hills in Lanjigarh tehsil area of Kalahandi district in Orissa. As per the agreement, Vedanta Alumina Limited has already set up an Alumina Complex, which includes 1 MTPA (million tonne per annum) Alumina Refinery Plant, 3 MTPA of bauxite mining and 75 MW Captive Power Plant at Lanjigarh at an aggregate investment of Rs 400 billion. In August 2008, the company could manage to get the approval of the Supreme Court of India to mine bauxite from the Niyamgiri hills. Very recently, the Ministry of Environment and Forest of Government of India has refused stage II environment clearance to Vedanta's mining proposal in the Niyamgiri area stating that it has violated Forest Rights Act and Environment Protection Act. This is based on the report of N.C. Saxena Committee on Vedanta. However, both the State Government in Orissa and the ruling party feel that Centre's stalling of Vedanta mining of Niyamgiri hills for bauxite is unjust as the mining project is important for the people of Orissa to develop the backward tribal region (http://news. outlookindia. com/item.aspx?691419).

Similarly, the Aditya Aluminium Project has planned to mine 3 MTPA bauxite at Kodingamali in Koraput district. The company will set up 1 MTPA Alumina Refinery at Kansariguda village of Kashipur region of Rayagada district (VIMTA Labs 2004).

However, the tribals and other marginalised people do not see any bright future for them in the wake of industrialisation of the region. Majority of them, being illiterate or semi-literate lacking technical skill, would not certainly be absorbed permanently in the proposed mines and industrial complexes. Conversely, they would lose their precious forest and life sustaining natural resources of the region. Consequently, tribal protest movement for a justified living in a natural surrounding has gained momentum in recent years and members of civil society and political parties have also come forward in their support. The tribal leaders fail to understand the rationale of the government which has so far done very little for their development in terms of education, health or other basic infrastructure and is now asking them to 'sacrifice' their livelihood for the sake of 'development'. The long-term ecological costs of such 'development' like gaping holes in the forest including damaged streams and ground water sources would permanently render the forest unfit for habitation. It would convert the entire region into desert and barren land after the exhaustion of bauxite ores. The tribals resent that in spite of the area being governed by the Fifth Schedule and in spite of the victims being *adivasis* (tribals), the government insists on going ahead with the project without consulting them and without devising any concrete R&R policy for their sustenance.

It is worth mentioning here that on 2 January 2006 Orissa witnessed massive tribal uprisings in the Kalinganagar industrial area of Jajpur district when efforts were made by the Tata Company officials to erect a boundary for the acquired land for their 6 million tonnes integrated iron and steel plant. The tribals were demanding higher compensation for the land acquired from them at the prevailing market price in place of Rs 25,000 to Rs 50,000 paid to them per acre of land around 10 years back. This finally culminated into strong violent protests by the land-loser tribals and axing to death of a policeman on duty by one of the protesters. After the death of policeman, the venue of the Tata's steel plant turned into a battleground. Sudden burst of anger by the armed police resulted in reckless firing on the protesting mob and killing of 12 innocent tribal men and women on the spot. Since then, the entire tribal belt of Orissa is in turmoil and despite subliminal state of living people do not like setting up of large mineral-based industries in any part of the state.

Even the mineral-rich Keonjhar district of Orissa, which did not have any history of recorded mass protests against mineral exploitation earlier, witnessed massive protests. In June 2007, people of nine villages in four Gram Panchayats of this district decided to oppose the Rs 125 billion Sterlite Steel Plant at Mahadeijoda. The villagers apprehended that the project would affect more than 1,000 acres of fertile agricultural land, rivers, streams and plantations. The *Bisthapan Birodhi Manch* (Displacement Opposition Front) feels that in the wake of coming up of the 5.1 million tonnes steel plant, as many as 12 minor irrigation projects, nine lift irrigation projects, Hemrada and Machhakandana rivers and four streams presently helping people of the region in growing a huge quantity of crops and vegetables will dry up. According to the blueprint of the project, it would acquire 2,160.89 acres of private land and 1,217.18 acres of government land and would lead to displacement of 173 families of four panchayats.

Aggrieved at the inadequate compensation and loss of their hundreds of acres of land to Mahanadi Coalfields Limited (MCL) in the mid-1990s, the villagers of Kulhapada in Sundargarh district have been staging protests and resorting to blockades off and on in front of the Basundhara mines office demanding higher compensation and jobs to the displaced persons. It is reported that many displaced persons have not been paid adequate compensation or given employment by the MCL authority for the loss of their land. Some of the tribal oustees report that although the Basundhara mines in Sundargarh district started operating five years ago, many displaced persons have not been given any employment and their compensation dues have not been settled yet. They have been drawing attention of the district administration and the MCL since long. But none of their grievances has been redressed and the plight of the oustees continues as before. Very recently, therefore, the oustee villagers of Kulhapada had resorted to blockade of coal production and transportation from Basundhara mines for more than five days.

Like Basundhara mines of Sundargarh, the sleepy hamlets around Punkhri-Barwadih in Jharkhand have witnessed people's violent resistance to the prospect of losing their fertile farmland to an industrial venture of National Thermal Power Corporation (NTPC). Apart from the loss of over 10,000 acres of well-irrigated three-crop farmland, and dense forests, NTPC's planned opencast captive coalmine project might displace some 14,000 families. In November 2006, a mob of thousands of farmers tore down NTPC's project site office at Barkagaon. In order to show their protests and resentments against the land acquisition, the affected villagers have formed the anti-land acquisition organisation *Karnpura Bachao Sangharsh Samiti* (KBSS) and the *Karanpura Bisthapita Morcha* (KBM). Those set to lose their homes, farmlands and forest-based livelihoods are largely small farmers belonging to the ST and SC communities. It is reported that rivulets crisscrossing the agricultural landscape around the villages supply enough water to produce three crops every year, while the forests – consisting mostly *Saal* (Shorea Robusta) trees – provide ample sustenance with their leaves and myriad fruits. In this situation of a rich ecological base, it is natural and obvious that people's temper will reach high in the case of dispossession from the land. The protesters say that they would rather die fighting for their land but will not give it away to NTPC or any other company while alive (Das 2007).

In the aftermath of Kalinganagar incidence, protests of the tribals and other ecosystem people against mining-based industrialisation and development became more intensified. It is also not a mere coincidence that all tribal districts in the three states of Chotanagpur region such as Orissa, Jharkhand and Chhattisgarh today are witnessing ultra-left movements. These districts have now become the breeding ground of Maoists or Naxalites as the tribals feel threatened to their sustainable means of subsistence from nature. The gloomy experience of 'development of underdevelopment' of the tribals has provided fuel for the growth of Maoist movements. As compared to the 'greedy' efforts of MNCs and the Indian corporate houses, and state's failure to protect their interest or even to provide them basic minimum facilities, the tribals indeed see Maoists as their saviours and extend them all implicit supports.

The movement of ecosystem people in Orissa, Jharkhand and Chhattisgarh has also spread to industrially advanced West Bengal leading to final disbanding of Nano car project of Tata at Singur and the stalling of SEZ project at Nandigram in Midnapore district (Meher 2010). Similarly, the fate of high value (Rs 51,000 crore) Posco project by the steel giant MNC of South Korea in Paradeep area of Orissa and the two iron and steel projects of ArcelorMittal in Orissa and Jharkhand has been hanging since 2005. Land for the Posco project and the two other mega iron and steel projects of ArcelorMittal in Keonjhar district of Orissa and Khunti and Gumla districts of Jharkhand has not been possible to acquire despite strong support of the state governments in these two states. Also, in Chhattisgarh, the mega iron and steel project of Tata is facing strong resistance of the tribals of Bastar region.

Conclusion

This paper clearly shows the inadequacy of resettlement and rehabilitation measures adopted in the case of oustees of mega development projects. The project oustee populations in different parts of the country carry discontentment current in their hearts even after long years of their relocation/resettlement in the new sites/habitations. Hence, there have been intermittent and often violent protests shown against the project authority/government for rightful shares of benefits and cash/land compensation.

Interestingly, even after fifty years of displacement, displaced persons of Rourkela Steel Plant in Orissa have joined protest movement and economic blockades so as to demand return of the unused surplus land and jobs for the uncovered displaced families. This type of protest movement has further ignited the oustee population of similar other project-affected families with the support of local NGOs and civil society organisations. No doubt, the mega river dam projects, iron and steel plants, heavy electrical plants and the like have become the symbols of India's economic progress. However, the inadequacy of R&R policy measures to rehabilitate the victims of involuntary displacement has generated new poverty and miseries and belittled the gains of such development projects. Over the years, the development euphoria of people was turned into disillusion, as more and more oustee population in the country, particularly the vulnerable groups like tribals and dalits, has increasingly become pauperised and homeless due to ad hoc R&R package and half-hearted project-specific policy measures including cash compensation given by the government.

Development, as it is understood in the contemporary world, should not be exploitative for the downtrodden and marginalised people, nor should it be resource exhaustive. It appears that development projects that require large-scale involuntary displacement of human population should not be taken up at all, unless the oustee people develop full confidence to become the prime beneficiaries of such projects. This can be possible if the local human capital in the project area is developed as per the requirement of new projects. In a populous country like India, development project should not be based on high technology that minimises employment of human labour and puts strain on natural resources. Benefits of such development are cornered by the privileged sections of society in terms of jobs, access to new gazettes and consumer durables and the like. The downtrodden people affected by mega projects hardly benefit from such development. For any balance development, it is therefore necessary to ensure food and employment security for a healthy living of project-affected families. These people need development of health care facilities, skill-based education and sustainable food supply to improve their quality of life. This can be achieved by going for a sustainable development model that ensures 'growth with equity' and provides employment to all.

Notes

1. The term 'ecosystem people' refers to indigenous tribal and rural population deriving their sustainable means of subsistence from nature. The term is coined by Gadgil and Guha (1995) in their study.
2. KBK region is considered as one of the most backward regions in India with a very high percentage of tribal and other depressed category population. The region is called KBK based on the initial letters of three old and undivided districts of Orissa, namely, Kalahandi, Bolangir and Koraput. This region now comprises of eight districts such as Kalahandi, Nuapada, Bolangir, Sonepur, Koraput, Malkangiri, Rayagada and Nawarangpur and it is infamous for its high incidence of poverty and distress seasonal migration.

References

Areeparampil, M. 1989. 'Industries, Mines and Dispossession of Indigenous People: The Case of Chota Nagpur', in W. Fernandes and E. Ganguly Thukral (eds.), *Development, Displacement and Rehabilitation* (13–32). New Delhi: Indian Social Institute.

Baboo, B. 1992. *Technology and Social Transformation: The Case of the Hirakud Multipurpose Dam Project in Orissa*. New Delhi: Concept Publishing Company.

Baviskar, A. 1995. *In the Belly of the River: Adivasi Battles over River in the Narmada Valley*. New Delhi: Oxford University Press.

Bhanot, R. and M. Singh. 1992. 'The Oustees of Pong Dam: Their Search for a Home', in E. Ganguly Thukral (ed.), *Big Dams, Displaced People: Rivers of Sorrow Rivers of Change*. New Delhi: Sage Publications.

Blaser, M., H.A. Feit and G. Mcrae (eds.). 2004. *In the Way of Development: Indigenous Peoples, Life Projects and Globalisation*. London and New York: Zed Books.

Cernea, M.M. 1996. *Eight Main Risks: Impoverishment and Social Justice in Resettlement*. Washington, DC: The World Bank, Environment Department.

——. 2000. 'Impoverishment Risks and Reconstruction: A Model for Population Displacement and Resettlement', in M.M. Cernea and Chris McDowel (eds.), *Risks and Reconstruction: Experiences of Resettlers and Refugees*. Washington, DC: The World Bank.

CSE. 1985. *The State of India's Environment 1984–85: The Second Citizens' Report*. New Delhi: Centre for Science and Environment.

Das, Anand S.T. 2007. 'Public Sector Displacement: A Singur in the Making', February 03. *http://www.tehelka.com*.

Dreze, J., M. Samson and S. Singh (eds.). 1997. *The Dam and the Nation: Displacement and Resettlement in the Narmada Valley*. New Delhi: Oxford University Press.

Ekka, Alex. 2008. 'Mining and Displacement of Tribals in Jharkhand'. Unpublished Paper presented at the Workshop on "Land Acquisition for Development Projects in Scheduled Areas, Increasing Land Alienation among Tribals and PESA", Lal Bahadur Shastri National Academy of Administration, Mussorie, 03–04 March.

Engineer, Rusi. 1990. 'The Sardar Sarovar Controversy', in B.D. Dhawan (ed.), *Big Dams: Claims, Counter Claims* (155–74). New Delhi: Common Wealth Publishers.

Fernandes, W. 1994. *Development-induced Displacement in the Tribal Areas of India*. New Delhi: Indian Social Institute.

Gadgil, M. and R. Guha. 1995. *Ecology and Equity: The Use and Abuse of Nature in Contemporary India*. London and New Delhi: Routledge and Penguin Books India.

Government of Chhattisgarh. 2008. 'Chhattisgarh State: State Investment Promotion Board'. *http://chhattisgarh.nic.in/departments/siph/MOU_LIST.pdf*.

Ghosh, Arun. 1990. 'A Plea for Open Government: Case of Narmada Project', in B.D. Dhawan (ed.), op. cit. (55–60).

Government of India. 2002. Tenth Five Year Plan (2002–2007), Vol. II, Sectoral Policies and Programmes. New Delhi: Planning Commission.

——. 2009. *Report of the Expert Group to Review the Methodology for Estimation of Poverty*. New Delhi: Planning Commission. Available at *http://planningcommission.gov.in/reports/genrep_pov.pdf*.

Government of Madhya Pradesh. 1959. *Socio-Economic Survey of Bhilai Region*. Part I (First Round 1955–56). Bombay: Popular Prakashan.

——. 1967. *Socio-Economic Survey of Bhilai Region*. Part II (Second and Third Rounds 1957–59). Bombay: Popular Prakashan.

Kothari, A. 2001. 'Against a People's Movement', *Frontline*, 18 (15). Available at *http://www.hinduonnet.com/fline/fl1815/index.htm*

Mahapatra, L.K. 1999. *Resettlement, Impoverishment and Reconstruction in India*. New Delhi: Vikas Publishing House.

Mathur, H.M. 2008. 'Development and Displacement: Introduction and Overview', in H.M. Mathur (ed.), *India Social Development Report 2008: Development and Displacement* (3–13). New Delhi: Council for Social Development and Oxford University Press.

Mathur, H.M. and D. Marsden (eds.). 1998. *Development Projects and Impoverishment Risks: Resettling Project Affected People in India*. New Delhi: Oxford University Press.

Meadows, D.H., D.L. Meadows, J. Randers and W.W. Behrens III. 1972. *The Limits to Growth*. New York: Universe Books.

Meher, R. 2001. 'Degeneration of the Periphery under Hegemonic Development: The Case of Marginalisation of the Aboriginal in a Tribal Region', *Indian Social Science Review*, 3 (2): 289–326.

——. 2003. 'The Social and Ecological Effects of Industrialisation in a Tribal Region: The Case of the Rourkela Steel Plant', *Contributions to Indian Sociology* (n.s.), 37 (3): 429–57.

——. 2004. *Stealing the Environment: Social and Ecological Effects of Industrialization in Rourkela*. New Delhi: Manohar.

——. 2010. *How Mineral-based Industrial Development Marginalizes and Displaces People in India: Three Case Studies*. Lewiston, New York: Edwin Mellen Press.

Oommen, T.K. 2004. *Development Discourse: Issues and Concerns*. New Delhi: Regency Publications.

——. 2006. 'Coping with Development Pathologies: Resistance to Displacement', *Sociological Bulletin*, 55 (2): 267–80.

Ota, A.B. 1999. *Resettlement and Rehabilitation Policies of Different Sectors for the Affected People in the State of Orissa*. Bhubaneswar: Department of Water Resources, Government of Orissa.

Pandey, B. 1998a. *Depriving the Underprivileged for Development*. Bhubaneswar: Institute for Social and Economic Development.

——. 1998b. 'Impoverishing Effects of Coal Mining Projects: A Case Study of Five Villages in Orissa', in H.M. Mathur and D. Marseden (eds.), op. cit. (174–92).

Reddy, I.U.B. 1992. *Displacement and Rehabilitation*. New Delhi: Mittal Publications.

——. 1994. *Industrial Development and the Problem of the Uprooted.* Jaipur: Rawat Publications.

Roy Burman, B.K. 1968. 'Social Processes in the Industrialization of Rourkela', *Census of India 1961*. Vol. 1, Monograph Series, Monograph No. 1, Part XI E. New Delhi: Government of India, Registrar General and Census Commissioner.

Sahu, B. 2000. *Development and Displacement: A Case Study of Rengali Dam Project in Orissa.* Unpublished PhD Thesis, Utkal University, Bhubaneswar.

Sharma, M. 2009. 'Passages from Nature to Nationalism: Sunderlal Bahuguna and Tehri Dam Opposition in Garhwal', *Economic and Political Weekly*, 44 (8): 35–42.

Shukla, J.P. 2001. 'Damming the Protests', *The Hindu*, April 29. Available at *http://www.hinduonnet.com/2001/04/29/stories/05291349.htm.*

Srinivasan, N.R. 1984. *The History of Bhilai*. Bhilai: SAIL, Bhilai Steel Plant.

Taylor, B.R. (ed.). 1995. *Ecological Resistance Movements: The Global Emergence of Radical and Popular Environmentalism*. Albany: State University of New York Press.

Viegas, Philip. 1992. 'The Hirakud Dam Oustees: Thirty Years After', in E. Ganguly Thukral (ed.), op. cit. (29–53).

VIMTA Labs. 2004. *Resettlement and Rehabilitation Action Plan for the PAPs of Alumina Refinery Project at Kansariguda*. Hyderabad: VIMTA Labs Ltd.

12

Policy Planning in Development Projects

Processes and Limitations

Manish K. Verma

The gigantic urge of development activities saw man reaching to such a threshold where their endless craving results in the exclusion and under-development of their fellow brothers. Every development project requires large chunk of land, which can be easily available and grabbed in the remotest rural and tribal part of the society, and hence the planners generally fall back to these areas. Consequently, the victims of industrial development overtly lose their dwelling and livelihood and covertly their culture, civilisation and bonding with the natal place. The condition becomes more pathetic when the project-affected persons (henceforth PAPs) are not even consulted before, during or after the whole process. Ironically, they remain ignorant and unaware about their future and oscillate between hope and despair. At times, with great amount of expectations, they dream hefty package from the rehabilitation agencies and on un-accomplishment of wishes and desires, they show intense resentment. This swiftly brings our sharp attention towards the process governing the planning of such development projects and its underlying limitations in the form of resettlement and rehabilitation at the level of policy, planning and administration.

In this background, the main objective of the paper is sociological interpretation of involuntary displacement particularly in Singrauli region, which awfully disrupts the entire environment of the affected community. In fact, the paper is an attempt to focus on the tribulations which mounted during project execution and the manner in which such problems were dealt with by various rehabilitation agencies. The whole exercise is done in the background of the policy guidelines of National Thermal Power Corporation (NTPC), World Bank and other government organisations concerned with the execution of project in the Singrauli region. The paper also brings into sharper focus the effectiveness of various resettlement and rehabilitation (henceforth R&R) policies, the kind of changes and modification done to it during past decades to suit the changing circumstances, the role played by rehabilitation personnel and the intrinsic troubles experienced by inhabitants due to all these. In other words, it is an endeavour to introspect into various policies of displacement and its adequacies from people's perception.

To carry out a systematic study, two NTPC projects – Vindhyachal (VSTPP) and Rihand Super Thermal Power Project, RSTPP) – situated in the Singrauli region of Uttar Pradesh state of India, were selected. These projects required vast amount of land for their inception and erection, which naturally displaced thousands of inhabitant rural people. Land oustees are forced to resettle at other places. The study includes analysis of these PAPs living at the new location sites. For the purpose of analysis, 250 heads of the household were selected for interview on the basis of random sampling. Apart from this, focused group discussion and the method of non-participatory observation were used for the collection of primary data. As usual, the secondary sources include books, journals, newspapers, coupled with demographic data from the local *Sarpanch* office and the voter list.

For the convenience of analysis, the paper is broadly divided into four sections. The first section provides an overall glimpse of the development-induced displacement scenario in India as well as worldwide under the title, 'Development-Induced Displacement: Singrauli and Others'. The second part, 'Policy Planning' discusses in length the origin and evolution of various resettlement and rehabilitation laws in India with its highlighted significance. The third section, 'Administrative and Policy Limitations' critically analyses the effectiveness and usefulness of the resettlement and rehabilitation policies discussed in the previous section. The fourth and the last segment is devoted to the 'People's Perception and Resentment' towards the whole issue. The way general masses conceive these policies and the kind of reactions they demonstrate against the atrocities done to them are analysed.

I

Development-Induced Displacement: Singrauli and Others

Development-Induced Displacement: An Overview

The outburst in development-induced displacement is one of the most serious issues plaguing development planners, causing widespread concern and demanding immediate attention. The phenomenon of project-induced displacement has compounded many of the problems of social development. It has relegated social objective to the background, which government was committed to until recently, of ensuring land rights and carrying out land reforms and land distribution. By impoverishing the large masses of displaced people, it has aggravated the already complex problem of alleviating poverty. It has also become a major source of the deprivation of basic human rights in the society.

In the mistaken priority to accelerate growth, mainly through mega projects undertaken by private companies, the government has generally taken the side of these companies at the cost of displaced persons. Relocation has seldom been regarded as human problem involving fundamental rights, but considered a simple law and order problem with oustees always been on the wrong side of the law. As a result, any reluctance to part with land has been regarded as violation of law and protests against displacement have been ruthlessly crushed as in case of dam construction in Narmada and Tehri involving more than one states; power projects like NTPC; mining industries in the form of CIL or more recently, Nandigram and Singur in West Bengal and in Kashipur in Orissa. Upendra Baxi (2008: 17) has therefore rightly remarked that "no development without displacement" is the mantra of the developers everywhere.

If we peep into the history of development-induced displacement, we find that earlier displacement was caused largely by multi-purpose river valley projects like dams and mining activities. There are signs suggesting displacement from the age of the Gupta dynasty. In the middle ages projects such as the Jai Samand Lake built near Udaipur in the 18th century affected many families. However, displacement did not disrupt people's lives completely because the population was then small and land was abundant. The displaced families could resettle themselves not far from their original habitat. Displacement was also caused in the colonial age in the pursuit of raw material for the Industrial Revolution in

England. Right from the 19th century, the colonialists in pursuit of this goal opened coal mines in Raniganj, tea gardens in Assam, coffee plantations in Karnataka etc. (Fernandes 2008: 89). Displacement became a serious issue in the colonial age, intensified after independence, and caused bigger problem in the context of globalisation today. Now, the land is being acquired for private companies for building factories, malls, parks, swimming pools, hotels, and night clubs (Dubey 2008: xv).

Worldwide experience with resettlement has shown that people who are displaced do not easily recover, much less improve, their previous standard of living. Resettlement studies have vividly documented the devastating consequences of failed resettlement projects, which create new pockets of poverty where none existed before. The fact is that for those affected, development has been too often experienced not as an opportunity, but as disruption and impoverishment. Such displacement not only puts affected people to grave impoverishment risks, but also causes a setback to the entire poverty reduction effort. As one observer puts it, "truly, development is a very contradictory affair if it reinforces the very poverty that it aims of eliminate" (Mathur 2008: 3–4).

Singrauli Region: A Retrospect

After detailed overview of India and worldwide, we will now focus on micro level and discuss the Singrauli scenario – our main focus of attention. In the past, Singrauli (GHK/MRM International et al. 1994; Electricite De France 1990; NTPC 1994) was an isolated little known and economically backward rural area with very less population living in small and scattered settlements. Forest and small fence characterised the hilly and undulating landscape, and the locals were mainly engaged in collecting minor products or in subsistence agriculture. After independence, the region started getting the attention of the planners basically for its large coal deposits which could be utilised for generation of power for urban/industrial development of the country. In conformity with the national goal, Singrauli region was opened up by railroad connection.

The first blow to their serene existence was in the form of land acquisition for Rihand Sagar dam in the beginning of the 1960s. The whole region came under chaos and turmoil and underwent pathetic experiences apropos loss of everything in the stream of dam. The compensation given was far inadequate in comparison to the loss incurred. Somehow, PAPs settled down, not fully but partially, in the vicinity. They thought, it is once for all and now, no one will disembark in future to infringe their privacy. But, the beginning of the 1980s earmarked another doom day in their life. Now, they had to forego the present patch of land to government agencies, on which they were lately living, for the sake of national goal. Naturally, they got displaced for the second time within the span of 20 years and came across same awesome encountering of distress, agony and anxiety.

II

Policy Planning

Policy guideline is essential for the success of any project. Development-induced displacement also solicits direction in the form of National R&R Policy of India, R&R Policy of NTPC, Land Acquisition Act of India, guidelines of donor agencies such as the World Bank etc. This section will analyse and evaluate the policy planning incorporated in the power projects of NTPC.

Land Acquisition Legislations in India

If we go through the history of land acquisition legislations (MARG 1990; The Land Acquisition Act, 1995) in India, it dates back to 1824. The Regulation I of 1824 was the first legislation of its kind. It empowered the government to acquire immovable property at a fair and reasonable price for construction of roads, canals or other public purposes. Act VI of the 1857 was the first full enactment, which had application to the whole of British India. It repealed all previous enactments relating to acquisition and its object. Through this Act, the principle of arbitration was introduced for the first time. Collector was empowered to fix the amount of compensation by agreement, if possible. If there was no agreement, the dispute had to be referred to arbitration. Later, in the 1870 Act, a detailed procedure for the acquisition of land was provided for the first time. Yet, the provision of this Act did not satisfy the needs of the day and eventually the Land Acquisition Act, 1894 was enacted.

Nearly a hundred years later, in 1984, the Act governing land acquisition in India took another shift and at least on paper, the effort was made to make it more people-friendly rather than government-friendly. Prior to 1984, the Land Acquisition Act was not applicable to the states of Jammu & Kashmir, Rajasthan, Kerala and Nagaland, which had their own self-contained Land Acquisition Acts. In 1984 the Land Acquisition (Amendment) Act was passed and became applicable to the whole of India, except Jammu & Kashmir.

The process of land acquisition starts with the Section 4(1) notification. By this, a preliminary notification by the government is made to the effect that land in a particular locality is needed or may be needed for any public purpose or for a company. A notification to this effect is also published in the official gazette and in two daily newspapers circulating in that locality of which at least one shall be in the regional language. Apart from this, the Collector shall paste public notices at convenient places in the said locality.

Then comes Section 5–A by which, within 30 days of the publication of the notification, anyone can file objection to the said acquisition of the land. Every objection shall be made to the Collector in writing who, in turn, shall give the objector an opportunity of being heard. Vide Section 9, the Collector issues public notice and individual notices to persons interested to file their claims for compensation. By Section 11, the Collector enquires into claims by the litigants. Finally, through Section 11 itself, the Collector awards the compensation.

The Government of India drastically amended 1894 Act in 1984. The Amendment Act of 1984 has resulted in the setting down of a time limit for the completion of all formalities between the issue of preliminary notice vide Section 4(1) and the issue of the declaration of intended acquisition vide Section 6(1). This period was three years. Another amendment gave an opportunity to those dissatisfied with the Collector's award to apply to him for a re-determination of the compensation payable to them on the basis of an order for higher compensation obtained by any one of them from the reference court by Section 28A.

These changes introduced by the Amendment Act of 1984 are beneficial to those who seek to minimise the undue delays that characterise acquisition proceedings and compensation payment on a realistic basis. The main point which emerges from the whole process of land acquisition is the immense power that has been conferred to the Collector. He is the sole authority and even the judiciary does not have much say in this regard. Once the Collector has taken a decision with regard to the land acquisition, it is final and binding on every one.

R&R Policy in India

Beginning of the 1980s observed sensitisation towards the ever-growing and all-pervasive problems of resettlement and rehabilitation. Opinion of the donor agencies as well as national and international organisations concerned with the social cause shifted towards protection of human rights. As a result, there were lots of hue and cry favouring for enactment of a sound National Resettlement and Rehabilitation Policy (GoI 1995; 1996) in India, ingenious enough to solve the problems of the oustees. As such, efforts were constantly paving toward the composition of a national policy.

Till now, there are very few states that have enacted state-wise R&R policies. "Till 2003, Maharashtra, Madhya Pradesh and Karnataka had rehabilitation laws for irrigation displaced persons. Rajasthan and Orissa had promulgated policies between 1994 and 1998" (Fernandes: 2005:123). Apart from that, some other states have issued government orders/resolutions. The Government of Maharashtra has developed a progressive policy to deal with people not successfully rehabilitated under previous water projects. There are also company-wise and sector-specific policies, such as those developed by the National Thermal Power Corporation (NTPC 1993), Coal India Ltd. and more recently by some other private and government infrastructure companies.

The attention of the NGOs (non-government organisations), particularly those concerned with tribal rights, as well as that of some donor agencies, have been drawn to the issue surrounding displacement due to increasing interest in matters of sustainability and human rights. These focused around the Sardar Sarovar Project during early 1990s.

There was pressure from the World Bank, other major donor agencies as well as national and international organisations concerned with the rights of the displaced. They expressed the need for a national policy. As a consequence, the Government of India initiated formulation of a sustainable policy on R&R. Thus, draft of a national resettlement policy has been the subject of widespread consultation amongst state governments and within the NGO community in many parts of the country. In 1989, a National Working Group on Displacement was formed through an NGO initiative which involved government officials also. Draft National Policy on Developmental Resettlement of Project Affected Persons was prepared. Since then, many more drafts have been prepared encompassing an ever-widening group of people – from 'oustees' of 'river valley projects' to 'persons affected by reservoir projects,' and now to the 'rehabilitation of persons displaced as a consequence of acquisition of land'.

The Ministry of Rural Development prepared the draft of a national policy for rehabilitation of persons displaced as a consequence of land acquisition.[1] Responsibility for the progress of government discussions lies with the Ministry of Rural Areas and Employment which has been designated as the nodal ministry for the execution of the policy. This shift in responsibility was perhaps one indication that the responsibility for successful R&R cannot really be given to a particular ministry, but is central to the agendas of many. The draft has been circulated to 15 ministries including the Planning Commission. This document has been used as a basic text by various NGOs over past years to produce a draft alternative R&R policy after widespread regional discussion. This draft alternative has also been submitted to the Ministry of Rural Areas and Employment for their consideration.

The circulating government draft emphasised equity, fairness, justice and equality on the distribution of burdens and benefits. The draft recognised the right to settle and reside in any part of the country, the special rights of tribal, the customary rights to common property resources of those dependent on the forests, and also those classified as 'encroachers'. It recognised that the 'displaced' are actually 'uprooted from the soil'. It emphasised the need to ensure rehabilitation in any displacement process and stressed the need to ensure that the displaced persons actively participate in their own rehabilitation. It was also recognised in the draft that the adverse impacts of involuntary displacement are much wider than those just associated with loss of land. The revised Land Acquisition Act indicated that R&R is likely to remain a necessary activity, which has to be undertaken prior to developments.

In 1993, in the wake of World Bank withdrawal from Sardar Sarovar Project due to severe negligence on R&R activities, the Ministry of Rural Development prepared a draft policy in 1993 which was revised many a time after that. After nearly 19 years of continuous debate and discussion, the Government of India notified a national rehabilitation policy on 17th February 2004 known as National Policy on Resettlement and Rehabilitation (NPRR) 2003 (GoI 2003). Its main feature was that it applied to such projects which were displacing more than 500 families en masses in the plains and 250 in the hills or the schedule area. The policy says that each project-affected families (henceforth PAF), whose house has been acquired, will get a site free of cost. Those families who are below poverty line will be given a one-time grant of Rs 25,000 for house construction. Land losers will be given one-time grant of Rs 10,000 per hectare for land development and Rs 5,000 per family for agricultural production. The best part of the policy was that it made provision for the payment of monthly allowance of 20 days minimum agricultural wages for one year up to 250 days of minimum agricultural wages to the PAFs. Apart from that, a PAF whose entire land is acquired will get one-time financial assistance equivalent to 750 days of minimum agricultural wages for loss of livelihood. Lastly, the policy says that each rural artisan, small trader and self-employed PAF will get financial assistance of Rs 10,000 for construction of shops or working sheds.

The positive aspects underlying NPRR 2003 was its broad definition of 'PAF' and 'agricultural family'. It made provision of separate rehabilitation agency for the execution of R&R work. Lastly, it restricted R&R benefit to those who have resided in the affected area for three years before the notification under Section 4(1) of Land Acquisition Act. By this provision, it prevented outsiders from buying land in the affected area and in turn grabbing most of the rehabilitation benefits.

R&R Policy of World Bank in Retrospect

World Bank (The World Bank 1980; 1990; 1991; 1993; 1994) was the first agency to formulate an approach to the resettlement question. In 1980, it issued for its staff a statement outlining a policy to guide operations in this sensitive area with the aim of protecting the interests of displaced persons. Since then, the Asian Development Bank, the Inter-American Development Bank and the Organisation for Economic Cooperation and Development laid down policies for projects requiring resettlement. As a result, every part of the globe has slowly sensitised towards the lives of millions as natural atonement of development.

The World Bank policy on resettlement has undergone several revisions since it first came into existence. Its first revision took place in 1986. A new version of the policy document appeared in 1988. This, too, underwent some revisions lately and an updated operational directive has been in effect since 1990. The Bank policy rests on a number of basic principles, such as minimising displacement, government responsibility towards the relocated, participation of stakeholders, the rights of victims of displacement, protection of host populace interests, a forward-looking definition of objectives of resettlement and so on. Further, the guidelines caution against viewing resettlement as a mere environmental issue. Therefore, the correct understanding of the sociological nature of involuntary resettlement, with its cultural, economic and psychological ramifications, much exceeds the environmental aspects. It leads to a different course of action on addressing resettlement than if it is regarded only as an environmental problem.

The Bank policy recognises that in any involuntary resettlement situation, some human suffering is inevitable. As its very first requirement, the policy therefore states that involuntary resettlement must be avoided wherever possible. When it is unavoidable, it must be minimised. Moreover, as Marsden argues:

> Emphasis is on providing resettled people with new and better economic opportunities. The policy states that the families affected by a Bank-financed project should share in benefits from the project and as a result be better off than before. The idea is that since involuntary resettlement dismantles existing production system, all resettlement programmes must at the same time be development programmes. Emphasis in the policy on preparation of resettlement plans in advance is intended to ensure that the people affected by projects are helped effectively in their rehabilitation. Specifically, the plans are to provide for compensation in full before departure to the new locations; and assistance in moving to the relocation site and support during the transition period; and see assistance in efforts to improve their living standards. (1996: 6–7)

It is a matter of great concern that the projects designed and appraised in the past had no provision for resettlement and rehabilitation in their guidelines. Subsequently, when it was discovered that resettlement would be necessary, the lack of resources for the purpose only complicated the implementation of otherwise sound projects. In order to prevent recurrence of such cases, the Bank guidelines insist that initial planning of any project construction should accompany the budget of R&R and other development activities. As resettlement-planning decisions impinge on the lives of the displaced groups, agencies concerned are enjoined to encourage community participation on planning and implementing resettlement. A related recommendation concerns the involvement of local groups and NGOs. Being closer to the people, they are in a better position to articulate resettlers' needs and defend their rights.

The Bank policy regards as of particular importance the welfare and development of the indigenous groups, ethnic minorities, pastoralists and other marginalised groups, such as women. Even without legal title, these adversely affected groups are to be eligible for full compensation as well as resettlement. Women and dependents even though adults have always been debarred from the resettlement benefits. So is the case with the marginal communities such as tribal and other downtrodden citizenry placed at the fringe of the power matrix.

R&R Policy of NTPC

Production of power requires setting up of massive plants, which necessitate involuntary displacement of the local population. Each 2000 MW power plant requires about 4,500 acres of land and as a consequence the relocation causes profound economic and cultural dismantling of the social fabric of local communities. The core area where the project gets incepted is the root to change. The cost of development is largely borne by few affected people for the larger benefit of the mankind and the nation. NTPC (NTPC 1993; 1994; 1996) recognised this suffering and sacrifice of the inhabitants and made efforts to ensure that PAP should improve or at least regain their previous standard of life.

Keeping this aspect in mind, NTPC is providing limited facilities for displaced people since inception and framed guidelines in 1980. It pays compensation for the assets acquired; apart from that, solatium, i.e., disturbance allowance, is also paid to the oustees. NTPC realised that forced relocation generally debars the residents from their dwellings. Thus, provision of plot and other necessary infrastructure facilities were provided in the resettlement colony. Loss of livelihood was tried to be compensated with the provision of employment, petty contracts, shops and vendor licences etc.

By 1991, NTPC started executing more and more projects, and thus need was felt to streamline the R&R activities. 1991 saw a formal NTPC policy on rehabilitation and resettlement, which was again revised in 1993. Remedial Action Plan (henceforth ReAP) for the old projects was initiated which encapsulated written guideline for the rehabilitation and resettlement of the land oustees of the earlier projects. Earlier, family (PAFs) was considered as a unit for rehabilitation activities. But since 1993, each and every adult person (PAPs) has been considered as 'project affected' and benefit went to him or her separately. The main feature of the changed policy, which invited widespread acknowledgement, was that even the landless and other affected persons, who were directly or indirectly deriving livelihood from the land acquired, were included in the new NTPC package. The stipulation of 'land for land' option was also provided in the revised policy, but it was viable only in case of willing seller. Assistance for self-employment schemes such as loan, venture capital, vocational training, etc., was provided. The main demarcation in the latest guideline from the earlier policy was that the policy of 1980s stated that the displaced person should regain if not able to improve their previous standard of life. The emphasis of the revised policy of 1993 was that the displaced person should improve or at least regain their previous standard of life.

1994–95 saw a new era in rehabilitation and resettlement activities where the orientation took a shift from welfare to necessity. Earlier, R&R activities were considered as welfare and charitable, but now it had become a nodal activity, which was essential and must. As per the policy, land oustees were given equal rights and were consulted in the development activities. They were involved and consulted, prior to the formulation of plans. It became possible due to the formulation of Village Development Advisory Committee (VDAC) and Public Information Centre (PIC). On the administrative level, reform took place in the form of recruitment of sociologist for better co-ordination between PAPs and NTPC. Apart from this, adviser from social science background was appointed at the corporate centre to advise NTPC. In addition, NTPC appointed consultants for various income-generation schemes (henceforth IGSs) and involved NGOs for effective and earliest solution to the problems of the land oustees.

New millennium perceived a shift in NTPC's policy on R&R. Due to continuous pressure from the victims of displacement, human rights activists and national and international NGOs, the year 2001 experienced the formation of Independent Monitoring Panel (IMP). The panel comprised of neutral and renowned persons, to expedite the matters concerning R&R and to provide solution to the ever-growing problems concerning rehabilitation package. This package was meant for the PAPs of the stage II. The main idea behind the formulation of IMP was to avoid further confrontation with the PAPs by providing them one-time benefits. Thus, the package envisaged handsome benefits to the PAPs. Those who received the IMP package, had to sign an agreement written on a proforma, with the affidavit on stamp paper by a lawyer that they would not ask for permanent job, contract or labour-intensive work from NTPC in future. This meant NTPC does not have any liability for these oustees in future.

III

Administrative and Policy Limitations

Sometimes, watertight planning becomes null and void in the absence of competent administration. It is the responsibility of the administration, as a nodal agency, to execute the work which was promised earlier at planning stage. Various policies governing R&R, which I have discussed earlier, will be evaluated in this section. In the latter part, the main focus will be on the assessment of efficacy of various R&R policies in terms of administration and governance. The main cause of concern will be to appraise how far it became able to solve the problems of the land oustees.

Lacunae in the Land Acquisition Act of India

The Land Acquisition Act does not give victims any rights to prevent the acquisition of their land. One can only delay acquisition by raising objections. The government is empowered to acquire land for public purpose. But, the term 'public purpose' is nowhere defined in the Act. Objections can be made to the proposed acquisition on the ground that the purpose is not a public one, or that the land is not suited to such public purpose. If someone wishes to argue that the intended purpose is not a public one, he/she has to require wider information about the project to substantiate his/her arguments. But, as the time prescribed for raising such objections is only one month, the whole exercise becomes obsolete due to inability on the part of victims to do the needful. Even if a person is able to do so, the Collector's decision on his/her objections is final. It is hard to imagine any situation in which the Collector goes against government planning and accepts the litigant's objections. Raising objections is therefore not a very successful exercise in preventing acquisition as it happened in the case of Narmada, Tehri, Koel Karo, NTPC and other projects of this nature. However, one can delay the process, which may make the project too expensive to be profitable.

The civil court does not have the power to decide whether the purpose behind the acquisition was a public purpose. It can only hear the litigant, if the Collector does not consider his/her objections. All that the court can do is to direct the Collector to hear the litigant. It cannot decide on merits of the case.

The government is also armed with emergency/urgency power, with which it can cut short the entire process of notices and objections. The term 'agency' is nowhere defined in the Act. Likewise, the term 'emergency' is also not defined. If someone's land is acquired in case of an emergency or urgency, he/she cannot raise objections. Nor can the court question whether there was really an urgency or emergency. A study of the Land Acquisition Act and the rest of the existing legislations shows that the present legal system favours the state and the industrialists, and ignores the right of the livelihood of the people who depend on the common property resources (CPRs) such as forest (Fernandes 1996: 3).

Lacunae in NPRR, 2003

It appears that on paper the government is serious about the rights of the victims of various development projects and also towards its responsibilities to the sufferer. But a closer scrutiny of the vicious problems debunks entirely different picture of the situation. It is still assumed that the efforts made towards rehabilitation are ad hoc, reactionary, charitable and are not the rights of the victims. Thus, to begin with, the Ministry of Rural Development that drafted the NPRR 2003, stated that it would be finalised after a dialogue, but it has been promulgated without it. The members of the civil society vehemently criticised the policy by stating that the benefits it announces can at best keep the PAPs poor and at worst push them below the poverty line. It neither accepts rehabilitation as right nor makes it mandatory. It only says that PAFs may be resettled if the project so desires. As per the provision of NPRR 2003, only individual land losers will get 'land for land' and other allowances to develop it. The remaining PAFs will get only one-time allowance for a certain number of days of minimum agricultural wages.

Again, the NPRR 2003 created much trouble to the land losers by stating that land will be provided subject to the availability of government waste land. In addition to this, the prejudiced approach of the policy appears in the arrangement that "a free plot will be given to those who own a house" seems to exclude tenants and other landless PAFs. Only such families who were below poverty line were entitled for Rs 25,000 to build a house.

The critics denounced NPRR 2003 by stating that the laws enabling displacement is unacceptable and so is the public purpose. Exponents of civil society[2] demanded that while displacing, people's livelihood should become basis of all decisions. The principle of compensation should be 'replacement value' and not the 'market value' or present 'depreciation value' of assets. Replacement, according to them, includes the economic cost as well as social and psychological trauma experienced by the affected persons. PAPs should be the first beneficiary of the development plan and assurance of permanent income from the project is the responsibility of the planners. Rather, the PAPs may become the shareholders of such projects so as to ensure them permanent source of income. The policy should also not be tribal, dalit and gender bias (Fernandes 2004). Last, but not the least, regional planning was strongly solicited to avoid the problem of multiple displacements.

Lacunae in the R&R Policy of NTPC

In the beginning of the 1980s, when NTPC was launching its first project at Vindhyachal, the concept governing the policy of resettlement and rehabilitation was in infant stage. General masses as well as the national and international community were not sensitised enough to take it seriously. The time when NTPC invaded the land of Singrauli, the concepts like socio-economic survey (SES) and the formulations of RAP (Rehabilitation Action Plan) and ReAP (Remedial Action Plan) were not known. In the absence of any policy guidelines, the residents of the locality were evacuated from their land without any prior SES and RAP. First SES of the Vindhyachal Stage-I took place nearly 10 years after the inception of the project. The research team authorised with the responsibility of the SES could not trace the oustees. During the gap of more than 10 years, victims had migrated to distant places in search of livelihood. Hence, it was very difficult to find out the exact social and economic conditions of the people ousted. As a result, the SES conducted lacked on various accounts. References made about the whereabouts of the residents do not match with the real situation persisting over there. A glance of the SES easily deciphers that it was just an effort to accomplish the necessary obligation. Due to this, in case one search for detail records pertaining to R&R, either no record is available or the documents lying in the offices of NTPC spell contradictory information.

In the absence of accurate estimate, surplus land was acquired for the project, township, ash-dyke and other infrastructure requirements of that time. Consequently, a vast patch of land, which earlier provided sustenance to common people, remained unused for years. After a passage of 15–20 years, these lands were utilised by NTPC, in the second stage of the project. This has constantly soured the feelings of the PAPs. Unused land debarred them from the opportunity to work in order to fetch livelihood for the family.

Moreover, plot measuring 60 by 40 feet was allotted to the oustees in the resettlement colonies in lieu of the acquisition of the homestead. On paper, planning for the development of resettlement colonies looked fair enough in the background of the urban atmosphere. But, in reality, the same situation became inappropriate for those who lived in the rural milieu. The planners forgot while planning that the small patch of land in the resettlement colony could no longer solve the problems of those living in purely rural areas. The small plots allotted to the PAFs were tiny enough to accommodate big joint families running into double figure. There was no provision for the cattle, which is an essential part of the rural household. Dearth of grazing land, open fields, orchards, open and airy space, ponds, lakes, wells, assembly places etc. suffocated the rural, who were habituated for that kind of living. Sanitation and infrastructure facilities were giving a dismal look in the resettlement colonies. Due to these problems, a large number of families migrated to other places.

At the time of acquisition, permanent employment was promised to at least one male member from PAF. During the latter stage, it was felt that due to technical nature of jobs available with the organisation, it was not possible to employ large numbers of oustees. Thus, NTPC drifted from earlier promise and started emphasising on income-generation schemes (IGSs). For this, they employed renowned expert as consultant in IGSs. In the beginning, PAPs showed reluctance towards the whole process. They were not born entrepreneur and scared about indulging in a completely alien business. However, due to constant pressure, and also because of lack of alternative source of livelihood, few PAPs dared to venture into new occupations. But, the whole process failed to take off smoothly for PAPs in the absence of substantial knowledge and experience. As a result, those brave enough to invest money in such business lost capital and further got pauperised.

The second most viable alternative to permanent employment for NTPC was to provide agricultural land at some other place. Accordingly, NTPC armed its policy with 'land for land' option on 'willing buyer, willing seller' basis. But meagre amount of compensation received by PAPs from NTPC in lieu of the agricultural land and homestead was not sufficient to buy land for them in the surrounding locality. Due to breach in demand and supply, price of land soared very high. Consequently, the option became null and void. In case of forced acquisition, it would have triggered off irreversible chain of forced displacement. Thus, the option provided in the resettlement and rehabilitation policy of NTPC in the form of 'land for land' alternative failed to take off.

Role of NGOs

Two main NGOs showed presence in the Singrauli region at the time of my fieldwork. The first one, namely, Govindpur Ashram, was led by Prem Bhai. Based on the Gandhian philosophy, it was founded in 1950s and established some 10 km to the north of Miurpur on an estate of 240 hectare. The second NGO, Srijan Lokhit Samiti, is situated at Navjivan Vihar near VSTPP. Established by Sri Awadhesh Prasad, it has been working since the inception of the Vindhyachal Project in the region.

On close observation, it was realised that both the NGOs were not working for the rehabilitation of the PAPs of NTPC. Govindpur Ashram had become inactive after the death of its founder Prem Bhai, though it still exists in the region. On the other hand, Srijan Lokhit Samiti does not have any assignment concerning R&R activities of NTPC. At present, it is busy with the development work of the NCL oustees situated in the same region. When enquired from the Director of Srijan Lokhit Samiti, he admitted that atrocities were caused to the PAPs by NTPC. He however emphasised, "Earlier, the PAPs were quite innocent and consequently paid the price of development. But with the advancement of time, they have become quite cunning and know it precisely how to pressurise NTPC to fetch better compensation. Now, the PAPs have developed dependency syndrome. During years, after the acquisition of agricultural land, many PAPs have become completely inactive and for urgent needs depend on NTPC. Because of this, most of the development plans meant for the progress of the land oustees, is not able to yield desirable results".

Contrarily, the PAPs were annoyed with the performance of these NGOs in the Singrauli region. They were largely dissatisfied with the role of these NGOs and blamed them for indulging in money making. Oustees attributed the cause of miseries in the form of weak and ineffective NGOs and blamed them for being responsible for the misuse of the funds meant for their development.

IV

People's Perception and Resentment

To derive a comprehensive understanding of the entire situation, it is important to have the opinion and perception of the victims of the project. Since they are the sufferers, they can better illustrate the lacunae and discrimination inherent in the policies from their first-hand experience. After a detailed discussion about various R&R policies and its adequacy, we are in a position to analyse the inherent problems in the approach and attitude of the project personnel from the perspectives of the land oustees.

About NTPC Policy of R&R

Resettlement colonies were equipped with infrastructure and sanitation facilities such as handpumps, wells, drainage, electricity, roads, streets etc. But, the researcher found most of the facilities in extremely poor condition. When verified, the inhabitants blamed that though NTPC and state government provided these facilities, maintenance work is lacking. In the absence of proper maintenance, infrastructure and sanitation facilities have become mostly dysfunctional and do not serve any purpose of the residents. When interrogated, officials admitted continuation of poor conditions and counter-blamed the villagers for this pathetic condition. They opined that once the facilities are granted in the resettlement colonies, it becomes the responsibility of the residents to look after the maintenance work. So, in the absence of clear guidelines, both parties are blaming each other for the poor maintenance and the ultimate sufferers are the residents of those resettlement colonies. The same situation persists with community facilities, hospitals and schools. Most of the buildings meant for these facilities are in dilapidated conditions. Doctors and teachers are not available. Even those posted here on paper, seldom come to the office. In the absence of proper medical facilities, PAPs have to go to distant places for medical assistance. Schools running in the NTPC premises are generally meant for the wards of the NTPC employees and the fee charged by them is too high. PAPs, being poor, could not afford sending their children to such schools. Overall, the educational facilities provided in the locality were not sufficient enough to satiate the requirements of the oustees.

The year 1994–95 earmarked change in NTPC policy from welfare and charitable to essential and rights of the victims. As a consequence, major instrumental change occurred in the approach towards dealing with the problems. Participatory mechanism was adopted for the first time which paved way for the genesis of Village Development Advisory Committee (VDAC) and Public Information Centre (PIC). Besides, the idea of the induction of the consultants and advisors from social science background was meant to initiate a shift in approach from monologue to dialogue and inculcate humanist approach. VDAC was meant to provide a single platform to the representatives of oustees, state government and local NGOs where they can discuss and debate various developmental issues. But to the dismay, it was detected as non-functional entity. Even if the meeting took place, it was heavily loaded in favour of NTPC, and denied entry of the opposite faction selectively, either by not inviting or informing them quite late. PIC building was found closed. There was no one in the premises to look after the library. Because of being unutilised since a long time, livestock have converted the place as their residence. Sociologists were not present at the time of visit. Villagers informed that since evacuation process has completed for the second stage of Vindhyachal and Rihand projects, sociologists are no more needed. Villagers expressed adverse opinion about the role played by the sociologists. Ideally selected for bridging the distance between the PAPs and the officials, sociologists were entrusted with the responsibility to get the land vacated from the residents. Contrary to their ideal role, sociologists were acting as agents of NTPC for spying and to dent into the unity of the locals. Advisor, an expert from social science background, was no more employed, as planned by NTPC. NTPC failed to apprehend that R&R is a long-lasting and forbearance episode and needs patience to deal with the whole problem for longer span of time.

The oustees complained that the provision of petty contracts is not able to serve the purpose as most of the contract jobs, meant for the victims, are provided to the outsiders. Shops allotted to the oustees, in most of the cases, located at remote and deserted places and were not viable for business purpose. In a nutshell, the efforts of NTPC to rehabilitate the oustees could not produce desirable result; contrarily, it enhanced the miseries of the victims.

Initially, NTPC used 'PAF' (project-affected family) as the basic unit to procure compensation. Under in this rule, only head of the household from the joint family was eligible for the allotment of plot, job as well as other compensation package. The small patch of land was not able to accommodate such big joint families. Apart from that, there was quarrel in the family for the distribution of compensation package. Little amount received as compensation was not sufficient to manage the whole family. So, there was large-scale dissatisfaction among the land oustees against the policy of PAF. Consequently, under the public pressure, NTPC had to change the previous policy into the benchmark of 'PAPs', i.e., project-affected persons. In the newer scheme, all the adult male members belonging to the same dwelling were considered as separate entity for the benefit of displacement. Surprisingly, at a time when the whole world is getting gender-sensitised and trying to empower and strengthen the fairer sex, NTPC forgot to address the rights of the female in its R&R policy as no adult females of the PAP's family were considered eligible to receive compensation from NTPC like other male family members. The new policy made several members of the same family eligible for compensation. This has created rift between the erstwhile PAF and the latter category of PAPs. The main cause of concern among the PAFs was that they were served notice simultaneously with the PAPs,[3] but since they readily agreed and vacated the land earlier, it devoid them with the facilities, what their counterparts are now receiving. So, under Section 4 families are treated differently with the changing policy of NTPC. This has created deep-rooted feeling of animosity and frustration among the oustees and divided them completely.

In 2001, the R&R policy of NTPC received another blow in the wake of the continuous agitation of the victims, who had not vacated their land till then. The latest move took place when Independent Monitoring Panel (IMP) was set up with the involvement of distinguished and learned persons from outside NTPC under the chairmanship of a retired Supreme Court judge. The terms of reference given to the panel were based on the formulation of a just compensation package. The idea was to offer such a lucrative package to Stage II people, not willing to vacate land on the basis of rehabilitation package proposed earlier, which, to their mind, was quite inadequate. A clause of the package compelled the PAPs to sign an agreement with NTPC that they do not have any future liability on NTPC. The panel came out with a very attractive package[4] and everyone was willing to accept. But since this was meant only for the PAPs of the Stage II who did not vacated land till date and posed stiff resistance against displacement, rest of other Stage I people who received compensation under the earlier policy, considered being cheated. This has created another divide between the Stage I and Stage II people. It becomes apparent that NTPC continuously divided people on the basis of twists and turns in its R&R policy through which those who received less compensation considered others their enemy and started fighting with them as well as NTPC to receive more or at least equal compensation with them.

The President of *Chetriya Vikash Yuva Samiti*, an assembly of some PAPs in Rihand to fight against the atrocities caused due to forced relocation, says, "Right from the beginning, NTPC adopted the policy of 'divide and rule' as well as 'appeasement' to those trying to raise voice against the system. In their latest move, NTPC with the offer of IMP package to the Stage II people, created another divide between brothers. The oustees not being given IMP package are fighting relentlessly with NTPC, for the demand of equal treatment. But DGM (R&R), Rihand is not willing to give ear to the plea of the victims. Those gentlemen, who bowed down in the beginning by vacating their land, are paid quite less than those preferred to show resistance".

The entire experience of shortfall of R&R clearly establishes that NTPC management has failed to realise that its officers are not competent enough to deal with the vicious problem of R&R. Engineers and managers always solicit for short-term solution of the problem without understanding the symptoms of the disease. They want their work to be executed at the earliest, even if it is costing to the masses. They know that delay in project execution will diminish the monetary profit of the organisation. They failed to understand that the work of R&R is entirely different from the project execution, where one has to deal with the emotional human beings and not heartless and soulless bricks, iron, sand and other such construction materials. Though, during 1994–95, NTPC realised this aspect and employed sociologists and consultants, but they did not involve them for a long time. In the absence of the experts from sociological and anthropological background to resolve such a vicious problem that requires human touch, the nemesis does not appear to be resolved in near future.

About Land Acquisition Act of India, 1984

The Amendment Act of 1984 has not changed the picture substantially. The basic position remains the same. In some ways, power of government officials has been increased. In other ways, the position on money compensation has been eased for the landholder. The Amendment Act of 1984 throws few consolations to the landholders: The whole process from first notice vide Section 4(1) to the final award vide Section 11 has to be completed within three years. Before 1984, the time difference between the two notices under Sections 4 and 6 alone could be three years. As compensation is computed in terms of value of land on the date of the notice vide Section 4, it is hoped that a more rapid settlement will keep down the difference between the compensation awarded and the market prices on the date of the award. But inherent in this facility is the cause of great worry for the people. If the whole process, right from Section 4(1) notification to the final award by Section 11, does not complete within the stipulated time of three years, then it needs to be re-initiated. In case of re-initiating, the process repeats as in the previous attempt. It becomes a long-lasting and painful experience for the victims as in case of Section 4 notification, development as well as sell-purchase activities receive a dead halt in the region.

The amount of solatium (disturbance allowance) has been increased from 15 per cent to 30 per cent. In case of acquisition under emergency or urgency powers, 80 per cent of the compensation estimated by the Collector must be paid on the spot, though the award itself will follow. If one person gets the award enhanced by court, others can now take advantage of the court order, and ask the Collector to re-assess the amount paid to them. But all these are monetary gains. The basic power of the state to acquire land has not been curtailed in any way. On the contrary, it has increased.

The Land Acquisition Act, the solitary law responsible for the acquisitions of land in India, is heavily biased against the rights of the women. According to Thukral, "Land Acquisition Act, the main law of acquisition, reveals a gender bias which seems to reinforce the existing situation of women's lack of ownership of land and property. Section 42(2) of this Act specifies that if the 'person interested' is not available to receive the notice for acquisition, then it may be handed over to, or served on, any other *adult male* member of the family who resides with him. If no 'adult male' is present, then the notice may be served by affixing a copy of the notice on the outer door of the house, or in some conspicuous place in the office of the Collector or court house, etc. To put it plainly, *if the notice is served on a woman, it is not legal.* The Act does not mention what is to be done if the 'person interested is a woman' or one of the 'persons interested' is a women in case of joint ownership or does it merely reinforce the fact that in reality women seldom have ownership?" (Thukral 1995: 24). The Act is also weighted in favour of the affluent. Because land can be easily acquired for the public purpose of hotels, it can be acquired for the public purpose of cooperative housing societies of lawyers, government servants and other professional.

Conclusion

The present investigation has been initiated with an effort to locate the historical evolution of R&R policies and various other guidelines concerning the acquisition of land and the methods of rehabilitation of the land oustees. The entire effort has been done in the domain of evaluation of attitude of rehabilitation agencies and the experiences recounted by sufferers. Conclusions drawn suggest that in the absence of a watertight policy, planners went for ad hoc and part-time solutions of the problem depending on their own wisdom. As a result, biases and prejudices erupted into the proceedings of rehabilitation. For example, the NTPC policy continuously changed during the last couple of decades leading to differences between land oustees of Stage I and Stage II. On closer observation, it became evident that the policy of NTPC lacks any clear guideline on innumerable issues and is unable to solve the problems of the oustees. Modifications in the policy to suit the changing demands of the situation itself became a great cause of concern for the management. PAPs assumed that NTPC is adopting the policy of divide and rule and thus discharged biased approach towards those who vacated the land earlier. It was established that NTPC still deals the issue with the nodal mechanism set-up of engineers and managers, who rather than going for the symptomatic solution, opt for quick and ad hoc measures. They forgot to realise that R&R needs to be dealt differently than machines and as such requires induction of experts from sociological and anthropological background (Verma 2004). NGOs present in the area are not able to produce desirable result and shun people's trust. PAPs are completely dissatisfied with them. In a nutshell, efforts of resettlement and rehabilitation in the case of NTPC failed on all the fronts – policy, planning and administration.

The Land Acquisition Act of India is still in the archaic nature and the Collector has been given immense power to acquire the land against the will of the victims. It is hard to imagine a circumstance in which land acquisition is abandoned due to pressure from land oustees. One can only ask for enhanced compensation or can delay the acquisition. General masses could only, in case of objection, delay the process of acquisition by giving petition to the Collector. In return, the Collector would look into the matter and pass the judgement, which will be mandatory and binding to the party. Even judiciary does not have much say in the proceedings of the land acquisition. International organisations like the World Bank, concerned with the issue of sustainable development, are also not able to do much. At times, under the pressure from them some modifications took place in the R&R policies, but that was only giving temporary respite. Such efforts could not produce any visible result as the planners had a close-shop mentality towards a 'given agenda of 'development' without any regard for their societal responsibilities.

It is time now to learn from these mistakes and get on with serious R&R planning and execution with the involvement of victims as well as social science experts forming part of the administrative machinery. Government should take serious view of such a vicious problem and chalk out a watertight and people-friendly rehabilitation policy. The

Land Acquisition Act also needs modification so that it could become more people-friendly. Social science experts should accompany administrative machinery in providing a humanitarian approach. PAPs should be involved in the resettlement process right from the beginning. Most importantly, planning should be done keeping in mind the rural people and their surrounding milieu, so that it could suit to their temperament. We are part of a democratic world, where we cannot live in monologue. In the absence of these guidelines, suffering of poor and innocent masses will prolong and they will have to incessantly pay the price for nation's development.

Notes

1. National Policy on Rehabilitation and Resettlement Bill 2007 was passed by Lok Sabha and placed in upper house of parliament but it lapsed due to expiry of 14th Lok Sabha. The Bill is yet to be passed in the Lok Sabha.
2. Though many policies were drafted under the World Bank pressure, the civil society too has played a major role in them. In 1988, the National Working Group (1989) supported by Narmada Bachao Andolan drafted the first policy. However, this civil society alliance got very little cooperation from the ministries (Fernandes 2005: 124–25).
3. In the beginning of the 1980s, NTPC served notice to the locals regarding acquisition of land. That time, NTPC adopted the policy of PAF and considered only the head of the household as eligible to receive compensation. Later on, with the shift in the R&R policy of NTPC, PAF was replaced with PAPs in which all the adult male members of the same household were considered eligible to receive compensation. That means, those shifted earlier vide the policy of PAF could not garner much benefit whereas rest of others who posed resistance to evacuation and shifted later got much more benefits from NTPC as more than one adult family member was eligible to receive compensation from the same household.
4. IMP package had the following provisions:
   - Landless person or loss of only house – compensation of Rs 70,000 and Rs 20,000 as rehabilitation allowance.
   - Loss of 2 acres of land – money of 2 acres of land @ Rs 70,000 per acre and Rs 20,000 as rehabilitation allowance.
   - Loss of 2 acres to 5 acres of land – payment for actual loss @ Rs 70,000 per acre and Rs 20,000 as rehabilitation allowance.
   - Loss of 5 acres or more land – compensation for 5 acres only @ Rs 70,000 per acre and Rs 20,000 as rehabilitation allowance.

— Rs 15,000 extra in the above mentioned cases, if the person is not willing to take the plot, already allotted in the resettlement colony.

— If the PAP wants to buy land elsewhere with the use of compensation money, then the registration money, i.e., stamp charge and maintenance of the land @ Rs 10,000 acre will be borne by NTPC.

— Those who received the IMP package had to sign an agreement with notary that they would not ask for a permanent job, contract and labour intensive work from NTPC in future.

References

Baxi, Upendra. 2008. 'Development, Displacement, Resettlement: A Human Right Perspective', *India Social Development Report 2008* (17–26). New Delhi, Council for Social Development: Oxford University Press.

Dubey, Muchkund. 2008. 'Foreword', *India Social Development Report 2008* (xv–xvii). New Delhi, Council for Social Development: Oxford University Press.

Electricite de France International and Group Charbonnages de France. 1990. NTPC Environmental Study of Singrauli Area, Chapter 3, Socio-Economics, EDF and GCF.

Fernandes, Walter. 1996. 'Displacement and Rehabilitation: Principles of the NGO Alternative', paper presented in a Workshop organised by the World Bank, NDO, March 12–14.

——. 2005. 'Rehabilitation as a Right: Where is the Policy?', *Social Action*, April–June, 55 (2): 123–37.

——. 2008. 'Sixty Years of Development-induced Displacement in India: Scale, Impacts and the Search for Alternatives', *India Social Development Report 2008* (89–102). New Delhi, Council for Social Development: Oxford University Press.

GHK/MRM International et al. 1994. Singrauli Development and Environmental Management Strategy, Displaced People Action Plan, GHK/MRM.

Government of India. 1995. National Policy on Resettlement and Rehabilitation, Ministry of Rural Area and Employment, Government of India.

——. 1996. National Policy on Resettlement and Rehabilitation, Ministry of Rural Area and Employment, Government of India.

——. 2003. National Policy on Resettlement and Rehabilitation, Government of India.

Marsden, David. 1996. 'Resettlement and Rehabilitation in India: Some Lessons from Recent Experiences', paper presented in the Workshop organised by the World Bank, NDO, March, 12–14.

MARG. 1990. *The Land Acquisition Act and You*. Delhi: Pauls Press and Jain Book Agency.

Mathur, Hari Mohan. 2008. 'Introduction and Overview', *India Social Development Report 2008* (3–13). New Delhi, Council for Social Development: Oxford University Press.

NTPC. 1993. Resettlement and Rehabilitation Policy. New Delhi.

——. 1994. Workshop on Sustainable Development in Singrauli Region, Proceedings and Paper Presented, November 11–12, NTPC Shaktinagar, Sonebhadra UP.

——. 1996. Checklist on Resettlement and Rehabilitation for New Projects. Corporate R&R Group, NTPC Corporate Centre, New Delhi.

Thukral, Enakshi Ganguli. 1995. 'Development, Displacement and Rehabilitation: Is there a Need for a Gender Perspective', *Mainstream*, November 11: 24–26.

The Land Acquisition Act and You with Short Notes. 1995. Delhi: Universal Law Publishing Company Pvt. Ltd.

The World Bank. 1980. Social Issues Associated with Involuntary Resettlement in Bank Financed Projects (Operational Manual Statement No. 2.33). Washington, DC.

——. 1990. Operational Directive 4.30, Involuntary Resettlement. Washington, DC.

——. 1991. Operational Directive 4.20, Indigenous People. Washington, DC.

——. 1993. 'Introduction to Environment and Social Assessment and Requirements and Procedures for World Bank Financed Projects'. Environment Department, Washington, DC.

——. 1994. 'Resettlement and Development: The Bankwide Review of Projects Involving Involuntary Resettlement, 1896–1993'. Environment Department, Washington, DC.

Verma, Manish Kumar. 2004. *Development, Displacement and Resettlement*. Jaipur: Rawat Publications.

13

From Alternative Development to Developmentalism?

A Narrative of the People's Science Movement in Kerala

Shoma Choudhury Lahiri

Development is an 'unstable' and an ambivalent term in social science discourse today and yet it continues to generate a lot of debate because of its alleged promise. While the state derives its legitimacy from the idea of development, other actors like the civil society, social movements and the non-governmental organisations engage with it, in order to recreate and recast it, according to their own vision, needs and contexts. Development appears to be self-consciously and inextricably linked to the idea of modern existence and in fact the term's association with "a faith in progress and an assumed capacity to improve one's conditions of existence" (Edelman and Haugerud 2002: 3) makes it quite impossible to think of a world without it.

The theoretical field of development is strewn with multiple paradigms. Most notable among them are the proponents of development as modernisation symbolised in the work of Rostow, Talcott Parsons and others, to those who critique this mainstream position and search for varied alternatives in development through participatory action research, in grassroots development, conscientisation, liberation theology, eco-feminism, cultural diversity and so on (Pieterse 1998) to the more recent post-development position espoused by Escobar, Rahnema, Esteva, Sachs and others who see in social movements 'an analytical and political terrain' which can offer a challenge and even displace the dominant discourse of development and modernity (Escobar 2005).

This paper attempts to look at the development discourse of a social movement, the people's science movement in the context of Kerala – a state known for the paradoxical nature of its development. The paradox of Kerala's development lies in the fact that the state has high developmental indices reflective of a higher quality of life, despite low levels of economic development. The movement in question was initiated in the early 1960s by a group of scientists, science writers, school and college teachers, who came together to form the Kerala Sastra Sahitya Parishad[1] (henceforth KSSP) in order to popularise science in the vernacular. Initially, the activities of the organisation were restricted to science popularisation through the spoken word. Subsequently, it expanded considerably and over the last 50 years of its existence, the People's Science Movement has worked towards 'taking science to the people' and in the course has intervened in the fields of education, environment, health and, more recently, local level planning and democratic decentralisation in the state.

The first section of the paper looks at the KSSP's engagement with Kerala's development and maps the continuities and discontinuities with the dominant Nehruvian discourse[2] on the nation's development. This is followed by a section which looks at some of the 'alternatives' that the movement offers both at the level of discourse and practice in the field of environment. Here I discuss the people's science movement's attempt at formulating an environmentally-sensitive developmental paradigm, as well as its interventions during the anti-nuclear movement at Peringom district in northern Kerala. I argue that these alternatives do not question the larger philosophical framework of development; they in fact create space within the existing framework of the techno-scientific development, thus reaffirming the spirit of developmentalism. This paper is based on my two-year long fieldwork on the people's science movement for my PhD. I followed several techniques like interviews, content analysis of their texts and survey of the activists to know their social background to construct the ethnography.

KSSP and Kerala's Development

The state of Kerala represents a unique case within India, because despite low economic development, it has achieved relatively high levels of social development and a better quality of life. The social development is signified by the prevalence of high literacy rates, spread of basic education, a high average life expectancy, low infant and maternal mortality rates, low death rates and the acceptance of a small family norm by a large proportion of the population. As these developmental indices compare favourably with the developed countries, Kerala has been upheld as a 'model' for developing countries.

In the post-independence period, within the larger framework of the Nehruvian model, Kerala's experience has been understood as a development with 'a human face'. There are several reasons attributed to this fact. While some have referred to the role of female literacy (Panikkar and Soman 1984; Mari Bhat and Irudaya Rajan 1990) and girls schooling (Caldwell 1986), others have emphasised the role of public action in promoting a range of social opportunities relating to elementary education, the widespread and equitable provision of health care and other public services as well as to the role of women in society (Ramachandran 1996).

But, the journey of the Kerala model has been very uneven. In the recent years it has been criticised from the perspectives of the 'outliers', i.e., the fishermen (Kurien 1995), the tribals (Rammohan 2008) and the lower castes (Omvedt 1998), and on questions of sustainability and replicability (Parayil 2000). In the 1990s though the model had been held out as a possible alternative to the growth-only model, in an increasingly unipolar world, we notice that this 'development defined Malayalee identity' being thrown into a crisis due to the resurgence of the *Hindutva* ideology, and a resurgence of ritualism and *savarna* identity on the one hand and an assertion of the hitherto marginalised identities on the other (see Devika 2007). Amidst all this, it would not be off the mark to say that development has been the frame through which Kerala has been constructed over and over again.

Though there exist differences between the regional experiences across the country within this growth-mediated notion of development, continuities with the Nehruvian model of nation-building exist. This continuity is manifest in 'the desire for development' that seems to animate the self-perception of the Malayalees in the region. In fact, recent literature (Devika 2007) shows how the consensus for development in Kerala was forged in post-50s and 60s through the demands and negotiations for *Aikya Kerala* (United Kerala), mirrored in the varied debates in art, literature and poetry and in the leftist evocations of development and of how developmentalism[3] became an article of faith which would enable the Malayalee people to tide over the feelings of fear and marginality constituted by a lack of numbers, capital and land.

KSSP has been concerned with Kerala's development rather indirectly since the 1970s. In its early interventions and writings in the field of education, health and environment, development emerges as a subtle and yet a persistently occurring idea though not clearly articulated as progress. It is only in the decade of the 90s that the people's science movement ostensibly makes development its 'politics'. There are various elements to the science movement's discourse of development, some of which mark its continuities with the Nehruvian model, and yet there are other aspects which make it rooted in the local/regional concerns and hence distinctive.

In its understanding of development we find that the people's science movement draws upon two strands of thought. The first is the idea of a general, overarching, universal history of the development of man, and of society expressed through an analogy with the laws of nature. The second strand, more attuned to the scientific, developmental paradigm, emerges out of the movement's engagement with the specific issues, concerns and controversies in Kerala. The first idea speaks of evolution as progressive development and the inevitability of change and transformation. This transformation is from a lower stage to the higher and is couched in the language of science.

> What characterises matter and hence the Universe, is constant movement, from one state to another. Everything around us from the smallest electron to the largest galaxy is in constant motion and is undergoing change always ... Movement is inevitable and evident in the external, physical growth and in the internal transformation of a human body, within the plant and the animal kingdom and in the environment around, in the formation of soil and minerals, and in the many different kinds of invisible movement in nature. Change is another name for motion. It is the law of life. There is nothing that is 'changeless' or motionless. (Kumar 1984: 25)

Despite the ubiquity of change, it is not directionless however. In the imagination of the KSSP ideologues M.P. Parameswaran and Other (1976: 28), evolution entailed step by step, gradual change from simple to complex to more advanced form of life. The process of evolution has been a slow one, from uni-cellular to multi-cellular organisms, from simple to complex organisms, eventually leading to the evolution of mammals and quadrupeds, apes who gradually evolved into human beings after hundreds of thousands of years. Thus, "the story of our ancestors is the story of transition from apes to man". This is also the basis for the KSSP to argue that society is also subject to constant change, and it is man who is the agent of this social transformation.

Social transformation is said to have been made possible due to two kinds of developments: (a) the ability of man to produce tools in order to procure food, and (b) the development of language. Inspired by Engels' 'The Role of Labour in the Transformation from Ape to Man', the KSSP reiterates that these two factors made society and collective existence possible. In the process of making tools, man lived in groups, developed language, and these ape men became real human beings. "The labour they did with their hands, their ability to do collective work and their ability to communicate using language led to a further development of their abilities and intelligence … . Man became more capable than all other animals, but it took many more years for man to reach this present state of development" (Kumar 1984: 32). At this stage all men were equal; they were organised into primitive classless society.

The increase in human population, the origin of settled agriculture, the transition from food gathering to food production, the organisation of human beings into settlements, and subsequently the making of new tools for cultivation, gradually the emergence of a group who did not participate in food production creating an elementary form of social stratification, development of the idea of private property leading to conflicts and wars over land and produce, the creation of a class of people as artists, sculptors and scientists, the need for agriculture to look for fertile lands leading to the development of river valley civilisations, the discovery of metals, development of iron tools, the transition from slavery to feudalism and eventually the overthrow of feudalism and monarchy by the Industrial Revolution and the French Revolution ushering in a new social order called capitalism. Capitalism saw the growth of the factory system of production, production of large quantities of goods, new machines, leading to the far-reaching changes in science and technology. All these changes were made possible by human labour, and hence labour or human agency constitutes an important frame of understanding the development of man and society.

Thus, what we have here is a historical materialist account of the development of society, and a grand narrative of development, articulated within a Marxist teleology, in the form of universal statements about the emergence and development of life and man, the emergence of science in and through the activities of man (i.e., through the labour process) and consequently the capacity of man to transform his reality through the use of science (knowledge) and technology. An important aspect is the constant reinforcement of the idea of a universal history of civilisation and mankind and its progress through stages. The experience of Kerala is understood and analysed as being located in a particular stage of history in this linear development of societies. The problems and contradictions are both problems of the particular and the general nature of the developmental process.

A specifically significant problem that has plagued Kerala concerns its low levels of economic development. This has been variedly attributed to the technologically backward industrial structure, low labour productivity, militant trade unionism, alleged Indian government's discrimination against distribution of central funds, and so on, from time to time (see Rammohan 2000). This has been a cause of anxiety of the average modern Malayalee in Kerala, and has even found expression in the leftist evocations of development as a way towards building a modern Kerala (Devika 2007). In fact, here, it would be instructive to remember E.M.S. Namboodiripad's vision of an ideal Kerala of the future, "thickly populated with large-scale industries, scientifically reorganised and managed farms and forests and hydel projects, enlisting its labour force rationally in productive activities, zestfully promoting scientific research and technical education, to fashion nothing less than a modern Malayalee culture" (cited in Devika 2007: 21).

In the writings of the KSSP during mid-70s[4] a similar trend is noticed, where the expert-activists are of the view that Kerala lags behind considerably as far as its degree of industrialisation is concerned. Large industries in the state are very few and contribute to merely 2 to 3 per cent of the national income. The state primarily abounds in traditional industries, namely, coir, cashew, tiles, brick, bidi and weaving. It is said that "the characteristics of traditional industries are appropriate technology, low energy utilisation, less capital investment and hence low productivity among other reasons" (Parameswaran et al. 1976). Therefore, the activists of the science movement were of the view that Kerala should "industrialise or (it would) perish!" It is through industrialisation and development that Kerala can overcome its fears of economic marginality and move towards its goal of development. This has been the reason for the ambivalence of the people's science movement even when it forges an 'alternate' developmental vision which attempts to incorporate environmental concerns of the region, as we would see in the next section of this narrative. Even when it goes on to draw up multiple, locale specific alternatives, it does not ostensibly oppose development; rather it seeks to modify and work within its framework.

This brings us back to the next building block of development, i.e., science as the cornerstone of the 'developmental modern'. The commitment to science as a cornerstone of social development lies at the heart of the KSSP's vision. This is also the basis of continuities between the Nehruvian model of development and the people's science movement's vision. Science and technology is to be the basis of a new technical, rational future. But science also has another important role, as in the words of KSSP, "it has a determining role in preparing the people for social revolution". The primary duty of science is to create a new culture, which would foster a scientific attitude and a temper. We can find here resonances of the attempt by our scientists in 1981 to formulate 'a scientific temper' for the people of India.

Although science and technology has grown and proliferated enormously, the structure of the society under capitalism has ensured that scientific knowledge and the access to technology remains concentrated in the hands of a few. Hence, the KSSP feels that its role is to enable or to make the poor and the exploited capable enough to respond 'scientifically' to their surroundings, to impart a scientific understanding/knowledge about the vast social reality so that it enables them to transform it according to their convenience. Thus, in KSSP's scheme of things science and technology are for the masses, and herein lies the movement's role, its raison d'être.

Realising that the conditions were not ripe for a structural change, the only revolution that the KSSP feels can be envisaged is a cultural revolution. For a cultural revolution, popular culture has to be scientised; the intellectuals have to be linked to the masses and thus a broad base for creative initiatives has to be created. Through this, the process of 'evolutionary development of society' can be speeded up. KSSP sees itself in being engaged in this task of ushering in a cultural revolution, of bringing about a qualitative change by intervening at the level of people's consciousness, so that it would enable people to transform their social experiences.

> ... the people should be given the self-confidence to realise that they have the capacity to transform their social realities (which were thought

to be based on beliefs and rituals), in ways they want, according to their convenience. They should also be enabled to understand their own problems scientifically, to examine their own experience and think of other alternatives systematically. (KSSP 1981)

Thus, the creation of a modern, developed Kerala is dependent on intervention both at the levels of the individual and the collective. While individuals needed the 'self-confidence' to turn away from their traditional beliefs, which were termed as 'superstitious', or 'feudal' or 'elitist' as the case may be, and become rational, popular culture needed to be emptied out of its religious and cultural elements and channelised 'scientifically' for this new reconstruction of the developmental modern.

In creating the developmental state, it would be the 'organic intellectuals' who would provide leadership. These organic intellectuals, revolutionary in character, would be ready to go to the people to initiate activities, which would enable the masses to be conscientised and organised. It would also require a public (masses) who are interested and ready to respond according to the framework/interpretation given by the intellectuals. This articulates the KSSP's conception of its own role vis-a-vis Kerala. It is as organic intellectuals undertaking the task of conscientisation that the activists explain and carry out their historic task of social transformation. This is undertaken through a process of conscientisation in which different kinds of pedagogic tools are used to inculcate the notion of science for social revolution. This also marks the creation of the expert as an activist, and the people's science movement as a space for the 'new elite', both "the technical expert and the modern educated intellectual, the recognised purveyors of the Indian modern" (Devika 2007) to blend in as if almost seamlessly, working for the cause of Kerala's development.

Keralathinde Sampattu: Creating an Alternative Discourse?

During 1970s, development of Kerala became one of the much discussed issues in different forums. This was the time when the 'Kerala model of development' also came into existence and gradually got institutionalised following a study commissioned by the UN and undertaken by the Centre for Development Studies, Trivandrum. In another forum, in 1976 a group of experts (mainly scientists and economists from Kerala), some of whom were activists in the science movement, wrote a book in Malayalam, which attempted to answer the question, Why were the Malayalees so poor while the state of Kerala was rich in both physical and human resources? The monograph, called Keralathinde Sampatthu (or The Wealth of Kerala), was the first attempt by a social movement like the KSSP in articulating a developmental perspective. Subsequently, in 1976–77, the KSSP carried out a campaign, across the villages of Kerala, taking the ideas of this monograph to the people.

The monograph was based on an elaborate account of both the human and physical resources (forests, water, fisheries and mineral wealth), nature of land use and agricultural production in the state. Kerala's wealth *(sampattu)* lay in its resources, and this was the basis of making a claim for its exceptionalism. There are two parallel strands of thought that run in this monograph which makes for the movement's ambivalence regarding environment. While one of the concerns was to make a realistic assessment of the resources available, articulated primarily in terms of their capacity for generating revenue and suggest ways to maximise their use for increasing their productivity and the economic development of Kerala, the second parallel and consistent concern is about the environmental degradation that development would bring about. The document reflects the view that at a very fundamental level the survival of man and his evolution involves an increasing pace of interaction with other human beings and with the environment around him, during the course of which nature is irrevocably transformed. This interaction, situated within the physical and territorial environment of Kerala, provides the actual context and space of this interaction for the Malayalees. The process of development is actually a manifestation of this interaction between man and his environment and its progressive transformation. KSSP recognises that this transformation has not been favourable for man in the long run. Industrialisation and urbanisation have been detrimental and have led to environmental problems. Therefore, a critique of the existing notion of development is found in the discourses of the movement. But alongside, the problem according to the activists lay not in the idea of development as such, but in the nature of consumption patterns and resource use, which they thought, would change, when the structure of the society changes.

The understanding of the movement, regarding environment vis a vis development, can be understood better by M.K. Prasad's position that over time, the increasing pace of interaction (resource extraction) has resulted in consuming nature's resources at an alarming rate, which has led to environmental degradation and depletion of resources. Although mankind today has a better understanding of nature's laws and can anticipate both the immediate and remote consequences of his interaction, this remains merely academic knowledge. Prasad notes:

> To understand this we have to investigate not only changes in biophysical environment but also his (man's) socio-economic environment. It is this socio-economic environment that determines man's interaction with the biophysical environment and, in turn, is modulated by his cultural environment. (1984: 125)

In this formulation it is the resource-intensive, capitalist system of production, which is implicitly responsible for the depletion of natural resources at such an exponential rate. Only a transformation in the structure of social and productive relations (to a socialist society) that underlie the socio-economic environment would transform the relation between man and nature.

Kerala is a state, which mainly depends on the primary sector. It is largely agricultural in terms of land use and "the share of agriculture in the national income is much more in Kerala, than that of industry" (Parameswaran et al. 1976). In developmental parlance, therefore, it is considered to be an economically backward state. This has been a cause of anxiety for the Malayalee people and finds a resonance in many quarters, in the social science literature written on Kerala as well as in the exchanges within the movement even today, justifying the necessity of development.

Finally, the most important resource of Kerala is its human resource, which is known for its high levels of education and technological expertise on one hand and an equally high level of unemployment on the other. Kerala is a densely populated state, where the density of its population (i.e., 819 in 2001) is said to be three times higher than other southern states. According to the experts, the high population of the state is nothing but a potential resource. The characteristics of this human resource in terms of its high standards of education, technological expertise etc. should be especially taken into consideration. This human resource can be planned and organised and run on a small scale into small units with the help of small amount of capital. Hence, importance should be given to micro-enterprises. The physical resources of the state, namely, forest and its resources, like rubber, tapioca, and such agricultural products, are used to produce paper, rayon, cloth, glucose and such other products. These small-scale industries should be encouraged through incentives. It would fall on the state to undertake development on behalf of its people.

For example, in Chapter 7 of the monograph *Keralathinde Sampattu*, on the Forest Resources, it is stated:

> The forest has been a home to man. Man was born and brought up in the forest.
>
> With the onset of agriculture, there grew an enmity between man and forest. At the same time the domination over the forest increased.
>
> The forest is an important ecological element in the maintenance of the ecological balance of the region.
>
> The destruction of forests has caused soil erosion, flood, drought, the drying up of water holes (resources) etc.
>
> The importance of forest conservation increases when we take into consideration the fact that forests regulate the climate of a region, purify air that we breathe and render many such indirect services.
>
> The development of the forests should not be geared towards the export of their genetic material to facilitate research and new forms of knowledge. Ecological problems should gain priority (KSSP 1981).

Similarly, in the use of water resources in the state, the above document says that water has manifold uses especially for the development of the state. Although the state has an abundant access to water resources, many problems in the use of water may arise in the future. Therefore, it should be made available at the time and in the form in which it is required. This requires the mediation of technology whose adoption and utilisation has been rather limited and also beset with a number of problems. Further, the increasing pace of human interaction with the environment also places considerable pressure on the available water resources. A scientific land and water-based management system should be devised, which can ensure that the available sources are managed properly (Parameswaran et al. 1976).

The movement's activists speak in a double voice. On the one hand, they echo the dominant developmental view that the state of Kerala needs to develop through the process of industrialisation, but on the other hand, they speak of the need to give priority to the ecological aspects of development. Therefore, the resolution lies in what the movement calls as 'the management of natural resources' by developing a scientific and an efficient system of land, water, forest management.

The people's science movement was one of the earliest independent attempts to articulate a developmental perspective for Kerala, which incorporated environmental values into the developmental paradigm. It argued that a reconciliation of environmental and developmental concerns was necessary for development to continue and in this sense went beyond the environment versus development debate in Kerala. But, the needs on the ground, i.e., Kerala's industrial backwardness and the anxieties of the Malayalee society around it, an increasing pressure of population on natural resources, a higher demand for economic productivity and the attendant necessities of power and labour which facilitate it – all these lead the movement activists to reaffirm their faith in the idea of a different model of society altogether. They believe that a transformation to a society based on the socialist model would bring about a change in the attitude towards production, labour, and to the natural resources – a claim that has not been testified by history so far.

Thus, we find a gradual shift towards what Pieterse says, the difference between alternative and mainstream development becoming merely 'conjunctural' and 'not really a difference in principle, although it tends to be presented as such' (1998: 349). He alleges that when it began, the rise of environmental thinking questioned and managed to weaken the growth-oriented paradigm, but over the years we find the distinctions between mainstream and alternative development blurring, as sustainability as an idea, has been incorporated to some extent within the mainstream developmental paradigm today. KSSP's alternative view of development emerges from a local understanding of Kerala's needs and specificities as we find in the above mentioned document *Keralathinde Sampattu* as well as from the idea of incorporating environmental sustainability into the developmental paradigm, when the idea of sustainability itself was not commonly articulated. Further, their idea of development being guided or directed by the activist-experts also appeared novel in a context where all decisions regarding development were taken in a top down manner. But the politics of accommodation within a socialist model of development, as we find in the imagination of the people's science movement, robs it of its value and limits the potential of an alternative vision. What emerges is a techno-scientific and a developmentalist vision of things.

Alternatives in Development? The Peringom Anti-Nuclear Controversy

Another contentious issue of energy vis-à-vis development in Kerala that pitted the issues of power generation against that of the security of the people and dangerous forms of development endorsed by the state in underdeveloped countries was regarding the building of a nuclear reactor in the Peringom panchayat in the Cannanore district of Kerala in the early 1990s. The Peringom-Vyakkara region was selected as site because about 1,000 acres of barren, rocky and sparsely populated area were available here. Within 1.6 km area around it, not many people would have to be evacuated. The Konkhol 110 KV sub-station was situated within 10 km; a 66 KV electricity line could be drawn for the purpose of the nuclear reactor. Apart from this, work on the Kakkadavu hydel project which was to begin soon would enable the supply of large amounts of water, necessary for the reactor.

Like all major decisions, even this decision to go ahead with the establishment of the reactor was taken unilaterally by the government; the people did not have any role in it. The CPI (M) government in power was in favour of civil uses of nuclear energy and its State Committee even passed a resolution that work at Peringom should begin immediately. But when the decision was made public, it sparked off huge protests, attracting the attention of prominent people, literary figures, environmentalists and scientists[5] who spoke in various public forums against the project. Between July–August 1991, a number of conventions were organised in Peringom and Payannur where anti-nuclear activists from different parts of Kerala came and addressed the public. Classes, rallies and even a door-to-door campaigns were organised to make the common people aware of the dangers of such a project and seeking their participation. At these meetings, the people were told some facts about the project which they had not been told earlier.

> A survey in Kota, Rajasthan revealed that most of the nuclear installations (about 90 to 95 per cent) had ill-effects. During its normal working, too, there would be a presence of radioactive materials in the environment, which are usually not revealed during small accidents. Chernobyl could not be concealed because of the extent of the radiation leak. Evacuation is also not possible under such circumstances because the area around Peringom is thickly populated. The people need to be told all this because there is no transparency in such decisions, which concern the public. (Peringom Anti-Nuclear Samithi n.d.)

Conscientisation also involved making the people aware of the risks (environmental and health) entailed in the building of nuclear reactors. In the course of an interview, Dr Surendranath, who was formerly with the KSSP, said,

> Such projects, which are taken up under the slogan of 'Atom for Peace', are usually justified in the name of 'national interests'. But atoms are only used for destruction, never for peace. Only 2 per cent of nuclear energy is used for purposes of energy. But the effect of radiation can be felt across generations over a long period of time. Moreover, if it is for the betterment of people, why is there a secrecy associated with the project? Secondly, it has been found that the life of a nuclear power plant is merely for 25 years. Countries, which have such nuclear plants, face a problem about how to dismantle and dispose them. Only big accidents have been reported so far, but even nuclear energy is polluting. Plutonium, which is necessary for nuclear fusion, is not only a deadly weapon, but even a millionth of a gram can cause lung cancer. Every year about 650 kg plutonium is produced in India.[6]

On August 6th, 1991, observed as Hiroshima Day, all state offices in Peringom remained closed and thousands of people in large numbers from the neighbouring areas courted arrest in symbolic protest against the project. A People's March to the District Collectorate was organised between November 1st and 4th in 1991, which became historic because of the number of people it attracted.

In the words of one of the local KSSP activists Dr D. Surendranath, a medical doctor who led the mobilisation as the Chairman of Peringom Anavanilaya Viruddha Samithi (Peringom Anti-Nuclear Forum), these initiatives to go to the people had an impact. He said,

> There was an overwhelming response from the local people of Peringom, people of different religions, small farmers and agricultural labourers, who forgot their own politics and came together to protest against the project. This was remarkable in a politically divided society like Kerala. The media, which was surprised by the spontaneous enthusiasm of the people, also joined the people to highlight the issue.

The People's Front received help from groups outside the state. Under the auspices of Sampurna Kranti Vidyalaya of Gujarat, a national meeting and a cycle yatra was organised from Gujarat to Peringom to express their solidarity over the issue. Activists from Gujarat also came and spoke in the meetings organised to shape public opinion. Eventually, the people won this fight and the plan to build the nuclear reactor was dropped.

The mobilisation over the nuclear issue brings to light a few contradictions within the people's science movement. D. Surendranath, who lives at Peringom, was the State Chairman and the District Convener of the Health Wing of the KSSP. He was involved in the fight closely right from the beginning. To quote him:

> When the issue came up, I tried to convince the District Committee of Parishad to take up the issue, but they did not take much interest. They (the District Committee members) said that it would be a 'shadow fight', as the reactor would not come up in the area. I even produced evidence about the project ...

The KSSP came into the scene quite late – to undertake a study on the issue. They were not involved in the people's mobilisation and were not sure of how the locals would respond to their entry at Peringom at a later stage. Hence, they tried to organise a public meeting independently, at Trikkeripur, to speak to people about the Peringom plan in the context of the energy needs of Kerala. People came to attend the meeting and also participate in the study classes organised by the KSSP's local unit. It was quite reluctant to join the people's mobilisation, and its role remained restricted to 'educating the public' on the issue. Much later, after a period of deliberations within the movement, the KSSP took a stand against the issue. Dissatisfied by its position on the issue, Dr Surendranath left the organisation and got involved in the fight frontally. Dr Surendranath's views are distinct from the KSSP's views and he is totally against the harnessing of the nuclear energy and used the logic of science to reinforce his position, whereas the KSSP was initially cautious and later on decided to take a scientifically tempered position about the issue.

The power crisis in Kerala continues till today. In fact, the increase in population has intensified the demand for energy and the stalemate over the energy issue has not been resolved. Since the Silent Valley project there is a division within the Left between the supporters of KSEB and the trade union lobby (led by E. Balanandan) who believes in energy-intensive development and the KSSP which in principle believes that nuclear energy offers a cheap option for energy, though there is no place for a nuclear reactor in a densely populated state like Kerala. The KSSP is committed to an environmentally-sensitive development for the state. The old fight has erupted time and again with the former character ising the KSSP and its supporters as an anti-development force. In order to counter this, Dr M.P. Parameswaran and Dr R.V.G. Menon of the KSSP have gone to great lengths to assess the needs of people of Kerala and also put forth alternative ways of fulfilling those needs. But these alternatives have not been explored by the State Electricity Board as yet. On the other hand, they continue to assign responsibility for the energy crisis in Kerala to the organisations/forces which argue for environmental preservation. The KSSP since 1975 has been asking for the establishment of thermal power stations for generating electricity in the region, which the Kerala State Electricity Board (KSEB) is opposed to, because it is said to be more polluting than nuclear energy.

As the power crisis in Kerala continues, the KSSP has been speaking at different forums, trying to convince the people that the crisis in the state needs immediate attention. According to the KSSP, this crisis cannot be solved through projects like Silent Valley(s) or nuclear power stations. The state needs to rely on different possible sources and forms of energy such as hydroelectric, thermal and even possibilities of mini-micro hydel projects should be utilised to the maximum. Apart from this, the projects, which have been undertaken and are half way through, should be completed on a war footing. Thus, the KSSP has demanded that the Kayankulam project, followed by Brahmapuram, Kasargod, Kozhikode diesel-based power stations and Trikkeripur, Vypeen thermal power stations, should become a reality. The 500 MW thermal power stations of Cochin Refineries should also be completed. Alongside, optimal utilisation of energy should be encouraged for purposes of energy conservation. An attempt should be made to minimise the loss of transmission of electricity as much as possible. Finally, the KSSP also feels that in order to facilitate the efficient distribution of electricity across the state, the KSEB has to be restructured and reorganised.

In the case of Peringom, we not only find divergent viewpoints of the experts (within the KSSP), but also a fair degree of uncertainty about the implications of nuclear energy, which leads the people's science movement to undertake a study on the nuclear issue. Being committed to the view that the generation of energy is a necessary prerequisite for industrialisation and development, the movement was reluctant in the beginning to oppose the idea of nuclear energy, though eventually they take a position against it. This in turn is subjected to criticism by other groups who look towards the expert groups for leadership in such situations. An activist from the People's Health Forum[7] in Kannur said,

> In Kerala, the Parishad could have had an influence at different levels in society. But it is itself influenced by the Communist Party and works closely with it. It often takes a technical position. Therefore, it has not

been able to provide leadership to the environmental struggles in Kerala.

Another activist, who joined the conversation said,

> When people come together and become conscious, we should educate the people about the issue; but when people are ready to fight the battle, we should be with them. The Parishad was not there to organise the people about the nuclear issue, their role was limited to educating them.

Thus, the controversy against the nuclear reactor at Peringom highlights how the KSSP is caught between its ecologically sensitive position on the one hand and its nuanced and qualified notion of development which earns it several epithets of being 'anti-people', 'anti-development' and so on.

The KSSP's attempts towards intervening in Kerala society began as a progressive alternative in the early 1960 in their efforts to teach science in the vernacular, in mobilising school teachers and college teachers to devise new methods of teaching science, in using different traditional art forms of Kerala to disseminate the message of development and change and in many other ways. It was people-centric, participatory and rooted in the regional cultural ethos, though not limited to a particular community. But, over the years, its positions have become closer to a form of developmentalism – an idea that characterises the dominant ethos of Kerala, testifying to what Pieterse says about alternative development, as "partaking of the momentum of modernity and the everlasting hope that the future will redeem the present" (Pieterse 1998: 349). Hence, the notion of 'alternative' is no longer an alternative; it gets subsumed within the idea of mainstream developmentalism to which it arose as the counterpoint. We are reminded here of what Habermas (1987) said in his analysis of the relation between knowledge and interests in advanced capitalist societies. The production of empirical/analytic knowledge about the world around us legitimising the imperative of development actually gets tied to a technical interest of controlling the environment and produces an instrumental view of the world.

We find that despite its critical currency, development as modernity, with all its ambivalences, continues to be imbricated in the everyday lives, choices, strategies adopted by the various constituencies of the Malayalee people. In this it continues to be created anew. The people's science movement's attempts towards furthering a consensus for development should be understood in this context.

Notes

1. KSSP literally translates as a Council of Science Littérateurs engaged in the production of scientific literature.
2. The Nehruvian model of development is characterised by a commitment to large-scale, planned industrial development, with the aid of scientific and technological expertise. In the early years after India gained Independence, Nehru envisaged a mixed economic model that would provide space to both the public (state-based) and private enterprise, with a commitment towards both production and redistribution. While on the one hand the Nehruvian model, led to the growth of infrastructure, and enduring institutions, many felt that due to an overwhelming importance of industry and the public sector, the agriculture-based economy grew at a slower pace and also could not achieve much towards removing poverty and social inequalities.
3. Developmentalism then refers to faith: The faith in the effectiveness of specifically modern interventions in all spheres of life in transforming all the diverse peoples and societies of the world in the image of the industrially advanced, socially rationalised, politically powerful ideal of society rooted in Enlightenment modernity (Devika 2007).
4. See Parameswaran et al. 1976.
5. Some among them were the noted poetess Sugatha Kumari, A. Mohankumar, the environmentalist, activists like Subramaniam of the Peoples' Health Forum, Dr Surendra Ghadilkar of SEEK, literary figures like M.T. Vasudevan Nair, Dr Sukumar Azhikode, public figures like Justice V. Krishna Iyer, scientists like M.P. Parameswaran and Dr R.V.G. Menon of the KSSP and political figures like the ex-Chief Minister of Kerala, Sri C. Achuthanandan of the CPI.
6. Interview with Dr D. Surendranath, 25th January 1996.
7. Interview with Subramaniam, People's Health Forum, April 1996.

References

Caldwell, J.C. 1986. 'Routes to Low Mortality in Poor Countries', *Population and Development Review*, 12 (2): 171–220.

Devika, J. 2007. 'A People United in Development: Developmentalism in Modern Malayalee Identity'. Working Paper, Centre for Development Studies, Trivandrum.

Edelman, Marc and Angelique Haugerud (eds.). 2005. *The Anthropology of Development and Globalization: From Classical Political Economy to Contemporary Neoliberalism*. USA: Blackwell Publishing.

Escobar, Arturo. 2005. 'Imagining a Post Development Era', in M. Edelman and A. Haugerud (eds.), *The Anthropology of Development ad Globalization:*

From Classical Political Economy to Contemporary Neoliberalism. USA: Blackwell Publishing.

Habermas, Jurgen. 1987. *The Theory of Communicative Action*. Vol. 2, Boston, MA: Beacon Press.

KSSP. 1981. 'Notes for the Cadre Camp'. Trivandrum. KSSP (Pamphlet in Malayalam).

Kumar, Krishna. 1984. *Prakriti, Sastravum, Samuhavum* (Nature, Science and Society). KSSP: Trivandrum (Malayalam).

Kurien, John. 1995. 'The Kerala Model: Its Central Tendency and the Outlier', *Social Scientist*, 23 (1–3): 70–90.

Mari Bhat, P.N. and S. Irudaya Rajan. 1990. 'Demographic Transition in Kerala Revisited', *Economic and Political Weekly*, 25 (35 & 36): 1957–80.

Omvedt, Gail. 1998. 'Disturbing Aspects of Kerala's Society', *Bulletin of Concerned Asian Scholars*, 30 (3): 31–33.

Panikker, P.G.K. and C.S. Soman. 1984. *Health Status of Kerala: The Paradox of Economic Backwardness and Health Development*. Trivandrum: Centre for Development Studies.

Parameswaran, M.P. et al. 1976. *Keralathinde Sampattu* (The Wealth of Kerala). KSSP: Trivandrum.

Parayil, Govindan (ed.). 2000. *Kerala, the Development Experience: Reflections on Sustainability and Replicability*. London and New York: Zed Books.

Pieterse, Jan Nederveen. 1998. 'My Paradigm or Yours? Alternative Development, Post Development, Reflexive Development', *Development and Change*, 29: 343–73.

Prasad M.K. 1984. *Environment and Development: KSSP's Approach in Science as Social Activism*. Reports and Papers on the People's Science Movements in India (123–28). KSSP: Trivandrum.

Ramachandran, V.K. 1996. 'On Kerala's Development Achievements', in Jean Dreze and Amartya Sen (eds.), *Indian Development: Selected Regional Perspectives* (205–356). Delhi: Oxford University Press.

Rammohan, K.T. 2000. 'Assessing Reassessment of the Kerala Model', *Economic and Political Weekly*, April 8: 1234–36.

——. 2008. 'Caste and Landlessness in Chengara', *Economic and Political Weekly*, Sept 13: 14–16.

Section V

Society, Community and Development

14

Social Development, Deprivations and Social Movements in India

Debal K. SinghaRoy

Contemporary world has borne witness to a paradoxical societal progression reflected in the unprecedented economic growth in many parts of the developing world (notwithstanding the very recent global economic slowdown) on the one hand and unabated continuation, reshaping and resurfacing of varieties of social, economic and political deprivations and exclusion, on the other. The fast process of economic globalisation, phenomenal expansion of information and communication technologies, proliferation of knowledge economy, global and local connectivity (Giddens 1991), phenomenal economic growth and material prosperity, have seldom facilitated the eradication of poverty, livelihood insecurity, malnutrition, unemployment, illiteracy, ill-health, social inequalities, divides and exclusions and disempowerment of the largest segment of the population. It has been widely realised by now that economic development does not necessarily lead to social development; and that the growing imbalances not only threaten social cohesion but also pave the way for social discontents and social movements. As against this backdrop, the central thrust of this paper is to delineate the linkages between development, deprivations and social movements. It focuses on India and explains these relationships in the context of contemporary transition of Indian society.

Social Development: Emerging Perspectives

For centuries, development has been equated with economic growth. This growth perspective has been widely nurtured as a panacea to all social ills, and accordingly got a place of paramount significance within the developmental discourses of capitalism, economic modernisation and globalisation. However, with the increasing disjunction between economic growth and social development (that envisages ensuring livelihood security, employment, education, health, clothing, shelter and basic civil rights of all sections of the population), collective endeavour to redefine the course of development has emerged to be a reality. The facts that social development is an inalienable part of economic development, that economic development is relational and not autonomous of social development and that economic development is a means to social and human development have got wide recognition is recent years.

Though the ideals of social and human development are of relatively recent origin, these have widely nurtured for long within the welfare perspective of the state. In the wake of globalisation and adoption of Structural Adjustment Programme (SAP) in most parts of the world, the developmental perspectives have undergone a paradigmatic shift. More importantly, the human development perspective has brought a strategic shift in discourses on development. This shift has been those of from viewing economic and material well-being as an end in itself to recognise it as the means to ensure livelihood security, equity, freedom and peace, increasing access to education, health care and employment opportunities, widening the scope of democratic practices, political participation, cultural freedom, and social widening choices of the marginalised people (Sen 1999; UNDP 1990). In order to ensure the changing social objectives of development, there have been varieties of initiatives by the state, civil societies, grassroots organisations and international bodies.

It is widely acknowledged that capital, infrastructure, organisation of production (entrepreneurship), technology, social policies and institutions like market, as instruments, play a decisive role in development. Significantly, these instruments are the product of human's own initiatives and are not independent determinants of development. In essence human beings are the embodiment of the capacity from within to produce those instruments for development. Developmental process releases, organises and coverts human energy into social capacity and material results that have a social purpose. Within these broad understandings the perspective on social development shifts the focus from 'instruments' to the 'creators of these instruments'. Ideally, social development should generate a framework around which all knowledge of the factors, instruments, conditions, agencies and processes of development can be integrated. Though human development cannot be devoid of economic growth, one must see beyond it. Amartya Sen largely points out, "The end and means of development require examination and scrutiny for a fuller understanding of the development process; it is simply not adequate to take as our basic objective ... just maximisation of income or wealth .... Development has to be more concerned with enhancing the lives we lead and the freedom we enjoy" (Sen 1999: 14).

The broad perspective on social and human development also looks for transforming the institutional arrangements of society for greater inclusion, cohesion and accountability with the goal to empower poor, vulnerable, marginalised women and men, with a view to promote equality of opportunity, to redress inequality and discrimination practices based on caste, race, gender, ethnicity and class, to integrate the society both vertically and horizontally by distributing the benefits of development, to promote equal access to opportunities to enable people to contribute to social and economic progress, to share its rewards, to enable people to work together, to address common needs, to overcome common constraints and consider diverse interest, to promote inclusive institutions, accountable and transparent institutions to respond to public interest through effective, efficient and fair manner and to economic growth for a better quality of life (World Bank 2005).

Developmental Perspectives on the Move

Though the concepts of human and social development have got wide coinage in recent years, the essence of these concepts has got reflected in the UN resolutions and several of the covenants, summits and reports. India, as a member of the UNO, has been part of these processes. The United Nations has formulated from its very inception the broad perspective on social development as moral obligation of the member-states to evolve social and legal frameworks and conditions for ensuring equality, fraternity and justice to all citizens. For example, the Universal Declaration of Human Rights, 1948 recognised that:

> All human beings are born free and equal in dignity and rights ... everyone, as a member of society, has the right to social security and is entitled to realization ... of the economic, social and cultural rights indispensable for his dignity and the free development of his personality. (United Nations 1948)

The International Covenant on Economic, Social and Cultural Rights, 1966 also recognised:

> ... the right of every one to an adequate standard of living for himself and for his family, including adequate food, clothing and housing, and to the continuous improvement of living conditions.

These universal rights are again re-emphasised in the Right to Development formulated by the United Nations General Assembly in its resolution 41/128 of 4th December, 1986. It has resolved that,

> ... the human person is the central subject of development and should be the active participant and beneficiary of the right to development .... The States have the right and the duty to formulate appropriate national development policy that aim at the constant improvement of the well-being of the entire population. (United Nations 1986)

Significantly, these proclamations for social rights have been widely represented in the successive Human Development Reports of the United Nations Development Programme (UNDP) since 1990 with in-depth interlinkages with the process of economic liberalisation. In these reports the UNDP has posited human development as a "process of enlarging people's choices to live a long and healthy life ... to be educated and to have access to resources needed for a decent standard" (UNDP 1990: 1–3). The UNDP has formulated the perspective on human development in the backdrop of economic globalisation, initiation of SAP by the World Bank and the International Monetary Fund and the Washington Consensus (1990). It has also been underlining from the very inception of the Human Development Report in 1990 the need to not only develop strong linkages between economic growth and human development, but also for the involvement and cooption of the civil society and integration of the market dynamics with the processes of human development. Human development requires economic growth – for without it, no sustained improvement in human well-being is possible. It aims to ensure human security and sustainable human development through partnership between state, markets and civil society (UNDP 1993, 1997, 2002, 2006, 2008). Indeed this perspective has been explicit in the resolution of the Social Development Summit and the GATT and GATS (Chanda 2002).

The World Summit for Social Development (1995), Copenhagen recognised several opportunities and challenges to the philosophy of human development within the processes of expansion of free trade, ICTs and globalisation. Civil society has emerged as a sensitive partner of social development in the contemporary world (Bläney and Pasha 1993). The World Bank has also been constantly emphasising on the increasing roles of the civil society and the market in social development. To the World Bank (2000),

> The world is changing, and with it our ideas about the state's role in economic and social development ... . The global integration of economies and the spread of democracy have narrowed the scope for arbitrary and capricious behaviour ... . Technological change has opened new opportunities for unbundling services and allowing a larger role for markets. These changes have meant new and different roles for government who is no longer as sole provider but as facilitator and regulator.

Changing Development Policies in India: From State to Market Drive

Immediately after independence, to restructure the society and to accelerate the process of economic growth, India initiated the programmes of radical land reforms, community development and state-sponsored heavy industrialisation in 1950s, and introduced new technology for Green Revolution in late 1960s and 1970s. Herein initiation of social welfare activities has remained predominantly the obligation of the state; and economic protectionism was the state philosophy. Significantly, India has well articulated its broad perspective on social development as the rights of the citizens and as the moral obligation of the state in the Directive Principles of the State Policy of the Constitution in 1949.

The Fundamental Rights embodied in the Indian Constitution guarantee all Indian citizens right to life and dignity and ensure that they will lead their life in peace, enjoy civil liberties, such as equality before the law, freedom of speech and expression, freedom of association and peaceful assembly, freedom of religion, and the right to constitutional remedies. The Directive Principles of State Policy suggest that it is the moral obligation of the state to "strive to promote the welfare of the people by securing and protecting as effectively as it may a social order in which justice, social, economic and political, shall inform all the institutions of the national life" (GoI 1982). It is also stated that the state shall, in particular, direct its policy towards securing equality among citizens, adequate means of livelihood, equal pay for equal work, health and strength of workers and the tender age of children, protection against exploitation and against moral and material abandonment. The Constitution has adopted the policy of protective discrimination to promote the social and economic interests of the Scheduled Castes (SCs), Scheduled Tribes (STs) and other weaker sections of the society. These have got re-emphasised in several constitutional amendments, enactment of new laws and formulation of new social welfare policies and have got strategised in the successive Five-Year Plans. Accordingly, the state envisaged "to initiate a process of development which will raise living standards and open out to the people new opportunities for a richer and more varied life" (GoI, First Five-Year Plan 1951), and "sought to rebuild rural India, to lay the foundations of industrial progress, and to secure to the greatest extent feasible opportunities for weaker and underprivileged sections of our people and the balanced development of all parts of the country" (GoI, Second Five-Year Plan 1956).

In the 1960s the focus was on growth with equity. Thus, the Third Five-Year Plan envisioned that "economic activity must be so organised that the tests of production and growth and those of equitable distribution are equally met". It explicitly talks about the foundation of a socialist pattern of society (GoI, Third Five-Year Plan 1961).

In the 1970s and 1980s the focus was on equity, social justice and self-reliance. State policies were directed towards "a rapid increase in the standard of living of the people, through measures which also promote equality and social justice" (GoI, Fourth Five-Year Plan 1969); and emphasis was placed on the common man, the weaker sections and the less privileged. In view of imbalanced economic development and proliferation of social unrests and radical movements in several parts of the country, the second phase of land reforms was initiated in early 1970s. The objectives were removal of poverty and achievement of self-reliance (GoI, Fifth Five-Year Plan 1974), removal of unemployment and inequalities (GoI, Sixth Five-Year Plan 1980), building "a new India free from the fear of want and exploitation to move forward at a still faster pace on the road to progress, prosperity, social justice and self-reliance" (GoI, Seventh Five-Year Plan 1985). Since early 1990 focus has been oriented to participation of people, civil society and private partners in achieving the objectives of development. It planned "to work out the ways and means of involving people in the developmental task and … participation of people at all levels; empowerment of women and socially disadvantaged, promoting people's participatory bodies like Panchayati Raj institutions, co-operatives and self-help groups …" (GoI, Eighth Five-Year Plan 1992).

It also proposed to "usher in a new era of (economic) growth with social justice" with the involvement of the 'public and private sectors' (GoI, Ninth Five-Year Plan 1997).

In the new millennium the perspective on development has been oriented to human well-being and inclusive growth. Significantly planning process now aims to "represent a visible shift in the focus of development planning from the mere expansion of production of goods and services, and the consequent growth of per capita income, to planning for enhancement of human well-being" (GoI, Tenth Five-Year Plan 2002).

Now, in view of impressive economic growth on the one hand and glaring socio-economic disparities in the country on the other, the Eleventh Plan aims ... to build on our strengths to trigger a development process which ensures broad-based improvement in the quality of life of the people, especially the poor, SCs/STs, other backward castes (OBCs), minorities and women ... . This growth is to be achieved in an environment in which the economy is much more integrated into the global economy (GoI, Eleventh Five-Year Plan 2007).

In India, the emerging development has envisaged state partnership with free and representative organisations of civil society, and strengthening of the abilities and opportunities of civil society and local communities to develop their own organisations, resources and activities. The 73rd amendment to the Constitution of India has made revolutionary changes in rural society by transforming Panchayati Raj Institutions (PRIs) into statutory bodies, introducing 33 per cent reservation for women in these elected bodies, and empowering these bodies to formulate and implement development initiatives at the grassroots. As an institution of democracy, it holds the key to elect three million people's representatives every five years, of which one million are women and little less than this SCs and STs. The rural development programmes, namely, National Rural Employment Programme, Pradhan Mantri Gram Sadak Yojana, Swarnjayanti Gram Swarozgar Yojana, Sampoorna Grameen Rozgar Yojana, Mahatma Gandhi National Rural Employment Guarantee Programme and National Social Assistance Programme etc. are being initiated and implemented through the PRIs. Indeed, these have generated strong waves of social and political activisms at the grassroots in most parts of the country as these have provided the scope of alternative livelihood security for the rural poor.

Moreover, with continued economic liberalisation, India has emerged as a favourable destination for the foreign direct investment (FDI). As per the global survey of corporate investment plans carried out by KPMG International (a global network of professional firms providing audit, tax and advisory services), released in June 2008, India will see the largest overall growth in its share of foreign investment, and it is likely to become the world leader for investment in manufacturing. Its share of international corporate investment is likely to increase from 8 per cent to 18 per cent over the next five years. It will help India to rise to the fourth, from the seventh position, in the investment league table, pushing Germany, France and the UK behind. In spite of the global meltdown, in fiscal year 2007–08, about US$ 32.4 billion as foreign investment had poured into India. The country posted a 45 per cent growth in FDI with US$ 23.3 billion between April and December 2008, over the same period last year. The FDI inflows between April and November 2008 stood at US$ 19.79 billion (www.ibef.org).

Notwithstanding all the developmental initiatives and increase in the local–global connectivity, rural India has remained the breeding ground for several social ills with the concentration of the problems of unemployment, poverty, illiteracy, high infant mortality, low longevity, inadequate safe drinking water, lack of proper roads, drainage, health care facilities, domination of traditional authority, caste hierarchy, conservatism and fractional politics.

Glimpses of Socio-Economic Disparities

Despite the broad directives of the United Nations, noble provisions in the constitutions, formulation of new policies in the successive Five-Year Plans, socio-economic disparities in India are on the rise. These are discussed under the following headings:

Informalisation of Labour and Consumption Disparities

Though India stands on the threshold of a new economic order, which is reflected in the fast economic growth, informalisation of work participation has been the emerging trends of Indian economy. The report of the Commission for Enterprises in the Unorganised Sector, Government of India (Sengupta 2008) points out that about 92 per cent of the total workforce of about 457 million (as of 2004–05) is engaged in the unorganised economy. This sector of the economy, according to the report, is overwhelmingly represented by the poor and vulnerable population of otherwisely shining India. The increasing quantum of disparity in Indian society has been revealed in this report:

> India's real national income grew by 125 per cent during the economic reform period of 1992/93 -2005/06 ... the per capita income increased by 77 per cent during 1992/93 – 2005/06. There has been a heightened sense of buoyancy in the economy during the last three years with the growth rate exceeding 9 per cent per annum .... The savings rate of the economy has risen form a long time average of 22–24 per cent to 30 per cent, ... growth in exports has averaged to around 20 per cent per annum, ... increasing flow of foreign investments has swelled the foreign exchange reserves to more than 200 billion US dollars ... However, a majority of the people, who did not have even Rs 20 a day for consumption, were not touched by this euphoria. At the end of 2004–05, about 836 million or 77 per cent of the population were living below Rs 20 per day and constituted most of India's informal economy. About 79 per cent of the informal or unorganised workers belonged to this group without any legal protection of their jobs or working conditions or social security, living in abject poverty and excluded from all the gory of a shining India. (ibid.: 1)

The report further shows that 87.8 per cent of the SCs and STs, 79.9 per cent of OBCs, 84.5 per cent of the Muslims and 54.8 per cent of the general category workers in the unorganised sector are poor and vulnerable. Besides, the conditions of work and lives of the unorganised workers are utterly deplorable and livelihood options extremely few. Such a sordid picture co-exists uneasily with a *Shining India* that has successfully confronted the challenges of globalisation powered by increasing economic competition both within the country and across the world (ibid.).

Increasing Marginal Land Holding

Despite occupational diversification, 52 per cent of Indian workforce is dependent on agriculture for the mainstay of their livelihood. Land holding per household has declined from 1.78 hectare in 1961–63 to only 0.73 hectare in 2003. In rural India, though there has been a significant decrease in the number of landless households, there has been steep downward mobility of the lowest segment of the rural population. It is evidenced at the lower strata and is reflected in patterns of land holding and work participation. In rural India 10.5 per cent of the households are landless. The landless and semi-landless households (having less than

0.04 hectare of land which is mostly for residential purposes) altogether form 40.2 per cent of the rural households. The semi-marginal and the marginal cultivators, who altogether formed 62 per cent of the rural landowning households in 1981, constituted 80 per cent of these households in 2003. The landless, semi-landless and the marginal cultivators (owning less than 1 hectare), who altogether form over 90 per cent of the rural household, have emerged to be highly economically vulnerable (NSSO 2003).

Increase in Agricultural Labourers

The proportion of cultivators as main workers has declined from 51 per cent to 40 per cent whereas the proportion of agricultural labourers has increased from 29 per cent to 33 per cent during the period 1981 to 2001. The decline in the category of cultivators and increase in the category of agricultural labourers is related to the issue of increasing unemployment and underemployment in rural areas and increase in the quantum of rural–urban migration. It has been visibly marked in the increase in the category of 'marginal workers' (getting less than 180 days of employment) from 4 per cent in 1981 to 11 per cent in 2001. These have generated instability in the rural economy, causing horizontal mobility and migration. According to the NSSO 2000 report, about 27 per cent of the Indian population was migrants and the proportion of migrants in the urban areas and rural areas were to the extent of 33 per cent and 24 per cent respectively. Among the urban migrants 59 per cent of the males and 58 per cent of the females were from rural areas (NSSO 2000). About 67 per cent of the households migrated from rural to rural areas and 60.2 per cent migrated from rural to urban areas for the purpose of employment (NSSO 1999).

Sustained Poverty and Unemployment

The NSSO (2005a) reports that 28.6 per cent of Indian population lives below the poverty line. However, according to the revised estimate of the Tendulkar Committee, 37 per cent of Indian population lived below the poverty line in 2004–05 and this estimate is based on a new methodology wherein expenditures on education, health and clothing are calculated along with food. Similarly, the Ministry of Rural Development committee on BPL surveys (called Saxena Committee), in its report submitted in July 2009, has recommended that 50 per cent of India's population be given below-poverty-line cards. According to the UNDP (2008), 34.3 per cent of Indian population earns less than a $1 per day and cumulatively 80.4 per cent less $2 a day. In terms of share of income or expenditure, the poorest 20 per cent have access over only 8 per cent while the richest 20 per cent have access over 45.3 per cent.

In India unemployment rate has gone up despite phenomenal economic growth during the period between 1993–94 and 2004. While the unemployment rate for males has increased from 5.6 per cent to 9 per cent in rural areas, the corresponding figure for urban areas was from 6.7 per cent to 8.1 per cent. In the financial year 2004–05, unemployment grew at the rate of 8.3 per cent and the GDP growth rate was hovering around 8 per cent.

Increasing Vulnerability of the Marginalised

Within the emerging processes of spatial and occupational mobility, the socio-economic position of the marginalised sections of the society has emerged to be highly vulnerable. Among the SCs, there have been fewer cultivators than agricultural labourers with 23.47 per cent and 52 per cent respectively. While among the STs, the proportion of the cultivators is more with 47 per cent than the agricultural labourers. However, the STs have the highest extent of work participation as agricultural labourers among all social categories because of the predominance of sub-marginal and marginal land holdings among them. The incidence of poverty is also highest among them with more than 47.3 per cent living below the poverty line. Among the SCs around 37 per cent live below the poverty line; and for the general category 28.3 per cent live below the poverty line as per the old NSSO (2005a) estimate.

While there has been a predominance of sub-marginal and marginal holdings in the agrarian society, the extent of such holdings has been very preponderant among the SCs and STs. Due to these emerging patterns of land holding and downward mobility, the extent of work participation as agricultural labourers among them has increased in recent years.

Increased Productivity vis-à-vis Sustained Hunger and Downward Mobility in Agriculture

In India, there has been phenomenal increase in agricultural production from less than 10 quintals in 1960s to over 24 quintals in 2003 (CMIE 2004). However, the proportion of the rural population unable to access required 2,400 calories a day has climbed from 75 per cent in 1994–95 to a record 87 per cent by 2004–05 (*The Times of India* 2009). According to

Global Hunger Index, India ranks 94 among 119 countries of the world with 230 million of its rural population being undernourished – the highest for any country in the world. More than 27 per cent of the world's undernourished people live in India, and 20 per cent of India's population is undernourished. Significantly inflation in food prices continues to rise from 5 to 11 per cent during July 2008 to January 2009 even though the general inflation rate has reported to have come down significantly (International Food Policy Research Institute 2008). Again, this economic growth has not been able to provide social security to the farmers. According to a report presented in the Lok Shaba, 1,37,621 farmers committed suicide in only 2006 because of indebtedness, crop failure, food insecurity and so on. The farmers' suicide constitutes more than 15 per cent of the total suicides in the country (Sainath 2009).

Health and Nutrition

While examining the area of child health and nutrition, one easily finds that more than 43 per cent of the below 5 years of age children are underweight, 51 per cent are underheight, and 30 per cent are with low birth weight (UNDP 2008). More than 70 per cent of children of this age group suffer from anaemia, and 80 per cent do not get vitamin supplement. Malnutrition accounts for nearly 50 per cent of the child deaths in India as every third adult (15–49 years) reported to be thin. More than 1.5 million rural children are at risk of becoming malnourished (International Food Policy Research Institute 2008). The UNICEF (2008) data reveal that in India one million infants die every year and 40 per cent of them die in the first week after birth. According to the NSSO report (2006), between 1998–99 and 2005–06, the number of children suffering from nutrition has gone up from 15.5 per cent to 19.1 per cent and the number of the children under five with anaemia rose from 74.2 per cent to 79.2 per cent.

India's performance in the area of health care is dismally poor. Only 43 per cent of Indian population uses improved sanitation and 14 per cent is even unable to get access to safe water sources. The percentage of women with chronic energy deficiency is 40. According to the recommendation of Health Survey and Planning Committee (Mudalier Commission), there should be one doctor for every 3,500 persons and one hospital with one bed for every 1,000 persons. But, in reality, India continues to face a poor doctor to patient ratio with only one doctor available for 1,588 people in the country. The number of registered allopathic doctors in the country was

7,33,617 in 2009 (*Deccan Chronicle* 2009). India's public expenditure on health constitutes only 0.9 per cent of the GDP. There are enormous disparities in the maternal and child health care; for example, 84 per cent of the births of the poorest 20 per cent of India are not attended by skilled health personnel. Similarly, the incidences of infant mortality, underheight and underweight are substantially higher among the poorest segment than those of the richest one.

Literacy

Even after 64 years of independence and constitutional directives, India is yet to achieve full literacy. As per provisional data of 2011 census the adult (7 years and above) literacy rate in India is 74 per cent, and the adult literacy rates for male and female are 82.14 per cent and 65.46 per cent GoI 2011. The combined gross enrolment ratio for primary, secondary and tertiary education is 63.8 per cent in 2001. Indian expenditure on education has always remained very low – around 3.8 per cent of the GDP. It altogether formed 10.7 per cent of total government expenditure during 2000–04. India spent only 0.8 per cent of the GDP on research and development as against 3 per cent in developed countries. Per million population, India has only 119 researchers. The gross enrolment ratio in higher education in India (percentage of the 18–23 age group enrolled in higher education institution) forms only 11 per cent as against 25 per cent in many of the developing countries (GoI 2007).

Child Labour and Child Marriage

India has enacted progressive laws to ban child labour and child marriage. However, the practice of both the institutions is widely rampant. According to a report of UNICEF (2009) *The State of the World's Children-2009*, 40 per cent of the world's child marriages take place in India and that 45 per cent of women married before they turned 18 and 78,000 women die during childbirth every year. Due to persistent livelihood insecurity, the prevalence of child labour has emerged to be a reality in India, howsoever disgraceful and inhuman this practice may be. Though the government estimate on this shows only 12.6 million, the NGO estimate claims the presence of 70 million child labour in India. There is a strong relationship between poverty, illiteracy and the increasing incidences of child labour and child marriage.

Growing Slums and Urbanisation

In India, the extent of urbanisation has substantially increased with a decadal growth rate of about 31 per cent during 1981–2001. Now, 285 million (27.8%) of Indian population live in urban areas. Simultaneously, India's slum-dwelling population has been more than doubled, rising from 27.9 million in 1981 to 61.8 million in 2001 (GoI 1981, 1991, 2001). They altogether form 22.6 per cent of the total urban areas reported slums in 2001. The growth of slum is widely recognised as the natural extension of poverty, declining land-man ratio, resourcelessness, and unemployment and livelihood insecurity in the rural areas.

Growing Unemployment Among Educated Youth

The youth (15–29 years) form 29 per cent of total population in India and there has been substantial improvement in the level of education among them. However, the rate of unemployment is substantially high among them with 13 per cent in rural and 9.1 per cent in urban areas. Significantly, this unemployment rate is very high among the educated female population of this age group with 26.7 per cent among rural females and 20.8 per cent among urban females (NSSO 2005b). Even after phenomenal proliferation of service sector with 39 per cent of the workforce being employed in this sector, the newly literate youth are yet to get fully integrated with this economy. Indeed, the gap between the acquired qualifications and the requirement in the job market is very high in rural areas.

Gender Discrimination

India has been experiencing phenomenon of declining female sex ratio over the decades. It now has 940 females to per 1,000 males and alarmingly declining child sex ratio from 962 in 1981 to 914 in the year 2011 (GoI 2011). Significantly, in economically developed areas of the country, girl child sex ratio is sharply adverse in comparison to other areas. For example, for every 1,000 boys in 2001, Punjab had only 798 girls, Haryana 819, Delhi 868 and Gujarat 883 girls. It has widely been pointed out that the traditional preference for male child, high incidences of female illiteracy, practice of child marriage and early marriage, and of dowry, sustained low status of women (in terms of low access to productive resources, health, education and capacity building opportunities, lack or negligible participation in the decision-making processes etc.) and predominance of patriarchal values contribute to unfavourable sex ratio in India. The phenomena of female infanticide and foeticide also contribute to declining sex ratio. According to UNICEF (2009), 50 million girls and women are missing from India's population as a result of systematic gender discrimination in Indian society.

Criminalisation and Corruption

Criminalisation and corruption have taken a deep root in Indian society. These are as rampant in local officialdom as in the high corridors of power. A report prepared by National Social Watch Coalition (2006) reveals that as many as 518 out of 3,182 candidates across parties contesting for the 14th Lok Sabha election had criminal backgrounds. Again, 120 Members of Parliament, which is about one-fourth of the total elected to the 14th Lok Sabha, had been charge-sheeted in criminal cases. India ranked among the 30th most corrupt nations in the corruption perceptions index (CPI) in 2002. According to a report released by Transparency International, India turned out to be the 22nd most corrupt country in the world (Transparency International 2008).

National Crime Record Bureau of the Government of India (NCRB 2008) report that rate of violent crimes have increased in India from 18.4 per cent in 2003 to 19.8 per cent in 2008. In 2007, there were 971 cases of Naxalite extremism covering 156 backward districts of 13 states in India. Similarly, dowry deaths, rapes and female foeticides have taken endemic form in the society. NCRB (2008) report shows that there were about 8,172 dowry death cases registered in India in 2008 and during the last one decade, there has been 16 per cent rise in the incidences of such deaths. Again, since 1971, the rape cases have increased from one case a day to 53 cases a day in 2008. Female foeticide has emerged to be a serious concern in India. According to a recent report, more than 25,000 female foeticides are committed in India per annum and as indicated earlier such incidences are higher in the developed regions of the country. The incidences of crime against children, SCs, STs and other vulnerable sections have also increased in recent years.

Dismal Social Development

According to Human Development Report of 2007/2008 (UNDP 2007, 2008), India ranks 128th among 177 countries of the world in terms of its attainment of human development index. It stands far below Sri Lanka and Maldives while marginally above Bhutan, Pakistan, Bangladesh and Nepal (also see, Haq 1997).

It is apparent that India lives in a paradoxical platform. Contemporary social and economic transition has furthered those paradoxes. While with fast economic development it has emerged to be the world hub of trained manpower and prosperity, it has also remained backward with highest burden of poverty, illiteracy and unemployment. The disjunction between economic growth and social development has contributed to emerging social instability and perversion in many areas of social and economic lives. These are reflected in the paradoxical social momentum of fluidity, flux and deformities on one hand and consolidation on the other (Castells 1997).

The dismal state of social development, persisting injustice and inequality have widely resulted from the state's failure to adhere to the broad guideline of the United Nations, mandates of the Constitution and increasing gap between the policy formulation and implementations of these policies at the grassroots. Such scenario has persisted due to organised apathy of the power elite to implement the social welfare and reform policies on the one hand and ignorance of the marginalised about their rights and entitlement and lack of their organised voice on the other. Thus, the backward areas of the country have emerged to be the hot beds of protests and resistance of diverse varieties. All these provided the basis for regular mobilisation of rural population on several issues including land reform, self-employment, micro-credit, and poverty elevation. The emerging patterns of transition of society have profound implications on the processes of social mobility, social conflicts and collective mobilisation and largely on the culture of social movements in society.

Social Conflicts and Social Mobilisations

For long, India has remained a land of social discontent which has widely been reflected in the form of organised protests, collective mobilisations and social movements. Notwithstanding the decline of conventional class-oriented social movements, India continues to experience the proliferation of social movements of peasants, farmers, tribals, ethnic minorities, women, displaced persons, dalits, workers, human right activists, environmentalists, backward classes and the like. Significantly enough, most of these movements have emerged and sustained in Indian society due to objective conditions of economic deprivation, social exclusion, and political subordination of largest segment of the population of the country. The prolonged deprivation and increasing interactivity with the wider world has provided the foundation for subjective and perceived understanding of their historical and situational neglects in the society.

The perceived and substantive gap between constitutional mandate and policy formulation on one hand and their implementations at the grassroots on the other not only breeds social underdevelopment, exclusion and neglect of the marginalised in the society, but also reinforces the hegemony and domination of the powerful over them. As the violation of human rights of the marginalised, reflected in the form of denial of food, livelihood, security, right to life and equality etc., get institutionalised through the corrupt practices of the politicians, bureaucrats and the dominant segments of the society, the marginalised communities take recourse to organised social protest for social justice.

The positive co-relationship between social underdevelopment and social protest has remained rather obvious in Indian society. Though the state has tried to co-opt many of those in protest and simultaneously many of the protest movements have got institutionalised, the quantum of social underdevelopment has remained unchanged for the marginalised. Indeed, the process of marginalisation has been strengthened and extended to several areas of social, economic and political lives of the marginalised people. Since the conventional mode of protests based on secular value has failed, a large segment of this protest now reflects and takes primordial form in the shape of tribal, dalits and ethnic movements. Again, the persistent backwardness has pushed a certain segment of the marginalised to follow the path of extremism.

In rural India, issues like gender, minority, reservation, etc., are articulated to frame collective mobilisations against the hostile forces of patriarchy, feudalism, caste and ethnic hegemony. The practice of democracy at the grassroots has generated a space for self-assertion among the marginalised groups on diverse issues. These have contributed to the continuity of the culture of collective mobilisations and re-articulation of regional, ethnic and gender identities. These have redefined the paradigm of legitimacy of conflict, protest and collective mobilisation and processes of articulation of new interests and identities. For example, the Telengana region of Andhra Pradesh, which has seen a proliferation of peasant movements (viz., the Telengana movement between 1948 and 1952, the Naxalite movement from 1972 onwards), has now seen the growth of numerous collective mobilisations at the grassroots. For example, the resurgent separate Telengana statehood movement, based on the ethnic identity of the Telengana people, mobilisation of the agrarian poor and sustained agrarian conflict spearheaded by the CPI(ML) (Peoples' War Group) and various other Naxalite outfits, mobilisation for the protection of civil rights of citizens by the Andhra Pradesh Civil Liberties Committee (APCLC), Organisation for the Protection of Democratic Rights and Citizens Forum, mobilisation of Scheduled Tribes by Thudum Debba (a militant organisation of the Scheduled Tribes), mobilisation of Maadigga (a group of Scheduled Caste) by Maadigaa Reservation Porata Samithi (MRPS) for re-categorisation of the Scheduled Castes into four groups based on their contemporary educational and economic status for the purpose of reservations in jobs, education, etc.), mobilisation of cultivators by Roytu Seva Samithi, Jala Sandhana Samithi (demanding irrigation facilities for the peasants), anti-arrack movement to mobilise women against production and consumption of liquor and also for women's liberty, political participation and social development and so on are the contemporary realities of collective mobilisation in rural Andhra Pradesh (SinghaRoy 2001).

Similarly, in West Bengal, there have been the Tebhaga (1946–47), Naxalite (1967–71) and Operation Barga movements (1977–till late 1990s), Gurkhaland movements (1980s and onward), Kamtapuri movement (1980s and onward), resurgence of Naxalite extremism in the southern part of the state since early 2000, movements against acquisition of agricultural lands by the *Krishi Jami Suraksha Committee* (Committee to Protect Agricultural lands) in Singur and the *Bhumi Ucched Pratirodh* Committee (Committee to Prevent Land Displacement) in Nandigram, resistance to police oppression in the Midnapore district and several other grassroots mobilisations (SinghaRoy 2010a).

It appears that the state now has provided the liberal democratic space to articulate issues, interests and identities for collective mobilisations and also to co-opt the emerging discontents brewing at the grassroots. Within this available space many of the radical mobilisations have got transformed to be institutionalised, co-opted and have become partially reformative. Hence, the processes of institutionalisation of conflicts have been privileged by the state and society over radicalisation of the same. However, the persisting deprivation and injustice have failed to accommodate the discontents of the people who have got a victim position socially and economically in the contemporary society. More than 125 districts of 11 states of India are now under the grip of Naxalite extremism. The positive co-relationship between the social underdevelopment and extremism is now widely recognised both by the academia and the state (SinghaRoy 2010b).

The contemporary social movements are emerging to be highly eclectic. The extremism is reflected in the economic, ethnic and related identity politics. Varieties of social movements – the socialist, labour, women, nationalist liberation, peasant, ecology and even some religious movements – are taking shape within the capitalist world economy. Since late 1960s these have "primarily triggered by the sense that the old movements – the social democrat, the communist and the nationalists – had failed in many of their objectives ... and that there has been a major crisis in the anti-systemic social movements" (Wallerstein 2002). It is again pointed that the increasing failure of the state/political parties, labour movements/parties, socialism/Marxist parties as well as people's increasing refusal to be manipulated by these, now also increasingly draws the new other social movements (Frank and Fuentes 1990: 177).

Now, the situation has emerged to be very complex one. It cannot be explained by invoking another order of the phenomena – the laws of the capitalist development or the consequences of modernisation. It is also a different intellectual moment causing inability to the 'traditional left' to understand social and the political events of this era. Our most urgent need is to learn how to name and analyse the new social practices and the new forms of collective action which are shaping the societies of today and tomorrow (Touraine 2002: 11–12, 25).

In the changing society, while most of the social movements have remained institutionalised, working class movements in the traditional format are also on a decline and have emerged to be incapable of rising to the level of historicity to challenge the overall control of the major orientations of collective life. Yet, new forms of social movements are in the making to articulate new forms of identity and interests. The emergence of the new phase of economy, characterised by globalisation, has marked the proliferation of 'global movements' involving numerous struggles on the questions of environment, human rights, vision of 'another world', demand of recognition of cultural identities, and so on (Wieviorka 2005). With the emergence of multiplicity of social movements in the 'movement society', social movements are to encounter its inverted image – the social anti-movements which instead of promoting a social or a cultural identity, champion of some abstract entity, essence or symbol, and speak in the name of a purity or homogeneity. Again, instead of building relationships with other actors, agreeing on the principles of debates and negotiations, they champion absolutes, and adopt do or die attitudes. And if they appear in an arena where social movements also exist, they try to destroy these movements, and fight against them (ibid.:18).

In the contemporary phase of transition of Indian society the relationship between social underdevelopment, social deprivations and social movements have been positively correlated. Higher the extent of the state inefficiency, higher has been the extent of social underdevelopment, deprivation and social discontents. This situation has again been reinforced by corruption and criminalisation of politics. Though a vast body of social movements emerges to further economic interests, social movements predominantly construct an alternative sensitivity and new collective identity. These identities are indeed moral, emotional and pave the foundation of a just society by questioning the very foundation inequality, deprivations, exclusion and subordination in society. The process of shaping of counter hegemony through social protest is a product of sustained underdevelopment of the marginalised in society.

References

Blaney, D.L. and M.K. Pasha. 1993. 'Civil Society and Democracy in the Third World: Ambiguities and Historical Possibilities', *Studies in Comparative International Development*, 28 (1): 3–24.

Castells, M. 1997. *The Information Age: Economy, Society and Culture, Vol. II, The Power of Identity*. Malden, MA: Blackwell Publishers.

Chanda, R. 2002. 'GATS and Its Implications for Developing Countries: Key Issues and Concerns'. Department of Economic and Social Affairs, Washington: The World Bank. Shifting Perspectives on Social Development 105.

CMIE. 2004. *Economic Intelligence Service*. Mumbai: CMIE.

Deccan Chronicle. 2009. 'India Lagging in Doctor to Patient Ratio', July 10, New Delhi.

Frank, A.G. and M. Fuentes. 1990. 'Civil Democracy: Social Movements in Recent World History', in S. Amin et al. (eds.), *Transforming the Revolution: Social Movements and the World System*. New York: Monthly Review Press.

Giddens, A. 1991. *Modernity and Self-identity*. Cambridge: Polity Press.

Government of India. 1951. *First Five Year Plan 1951–56*. New Delhi: Planning Commission.

——. 1956. *Second Five Year Plan 1956–60*. New Delhi: Planning Commission.

——. 1961. *Third Five Year Plan 1961–66*. New Delhi: Planning Commission.

——. 1969. *Fourth Five Year Plan 1969–74*. New Delhi: Planning Commission.

——. 1974. *Fifth Five Year Plan 1974–79*. New Delhi: Planning Commission.

——. 1980. *Sixth Five Year Plan 1980–85*. New Delhi: Planning Commission.

——. 1981, 1991, 2001, 2011. *Census of India*. New Delhi: Ministry of Information and Broadcasting.

——. 1982. *The Constitution of India*. New Delhi: The Government of India Press.

——. 1985. *Seventh Five Year Plan 1985–89*. New Delhi: Planning Commission.

——. 1992. *Eight Five Year Plan 1922–97*. New Delhi: Planning Commission.

——. 1997. *Ninth Five Year Plan 1997–2002*. New Delhi: Planning Commission.

——. 2002. *Tenth Five Year Plan 2002–07*. New Delhi: Planning Commission.

——. 2007. *Eleventh Five Year Plan 2007–12*. New Delhi: Planning Commission.

Haq, M.U. 1997. *Human Development in South Asia*. New Delhi: Oxford University Press.

International Food Policy Research Institute. 2008. The 2008 Global Hunger Index. *http://www.ifpri.org/publiction/challenge-hunger*.

National Crime Record Bureau. 2008. *Crime in India*. New Delhi: Ministry of Home Affairs, Government of India.

National Social Watch Coalition. 2006. *India: Citizens' Report on Governance and Development*. New Delhi: NSWC. *www.infibeam.com*.

NSSO. 1999. *Report of National Sample Survey*. New Delhi: Ministry of Statistics and Programme Implementation.

——. 2000. *Report of National Sample Survey*. New Delhi: Ministry of Statistics and Programme Implementation.

——. 2003. *Report of National Sample Survey: Land Holding in India*. NSS 59th Round. New Delhi: Ministry of Statistics and Programme Implementation.

——. 2005a. *Report of National Sample Survey: Level and Pattern of Consumers Expenditure, 2004–2005*. NSS 62nd Round. New Delhi: Ministry of Statistics and Programme Implementation.

——. 2005b. *Employment and Unemployment Situation in India 2004–05*. 60th Round Survey. New Delhi: Government of India.

——. 2006. *Report of National Sample Survey: Level and Pattern of Consumers Expenditure, 2005–2006*. New Delhi: Ministry of Statistics and Programme Implementation.

Sainath, P. 2009. 'Farmer's Suicide', *India Together*, 6 November: 108.

Sen, A. 1999. *Development as Freedom*. New Delhi: Oxford University Press.

Sengupta, A. 2008. *Report on the Conditions of Work and Promotion of Livelihoods in the Unorganised Sector*. New Delhi: National Commission for Enterprises in the Unorganised Sector, Government of India.

SinghaRoy, D.K. 2001. 'Critical Issues in Grassroots Mobilizations and Collective Action', in D.K. SinghaRoy (ed.), *Social Development and Empowerment of the Marginalized Groups: Perspectives and Strategies*. New Delhi: Sage.

——. 2010a. 'Changing Trajectory of Social Movements in India: Search for an Alternative Analytical Perspective', in D.K. SinghaRoy (ed.), *Dissenting Voices and Transformative Actions, Social Movements in Globalising World*. New Delhi: Manohar Publication.

——. 2010b. 'Shifting Perspectives on Social Development: Changing Context and Emerging Challenges for India', in D.K. SinghaRoy (ed.): *Interrogating Social Development*. New Delhi: Manohar Publication.

The Times of India. 2009. February 24, New Delhi Edition: 17.

Transparency International. 2008. The Global Coalition against Corruption. *www.transparency.org*

Touraine, A. 2002. 'The Importance of Social Movements', *Social Movement Studies*, 1 (1): 89–95.

UN. 1948. *Universal Declaration of Human Rights*. Washington: United Nations.

——. 1986. *Right to Development*. Washington: United Nations.

UNDP. 1990–2006. *Shifting Perspectives on Social Development*. New York: UNDP.

——. 1993. *UNDP and Civil Society*. New York: UNDP.

——. 2007–2008. *Human Development Report*. New Delhi: Oxford University Press.

UNICEF. 2008. India: The Big Picture. *www.unicef.org/infobycountry/india_background.html*

——. 2009. *The State of the World's Children*. New York.

Wallerstein, I. 2002. 'Antisystemic Movements: History and Dilemmas', in S. Amin et al. (eds.), op. cit.

Wieviorka, M. 2005. 'After New Social Movements', *Social Movements Studies*, 4 (1): 1–19.

World Bank. 2000, 2005. *World Development Report*. New Delhi: Oxford University Press.

Website

www.ibet.org

15

Tribes and Development in India

Some Observations

Virginius Xaxa

India has a large population that is designated as tribal. As per the 2001 census, nearly 500 groups/communities described as tribes have been estimated at 88.8 million representing 8.6 per cent of country's population. Though they constitute less than one-tenth of the total population, they represent an enormous diversity in terms of size, language and linguistic traits, ecological situations, physical features, extent of acculturation, modes of making a living, level of development etc. Notwithstanding these diversities, they have all been described as 'tribes'. This shows that tribes have not been delineated in terms of some coherent and consistent characteristics. Officially, characteristics used to define tribes have been features like primitive traits, distinctive culture, shyness with the public at large, geographical isolation and social and economic backwardness (Verma 1990: 11).[1] Needless to say that the characteristics so delineated are not only stereotypical but also inadequate. They also fail to account as to how amorphous groups and communities at different stages of social development have been brought under the category of tribes. On close introspection, it appears that only characteristic the groups described as tribes seem to share in common is that they have all been at the point of their delineation outside of the Indian civilisation. This of course did not mean that they had no connection whatsoever with the larger society or civilisation. There was connection and it was this, which gradually led the way for the process of absorption of tribes into the larger Indian society. In fact, the growth and expansion of the Indian society and civilisation is explained primarily in terms of this process.[2] However, the relation, most often than not, was tenuous and tribes continued to live in relative isolation and social backwardness. The relation was on the whole cooperative and organic but become friction-ridden with the movement of traders, moneylenders and land-hungry non-tribal peasants into tribal areas during the colonial period. The movement resulted in loss of control over land and forest as well as of nerves. This article attempts to critically review the agenda of tribal development in India since independence.

So-called Tribal Policy

India being the state in which tribes as a whole lived at the dawn of independence, evolving an appropriate policy towards them assumed place of critical concern among the nationalist leadership. However, even before independence the nature of policy to be adopted had become an issue of heated debate between two scholars, viz., Verrier Elwin and G.S. Ghurye. The debate had its genesis in the publication of a book entitled *The Baiga*, which Elwin had published in 1939. The idea inherent in the book was forcefully carried forward in the pamphlet, *The Aboriginals* published later in 1944. Herein, Elwin had made certain suggestions regarding approach to be adopted towards tribes. The issue at the centre of the debate was whether tribes are to be kept in a state in which they are, namely, in isolation or to be drawn into the larger society so as to enjoy the fruits and benefits enjoyed by the larger section of the society. Elwin was charged with advocating the policy of isolation. The charge, Elwin (1960a) wrote later, was a result of suggestions badly put and unfortunate connotation of expression 'national park' used by him. The suggestion, he said, was made on desperation as the Baigas had very little left of their own when the book was written in 1939. It was not so much of preserving their culture as keeping them alive and away from exploitation and oppression, the single most development that was occurring among them. Since then, there had been shift in Elwin's position and he no longer held the policy of isolation. The policy, one finds on close introspection, was meant to be restricted to very small section of the tribal population. For the majority of the tribes, the policy he advocated was not different from those of the general population for he thought the problems they faced could not be considered apart from the general village population. Hence, what Elwin advocated was not of the same genre for the whole of the tribal population (Elwin 1960a). As against this, Ghurye advocated the policy of assimilation. His view was that the tribes were Hindus or to put it more aptly they were the 'backward Hindus'. He thought of them as inferior and backward because they stood cut off from the large mass of the Indian population. He also identified them as standing at a stage lower in the evolutionary scale, in fact not very different from the large mass of the Indian population. His considered view was that tribes are to be assimilated with the larger society so that they can be lifted out of their abject poverty and base lifestyle. This view placed tribals lowest on the tribe–caste–class continuum – a conceptual paradigm used to understand the processes of change in tribal life. For Ghurye, this continuum was to suggest a movement of the tribals from tradition to modernity, from pantheism to a higher form of religion, from a base and crude way of life to a life morally and ethically superior. This was a way of tracing the assimilation/integration stage of the tribals into the mainstream (Ghurye 1963).

Neither of the two policies was thought adequate in independent India by the nationalist leadership. This is evident from the nature and types of provisions laid down in the Indian Constitution for the tribals. The provisions pointed to an approach that was quite different from those propagated by the two scholars. The provisions included among other things the provision of statutory recognition, proportionate representation in the legislatures, right of using own language for education and other purposes, profess own faith and development according to their own genius. The Constitution had also clause that enabled state to make provision of reservation in jobs in favour of tribal communities. Alongside such provisions, the Directive Principles of the State Policy required that the educational and economic interests of the weaker sections of the society including tribals be especially promoted. Besides, there were provisions that empowered the state to bring area inhabited by tribes under the 5th or the 6th schedule for purpose of special treatment in respect of administration of the tribal people. The provisions laid down in the Constitution of India thus aimed at safeguarding, protecting as well as promoting the interests of the tribal people. Now, if one were to examine the provisions made in the Constitution a little more carefully, one finds that the Constitution clearly reflects articulation of the tribal problems in the direction of integration rather than isolation or assimilation without using the term and concept of integration even for a while. Indeed, there is no official document where the policy of integration finds an explicit formulation. Yet, this is what goes in the name of tribal policy in India, of course not without reason if one was to take note the provisions contained in the Constitution. In fact, the five principles mentioned by Nehru in the foreword to the book entitled *A Philosophy for NEFA* by Verrier Elwin (1960b) and proclaimed as the guide for tribal development was no more than an enunciation in the form of the principles of the provisions laid down in the Indian Constitution.[3]

The State Agenda for Tribal Development

It is against the above backdrop that the state's agenda towards tribals need to be examined and understood. The different measures taken for the upliftment of the tribal people are usually divided into three categories. These are: (1) protective, (2) mobilisation, and (3) developmental. The protective includes constitutional and legislative rights that safeguard the interests of the tribals. Mobilisation refers to the reservation extended to the tribals in different fields. Developmental means programmes and activities that are initiated for promoting the welfare of the tribal people. It is to this aspect of the state agenda that the scholars have given the greatest attention.

As a first step to developmental initiatives, special multipurpose development projects as a supplement to the community development projects were introduced in the tribal areas. The latter aimed at comprehensive development of the rural areas in general. A committee set up by the government under the chairmanship of Verrier Elwin in 1957 reviewed the scheme. On its recommendation the projects to be undertaken in the block were reduced in number. They were to concentrate mainly on four activities, viz., economic development, education, health and communication. This strategy was continued with some modifications here and there until the Fifth Plan period. The Fifth Plan is taken as a landmark in the task of tribal development. Not only it made shift in policy perspective from welfare to development but also introduced new concept of tribal sub-plan and integrated tribal development projects. The plan entailed a separate budgetary head for the purpose. The immediate objective of this strategy was to eliminate the forms of exploitation that existed in the tribal areas and accelerate the process of development. Hence, it recommended such programmes as integrated credit-cum-marketing services, marketing of agricultural and minor forest produce, supply of inputs and essential consumer commodities, credit for production purposes and consumption of social needs, and redemption of past debts through legislative and executive measures. Alongside these programmes, emphasis was also laid on the programmes for prevention of land alienation, restoration of alienated land, abolition of bonded labour, review of excise and forest policies, etc., as well as activities giving top priority to agriculture, such as land reforms, irrigation, improved method of cultivation etc.

The tribal sub-plan thus primarily concentrated on the area development with focus on improving the quality of life of the tribal communities and its main components were the integrated tribal development project (ITDP), modified area development approach (MADA), and pockets and primitive tribal group projects. The demarcation of the area for purpose of these development projects thus assumes crucial significance and the factors considered in delineation of these areas were to be predominance of tribal population, contiguity of area and the administrative viability. Thus, each ITDP comprised blocks, *talukas* or the whole district with 50 per cent or more tribal population. On a similar principle, the areas for the MADA were also identified. These areas comprise smaller pockets of tribal concentration having minimum total population of 10,000 with ST population of 50 per cent or more. Over and above 74 primitive tribes were identified which required special care for their development both at the level of planning and implementation.

Under the broad strategy of tribal sub-plan (TSP), a number of schemes have been introduced with a view to uplift the condition of the tribal people. Broadly, the schemes fall under two broad categories – economic and social. The issues taken up under the former include mainly activities such as employment and income generation, credit and market support mechanism, skill and vocational training etc. The social category schemes cover the domain of education, health and women and child development etc. The development schemes under the TSP have been at work now for about 35 years. Yet, the results are still very depressing. In 1993–94, for example, the proportion of the tribal population falling below the poverty line was 51.14 per cent, as compared with 35.97 per cent for the country as whole. By 2004–05, the share of the tribal population living below the poverty line had declined to 46.5 per cent, as compared with 27.6 per cent for the population as a whole (Mathur 2008a). Thus, although there has been a decline, the level of poverty in the tribal population is still much higher than the national average, and the gap between the two continues to be one of the major issues of concern in poverty discourse in India. The same is the case in respect of other indicators of social development such as education and health. In 1991, the literacy rate among the ST population was 29.60 per cent as compared to 52.21 per cent for the general population. The gap between the two was as high as 28.09 per cent. By 2001 the literacy rate for the general population had jumped to 65.38 per cent as compared to 47.1 per cent for tribal population. The gap between the two has been somewhat bridged, but the difference of 21.71 per cent is still very large (Planning Commission 2001, 2007). The picture is no different in respect of health of the tribal population. The percentage of institutional deliveries was mere 17.1 in case of tribal population as compared to 33.6 for the general population. As for ANC check-up, the figure was 56.5 for tribal population, the same being 65.4 per cent in case of the general population. Anaemia too is more among tribal women than other women. To illustrate, MMR is the highest in the tribal areas. Infant mortality and under-five mortality per thousand live births have been as high as 83 and 126.6 respectively as compared to 61.8 and 82.6 for the general population (Planning Commission 2000, 2001; IIPS 2000). In 2005–06, infant mortality and under-five mortality for the tribals has remained as high as 62 and 96 per cent respectively as compared to 49 and 59 per cent among the general population (Planning Commission 2007; IIPS 2007).

Constraints, Recommendations and Implementation

To sustain the constitutional safeguards meant for the tribals, a number of commissions, committees, working groups and study teams have been constituted from time to time to evaluate the condition and development problems of the scheduled tribes (STs). The annual reports of the Commissioner for the Scheduled Castes and the Scheduled Tribes from 1950 onwards are important documents in this connection. These reports have helped to reformulate the developmental strategies with reference to the tribals. But the most important have been those that were prepared by committees/commissions instituted to look into the specific problems of the development of the tribes. The earliest of the committees set up by the governments to look into the matter has been the Elwin Committee. The committee recommended reduction in the number of projects and simplification of administration in the tribal areas. The Scheduled Areas and Scheduled Tribes Commission, more popularly known as the Dhebar Commission (1960), noted the pace of development in the tribal areas as slow, investment and other protective measures inadequate and emphasised need for urgent attention. It called for comprehensive legislation to cover all tribals living within the scheduled areas and outside, and also a simple administrative system for the tribal areas. Yet, there was little change in so far as protective measures and development programmes were concerned. Another committee to review the developmental programmes was appointed in 1969 under the chairmanship of Shilu Ao. The committee observed that most of the recommendations of the earlier committees have not been implemented and emphasised their implementation without any delay. Most importantly, it found the block approach inadequate. In its opinion, it was too small to function effectively as a basic unit of planning and implementation. In fact, the main problems of the tribals was related to indebtedness, land alienation, economic backwardness and communication. Hence, these should be tackled on priority basis under the comprehensive development programmes. The tribal situation was again reviewed on the eve of five-year Plan by a Task Force on Development of Tribal Areas constituted by the Planning Commission. It noted that the deficiencies and shortcomings pointed by the earlier committees and commissions have not been attended to. Besides, one of the important factors for the failure of the developmental programmes was that the problems of the STs have been looked upon as 'welfare' problems as distinguished from the 'development' problems. The welfare of the STs has continued on small outlays under the backward classes sector and not on general sector outlays. The administrative structure lacks simplicity and beyond the comprehension of the tribals and therefore not suitable for taking up integrated development in tribal areas. It is of interest to note that the result of development projects has been somewhat better where there has been less division between recipient and local level bureaucracy. One can illustrate this by citing such case as literacy. Mizoram, Nagaland and Meghalaya, for example, show better results in this respect than Arunachal Pradesh, Assam, Tripura, etc., where the division between the two has been more glaring.

Interestingly, none of the commissions except the Task Force mentioned above has pointed to inadequacy of plan outlay for the tribal development. The STs have been enumerated at 7.5 per cent of the total population. But plan allocations for their development have invariably fallen far short of their population size. In fact, till the Fourth Plan the allocation has been less than 1 per cent of the total plan outlay. To be more precise, the outlay was 1.04 per cent in the First, 0.96 in the Second, 0.75 in the Third and 0.5 per cent in the Fourth Plan period. As mentioned earlier, a new strategy in the form of the tribal sub-plan (TSP) was adopted in the Fifth Plan, which resulted in unprecedented increase in plan allocation for tribal development. Thus, the inception of TSP strategy saw an increase from Rs 1,157.67 crore (3%) in the Fifth Plan to

Rs 3,640.25 crore (3.7%) in the Sixth Plan to Rs 6,744.85 crore (3.8%) in the Seventh Plan (Planning Commission 2001: 65). And yet the TSP strategy has not been able to bring about any perceptible improvement in the situation in the tribal areas. A number of factors seem to account for this shoddy state of affairs. Firstly, the resources earmarked for tribal development, though undergone increase, had been far from adequate. At no point of time the plan allocation has gone beyond 3.8 per cent. The only exception was the Eighth Plan period when the allocation was the highest at 5.2 per cent of the total outlay. In the Ninth Plan, allocation again had gone down to 3.7 per cent. Given the inadequate fund earmarked for tribal development, especially in the first four plan periods, could anything tangible have been expected in respect of tribal development? This is more so as there were wider processes at work which were detrimental to the interests of the tribal people. After all no fault of their own, they were steadily being squeezed out from their control over their life support system, viz., land, forest and other resources due to state sponsored projects of national development on the one side and alienation of land from tribes to non-tribes on the other. Since the Fifth Plan the allocation has been relatively better. Even then it has far short of their population size. Hence, the result even after the inception of TSP strategy has not been anyway impressive. A number of factors have responsible for it. Meagre plan allocation has already been referred to. But there were other factors too. One of them is that in the majority of the states, the emphasis under TSP has been on building infrastructural facilities. An average spending of 37 per cent of the TSP has been spent on the infrastructure. For example, in Maharashtra, as large as 80 per cent was spent on extending infrastructure. On an average, then, only 20 per cent of the TSP went for beneficiary-oriented schemes. The major achievement under TSP has been claimed in the field of education. As high as 95 per cent of tribal habitations are stated to have been covered with the primary school (Vaid 1992). Paradoxically, however, the achievement level of literacy as per the 1991 census remains at mere 29.6 per cent. Even in 2001, the rate did not increase beyond 47 per cent. The other problem that is associated with the TSP is that it has failed to go beyond the conglomeration of sectarian schemes.

Non-Governmental Organisations

One of the major drawbacks of the development programmes has been the lack of their effective implementation. The state agencies meant to implement the programmes somehow failed to deliver the goods. Hence, there had been rethinking since 1980s on the ways and modalities whereby programme could be more effectively executed. In this rethinking much sensitivity was shown by the state agencies for the role of the non-governmental organisations (NGOs). In fact, the involvement of the voluntary agencies in the governmental programmes was seen by the state as a part of its effort to make the administration more responsive to people's aspirations, needs and problems. The NGOs were expected to improve the effectiveness of developmental operations, especially in respect of poverty alleviation and sustainable development programmes. The initiatives of the voluntary organisations towards the development of the tribes could be traced back to the role of Christian missionaries. Later, Gandhi encouraged dedicated workers like Thakkar Bapa and Raghvaiya to work among the tribals. It was under his inspiration that the Adim Jati Sevak Sangh was formed. These organisations were primarily concerned with the social service oriented activities in the tribal areas. Today, there are a large number of such organisations working in the different parts of the country. These are mostly engaged in one or more of such issues and activities as agriculture, water, education, health, training, eradication of social evils, conservation of ecology, agitation and struggle against all forms of exploitation, political action for alternative process of development, people's organisation etc. Earlier work in tribal areas by the voluntary organisations was regarded as service in which the people in the area were involved only as beneficiaries. The contents of the welfare programme were drawn up by the social workers in their own light. The CAPART has come to occupy a position of principal promotional agency of voluntary action for rural or tribal development at the central level. It has now come to be realised that real development lies in doing away with dependency in any form on outside agencies whether they pertain to planning, implementation or evaluation. This can be done only through building up critical awareness, organisation and mobilisation. There are varied NGOs which are engaged in such tasks. These are more to do with what is generally referred to as rights and entitlements. Whereas some do it within the constitutional framework, others like the Maoist aim to do by radical reorganisation and transformation.

General Perspectives on Development

The reasons for the state of affairs in which tribes are situated are not confined to the problems of implementation as administrators and scholars tend to think and suggest. The reasons are structural too. In fact, issues taken up under the development schemes have often been the results of the kind of measures pursued under the national development. Hence, until the tribal problem is seen as one linked to national/regional development, the solution to the problem suffered by tribes is going to be partial and inadequate. In fact, development schemes have been acting more as a safety valve for the situations and conditions being created by the national and regional development. This dimension is however glossed over by the development planners, administrators and scholars. Alternately, they have generally held that the developmental programmes have failed to achieve the required results mainly due to factors inherent in the traditional socio-economic structure and cultural system of the people. Hence, the emphasis has invariably been made on introducing values, attitudes and institutions that would help them to take advantage of the fruits of development projects. In these perspectives tribes have been shown as backward, ignorant, superstitious, unable to overcome their worldview to recognise and exploit the wealth of resources present in the forest and the surroundings in which they live. Of late, however, it is increasingly being articulated that the development is expected to be more effective if the programmes and schemes are evolved in consonance with the ecology, social organisation and cultural values of the tribal people.

Approach to Tribal Development: Gap in Theory and Practice

At the heart of the problems of tribal development lies the discrepancy between theory and practice. The Constitution and the principles enunciated by Nehru say one thing, whereas the actual practice moves another thing. This gap in principle and practice has been carried on all through the Nehruvian era and continues even today. This has been so mainly due to the imperatives of national development, which included such activities as building up infrastructure, setting up industries, construction of dams for irrigation and power projects for electricity and light. It also included extraction and exploitation of mineral and forest resources. Interestingly, a substantial portion of these projects was undertaken in the areas inhabited by the tribal population, as the areas happened to be rich reservoir of mineral and forest resources. In fact, measures undertaken for bringing about rapid national development were seen as a kind of mechanisms whereby not only integration of the tribal society with the larger Indian society but also their development could be achieved. The integration it did achieve but not the development of the tribes. After all, the integration was built based on discrimination, exploitation and subjugation of the tribes. The national objective to build up productive structure for future growth and resource mobilisation was far more important than the issues that concerned welfare and interest of the tribes. The national development worked at loggerheads with the interest and welfare of the tribes and the interest of the latter was invariably sacrificed in the name of national development.

Social Consequences of National Development

The most important impact of the policy of national development was that it drastically altered the relationship of tribes with the natural environment and the resources lying therein, viz., land, forest, mineral and other resources. Traditionally, these resources were either individually or collectively owned. If they had no such rights, then, at least they had usufructuary rights over these. But, due to the measures followed by the state in the colonial period and later in the post-independence India, there has been steady erosion on control and use over these resources by tribes.

Of the resources that have most drastically affected the lives of the tribal groups, the most important are land and forest. The erosion of land rights of tribes began with the coming of the British rule. It was brought about by a combination of forces that were at work during the British period. Of these the most important were the introduction of the concept of private property in land and the penetration of the market forces. The two taken together opened up the way for large-scale alienation of land from tribes to non-tribes, especially after the tribal areas came to be linked by roads and railways. The mechanisms through which this was achieved were fraud, deceit, coercion and the most widely debt bondage. Despite much protective and even restorative legislation to stop land alienation in the post-independence period, there has been little success to this effect. Of course, the major source of land alienation in the post-independence period is not so much the encroachment of the non-tribals into the tribal land as the process of development that the Indian State has followed during the period. The large-scale industrialisation and exploitation of mineral resources and the construction of irrigation dams and the power projects that the tribal areas have witnessed during the period have been the single most factors that have uprooted more people out of their lands than the transfer of land from tribals to non-tribals on the individual basis. During the first three five-year plans, more than 50 thousand ST and 10 thousand SC families in Jharkhand area of Bihar (now, a separate state) were uprooted from their ancestral homes to make land available for the construction of public sector industrial projects alone. The total number of displaced families was to be much higher if one were to consider the private sector and coalmines at that phase were in the private sector. The progress of land acquisition for industrial purpose has remained high even after the first three plans (Sengupta 1979). It has been estimated that the total number of people displaced in India due to setting up of many modern development projects during the last 60 years has reached almost 60 million (Mathur 2008b).

Tribes underwent change not only in their relationship to land but also in their relationship to forest. Actually, they were greatly dependent on the forest for their day-to-day needs such as food, shelter, instruments, medicine and even clothing. But as long as tribes were in control of forest in the sense of unrestricted use of forest and its produce, they had no difficulty in meeting these needs. In turn, they preserved it, as it was their life support system. The entry of the British however drastically altered this relationship. To the British the forest was an important source of revenue and the commercial exploitation. Hence, the forest policy that was enunciated by the British not only introduced state control over forest resources but it also drastically curtailed the rights and privileges of tribals over them. The policy pursued by the British was continued in the post-independence era of economic development with even stricter regulation and enforcement. All these were justified on the ground that these were necessary for wider and national public interest. Besides affecting the rights of the tribal communities, the forest policy and its enforcement had other consequences. That is, it led to steady depletion of the area under forest. In 1854, the year of the first forest policy, the area under forest was estimated to be 40 per cent of the country's territory but in 1952 it was estimated mere 22 per cent. During 1980s, the estimated forest cover has gone down to 10 per cent of the country's area. Indeed, a large number of studies in recent years have highlighted the extent to which deforestation has occurred in different parts of the country (Fernandes 1996).

The issue of land alienation arising from the imperatives of national reconstruction process in the post-independence India, such as the infrastructure development (road, railways, irrigation, power etc.), industrialisation and exploitation of mineral resources, has been more specifically conceived as the problem of displacement rather than one of land alienation. And, given the fact that these projects have come up more extensively in the tribal areas than the non-tribal areas, there has been a great deal of attention to the problem of the displacement of the tribals. Yet, this attention to the issue of displacement is a more recent phenomenon though the problem had already begun in the first decade after independence.

These development projects have given way to other social processes as well in the tribal areas. To begin with, they opened up the tribal areas to the people from outside the region as never before. The tribal areas in almost all parts of India have seen a large influx of people from outside in search of employment in industry, mines, railways, transports, government and other ancillary activities like trade, commerce, transport that followed as a corollary of the activities referred above. These activities have not only given rise to increasing urbanisation of the tribal areas but also large-scale immigration of the non-tribal population in the tribal areas depriving tribals from the fruits of development that have come in the tribal areas. One of the tribal regions, which registered the fastest urban growth in the decades after independence, was the Jharkhand region. Yet, out of the total urban population of the region, only 17 per cent were SCs/STs as per the 1971 census. Indeed, the wave of immigration has been so fast and large that it has led to steady decline of the tribal population in the tribal regions. In Bihar, for example, the tribal population has declined from 10.07 per cent in 1951 to 7.66 per cent in 1981. The decline is more striking at the local level. In Dhanbad and Santhal Pargana districts of the Jharkhand, for example, the tribal population saw a decline from 15.65 per cent and 44.66 per cent in 1951 to 9.12 per cent and 36.80 per cent respectively in 1981. Even in the north-east, one finds in some states/union territories such as Tripura and Arunachal Pradesh a steady decline in the percentage of the tribal population to the total population of the respective states/union territories. In Tripura, for instance, they were even reduced to minority just within a decade, that is, from 50.09 per cent in 1941 to 32.24 per cent in 1951. This movement of the population from outside was not limited to mere movement for employment, trade and commerce. It also threw them open to the vagaries of greed, exploitation and even oppression. The result is that the tribes found themselves uprooted from their land and resources in a scale unprecedented in the history and were forced to move out of their place or even region outside their own for survival and employment. There was, for example, large-scale migration of the tribal population from eastern, central and southern India to tea plantations in Assam and Bengal all through the colonial period. The migration in the post-independence period has been to Sunderban in West Bengal and Andaman & Nicobar Islands especially by tribes from the Jharkhand region.

The other aspect is that these developments led to the 'development of underdevelopment' characteristics in the region. As has been noted that above tribal areas have been witnessed to large-scale expansion of industries, extraction of mineral resources, development of infrastructures such as power projects, irrigation dams, roads, railways etc. These have contributed to increasing industrialisation and urbanisation of the region and the diversification of the economy. No other tribal region reflects this phenomenon better than the Jharkhand region especially of that part that comes under Bihar. Yet they have been of little usefulness to the tribals. The industries and other development projects that came up have not made job available to them. Even where they could have been absorbed, people from outside the region have been preferred to the tribes. In fact, of the total number of workers in industry other than household industry, only 20 per cent were the SCs/STs, who mainly comprised the unskilled workers. Benefits arising out of power and irrigation projects have not reached the tribals. There are fewer tribal villages that find electrification and the land under irrigation is almost negligible. By March 1973, only 5 per cent of the villages in Jharkhand were electrified and only 7.2 per cent of the total area was under irrigation. Again, despite urbanisation of the tribal areas, the percentages of tribal people living in the urban areas as noted earlier are hardly visible (Sengupta 1979). In short, the fruits of development have not gone to the tribals but to the people from outside. Rather, with these developments, the conditions of the tribals have become worse. They find themselves increasingly subjected to impoverishment, exploitation and oppression. In fact, these have become the marked features of the tribal society in India at least in the region outside north-east. These being the general features of the tribes at large, it is not surprising that they have even come to be described as the 'fourth world' in the social science literature.

Resistance and Alternative to Development

The type of development projects pursued as a part of the national development has caused massive displacement of the tribals from their land and territory. This has adversely affected the cultural heritage and communitarian life of the tribals. Hence, a great deal of indignation has been shown towards such projects. The resistance against such projects by tribals can now be seen in other parts of the country as well. The *Narmada*

Bachao Andolan is a well-known example of such resistance. Some of the other project sites where resistance has been going on are Koel-Karo and Netarhat Field-Firing Projects in Jharkhand, Kashipur, Lanjigarh, Kalinga in Orissa, Nagarner in Chhattisgarh, Mehendikheda in Madhya Pradesh etc. The resistance against such projects has set into motion not only a critique of development but also a justification for alternative development. This has found renewed interest in the wake of ecological havoc that these projects have created at different levels. The articulation for alternative has also come from another angle, viz., depletion of the forest resources. Needless to say that there has been increasing exploitation of the forest resources in the tribal areas, especially of timber, which are required for the industrial and other infrastructural projects. The forest has also been an important source of the state revenue. Given this, a lot of restrictions and regulations have been imposed on the tribal people with regard to use of the forest resources on which they have remained so highly dependent for their livelihood. These have entailed curtailment/denial of such rights as collecting fuel, fodder, minor produce, grazing cattle, cutting timber for use, reclaiming land for cultivation etc. The customary rights that the tribals had over the forest were thus denied to the tribals. There has been in recent times renewed interest in the study of tribes and tribal communities, which stems not so much from the need to integrate and promote development but from the need to conserve and maintain ecological balance in the society. The issue at the centre today is development but without or minimal cost to ecological and environmental degradation and destruction. In this perspective, the tribes are seen as representing a storehouse of worldviews, systems of knowledge and way of life, which stands separate and opposed to the one governing the modern, industrial world. The tribal communities then stand as the 'other' in whom a search for an alternative is postulated. It is not surprising then that the increasingly emphasis is being laid on the need for conservation. In fact, a New Forest Act is already on anvil with conservation as being its main thrust. There is also increasing realisation in these studies that the conservation is not possible without participation of the rural and tribal communities. Hence, more and more emphasis is being given on the need for restoring rights and privileges to the tribals over the forest. Such a plea is made on the ground that tribes preserved the forest as long as they exercised control over the forest.

It is important to note that the alternative development has now come to be incorporated in the mainstream development paradigm.

Hence, rather than talking of alternative development, what has begun to be articulated is alternatives to development meaning development that is people-centric. In the literature on tribes and indigenous peoples, such development paradigm is referred to as self-determined development. Much of the organisations engaged in tribal struggles and resistance articulate such development paradigm.

Notes

1. See also Draft Tribal Policy worked out by the Ministry of Tribal Affairs, Government of India during the NDA government.
2. See D.D. Kosambi (1975) for details.
3. The principles as enunciated by Nehru were: (1) People should develop along the lines of their own genius and we should avoid imposing anything on them. We should try to encourage in every way their own traditional arts and culture. (2) Tribal rights in land and forest should be respected. (3) We should try to train and build up a team of their own people to do the work of administration and development. We should avoid introducing too many outsiders into tribal territory. (4) We should not over administer these areas or overwhelm them with a multiplicity of schemes. We should rather work through, and not in rivalry to, their own social and cultural institution. (5) We should judge results, not by statistics of the amount of money spent, but the quality of human character that is evolved.

References

Elwin, V. 1939. *The Baiga*. London: John Murray.

——. 1944. *The Aboriginals*. Bombay: Oxford University Press.

——. 1960a. 'Issues in Tribal Policy Making'. *Seminar*, 14.

——. 1960b. *A Philosophy for NEFA* (Reprint) with Foreword by Jawaharlal Nehru. Shillong: The Advisor to the Governor of Assam.

Fernandes, W. 1996. 'The New Forest Act: Conservation Orientation but Where are the People?', Mimeo.

Ghurye, G.S. 1963. *The Scheduled Tribes*. Bombay: Popular Prakashan.

IIPS (International Institute of Population Studies). 2000. *National Family Health Survey (NFHS-2)*. IIPS: Mumbai.

——. 2007. *National Family Health Survey (NFHS-3)*. IIPS: Mumbai.

Kosambi, D.D. 1975. *The Culture and Civilization of Ancient India in Historical Outline*. Delhi: Vikas Publishing House.

Mathur, Ashok. 2008a. 'An Overview of the Jharkhand Economy and Perspectives for Human Development', at National Seminar on Growth and Human Development in Jharkhand, July 4–5.

——. 2008b. 'Development and Displacement: Introduction and Overview', in H.M. Mathur (ed.), *India Social Development Report 2008: Development and Displacement* (3–13). New Delhi: Council for Social Development and Oxford University Press.

Planning Commission (Government of India). 2000. *Tribes in India* (A Data Sheet).

——. 2001. Report of the Steering Committee on Empowering the Scheduled Tribes for the Tenth Five Year Plan (2002–07).

——. 2007. Report of the Working Group on Empowerment of Scheduled Tribes for the Eleventh Five Year Plan (2007–12).

Sengupta, N. 1979. 'Class Structure in Jharkhand', *National Labour Institute Bulletin*, 5 (7–8).

——. (ed.). 1982. *Fourth World Dynamics: Jharkhand.* Delhi: Authors Guild Publications.

Vaid, N.K. 1992. *Tribal Development.* Delhi: Ashram Prakashan.

Verma, R.C. 1990. *Indian Tribes through the Ages.* Delhi: Government of India.

16

Towards Analysing the Muslim Situation in India

Perspectives from Community, Society and State

Sekh Rahim Mondal

> "Allah does not change the condition of the people unless they strive to change themselves."
>
> —Poet Iqbal

Religious pluralism, an important ingredient of cultural pluralism, of India is well known and ancient. Almost all major religions of the world are professed in this country. Yet, the persisting deep wedge, between Indic and non-Indic religions, is an important obstacle for the unity of India (Oommen 1986). The people who belong to religions of foreign origin, mainly Islam and Christianity, are often perceived as 'lesser Indians'. While only a minority among Hindus publicly articulates this, this seems to be the overall ethos. But, as Oommen (ibid.) rightly argues, India cannot build an authentic state by building a cultural mainstream that reduces the numerous collectivities of the periphery to the status of marginals. We can only have a nation-state with multiple cultural 'centres'. In pursuing this task, the different cultural collectivities should be encouraged to nurture and foster their specific identities. It is in this context that we need to understand the Muslim situation in India today.

Muslims constituted 13.4 per cent of India's total population as per 2001 census. They are the principal minority and are visible in the entire length and breadth of this country.[1] Despite having their rich heritage and innumerable contributions, even official reports find them to the level of one of the most backward and marginalised communities being alienated from the greater society and developmental initiatives of the country. The areas inhabited mostly by the Muslims suffer from acute infrastructural backwardness with regard to facilities like housing, tap water, schools, medical facilities and roads. The access of Muslim children to Integrated Child Development Services (ICDS) is also low and so is its overall coverage. All these clearly refer to the fact that "Muslim areas are being deliberately ignored in the state provision of public services of all kind" (Alam 2010: 215). The dismal Muslim situation in India has been established by several researches done by individuals, survey agencies, and even by the government committees. Justice Sachar Committee Report (SCR) submitted in December 2006 on social, economic and educational status of the Muslims in the country has particularly exposed such depressing state of affairs. SRC has clearly identified three types of interrelated issues, viz., inequality, identity and security, with which the Muslims struggle. Given such a context, this paper seeks to explore and analyse the Muslim situation in India from multiple perspectives. The study is based on facts gathered from primary and secondary sources and supported by author's own research experience on Indian Muslims for about three decades. There is every need to assess the nature, extent and causes of Muslim backwardness today so as to evolve appropriate strategies and policies to address them.

Muslim Situation in India as Reflected in Reports and Studies

Several officially sponsored studies have noted the problems of underrepresentation of Muslims in government employment and educational institutions. These studies, made by government appointed committees, commissions and agencies and even by individual researchers, have time and again pointed out the plights of Indian Muslims and their problems of backwardness as well as marginalisation. But for unknown reasons the problems remain unsolved till today. There are neither community initiatives nor state efforts to overcome the barriers. Let me begin the analysis by referring to some noted reports and studies on the Muslims in the country. Sir William Hunter (1971) has studied the Muslim situation in India during colonial era. The study noted the position of Muslims in government jobs and also recorded the other aspects of Muslim life including the causes of Muslim unrest in the country. In independent India, Kaka Kalelkar Commission on Backward Classes in India (1955) has noted the presence of Other Backward Classes (OBCs) among Muslims. It examined the extent of backwardness of many social groups among the Muslims. Dr Gopal Singh Committee, a high-power panel appointed by the Government of India in early 1980s, enquired about the socio-economic condition of Indian minorities including Muslims and made wide-ranging short- and long-term recommendations. Later, the Mandal Commission (1978), while giving due recognition to the problems of backward sections of Indian population, treated 90 per cent of Muslim population of the country as OBCs and proposed reservations in government jobs and educational institutions for them.

In 1996, a sub-committee of the Planning Commission submitted a report on minority presence in central services and banking sector. This committee noted that proportional representations of Muslims in central and state services were very low. Following this report, a Minority Commission was established in 1978, which again confirmed the deplorable condition of the Muslims and their poor representation in government jobs through field survey. The Commission therefore made some recommendations to rectify the situation. Likewise, the National Commission for Minorities, set up in 1988–99, proposed at least 15 per cent representation of the minorities (with a break of 10% for Muslims and 5% for other minorities taken together) in all Central Government employment. Several reports of the National Sample Survey Organisations (NSSO) have consistently voiced the poor conditions of Indian Muslims with particular respect to literacy, access to land and employment. There have also been attempts by many researchers and academicians to explore the deplorable conditions of Indian Muslims during the last few decades (Ahmed 1993; Ahmed 1980, 1983; Ansari 1989; Engineer 1985; Harris 2003; Hasnain 2006; Khalidi 1996; Mohammad 1999; Momin 2004; Mondal 1992, 1997, 2007; Shariff and Alam 2004; Siddiqui 2004; Waheed 2006; Zakaria 2004 etc.).

The setting up of the SCR in January 2006 by the United Progressive Alliance (UPA) government however signifies a different political and intellectual context. In the past the ideology of secularism had placed a constraint upon the issue of religion as the unit of analysis for framing policies. In fact, in 2004, when religion alone was taken as the basis of extending reservations to the Muslims in Andhra Pradesh, the action was struck down by the judiciary as being unconstitutional (Fazal 2010: 245–46). The SCR has clearly pointed out that the Muslims have been lagging behind in all aspects and the community exhibits deficits and deprivations in practically all dimensions of development (GoI 2006: 237). The SCR has brought out various indicators of Muslim backwardness and found that in the fields of education, economy, employment and representation in public services, they are worse off than other social and religious groups, including the Scheduled Castes (SCs) and often the Scheduled Tribes (STs). Bank credits are received by fewer Muslims (ibid.: 123–27) and districts having higher concentration of Muslims possess weak social and physical infrastructure (ibid.: 146–50). Even in a state like West Bengal, which is remarkably free of communal violence, Muslims suffer from acute development deficit. They therefore deserve special policy focus not only as a matter of right as citizens, but also through mechanism of inclusive programme of the state. The SCR has however noted considerable variations in the conditions of Muslims across states. For instance, the Muslims living in South India are found to be better placed as compared to others in the country. Yet, the community as a whole exhibits deficits and deprivation in almost all dimensions of development. Muslim development deficit can also be measured from the low status of women of this community. Factors like high indices of poverty, low level of educational achievements and poor access to health services particularly affect Muslim women.

The SCR has, for the first time, prepared a checklist of development with a religious community as the unit of analysis (Mahajan 2010: 18). It has also established that far from being a pampered minority, the Muslims were the worst off. Even some secularist has welcomed the report on the ground that it has rightly focused on the material and economic concerns of the community, and not just its religious and cultural needs. There are however questions regarding treating the entire community as a single cohesive unit given its internal differentiation and even hierarchy (ibid.: 23). It is a wide established fact that caste-like distinctions exist even within the Muslim community. It has also been argued that marginalisation can manifest in many different ways and cannot be compared or ranked along a single continuum. This is because different communities face different kinds of challenges (ibid.: 26–27). Notwithstanding the limits of the discourse on religion, community and development, the SCR has initiated a new logic to make the public domain more inclusive and empowering.

Notwithstanding such a vast body of literature on the plights of India Muslims, there is yet no definite move at the national level to implement the recommendations of at least officially sponsored committees. Before analysing the implications of any affirmative policy for the Muslims, it would be better to first examine the factors behind their backwardness and marginalisation. In the following section an attempt has been made to explore as well as analyse the reasons behind the present state of affairs of the Muslims.

Muslim Situation in India: An Analysis

Scholars have attempted to understand and interpret the Muslim situation in India from various perspectives. Some scholars consider that the Muslims are backward due to their inability to participate in modernisation and developmental process for historical reasons and social backgrounds. While some others hold the view that the Muslims are deprived, marginalised and disempowered by the ruling elite owing to their social position (minority status) in the country. Some have even argued that the root cause of Muslim backwardness or marginalisation is their lack of social and political empowerment under the dominant (mainstream) socio-political milieu of the state. Actually, it is difficult to ignore all these views, as there are some truths in all of them.

Muslim development deficits may be interpreted from the perspective of social exclusion and also from the point of power and security deficit. Construction of certain stereotypes images like 'non-indigenous', 'extra-territorial' or 'disloyal other' of the Indian Muslims by the society at large have created a psychological barrier and mental ghetto among them towards enthusiastic and holistic participation in developmental process. It is in this context that some Muslim leaders as well as the commoners have often raised the issue of denial and discrimination. It is normal for any citizen of democratic India to raise issues related to equitable distribution of national wealth and opportunity as well as express concern for affirmative action to protect the weaker sections including Muslims. Many human right activists and political leaders have often linked the issue of marginalisation of the Muslims since independence with state policy and more particularly the social practice of a section of power-wielding majority, i.e., the ruling elite of the country.

The issue of social exclusion of the Muslims is now been raised by the backward Muslim organisations like All India Muslim OBC Sangathan (AIMOBCS), All India Backward Muslim Morcha (AIBMM), Pasmanda Muslim Mahaz (PMM), Uttar Banga Anagrasar Muslim Sangram Samity (UBAMSS) etc. It is stated that in spite of indigenous origin of the bulk of Indian Muslims (occupational groups like Ajlafs and Arzals who did not seize political power during medieval period), they were excluded from the policy of protective discrimination of independent, democratic and secular India. The lower ranked Hindu occupational groups, identified as Scheduled Castes (SCs), were assigned constitutional privileges and this was also extended to the similar other groups who converted to Sikhism and Buddhism. But, the Muslim occupational groups of the same historical background were not allowed this constitutional benefit. Guru (2010) however argues that policy measures initiated for the SCs were a consequence of the political struggle of these groups and were related to historical injustices faced by them. In this context, the present situation of the SCs is not comparable with the Muslim community which did not wage a similar struggle for dignity and self-respect. No doubt, the issue is debatable on the question of 'caste' in Islam or in Muslim society, but one reason behind such exclusion is the notion of 'other' towards non-indigenous, i.e., non-Indic religious groups. It is in this context scholars have argued that Muslims in India are an incredibly disadvantaged minority who besides being poor, educationally backward and marginalised, face discrimination from the power holding authorities. The human rights activists are of the opinion that the exclusion of those Muslims who voluntarily converted to Islam (and even to Christianity) from the list of SCs is violative of two principals: (a) non-discrimination on the basis of religion, and (b) the principle of compensatory discrimination which takes into account the deliberate denial of opportunities to sections of people in the past and not their present affiliations to faith. Reservation benefits for SCs belonging to indigenous (Indic) religious groups like Hindu, Sikh and the Buddhist excluding the religion of foreign (non-Indic) origin has also affected the Muslim psyche.

Dalit Muslims today are raising their profile on the ground that the discriminatory exclusion of SC converts to Islam needs to be rectified for the sake of social justice. The findings of various empirical studies including that of the Sachar Committee have been used to reinforce the view that the status of Muslims is worse than that of the SCs. The findings of Sachar Committee may be used to corroborate the fact that Muslims in India are poorly represented in even Group 'D' employment, which does not require much qualification, and this is a fallout of the discriminatory practices followed so far by the state. Very recently, therefore, the Ranganath Misra Commission (GoI 2009) has called for adoption of a wide range of affirmative action programmes including reservation for certain Muslims, who have been historically surviving as 'occupational groups', categorising them either as backward or weaker section. There is no doubt that continued deprivation and discrimination of this section of Indians has by now led to frustration and alienation. Hence, Muslims in India deserve special policy focus not only as a matter of right as citizens but also to augment the goal of inclusive growth.

It is true that Muslims are not always deliberately discriminated against recruitments for various levels of government service as many of them may lack required qualification or training to compete for such jobs. But this is equally true that government initiatives to uplift the condition of the Muslims to compete in job market are not so appreciable. In this context, it is worth mentioning the populist measure on the part of the government to reform the Madrasa education. But, the reality is that major chunk of the Muslim students usually attends the governmental schools rather than Madrasas (Mondal 1997; GoI 2006). No doubt, Muslim education has some relation with the Madrasa; hence, there is a need of modernisation of Madrasa course curriculum due to demand of situation. But equating Muslim educational backwardness with Madrasa is not an empirical reality. Hence, the myth of Muslim educational backwardness and its linkage with Madrasa needs to be rectified.

It appears that the problem of social exclusion of the Muslims needs also to be analysed from the point of their lack of knowledge, skills and education. Contemporary societies stress on the quality of human resources to augment adaptability in competitive market. But unfortunately there has been a crisis of quality of human resources in the Muslim community in the country. Unless such qualities are substantially improved, Muslims would continue to remain in the periphery of developmental process. Hence, there is a need of inclusive and holistic developmental policies to improve the economic, educational and social condition of the Muslims. To make such policies successful, both state support and community initiatives are needed to a great extent.

Identity, Security and Ghettoisation of the Muslims

The issue of identity of the Muslims is a very complex one. It is because identities are not singular but multiple and are never formed once and for all time. They change over time as the actions and relationships change (Ghosh 2001). Identity is associated mainly with how members of a group think about themselves as people and also about other people around them. The notions of 'we' and 'they' are very much crucial in the context of construction of identity of a group. I would like to identify three major layers of identity of a group. First, the *individual identity* that a person develops through his/her interaction with people in a society. Second, the *social identity* that is developed by individuals sharing common social characteristics. Third, the *cultural identity* that indicates a sense of belonging to a certain ethnic group and its culture or sub-culture. The concept of identity also encompasses the notion of human agency implying that one can have some control in constructing the identity of his/her own group and also of the other group(s). We will now analyse the process of formation of identity among the Muslims in India.

The various sociological and anthropological studies on social structure of Muslims in India have noted the presence of descent based social stratification among them. The Census of India, 1901, had listed about 133 social groups (wholly or partially) among Muslims, which also reflects social stratification within the community. They are scattered across numerous and diverse ethno-cultural and linguistic regions in the country. There are also highly accomplished and successful people among the Muslims. Hence, as Alam (2010: 223) argues, widespread backwardness and high accomplishments make Muslims a 'unique and incomparable people'.

On the basis of history and social background, Muslims in India are also divided into four major groups: (i) Ashrafs who trace their origins to foreign lands, (ii) the upper-caste Hindus who converted to Islam, (iii) the middle caste converts who were or still are associated with clean occupations, and (iv) the converts from erstwhile untouchable castes. These four groups are usually placed into three broad categories, namely, Ashrafs (*Khas*), Ajlafs (*Aams*) and Arzals (*Raizals*). The Ashraf means noble and include all Muslims of foreign origin as well as the converts of Hindu higher castes. Ajlaf means the commoners and clean occupational groups. They are primarily the peasants and artisans. The Arzals are the low ranking converts dealing with unclean occupations. In India, these Muslim groups correspond roughly with the ranking of general castes, OBCs and SCs as in the case of Hindus.

It is worth noting that the Sachar Committee has also categorised the Muslims as Muslim General, Muslim OBCs and Muslim STs, i.e., the Muslims of tribal origin whose numbers are rather very small in India. The Muslim groups currently put under the categories of General and OBCs are essentially from Ashrafs and Ajlafs respectively. It may be noted that there are diversities of views even within the Muslim community with respect to their relative place in social hierarchy. It has also been noted that there exists relative hostility between groups within the community, i.e., Muslim OBCs and Most Backward Castes (MBCs) versus Muslim General on caste, class and community issues. As a corollary, backward and Dalit (Pasmanda) segments of Muslims are increasingly alleging discrimination at the hands of the traditional elites, i.e., so-called higher 'caste' Muslims and demanding reservations in government jobs.

It appears that the official categories of Muslims, i.e., Muslim General, Muslim OBCs, Muslim MBCs and Muslim STs along with their traditional social gradations like Ashrafs, Ajlafs and Arzals have created a complex problem for self-determination and self-identification of various groups within the Muslim community. Hence, the question of affirmative action for the Muslims is not an easy task. The official categorisation has generated debate and hostility not only on the questions of classes and castes in Muslim society, but also made them ethnic or caste conscious. For historical, political and cultural reasons, identities of the Muslims have got fractured into varied forms. And, it was done both by the Muslim themselves and also by the non-Muslims and even by the state. Identities like Ashraf, Ajlaf and Arazal are the construction of Muslim themselves. The notion of Muslim as a whole, as 'other' (*Mussalman*), is the construction of the mainstream Indian society owing to historical and socio-political processes. But, the notion of Muslim as 'minority' (*Sankhya Laghu*) is the construction of media and political parties and also to some extent of the state. Many Indians narrowly use the term 'minority' to refer to only religious minorities so as to identify the Hindus with the 'mainstream'. But, as Weiner (1997) has argued, this is not the way India's minorities define the problem and caste, tribal, linguistic as well as religious groups do often define themselves as 'minorities' depending upon situations.

The repetitive use of the term 'minority' to designate the Muslims and other religious groups smacks of a political process leading to 'minoritisation'. There are forces in India that constantly try to make fish out of troubled waters by intensifying ethnic and religious conflicts. It is worth noting here that despite India's experience of economic development and democratic governance in the last six decades, the presence of religion in the public sphere has also expanded. Democratic political processes have not only provided new modes of articulating development aspirations, they have given life and legitimacy to many 'old' identities

(Mahajan and Jodhka 2010: xi). The experiences of repetitive acts of communal violence since independence have proved that religion is not just a source of personal belief and practices in the Indian context, but it is also a readily available site of mobilisation. It is in this context, the notion of minority as a separate or distinct population has actually compelled the non-Muslims of Indian society to image the Muslims as an 'other'. The recent categorisation of Muslims as General, OBCs and MBCs has not only segmented them on ethnic or caste lines, but also generated a counterforce to strengthen their identity as a disadvantaged religious community in the democratic Indian state. All these have created isolation, seclusion, alienation and even ghettoisation of the Muslims as a religious community in India.

The Muslim problem should also be analysed in the context of persistent patterns of communal violence in India. These riots since early 1960s have served as a major source of some kind of pan-Indian unification of Muslim community in India in spite of their immense internal, linguistic and regional differences. A larger and common consciousness born out of these horrifying experiences has created a negative feeling of 'unwanted other' among the Muslims. Consequently, Samuel Huntington's thesis of 'clash of civilisations' (1993) in the wake of identification of the Muslims as 'other' in several parts of the world has caused deep scars in the community psyche and ultimately created emotional blocks to their participation in development process. This is in spite of the fact that Muslims in India today, unlike earlier, are in alignment with different secular forces in the different regions of the country. Yet, on cultural and religious questions, they show an uncanny affinity with Muslim orthodoxy across the world, taking to the streets in protest over slightest provocations. This hypersensitivity of the Muslim community shows a clear unease with the ongoing process of secularisation (Alam 2010: 209). Imaging Muslims as 'other' has not only made them conscious of victimisation, but also reduced their faith in the democratic and developmental process. Contrarily, the stereotype notion of Muslim appeasement as propagated by some Hindutva forces and the mindset evolved out of that is a major bottleneck for any inclusive programme for the Muslims. The notion of appeasement not only created a sharp social boundary between the Muslims and non-Muslims, but also helped in constructing their image as 'unwanted other'. The question that is validly asked in such a context is: How can a community, which is argued to be appeased by the successive governments, has reached the very bottom of Indian society in terms of socio-economic and development indicators?

Repeated terrorist attacks in different parts of the world including India and appearance of Muslim names in those violent activities created a very complex social environment consisting of suspect and mistrust towards the Muslims. It is true that a small section of the Muslim community has taken to wanton acts of terrorism. And slowly they have also managed to acquire international connections. It is however argued that terrorism among Muslims in India has post-Babri Masjid origins (Alam 2010: 210). This event and consequent pogrom like killings in Gujarat have opened up the opportunity for trans-border terrorists to trap India as a potential constituency for terrorist activities. Whatever may be the reasons, this ultimately motivated the communal forces in successfully constructing an image of the Muslims not only as 'unwanted other', but 'other' as enemy.

Muslims are suffering not only because of their economic and educational deficits but also because of their exclusion and alienation. For the plight of the Muslims the state, the community and the leadership all are responsible. Muslims in India and elsewhere appear to be victims of political process. The political parties as well as ruling elites are much concerned about the Muslim votes and less concerned about their development and change. It will be erroneous to put the blame only on the state, political parties and the society at large. The Muslim leadership in India cannot get away from their responsibility for the plight of the members of their own community. They, except a very few, have not shown sustained interest and effort towards development of the community members. It is very hard to see that the leaders of the Muslim community have organised demonstration or rally for removal of illiteracy, poverty and other problems of the community.

Another complex problem is that the conservative clerics or religious elites, who have become self-appointed spokesmen for the community, have assumed leadership role on the name of religion without paying any attention to the socio-economic issues and problems of the masses. It is matter of great shame that there has always been a linkage between the power elite and the conservative religious elite on the issues of Muslim community for the sake of vote-bank politics and this has damaged the progressive role of the state for the development of this community.

Besides, the issue of 'security' has also made the Muslim situation more problematic in the present juncture. Muslim socio-political activities since the time of partition has remained chiefly centred on the problem of fear psychosis and trauma. The isolation and seclusion of the community is primarily inflicted by insecurity. This issue is also politicised by the political parties for the share of their vested interest rather than to offer them a constructive path for security and development. In recent times the issues of citizenship and rights are very often raised in the context of Muslim situation in India. Since the notion of citizenship is linked to processes like democracy and freedom, the question being asked is: Are the Muslims in India, being haunted by questions regarding their Indianness and suffering from a deep sense of insecurity, free citizens of the country? Such questions are also linked to contemporary concerns for human rights of individuals. The Muslims in India, being the citizens of the country by birth, do have the right to safeguard their religious and cultural identity, and thereby lead a life with dignity.

It is unfortunate that the entire community today lives under a blanket of suspicion, cocooned in a miasma of fear for various reasons. When communal problem bursts into communal violence, it not only causes material damage and loss of life, but also shatters their hope and aspiration along with their faith on development process of the state. For fear psychosis, Muslims very often hesitate to assert their human, legal or citizenship rights making them indifferent to the authorities. The old popular identity of Muslims as the persons with cap and beard or a lady with *burka* or *hijab* is turned to symbols of terrorism in recent times. All these have structured the Muslim mind and that ironically affects their life ways.

There are many Muslims who live in urban areas. Though urban places are sociologically supposed to be more open, flexible and accommodating, irrespective of religious identities, but in India cities and towns are highly segmented on communal lines. It has been observed that even in a city like Kolkata, Muslims normally look for house or accommodation in Muslim localities. Such constraints allow little space for the development of secular identities particular among those who were denied entry into Hindu locality. One can equally see that Muslims are normally concentrated in low-income urban areas or slums (*bastis*) with poor services and amenities. Muslim settlements look highly dirty and congested due to high density of population and lack of proper civic amenities. Economic opportunities available to them are rather limited. They are mostly self-employed or work as labour force in the urban informal sector. But changes in our economic life today following introduction of post-Fordist strategy of industrial production and market internationalism in the era of globalisation have liquidated most of the traditional activities with which Muslims are traditionally involved. This has led to serious crisis of livelihood for them.

While such a situation calls for quick protective actions on the part of the state and other agencies, Muslims are dubbed as 'terrorists' and 'outsiders' for reasons beyond their control. It is obvious that situation of such a nature generated self-exclusion of the Muslims leading to ghettoisation of the community, i.e., separating them physically from the community at large. The process of ghettoisation has far-reaching consequences because it exhibits both social isolation as well as exclusion. The periodic communal riots and fear psychosis arising out of those have also strengthened the process of ghettoisation. There are instances of Muslims shifting from areas inhabited by the dominant community to avoid any untoward incidence leading to loss of life and property. Muslims feel that by living in ghettos they acquire a sense of security because of numerical strength; but in reality ghettoisation contributes to further alienation and loss of faith on the state and society at large. Because, Muslims are then forced to live in a space typically characterised by high density of population and consequent pressure on natural and man-made resources. Conversely, Muslims living together in concentrated pockets make them easy targets for communal lashes and also for neglect of the authorities. Ghettoisation, therefore, has multiple adverse effects on the Muslims. In a plural society like India, inter-community interactions at economic, social and political levels are of utmost importance in preserving and strengthening communal harmony and peace. Therefore, increasing ghettoisation of Muslims needs to be seriously and urgently addressed by the society and the state.

Towards Rescuing Muslims: Issues of Affirmative Action

In view of the above situation, the debate today is largely concentrated on whether Muslims should come under any state-sponsored affirmative action, including reservation. To some Hindu fundamentalists, quotas for Muslims will lead to separatism and minorityism. Contrarily, this is seen by many to be the best way of infusing a sense of security and justice among the excluded Muslims who have so far suffered from development deficit. This would, at least partially, minimise the inequalities, inequities and injustices that the second largest section of the Indian citizens has been facing. In the context of the recommendations of first the Sachar Committee and second the Ranganath Misra Commission for such affirmative actions, we may refer to three existing models to analyse the situation. Thus, to begin with, Kerala and Karnataka have extended the benefits of reservation to the entire Muslim population as a 'backward' segment of the society. In Kerala, a separate Muslim share was fixed at 10 per cent and later it rose to 12 per cent. The second model represents the case of Tamilnadu. This state government has done away with reservation on the ground of religion. Yet, nearly 95 per cent of the Muslims have been included within the fold of backward classes. In the third model, as in Bihar, the Muslim groups, depending upon their level of backwardness, have been included either in OBCs or in MBCs lists. Recently, following the recommendations of the Ranganath Misra Commission, the Government of West Bengal has also prepared a list of deserving Muslim OBCs and MBCs for extending the benefit of reservation to them.[2]

I aver in this context that the prevalence of caste-like divisions among the Indian Muslims is a debatable issue. This is because, on the one hand, the prominent social position of the Ashrafs and the privileges they used to enjoy in the medieval era and also to some extent in the colonial era have worn out in contemporary times. On the other hand, at least a small section of Ajlafs has been able to change their economic condition as well as social position in recent times. Hence, it is difficult today to differentiate the problems of poor Ashrafs from the plight of the poor Ajlafs and Arjals. The so-called 'creamy layer' may be seen among the Ashrafs as well as Ajlafs in differential numbers. Under such a situation, it is necessary to think very seriously about the 'caste' and 'class' questions for this disadvantaged community. It is true that in India family, caste and class issues are all tied with each other. Hence, for a secular and democratic state like India, the 'class' category has to be prioritised over the 'caste' categories. It should be noted here that when the All India Muslim Majlis-e-Mushawarat reiterated its long standing demand of separate reservation quota of 10 per cent for the Muslims, the claim was disputed by the Muslims backwards who resisted any move at the 'bundling of unequals' together (Fazal 2010: 229). These groups see reservation for all Muslims as detrimental to the interest of middle and lower caste Muslims whose underrepresentation and deprivation is argued to be far greater than the other Muslim groups. In order to get rid of these ambiguities, we feel that affirmative actions or policies and programmes for development of the Muslims should be based on income and level of backwardness of the family rather than on their position in a particular caste or caste-like group. The bifurcation of the Muslim backward groups into OBCs and MBCs would ensure that the more advanced among the backwards do not encroach upon the share of the relatively more deprived. It has been estimated that around 10 to 15 per cent of the Muslim population constitute the so-called 'creamy layer'. Any inclusive policy should cover the people of all social categories of the Muslim community except the one who may be called 'creamy' depending upon criteria like land ownership, government job, property and wealth. This would, on the one hand, address the issues of inter-group inequality among the Muslims and thereby strengthen Indian variety of secularism, on the other.

It should be noted that identification of Muslim OBCs/MBCs simply on the basis of traditional occupation is a very difficult task today and such endeavour would rather complicate the matter and create scope for political meddling. As of now, many of the Muslim groups have changed their traditional occupations. Further, several new occupations have also emerged among the Muslims where both poor as well as affluent sections within the same occupational groups persist. Therefore, instead of looking for caste-like divisions (based on occupations) for identification of Muslim OBCs/MBCs, we should identify them on the basis of certain commonly observable socio-economic indexes.

Concluding Observations

India is a multi-ethnic, multi-religious, multicultural democratic country. Owing to diversities of Indian population, the country is guided by the doctrine of unity in diversity. The Constitution of India is committed to 'equality' of all its citizens and considered the responsibility of the state to protect the rights of all. But, unfortunately, in spite of several attempts, inequalities rampantly characterise different spheres of our life including those among the socio-religious groups. Muslims represent the second largest religious group and the principal minority of this country. It is now widely recognised that a large section of Muslim population of this country is living at the margins and is often alienated from development initiatives of the state. Even though such discrimination is not always deliberate, the Indian state has to answer questions and find solution regarding their deprivation, discrimination and exclusion.

We have argued in this paper that the exclusion and alienation of the Muslims is the outcome of complex factors to which the issues of identity, security and inequality are deeply involved. These issues have deep relation with their social formation as well as their images and position in the Indian society. The state and its political machinery on one hand and activities of some political as well as religious elites of the community on the other have played a very crucial role in this process.

There are three major forces that characterise the Muslim problem in India, i.e., poverty, educational backwardness and socio-administrative mindsets of the ruling elite. Poverty, pollution and illiteracy are the common features of Muslim localities both in rural and urban areas. The failure of the Muslims to transform their society is not only due to their lack of knowledge, modern skills and capabilities in most areas of intellectual endeavour, but also due to lack of opportunities and resources which are supposed to be available to them as a free citizen of the country. Muslims also face trouble to get accommodation in non-Muslim areas or houses. Their obligation to the Indian state is also been questioned in some cases. For various reasons, Indian Muslims today have become conscious of their identity and existence. But, at the same time, it is also true that there are several 'Muslim factors' which are creating obstacle towards their social upliftment. Under such a context, development initiatives should primarily focus on two factors: (a) increasing standard of living of affected people through socio-economic development, and (b) creating conditions conductive to the growth of people's self-esteem. The latter element, in turn, would promote human dignity.

These issues must be recognised as the problems of the whole nation and not of Muslims alone. Hence, the state as well as the society at large must come forward to rescue the Muslims from their present state of affairs. Besides, self-correction and self-reliance of the Muslims are considered necessary for any desirable change. In this context, the role of the majority community in instilling self-confidence among the Muslims also seems very important. Hence, we may frame a model for socio-economic upliftment of the Muslims considering three basic aspects discussed above: Awareness (A), Motivation (M) and Participation (P). For a comprehensive and qualitative development of the Muslim community, the above set of 'AMP model' is very crucial. Given a context of eagerness of the Muslims at large to eke out a decent standard of living and join the process of nation building and citizen's politics in contemporary India, it is only desirable that different stakeholders including the state should come forward with appropriate policies and programmes to usher in a new *Bharat* (India) that is really *mahan* (great).

Acknowledgement

I acknowledge the useful and sincere contributions of Prof. Biswajit Ghosh in revising an earlier draft of this paper.

Notes

1. According to 2001 census, there are 11 districts in the country where the Muslim population is above 50 per cent and 38 districts where it is more than 25 per cent – approximately a third of the Muslim population lives in these areas. There are another 182 districts where the Muslim population is between 10 and 15 per cent and about 47 per cent of Muslims live in these areas. Apart from these districts, there are a large number of small and medium-sized towns with a sizeable Muslim population (Alam 2010: 214–15).
2. The Government of West Bengal has specified nearly 85 per cent of Muslims in the state as 'backward' in September 2010. A total of 53 Muslim groups have been included under the OBC category, of which 49 groups are put under the 'most backward' category. Due to such inclusion the OBC quota for government jobs will increase from the current 7 per cent to 17 per cent.

References

Ahmad, Ansuf. 1993. *Indian Muslims: Issues in Economic and Social Development*. New Delhi: Khama Publishers.

Ahmad, Imtiaz. 1980. 'The Problem of Muslim Educational Backwardness in Contemporary India: An Inferential Analysis', Occasional Paper.

——. (ed.). 1983. *Modernization and Social Change among Muslims in India*. New Delhi: Manohar Publications.

Alam, Javeed. 2010. 'The Contemporary Muslim Situation in India: A Long-Term View', in G. Mahajan and S.S. Jodhka (eds.), *Religion, Community and Development* (203–27). New Delhi: Routledge.

Ansari, Iqbal A. (ed.). 1989. *The Muslim Situation in India*. New Delhi: Institute of Objective Studies.

Engineer, A. Ali. 1985. *Indian Muslims: A Study of Minority Problems in India*. New Delhi: Ajanta Publications.

Fazal, Tanweer. 2010. 'Between Identity and Equity: An Agenda for Affirmative Action for Muslims', in G. Mahajan and S.S. Jodhka (eds.), op. cit. (228–47).

Ghosh, Biswajit. 2001. 'Contested Boundaries and Multiple Identities: Ethnicity and Politics in Modern India', *Bharata Vidya*, Vol. I: 86–93.

Government of India (GoI). 2006. *Social, Economic and Educational Status of the Muslim Community of India: A Report*. Prime Ministers High Level Committee (Justice Sachar Committee). New Delhi: Cabinet Secretariat, GoI.

——. 2009. *Report of the National Commission for Religious and Linguistic Minorities (Ranganath Misra Commission Report)*. Vols. I & II, New Delhi: Ministry of Minority Affairs.

Harris, White Barbara. 2003. *India Working: Essays on Society and Economy*. Cambridge: Cambridge University Press.

Hasnain, Nadeem. 2006. *Islam and Muslim Communities in South Asia*. New Delhi: Serials Publications.

Huntington, Samuel P. 1993. 'The Clash of Civilizations', *Foreign Affairs*, Summer.

Khalidi, Omar. 1996. *Indian Muslims since Independence*. New Delhi: Vikas Publishing House.

Mohammad, Noor (ed.). 1999. *Indian Muslims: Precepts and Practices*. Jaipur: Rawat Publications.

Mahajan, Gurpreet. 2010. 'Religion, Community and Development', in G. Mahajan and S.S. Jodhka (eds.), op. cit. (1–35).

Mahajan, Gurpreet and S.S. Jodhka. 2010. *Religion, Community and Development*. New Delhi: Routledge.

Momin, A.R. 2004. *The Empowerment of Muslims in India: Perspective, Context and Prerequisites*. New Delhi: Institute of Objective Studies.

Mondal, Sheikh Rahim. 1992. 'Muslims in India: An Enquiry into their Minority Status, Backwardness, Special Rights and Development Problems', *Journal of Indian Anthropological Society*, 27: 149–60.

——. 1997. *Educational Status of Muslims: Problems, Prospects and Priorities*. New Delhi: Inter-India Publications.

——. 2007. 'Sachar Committee Report and Beyond: A Critical Appraisal of Socio-Economic Condition of Indian Muslims', *Islam and Muslim Societies: A Social Science Journal*, 3 (1): 27–50.

Oommen, T.K. 1986. 'Insiders and Outsiders in India: Primordial Collectivism and Cultural Pluralism in Nation Building', *International Sociology*, 1 (1): 53–74.

Shariff, Abusatcha and M. Alam. 2004. *Economic Empowerment of Muslims in India*. New Delhi: Institute of Objective Studies.

Siddiqui, M.K.A. (ed.). 2004. *Marginal Muslim Communities in India*. New Delhi: Institute of Objective Studies.

Waheed, Abdul. 2006. *Muslim Artisans, Craftsmen and Traders*. New Delhi: Icon Publications Pvt. Ltd.

Weiner, Myron. 1997. 'Minority Identities', in Sudipta Kaviraj (ed.), *Politics in India* (241–53). New Delhi: Oxford University Press.

Zakaria, R. 2004. *Indian Muslims: Where Have They Gone Wrong?* New Delhi: Popular Prakashan.

Index

Index